Get the eBook FREE!

(PDF, ePub, Kindle, and liveBook all included)

We believe that once you buy a book from us, you should be able to read it in any format we have available. To get electronic versions of this book at no additional cost to you, purchase and then register this book at the Manning website.

Go to https://www.manning.com/freebook and follow the instructions to complete your pBook registration.

That's it!
Thanks from Manning!

Modern Fortran

BUILDING EFFICIENT PARALLEL APPLICATIONS

MILAN CURCIC

FOREWORD BY DAMIAN ROUSON

MANNING

SHELTER ISLAND

For online information and ordering of this and other Manning books, please visit
www.manning.com. The publisher offers discounts on this book when ordered in quantity.
For more information, please contact

> Special Sales Department
> Manning Publications Co.
> 20 Baldwin Road
> PO Box 761
> Shelter Island, NY 11964
> Email: orders@manning.com

Manning Publications Co.
20 Baldwin Road
PO Box 761
Shelter Island, NY 11964

Development editor:	Lesley Trites
Technical development editor:	Michiel Trimpe
Review editor:	Aleksandar Dragosavljević
Production editor:	Lori Weidert
Copy editor:	Frances Buran
Proofreader:	Melody Dolab
Technical proofreader:	Maurizio Tomasi
Typesetter:	Dennis Dalinnik
Cover designer:	Marija Tudor

ISBN: 9781617295287
Printed in the United States of America

contents

PART 3 ADVANCED FORTRAN USE 171

foreword

I was immediately excited to find out that Milan Curcic would be writing a modern Fortran book. Almost weekly, I meet people who express surprise that Fortran remains in use more than 60 years after its creation, so any signs of new life in a language so often written off as dead or dying are cause for celebration. I usually explain that Fortran has its strongest footholds in fields that embraced computing early. I go on to tell them that they almost certainly use the results of Fortran programs daily when checking weather forecasts. What makes Milan's work intriguing is the extent to which it connects established domains, where Fortran has long held sway, and emerging domains, where Fortran is rare. This book grew out of the unique perspective Milan brings from having been involved in bridging the divides that prevent many disciplines from writing Fortran and prevent most Fortran programmers from exploiting programming paradigms that have come into widespread use in other languages.

To Milan's credit, the book focuses on teaching Fortran programming rather than promoting the intriguing software libraries and applications to which he has contributed. The lucky reader who follows the links to his work and that of others will gain more than just an understanding of Fortran programming. Such a reader will embark on a journey that connects numerical weather prediction, a subject as old as computing, and cloud computing, a twenty-first-century innovation. Such a reader will also discover how to incorporate aspects of functional programming, a paradigm around which whole languages have been built, in Fortran, the language that's the ultimate ancestor of all high-level programming languages. And such a reader will be exposed to neural networks, a subject undergoing explosive growth and impacting technologies as disparate as autonomous driving and cancer diagnosis.

Milan has led or contributed to popular software in each of these areas, and some of the packages grew out of this book or vice versa. Cloudrun (https://cloudrun.co), a service he develops with others, for example, pioneered numerical weather prediction software-as-a-service (SaaS) using cloud computing platforms. The open source functional-fortran library (http://mng.bz/vxy1) provides utilities supporting a programming paradigm that hasn't penetrated the Fortran world as much as I would like. The open source Fortran Standard Library (https://github.com/fortran-lang/stdlib) aims to put Fortran on more even standing with other languages that benefit from large libraries considered part of the language. His neural-fortran (https://github.com/modern-fortran/neural-fortran), which grew out of his work on one chapter of this book, demonstrates the application of Fortran's scalable parallel programming model in a domain dominated by languages that lack built-in parallel programming models able to exploit distributed-memory platforms. Collectively, these projects are used by hundreds of developers worldwide, and the interplay between his work on this book and work on these projects informs and inspires the book's coverage of the language.

For the reader seeking proof of life for modern Fortran, Milan's work provides ample evidence of the language's ongoing role in technological modernity. This book is one of the more vibrant buds growing out of his work, and the interested reader will learn the features of the language that have proven useful in the aforementioned broad portfolio of Milan's projects.

—DAMIAN ROUSON,
PhD, P.E. President, Sourcery Institute, Oakland, California, USA

preface

When Mike Stephens from Manning first reached out to me in the summer of 2017, he wrote, "We saw some of your forum posts and GitHub repositories; would you consider writing a Fortran book with Manning?" Writing a book had never crossed my mind, nor did I believe I was cut out for the job. I closed my eyes and took a leap of faith. "Of course, I'd love to! Where do I send a proposal?" By the end of the summer, we had a contract and a tentative table of contents in place. Two development editors, two technical editors, four peer reviews, three chapter rewrites, two hurricanes, and almost three years later, we have the finished book.

Welcome to *Modern Fortran: Building Efficient Parallel Applications*! If you're holding this book, chances are you either want to learn Fortran programming for school or work, or you're an experienced Fortran programmer looking to brush up on the latest developments in the language. Either way, you've come to the right place. If you're just starting to learn, my goal with this book is to give you a straightforward, hands-on, practical approach to Fortran programming. If you have prior experience with the language, I want this to be a handy survival guide in the Fortran world. Forgot how to write functions that operate on both scalars and arrays? Wondering how to write your program for parallel execution? Practical projects and exercises with solutions are here to show you how.

I'm happy to have the opportunity to share with you what I've learned over the past 14 years. Thank you in advance for trusting me with your time and money. *Modern Fortran* is my way of giving back to dozens of you who taught me and helped me along the way. I hope you use this book to teach the next generation of Fortran programmers.

acknowledgments

It takes a village to make a great book. Mike Stephens was the acquisitions editor—he brought me on board and helped work out the table of contents, as well as getting clear on who this book is for. My development editors, Kristen Watterson and Lesley Trites, guided me along the way and diligently pushed me forward. Kristen worked with me on the initial drafts of nine of the chapters; then Lesley took over for the remainder and putting it all together. Technical editors Michiel Trimpe and Alain Couniot made sure to point out any mistakes in the code and confusing paragraphs that didn't make sense. Bert Bates chimed in on occasion to help me pull out the concrete from the abstract. Maurizio Tomasi was the technical proofreader and made sure that all the code in the book works as advertised. Melody Dolab was the final proofreader and Lori Weidert was the production editor. Also, the rest of the Manning staff who worked with me: Candace Gillhoolley, Ana Romac, Rejhana Markanovic, Aleksandar Dragosavljević, Matko Hrvatin, and others. Thank you all—I've learned a lot from you.

I also want to thank all of the reviewers: Anders Johansson, Anton Menshov, Bridger Howell, David Celements, Davide Cadamuro, Fredric Ragnar, Jan Pieter Herweijer, Jose San Leandro, Joseph Ian Walker, Kanak Kshetri, Ken W. Alger, Konrad Hinsen, Kyle Mandli, Leonardo Costa Prauchner, Lottie Greenwood, Luis Moux-Domínguez, Marcio Nicolau, Martin Beer, Matthew Emmett, Maurizio Tomasi, Michael Jensen, Michal Konrad Owsiak, Mikkel Arentoft, Ondřej Čertík, Patrick Seewald, Richard Fieldsend, Ryan B. Harvey, Srdjan Santic, Stefano Borini, Tiziano Müller, Tom Gueth, Valmiky Arquissandas, and Vincent Zaballa. Your suggestions helped make this a better book.

Arjen Markus provided thorough reviews and suggestions on every chapter as they became available in the Manning Early Access Program. Izaak Beekman, Jacob Williams, Marcus Van Lier-Walqui, and Steve Lionel provided helpful comments on early drafts of the book. Damian Rouson and his own books were an inspiration, and he encouraged me further along the way. Michael Hirsch helped with continuous integration of some of the GitHub repositories associated with the book. Finally, all my readers who trusted me and bought the book while still in the works—you helped me to keep at it and finish the job.

Last but not least, to my wife, family, and friends who supported me and were proud of me—I couldn't have done it without your love and help.

about this book

Modern Fortran aims to fill a glaring gap in the existing Fortran literature: a book that teaches modern Fortran through practical, hands-on examples, with extra attention on parallel programming and the latest developments in the language. This is a book for scientists and engineers who want to solve the challenging computational problems of tomorrow using mature, highly performant, easy-to-use technology. If you don't have a clue about Fortran and want to work on a Fortran project (new or existing), I believe this book is the easiest and fastest way to get you up to speed.

Modern Fortran isn't a complete reference on all features of the language. Instead, it's a straightforward and hands-on practical course on Fortran programming, covering the most essential features you're likely to use in your work. I also intend this to be a useful reference text for solving practical everyday problems in science and engineering. Examples in this book range from the more general, like a note-taking app and working with dates and times; to the specialized, such as stock price and weather data analysis; to the more sophisticated, such as parallel tsunami simulation. You'll find many examples and solutions to problems that are typically not covered by other books on Fortran.

Also, unlike most other Fortran books, this one gives extra attention to parallel programming. As of the 2008 release, Fortran is a natively parallel programming language, and the recent 2018 release only brings more to the table. In particular, this book will show you how to write parallel Fortran programs using coarrays, teams, events, and collectives, without relying on external libraries such as the Message Passing Interface.

However, parallel programming is an advanced topic, and most chapters in the book focus on gently introducing nonparallel language concepts. There's only so much material that we could fit in a single book, so important topics such as parallel algorithms and scaling aren't covered. Message Passing Interface, OpenMP, and OpenACC, while all important technologies in their own right, were simply out of scope for this book. Ditto for debugging, preprocessors, and working with legacy code. I'll provide references for further reading where appropriate.

Who should read this book

This book is primarily for readers who are new to Fortran and want to learn it. It will also be useful to experienced Fortran programmers who want to brush up on the latest in Fortran development through fun exercises. Whether you've had any contact with Fortran or not, I assume you have at least some experience programming and understand the basic concepts of source code, variables, and functions. Perhaps you're a proficient Fortran programmer looking to step up your parallel programming game. Maybe your company is embedding a large Fortran simulation codebase into the existing software stack, and the project fell into your lap. Whatever your story is, I believe you'll learn something new from this book.

I believe the following professions will benefit most from this book:

- Students and researchers in science or engineering, especially disciplines that involve computational fluid dynamics
- Meteorologists, oceanographers, and climate scientists, especially those who work on numerical prediction problems
- Data analysis professionals, such as data engineers and data scientists
- Machine learning researchers and practitioners
- Quantitative finance analysts
- High-performance computing system administrators
- Teachers and instructors in any of the above disciplines or anybody else curious about programming languages and computation in general.

A bit of Fortran history

Fortran is a compiled, statically typed, general-purpose programming language. It was developed by John Backus and his team at IBM, with the first release in 1957 for the IBM 704 computer. Originally called FORTRAN (FORmula TRANslation), it allowed programmers to write programs more easily compared to writing machine instructions of the era. Fortran was one of the first high-level programming languages in history and is the oldest language still in active use and development today. In that sense, Fortran was the very beginning of the modern computing that we practice today.

The language has since evolved through more than a dozen revisions and several ISO standards. Fortran remains the dominant language of high-performance computing (HPC), where many interconnected processors work together to solve huge problems. Fortran 2018 is the most recent iteration of the language. The next revision, with the current working name Fortran 202x, is in development and expected to come out in the next few years.

Today, Fortran is the leading programming language used in many areas of physical science and engineering. These include computational fluid dynamics, numerical weather prediction, climate science, aerodynamics, astrophysics and so on. Fortran is also used to benchmark the world's fastest and largest supercomputers (https://top500.org). Many universities still teach Fortran programming in science and engineering tracks because Fortran remains relevant in those industries. With the explosion of internet and mobile technologies over the past 20 years, it's evident that the Fortran ecosystem has fallen into the shadows, at least from the point of view of mainstream computing. However, its relevance never lessened on an absolute scale. In fact, Fortran compilers, Fortran libraries, and its open source community are stronger than ever. Fortran is the only standardized language with a native parallel programming model, expressed using an intuitive array-like syntax. With the current trend toward many-core architectures, it's safe to say that Fortran will be relevant for many years to come.

How this book is organized: a roadmap

Modern Fortran is organized in four parts and twelve chapters:

- *Part 1*—Getting started with modern Fortran
  - Chapter 1 will give you a taste of Fortran and what kind of problems it solves best.
  - Chapter 2 will guide you through a basic, yet complete Fortran program.
- *Part 2*—Core elements of Fortran
  - Chapter 3 will teach you to use procedures to simplify and reuse your Fortran program.
  - Chapter 4 explains how to organize your procedures and variables in modules.
  - Chapter 5 covers arrays and whole-array arithmetic.
  - Chapter 6 tackles input and output, and formatting numerical data as text.
- *Part 3*—Advanced Fortran use
  - Chapter 7 will show you how to use images and coarrays for parallel programming.
  - Chapter 8 covers derived types for working with abstract and complex data structures.
  - Chapter 9 explains how to write generic procedures that can work on arguments of any data type.
  - Chapter 10 covers user-defined operators for derived types.
- *Part 4*—The final stretch
  - Chapter 11 will teach you how to interface with existing C libraries from Fortran.
  - Chapter 12 covers advanced parallel programming concepts: teams, events, and collectives.

Part 1 will give you a taste of Fortran. Work through this part if you're new to Fortran. Even if you have some Fortran experience, if you'd like to work through the running example (a tsunami simulator), it's introduced in chapter 2. At the end of part 1, you'll be able to write, compile, and run basic working Fortran programs.

In part 2, I cover the core elements of the language: procedures (functions and subroutines), modules, arrays, and I/O. These are the features that you'll find in most Fortran projects and that are essential for writing clean, organized, and reusable code. At the end of part 2, you'll be able to write more complex Fortran programs and libraries to solve real problems. You can start here if you're proficient with one or more other programming languages. After working through this part, and with some practical experience, you'll be a functional and independent Fortran programmer.

Part 3 introduces parallel programming with coarrays (chapter 7), as well as derived types (chapter 8), generic procedures (chapter 9), and custom operators (chapter 10). Here, you'll write your first parallel program, model complex data structures with classes, and write generic procedures that can work with any data type. This part depends on concepts introduced in part 2. Become familiar with those concepts first. After you work through part 3, you'll be able to understand, reuse, and extend most of the existing Fortran code in the wild, as well as write innovative parallel Fortran solutions. This is the heaviest part of the book—approach it with patience and an open mind.

Finally, part 4 covers specialty topics: interfacing C code from Fortran (chapter 11) and advanced parallel features that were most recently added to the language—teams, events, and collectives (chapter 12). The former is important if you'll use Fortran for systems programming, networking, interfacing with instruments, or reusing existing C libraries for any task. The latter is the cutting edge of parallel programming in Fortran. I recommend working through these chapters only after you're familiar with the concepts covered in parts 2 and 3.

When it came to deciding on the order in which to organize different chapters and topics, we found that there's no obvious answer. Depending on your experience and interest, you may find that some more basic topics may be covered later in the book. If that's the case, feel free to skip ahead and come back at a later time. Just like any new creation, this book is an experiment. Choose your own adventure, and do what feels good.

About the code

This book develops quite a bit of source code, mostly organized in one large running example (tsunami simulator) and several miniprojects. All of the code in this book is organized in Git repositories at https://github.com/modern-fortran. The tsunami simulator and the miniprojects each have their own GitHub repository, so you can explore and tinker with them independently from one another. Miscellaneous examples and source code listings that don't belong to any single project are organized in the "listings" repository at https://github.com/modern-fortran/listings. I maintain these as active projects, so if you spot any issues or have a question about the code, feel free to open an issue in the appropriate repository.

Although all the code is available to download, I recommend that you type out the source code by hand as you work through this book. Doing this will get you accustomed to Fortran's syntax and help you develop muscle memory. However, if you still want to just download the code and run it, you of course can. If you're familiar with Git, the easiest way to get the code is to git clone each project repository from the command line. If you don't have Git or don't want to use it, just download the zip archive of the source code from the repository page. The README file in each project will instruct you on how to build it.

This book contains many examples of source code in numbered listings, in code snippets, and inline with normal text. In all cases, except code annotations, source code is formatted in a `fixed-width font like this` to separate it from ordinary text.

In many cases, the original source code has been reformatted; we've added line breaks and reworked indentation to accommodate the available page space in the book. Additionally, comments in the source code have often been removed from the listings when the code is described in the text. Code annotations accompany many of the listings, highlighting important concepts.

Requirements

To work through this book, you'll need a computer, ideally with Linux or macOS. If you work with Windows 10, you may already have access to the Windows Subsystem for Linux, which provides a native Linux environment, and I recommend using that. If you're on an older version of Windows, I suggest setting up a Linux Virtual Machine on your system. The advantage of Linux operating systems is that they're designed for software development. I worked with both Ubuntu 18.10 (desktop) and Fedora 28 (laptop) while writing this book. They're both great for Fortran development.

You'll also need working knowledge of a text editor with syntax highlighting to read and write source code, as well as knowing how to use the Linux/UNIX command line to compile programs. I'm a minimalist when it comes to text editors and prefer Vim (Vi IMproved). If you like more sophisticated editors like Sublime, Atom, or VS Code, those are fine as well. After all, an editor is just a tool. Pick one that gets out of your way of doing actual work. You'll find more info on text editors in appendix A.

Get involved

If you like Fortran, and this book inspires you to do more, consider joining the Fortran open source community and/or the Standard Committees:

- Fortran home on the internet: https://fortran-lang.org
- Fortran home on GitHub: https://github.com/fortran-lang
- Fortran Standard Library: https://github.com/fortran-lang/stdlib
- Fortran Package Manager: https://github.com/fortran-lang/fpm

- Proposals for the Fortran Standard Committee: https://github.com/j3-fortran/fortran_proposals
- US Fortran Standards Committee: https://j3-fortran.org
- International Fortran Standards Committee: https://wg5-fortran.org

The community is friendly and open to all newcomers with goodwill. We need help—join us!

liveBook discussion forum

Purchase of *Modern Fortran: Building Efficient Parallel Applications* includes free access to a private web forum run by Manning Publications, where you can make comments about the book, ask technical questions, and receive help from the author and other users. To access the forum, go to https://livebook.manning.com/#!/book/modern-fortran/discussion. You can also learn more about Manning's forums and the rules of conduct at https://livebook.manning.com/#!/discussion.

Manning's commitment to our readers is to provide a venue where a meaningful dialog between individual readers and between readers and the author can take place. It's not a commitment to any specific amount of participation on the part of the author, whose contribution to the forum remains voluntary (and unpaid). We suggest you try asking the author some challenging questions lest his interest stray! The forum and the archives of previous discussions will be accessible from the publisher's website as long as the book is in print.

about the author

MILAN CURCIC is a meteorologist and oceanographer. He studies ocean waves and turbulence and their importance for numerical weather and ocean prediction at the University of Miami. He's also working on enabling numerical weather prediction in the scalable compute cloud. A Fortran programmer since 2006, he has worked with teams from the United States Navy and NASA on developing and improving Earth system prediction models. He has authored several open source Fortran libraries and collaborates with the Fortran Standards Committee on developing the next Fortran release, as well as its standard library.

Milan lives with his wife, Evelyn, and son, Nolan, in Boca Raton, Florida. You can stay up to date and get in touch with him at https://milancurcic.com.

about the cover illustration

The figure on the cover of *Modern Fortran: Building Efficient Parallel Applications* is captioned "Ingrienne," which refers to a woman from the historical geographic area of Ingria, located along the southern shore of the Gulf of Finland. The illustration is taken from a collection of dress costumes from various countries by Jacques Grasset de Saint-Sauveur (1757–1810), titled *Costumes Civils Actuels de Tous les Peuples Connus*, published in France in 1788. Each illustration is finely drawn and colored by hand. The rich variety of Grasset de Saint-Sauveur's collection reminds us vividly of how culturally apart the world's towns and regions were just 200 years ago. Isolated from each other, people spoke different dialects and languages. In the streets or in the countryside, it was easy to identify where they lived and what their trade or station in life was just by their dress.

The way we dress has changed since then, and the diversity by region, so rich at the time, has faded away. It's now hard to tell apart the inhabitants of different continents, let alone different towns, regions, or countries. Perhaps we've traded cultural diversity for a more varied personal life—certainly for a more varied and fast-paced technological life.

At a time when it's hard to tell one computer book from another, Manning celebrates the inventiveness and initiative of the computer business with book covers based on the rich diversity of regional life of two centuries ago, brought back to life by Grasset de Saint-Sauveur's pictures.

Part 1

Getting started with
Modern Fortran

In this part, you'll get a taste of Fortran and a gentle introduction into the language.

In chapter 1, we'll discuss the design and features of Fortran, and the kinds of problems for which Fortran is suitable. You'll learn why parallel programming is important and when you should use it.

In chapter 2, we'll build a minimal working example of the tsunami simulator that we'll be working on throughout the book. This example will give you a taste of the Fortran essentials: variable declaration, data types, arrays, loops, and branches.

If you're new to Fortran, this is the place to start. At the end of this part of the book, you'll be able to write simple yet useful Fortran programs. More importantly, you'll be ready to learn about Fortran essentials in more depth.

Introducing Fortran

1

This chapter covers

- What is Fortran and why learn it?
- Fortran's strengths and weaknesses
- Thinking in parallel
- Building a parallel simulation app from scratch

This is a book about *Fortran*, one of the first high-level programming languages in history. It will teach you the language by guiding you step-by-step through the development of a fully featured, *parallel* physics simulation app. Notice the emphasis on *parallel*. *Parallel programming* allows you to break your problem down into pieces and let multiple processors each work on only part of the problem, thus reaching the solution in less time. By the end, you'll be able to recognize problems that can be parallelized, and use modern Fortran techniques to solve them.

This book is not a comprehensive reference manual for every Fortran feature—I've omitted significant parts of the language on purpose. Instead, I focus on the most practical features that you'd use to build a real-world Fortran application. As we work on our app chapter by chapter, we'll apply modern Fortran features and software design techniques to make our app robust, portable, and easy to use and extend. This isn't just a book about Fortran; it's a book about building robust, parallel software using modern Fortran.

1.1   *What is Fortran?*

I don't know what the language of the year 2000 will look like, but I know it will be called Fortran.

—Tony Hoare, winner of the 1980 Turing Award

Fortran is a general-purpose, parallel programming language that excels in scientific and engineering applications. Originally called FORTRAN (FORmula TRANslation) in 1957, it has evolved over decades to become a robust, mature, and high perfomance-oriented programming language. Today, Fortran keeps churning under the hood of many systems that we take for granted:

- Numerical weather, ocean, and surf prediction
- Climate science and prediction
- Computational fluid dynamics software used in mechanical and civil engineering
- Aerodynamics solvers for designing cars, airplanes, and spacecraft
- Fast linear algebra libraries used by machine learning frameworks
- Benchmarking the fastest supercomputers in the world (https://top500.org)

Here's a specific example. In my work, I develop numerical models of weather, ocean surface waves, and deep ocean circulation. Talking about it over the years, I found that most people didn't know where weather forecasts came from. They had the idea that meteorologists would get together and draw a chart of what the weather would be like tomorrow, next week, or a month from now. This is only partly true. In reality, we use sophisticated numerical models that crunch a huge amount of numbers on computers the size of a warehouse. These models simulate the atmosphere to create an educated guess about what the weather will be like in the future. Meteorologists use the output of these models to create a meaningful weather map, like the one shown in figure 1.1. This map shows just a sliver of all the data that this model produces. The output size of a weather forecast like this is counted in hundreds of gigabytes.

The most powerful Fortran applications run in parallel on hundreds or thousands of CPUs. Development of the Fortran language and its libraries has been largely driven by the need to solve extremely large computational problems in physics, engineering, and biomedicine. To access even more computational power than what the most powerful single computer at the time could offer, in the late 20th century we started connecting many computers with high-bandwidth networks and let them each work on a piece of the problem. The result is the *supercomputer*, a massive computer made up of thousands of commodity CPUs (figure 1.2). Supercomputers are similar to modern server farms hosted by Google or Amazon, except that the network infrastructure in supercomputers is designed to maximize bandwidth and minimize latency between the servers themselves, rather than between them and the outside world. As a result, the CPUs in

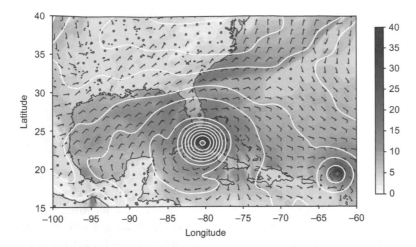

Figure 1.1 **A forecast of Hurricane Irma on September 10, 2017, computed by an operational weather prediction model written in Fortran. Shading and barbs show surface wind speed in meters per second, and contours are isolines of sea-level pressure. A typical weather forecast is computed in parallel using hundreds or thousands of CPUs. (Data provided by the NOAA National Center for Environmental Prediction [NCEP])**

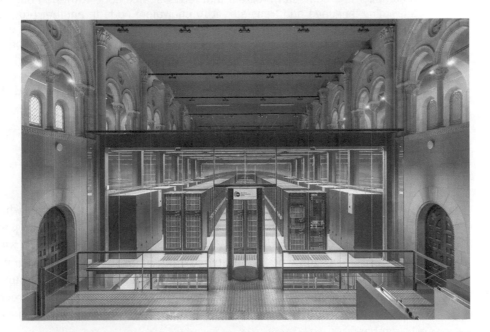

Figure 1.2 **The MareNostrum 4 supercomputer at the Barcelona Supercomputing Center. The computer is housed inside the Torre Girona Chapel in Barcelona, Catalonia, Spain. A high-speed network connects all of the cabinets to each another. With 153,216 Intel Xeon cores, MareNostrum 4 is the fastest supercomputer in Spain, and the 37th fastest in the world as of June 2020. (https://www.top500.org/lists/2020/06). It's used for many scientific applications, from astrophysics and materials physics, to climate and atmospheric dust transport prediction, to biomedicine. (Image source: https://www.bsc.es/marenostrum/marenostrum)**

a supercomputer act like one giant processor with distributed-memory access that's nearly as fast as local memory access. To this day, Fortran remains the dominant language used for such massive-scale parallel computations.

1.2 Fortran features

> *This is not your parents' Fortran.*
>
> —Damian Rouson

In the context of programming languages, Fortran is all of the following:

- *Compiled*—You'll write whole programs and pass them to the *compiler* before executing them. This is in contrast to *interpreted* programming languages like Python or JavaScript, which are parsed and executed line by line. Although this makes writing programs a bit more tedious, it allows the compiler to generate efficient executable code. In typical use cases, it's not uncommon for Fortran programs to be one or two orders of magnitude faster than equivalent Python programs.

> **What is a compiler?**
>
> A compiler is a computer program that reads source code written in one programming language and translates it to equivalent code in another programming language. In our case, a Fortran compiler will read Fortran source code and generate appropriate assembly code and machine (binary) instructions.

- *Statically typed*—In Fortran, you'll declare all variables with a type, and they'll remain of that type until the end of the program:

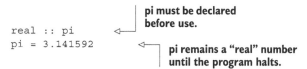

```
real :: pi
pi = 3.141592
```

pi must be declared before use.

pi remains a "real" number until the program halts.

You'll also need to explicitly declare the variables before their use, which is known as *manifest typing*. Finally, Fortran employs so-called *strong typing*, which means that the compiler will raise an error if a procedure is invoked with an argument of the wrong type. While static typing helps the compiler to generate efficient programs, manifest and strong typing enforce good programming hygiene and make Fortran a safe language. I find it's easier to write correct Fortran programs than Python or Javascript, which come with many hidden caveats and "gotchas."

- *Multiparadigm*—You can write Fortran programs in several different paradigms, or styles: imperative, procedural, object-oriented, and even functional. Some paradigms are more appropriate than others, depending on the problem you're trying to solve. We'll explore different paradigms as we develop code throughout the book.

- *Parallel*—Fortran is also a *parallel* language. Parallelism is the capability to split the computational problem between processes that communicate through a network. Parallel processes can be running on the same processing core (thread-based parallelism), on different cores that share RAM (shared-memory parallelism), or distributed across the network (distributed-memory parallelism). Computers working together on the same parallel program can be physically located in the same cabinet, across the room from each other, or across the world. Fortran's main parallel structure is a *coarray*, which allows you to express parallel algorithms and remote data exchange without any external libraries. Coarrays allow you to access remote memory just like you'd access elements of an array, as shown in the following listing.

Listing 1.1   **Example data exchange between parallel images**

```
program hello_coarrays

  implicit none                    Each image declares a local
                                   copy of an integer "a."

  integer :: a[*]      ◄─         Each image assigns its
  integer :: i                     number (1, 2, 3, etc.) to "a."

                                   Only image 1 will
  a = this_image()     ◄─         enter this if block.

  if (this_image() == 1) then  ◄─    Iterates from 1 to the
    do i = 1, num_images()      ◄─    total number of images
      print *, 'Value on image', i, 'is', a[i]   ◄─
    end do                              For each remote image,
  end if                                image 1 will get the value
                                        of "a" on that image and
end program hello_coarrays              print it to the screen.
```

The Fortran standard doesn't dictate how the data exchange is implemented under the hood; it merely specifies the syntax and the expected behavior. This allows the compiler developers to use the best approach available on any specific hardware. Given a capable compiler and libraries, a Fortran programmer can write code that runs on conventional CPUs or general-purpose GPUs alike. Listing 1.1 is meant for illustration; however, if you'd like to compile and run it, do so after following the instructions in Appendix A to set up your Fortran development environment.

- *Mature*—In 2016, we celebrated 60 years since the birth of Fortran. The language has evolved through several revisions of the standard:
  - FORTRAN 66, also known as FORTRAN IV (ANSI, 1966)
  - FORTRAN 77 (ANSI, 1978)
  - Fortran 90 (ISO/IEC, 1991; ANSI, 1992)
  - Fortran 95 (ISO/IEC, 1997)

– Fortran 2003 (ISO/IEC, 2004)

– Fortran 2008 (ISO/IEC, 2010)

– Fortran 2018 (ISO/IEC, 2018)

Fortran development and implementation in compilers have been heavily supported by the industry: IBM, Cray, Intel, NAG, NVIDIA, and others. There has also been significant open source development, most notably free compilers—gfortran (https://gcc.gnu.org/wiki/GFortran), Flang (https://github.com/flang-compiler/flang), and LFortran (https://lfortran.org)—as well as other community projects (https://fortran-lang.org/community). Thanks to Fortran's dominance in the early days of computer science, today we have a vast set of robust and mature libraries that are the computational backbone of many applications. With mature compilers and a large legacy code base, Fortran remains the language of choice for many new software projects for which computational efficiency and parallel execution are key.

■ *Easy to learn*—Believe it or not, Fortran is quite easy to learn. This was my experience and that of many of my colleagues. It's easy to learn partly due to its strict type system, which allows the compiler to keep the programmer in check and warn them at compile time when they make a mistake. Although verbose, the syntax is clean and easy to read. However, like every other programming language or skill in general, Fortran is difficult to master. This is one of the reasons why I chose to write this book.

1.3   *Why learn Fortran?*

There were programs here that had been written five thousand years ago, before Humankind ever left Earth. The wonder of it—the horror of it, Sura said—was that unlike the useless wrecks of Canberra's past, these programs still worked! And via a million million circuitous threads of inheritance, many of the oldest programs still ran in the bowels of the Qeng Ho system.

—Vernor Vinge, *A Deepness in the Sky*

Since the early 1990s, we've seen an explosion of new programming languages and frameworks, mainly driven by the widespread use of the internet and, later, mobile devices. C++ took over computer science departments, Java has been revered in the enterprise, JavaScript redefined the modern web, R became the mother tongue of statisticians, and Python took the machine learning world by storm. Where does Fortran fit in all this? Through steady revisions of the language, Fortran has maintained a solid footing in its niche domain, high-performance computing (HPC). Its computational efficiency is still unparalleled, with only C and C++ coming close. Unlike C and C++, Fortran has been designed for array-oriented calculations, and is, in my opinion, significantly easier to learn and program. A more recent strong argument for Fortran has come about through its native support for parallel programming.

What is high-performance computing?

High-performance computing (HPC) is the practice of combining computer resources to solve computational problems that would otherwise not be possible with a single desktop computer. HPC systems typically aggregate hundreds or thousands of servers and connect them with fast networks. Most HPC systems today run some flavor of Linux OS.

Despite being a decades-old technology, Fortran has several attractive features that make it indispensable, even compared to more recent languages:

- *Array-oriented*—Fortran provides whole-array arithmetic and operations, which greatly simplify element-wise operations. Consider the task of multiplying two two-dimensional arrays:

```
do j = 1, jm
  do i = 1, im
    c(i,j) = a(i,j) * b(i,j)
  end do
end do
```

With Fortran's whole-array arithmetic, you write

```
c = a * b
```

This is not only more expressive and readable code, it also hints to the compiler that it can choose the optimal way to perform the operation. Arrays lend themselves well to CPU architectures and computer memory because they're contiguous sequences of numbers, and thus mirror the physical layout of the memory. Fortran compilers are capable of generating extremely efficient machine code, thanks to the assumptions that they can safely make.

- *The only parallel language developed by a standards committee (ISO)*—The Fortran standards committee ensures that the development of Fortran goes in the direction that supports its target audience: computational scientists and engineers.

- *Mature libraries for science, engineering, and math*—Fortran started in the 1950s as the programming language for science, engineering, and mathematics. Decades later, we have a rich legacy of robust and trusted libraries for linear algebra, numerical differentiation and integration, and other mathematical problems. These libraries have been used and tested by generations of programmers, to the point that they are guaranteed to be almost bug-free.

- *Growing general-purpose library ecosystem*—In the past decade, Fortran has also seen a growing ecosystem of general-purpose libraries: text parsing and manipulation, I/O libraries for many data formats, working with dates and times, collections and data structures, and so on. Any programming language is as powerful as its libraries, and the growing number of Fortran libraries make it more useful today than ever before.

- *Unmatched performance*—Compiled Fortran programs are as close to the metal as it gets with high-level programming languages. This is thanks to both its array-oriented design and mature compilers that continuously improve at optimizing code. If you're working on a problem that does math on large arrays, few other languages come close to Fortran's performance.

In summary, learn Fortran if you need to implement efficient and parallel numerical operations on large multidimensional arrays.

1.4 Advantages and disadvantages

Many Fortran features give it both an advantage and a disadvantage. For example, it's all of the following:

- A *domain-specific language*—Despite being technically a general-purpose language, Fortran is very much a domain-specific language, in the sense that it has been designed for science, engineering, and math applications. If your problem involves some arithmetic on large and structured arrays, Fortran will shine. If you want to write a web browser or low-level device drivers, Fortran is not the right tool for the task.
- A *niche language*—Fortran is extremely important to a relatively small number of people: scientists and engineers in select disciplines. As a consequence, it may be difficult to find as many tutorials or blogs about Fortran as there are for more mainstream languages.
- A *statically and strongly typed language*—As I mentioned earlier, this makes Fortran a very safe language to program in and helps compilers generate efficient executables. On the flip side, it makes it less flexible and more verbose, and thus not the ideal language for rapid prototyping.

The comparison of Fortran to Python that follows will help you better understand its advantages and disadvantages in the general-purpose programming context.

1.4.1 Side-by-side comparison with Python

How does modern Fortran compare to a more recent general-purpose programming language? Python has had the most rapidly growing ecosystem in the past few years for data analysis and light number crunching (http://mng.bz/XP71). It's used by many Fortran programmers for postprocessing of model output and data analysis. In fact, Python is my second favorite programming language. Because of the application domain overlap between Fortran and Python, it's useful to summarize key differences between the two, as shown in table 1.1. If you're a Python programmer, this summary will give you an idea of what you can and can't do with Fortran.

Table 1.1 Comparison between Fortran and Python (CPython specifically)

Language	Fortran	Python
First appeared	1957	1991
Latest release	Fortran 2018	3.8.5 (2020)
International standard	ISO/IEC	No
Implementation language	C, Fortran, Assembly (compiler-dependent)	C
Compiled vs. interpreted	Compiled	Interpreted
Typing discipline	Static, strong	Dynamic, strong
Parallel	Shared and distributed memory	Shared memory only
Multidimensional arrays	Yes, up to 15 dimensions	Third-party library only (`numpy`)
Built-in types	`character, complex, integer, logical, real`	`bool, bytearray, bytes, complex, dict, ellipsis, float, frozenset, int, list, set, str, tuple`
Constants	Yes	No
Classes	Yes	Yes
Generic programming	Limited	Yes
Pure functions	Yes	No
Higher order functions	Limited	Yes
Anonymous functions	No	Yes
Interoperability with other languages	C (limited)	C
OS interface	Limited	Yes
Exception handling	Limited	Yes

From table 1.1, a few key differences between Fortran and Python stand out. First, Fortran is compiled and statically typed, while Python is interpreted and dynamically typed. This makes Fortran more verbose and slower to program but allows the compiler to generate fast binary code. This is a blessing and a curse: Fortran isn't designed for rapid prototyping, but can produce robust and efficient programs. Second, Fortran is a natively parallel programming language, with syntax that allows you to write parallel code that's independent of whether it will run on shared or distributed memory computers. In contrast, distributed parallel programming in Python is possible only with external libraries, and is overall more difficult to do. Finally, Fortran is a smaller language that focuses on efficient computation over large multidimensional arrays of a few different numeric data types. On the other side, Python has a much broader arsenal of data structures, algorithms, and general-purpose utilities built in.

In summary, whereas Python is akin to a comprehensive and flexible toolbox, Fortran is like a highly specialized power tool. Fortran thus isn't well suited for writing device drivers, video games, or web browsers. However, if you need to solve a large numerical problem that can be distributed across multiple computers, Fortran is the ideal language for you.

1.5   *Parallel Fortran, illustrated*

I'll illustrate the kind of problem where Fortran really shines. Let's call this example "Summer ends on old Ralph's farm."

Farmer Ralph has two sons and two daughters, and a big farm. It's the end of the summer and about time to cut the grass and make hay for the cattle to eat. But the pasture is big, and old Ralph is weak. His children, however, are young and strong. If they all work hard and as a team, they could get it done in a day. They agree to split the work between themselves in four equal parts. Each of Ralph's children grabs a scythe and a fork and heads to their part of the pasture. They work hard, cutting grass row by row. Every hour or so, they meet at the edges to sharpen their tools and chat about how it's going. The work is going well, and almost all of the grass is cut by mid-afternoon. Near the end of the day, they collect the hay into bales and take them to the barn. Old Ralph is happy that he has strong and hard-working children, but even more so that they make such a great team! Working together, they completed work that would take four times as long if only one of them was working.

Now you must be thinking, what the heck does old Ralph's farm have to do with parallel Fortran programming? More than meets the eye, I can tell you! Old Ralph and his big pasture are an analogy to a slow computer and a big compute problem. Just like Ralph asked his children to help him with the chores, in a typical parallel problem we'll divide the computational domain, or input data, into equal pieces and distribute them between CPUs. Recall that his children cut the grass row by row— some of the most efficient and expressive aspects of Fortran code are the whole-array operations and arithmetic. Periodically, they met at the edges to sharpen their tools and have a chat. In many real-world apps, you'll instruct the parallel processes to exchange data, and this is true for most of the parallel examples that I'll guide you through in this book. Finally, each parallel process asynchronously writes its data to disk, like taking the hay bales to the barn. I illustrate this pattern in figure 1.3.

Much like farmer Ralph, Fortran is old. This is by no means a bad thing! It's a mature, robust, and dependable language that isn't going anywhere. Although it does have some quirks of an old programming language, it's been improved over decades by generations of computer scientists and programmers, and has been battle-tested in countless applications where performance is critical. The ease of parallel programming with Fortran is key for high-performance apps, which is why I made it a central theme of this book.

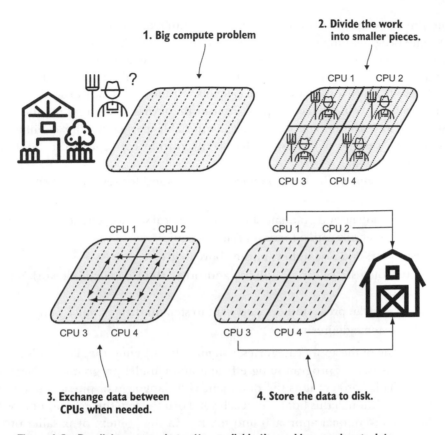

Figure 1.3 Parallel programming patterns: divide the problem, exchange data, compute, and store the results to disk

1.6 What will you learn in this book?

This book will teach you how to write modern, efficient, and parallel Fortran programs. Working through each chapter, we'll build from scratch a fully functional, parallel, fluid dynamics solver with a specific application to tsunami prediction. If you work through the book, you'll come out with three distinct skill sets:

- You'll be fluent with most modern Fortran features. This is a unique and desired skill in a robust, multibillion-dollar market that is HPC.
- You'll be able to recognize problems that are parallel in nature. You'll think parallel-first, and parallel solutions to problems will seem intuitive. In contrast, a serial solution to a parallel problem will become an edge-case scenario.
- You'll get a grasp on good software design, writing reusable code, and sharing your project with the online community. You'll also be able to adapt existing Fortran libraries in your project and contribute back. This will not only make your project useful to others, but can open doors in terms of career and learning opportunities. It did for me!

While I'm not expecting you to have prior Fortran experience, I assume you have at least some programming experience in a language like Python, R, MATLAB, or C. We won't go into detail about what is a program, a variable, a data type, source code, or computer memory, and I'll assume that you have an idea about these concepts. Occasionally, we'll touch on elements of calculus, although it's not crucial that you're familiar with it. We'll also work quite a bit in the terminal (compiling and running programs), so I assume you're at least comfortable navigating the command line. Whatever the case, to help ensure clarity, any Fortran concept in this book will be taught from scratch.

Given the theme of the book, I expect it will be ideal for several audiences, such as the following:

- Undergraduate and graduate students in physical science, engineering, or applied math, especially with a focus on fluid dynamics
- Instructors and researchers in the above fields
- Meteorologists, oceanographers, and other fluid dynamicists working in the industry
- Serial Fortran programmers who want to step up their parallel game
- HPC system administrators

If you fit in one of the above categories, you may already know that Fortran's main selling point is its ease of programming efficient and parallel programs for large supercomputers. This has kept it as the dominant HPC language of physical sciences and engineering. Although this book will teach you Fortran from the ground up, I will also take the unconventional approach and teach it in the context of parallel programming from the get-go. Rather than gaining just another technical skill as an afterthought, you'll learn how to *think parallel*. You'll recognize ways you can distribute the workload and memory to arrive at the solution more efficiently. With parallel thinking, you'll come out with two critical advantages:

1 You'll be able to solve problems in less time.
2 You'll be able to solve problems that can't fit onto a single computer.

While the first is at least a nice-to-have, the second is essential. Some problems simply can't be solved without parallel programming. The next section will give you a gentle introduction and an example of parallel programming.

1.7   *Think parallel!*

> *For over a decade prophets have voiced the contention that the organization of a single computer has reached its limits and that truly significant advances can be made only by interconnection of a multiplicity of computers in such a manner as to permit cooperative solution.*
>
> —Gene Amdahl (computer architect) in 1967

Parallel programming is only becoming more important with time. Although still positive, the rate of semiconductor density increase, as described by Moore's law, is limited. Traditionally we went past this limit by placing more processing cores on a single die. Even the processors in most smartphones today are multicore. Beyond the shared-memory computer, we've connected many machines into networks, and made them talk to each other to solve huge computational problems. Your weather forecast this morning was computed on hundreds or thousands of parallel processors. Due to the practical limits of Moore's law and the current tendency toward many-core architectures, there's a sense of urgency to teach programming parallel-first.

What is Moore's law?

Gordon Moore, cofounder of Intel, noticed in 1965 that the number of transistors in a CPU was doubling each year. He later revised this trend to doubling every two years. Nevertheless, the rate of increase is exponential and closely related to a continuous decrease in the cost of computers. A computer you buy today for $1,000 is about twice as powerful as one you could buy for the same amount two years ago.

Similarly, when you buy a new smartphone, the OS and the apps run smoothly and quickly. What happens two years later? As the apps update and bloat with new features, they demand increasingly more CPU power and memory. As the hardware in your phone stays the same, eventually the apps slow down to a crawl.

All parallel problems fall into two categories:

1 *Embarrassingly parallel*—And by this, I mean "embarrassingly easy"—it's a good thing! These problems can be distributed across processors with little to no effort (figure 1.4, left). Any function $f(x)$ that operates element-wise on an array x without need for communication between elements is embarrassingly parallel. Because the domain decomposition of embarrassingly parallel problems is trivial, modern compilers can often autoparallelize such code. Examples include rendering graphics, serving static websites, or processing a large number of independent data records.

2 *Nonembarrassingly parallel*—Any parallel problem with interdependency between processes requires communication and synchronization (figure 1.4, right). Most partial differential equation solvers are nonembarrassingly parallel. The relative amount of communication versus computation dictates how well a parallel problem can scale. The objective for most physical solvers is thus to minimize communication and maximize computation. Examples are weather prediction, molecular dynamics, and any other physical process that's described by partial differential equations. This class of parallel problems is more difficult and, in my opinion, more interesting!

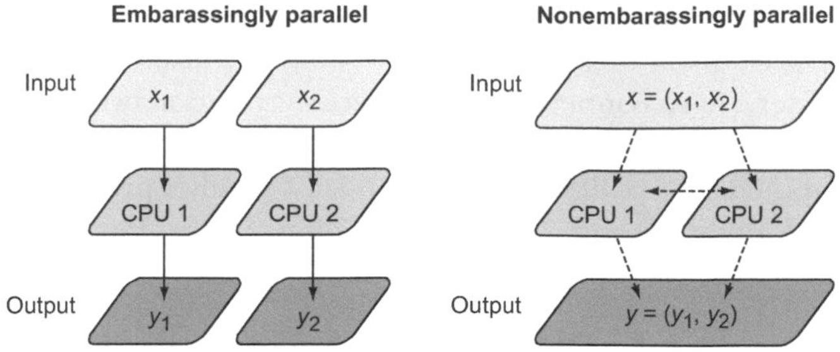

Figure 1.4   **An embarrassingly parallel problem (left) versus a nonembarrassingly parallel problem (right). In both cases, the CPUs receive input (x_1, x_2) and process it to produce output (y_1, y_2). In an embarrassingly parallel problem, x_1 and x_2 can be processed independently of each other. Furthermore, both input and output data are local in memory to each CPU, indicated by solid arrows. In a nonembarrassingly parallel problem, input data is not always local in memory to each CPU and has to be distributed through the network, indicated by dashed arrows. In addition, there may be data interdependency between CPUs during the computation step, which requires synchronization (horizontal dashed arrow).**

Why is it called embarrassingly parallel?

It refers to overabundance, as in an embarrassment of riches. It's the kind of problem that you want to have. The term is attributed to Cleve Moler, inventor of MATLAB and one of the authors of EISPACK and LINPACK, Fortran libraries for numerical computing. LINPACK is still used to benchmark the fastest supercomputers in the world.

Because our application domain deals mainly with nonembarrassingly parallel problems, we'll focus on implementing parallel data communication in a clean, expressive, and minimal way. This will involve both distributing the input data among processors (downward dashed arrows in figure 1.4) and communicating data between them (horizontal dashed arrow in figure 1.4).

Parallel Fortran programming in the past has been done either using the *OpenMP* directives for shared-memory computers only, or with the *Message Passing Interface* (MPI) for both shared and distributed memory computers. Differences between shared-memory (SM) and distributed-memory (DM) systems are illustrated in figure 1.5. The main advantage of SM systems is very low latency in communication between processes. However, there's a limit to the number of processing cores you can have in an SM system. Since OpenMP was designed for SM parallel programming exclusively, we'll focus on MPI for our specific example.

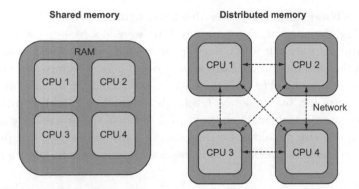

Figure 1.5 A shared-memory system (left) versus a distributed-memory system (right). In a shared-memory system, processors have access to common memory (RAM). In a distributed-memory system, each processor has its own memory, and they exchange data through a network, indicated by dashed lines. The distributed-memory system is most commonly composed of multicore shared-memory systems.

OpenMP versus MPI

OpenMP is a set of directives that allows the programmer to indicate to the compiler the sections of code that are to be parallelized. OpenMP is implemented by most Fortran compilers and doesn't require external libraries. However, OpenMP is limited to shared-memory machines.

Message Passing Interface (MPI) is a standardized specification for portable message passing (copying data) between arbitrary remote processes. This means that MPI can be used for multithreading on a single core, multicore processing on a shared-memory machine, or distributed-memory programming across networks. MPI implementations typically provide interfaces for C, C++, and Fortran. MPI is often described as the assembly language of parallel programming, illustrating the fact that most MPI operations are low-level.

Although still ubiquitous in HPC, OpenMP and MPI are specific approaches to parallel computing that can be more elegantly expressed with coarrays. This book will focus on coarrays exclusively for parallel programming.

1.7.1 Copying an array from one processor to another

In most scientific and engineering parallel applications, there's data dependency between processes. Typically, a two-dimensional array is decomposed into tiles like a chessboard, and the workload of each tile is assigned to a processor. Each tile has its own data in memory that's local to its processor. To illustrate the simplest case of parallel programming in a real-world scenario, let's take the following meteorological situation for example. Suppose that the data consists of two variables: wind and air temperature. Wind is blowing from one tile with a lower temperature (cold tile) toward another tile with a higher temperature (warm tile). If we were to solve how the temperature evolves over time, the warm tile would need to know what temperature is coming in with the wind from the cold tile. Because this is not known *a priori* (remember that the data is local to each tile), we need to copy the data from the cold tile into the memory that belongs to the warm tile. On the lowest level, this is done by explicitly copying the data from one processor to another. When the copy is finished, the processors can continue with the remaining computations. Copying one or more values from one process to another is the most common operation done in parallel programming (figure 1.6).

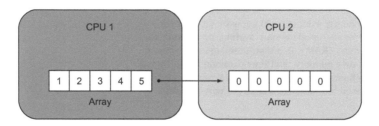

Figure 1.6   An illustration of a remote array copy between two CPUs. Numbers inside the boxes indicate initial array values. Our goal is to copy values of `array` from CPU 1 to CPU 2.

Let's focus on just this one operation. Our goal is to do the following:

1. Initialize `array` on each process—[1, 2, 3, 4, 5] on CPU 1 and all zeros on CPU 2.
2. Copy values of `array` from CPU 1 to CPU 2.
3. Print the new values of `array` on CPU 2. These should be [1, 2, 3, 4, 5].

I'll show you two example solutions to this problem. One is the traditional approach using an external library like MPI. Unless you're a somewhat experienced Fortran programmer, don't try to understand every detail in this example. I merely want to demonstrate how complicated and verbose it is. Then, I'll show you the solution using coarrays. In contrast to MPI, coarrays use an array indexing-like syntax to copy remote data between parallel processes.

MPI: THE TRADITIONAL WAY TO DO PARALLEL PROGRAMMING

As noted before, MPI is often described as the assembly language of parallel programming, and, indeed, that was its developers' original intention. MPI was meant to be implemented by compiler developers to enable natively parallel programming languages. Over the past three decades, however, application developers have been faster at adopting MPI directly in their programs, and it has become, for better or worse, a de facto standard tool for parallel programming in Fortran, C, and C++. As a result, most HPC applications today rely on low-level MPI calls.

The following Fortran program sends data from one process to another using MPI.

Listing 1.2   Copying an array from one process to another using MPI

```fortran
program array_copy_mpi

  use mpi              ◁——  Accesses MPI subroutines and
  implicit none              the mpi_comm_world global
                             variable from a module

  integer :: ierr, nproc, procsize, request
  integer :: stat(mpi_status_size)

  integer :: array(5) = 0                                  Which processor
  integer, parameter :: sender = 0, receiver = 1           number am I?

  call mpi_init(ierr)
  call mpi_comm_rank(mpi_comm_world, nproc, ierr)    ◁——
  call mpi_comm_size(mpi_comm_world, procsize, ierr) ◁——   How many processes
                                                           are there?
  if (procsize /= 2) then
    call mpi_finalize(ierr)                          Shuts down MPI and
    stop 'Error: This program must be run &          stops the program if
          on 2 parallel processes'                   we're not running
  end if                                             on two processors

  if (nproc == sender) array = [1, 2, 3, 4, 5]

  print '(a,i1,a,5(4x,i2))', 'array on proc ', nproc, &    Prints text to screen
    ' before copy:', array                                 with specific formatting

  call mpi_barrier(mpi_comm_world, ierr)

  if (nproc == sender) then
    call mpi_isend(array, size(array), mpi_int, &     Sender posts a
      receiver, 1, mpi_comm_world, request, ierr)     nonblocking send
  else if (nproc == receiver) then
    call mpi_irecv(array, size(array), mpi_int, &     Receiver posts a
      sender, 1, mpi_comm_world, request, ierr)       nonblocking receive
    call mpi_wait(request, stat, ierr)
  end if

  print '(a,i1,a,5(4x,i2))', 'array on proc ', nproc, &
    ' after copy: ', array

  call mpi_finalize(ierr)       ◁——  Finalizes MPI at the
                                      end of the program

end program array_copy_mpi
```

(Annotations in left margin:)
- Initializes MPI → (points to `call mpi_init(ierr)`)
- Initializes array on sending process → (points to `if (nproc == sender) array = [1, 2, 3, 4, 5]`)
- Waits here for both processes → (points to `call mpi_barrier(mpi_comm_world, ierr)`)
- Receiver waits for the message → (points to `call mpi_wait(request, stat, ierr)`)

Running this program on two processors outputs the following:

```
array on proc 0 before copy:     1     2     3     4     5
array on proc 1 before copy:     0     0     0     0     0
array on proc 0 after copy:      1     2     3     4     5
array on proc 1 after copy:      1     2     3     4     5
```

This confirms that our program did what we wanted: copied the array from process 0 to process 1.

Compiling and running the examples

Don't worry about building and running these examples yourself for now. At the start of the next chapter, I'll ask you to set up the complete compute environment for working with examples in this book, including this example. If you prefer, you can follow the instructions in appendix A now instead of waiting.

ENTER FORTRAN COARRAYS

Coarrays are the main data structure for native parallel programming in Fortran. Originally developed by Robert Numrich and John Reid in the 1990s as an extension for the Cray Fortran compiler, coarrays have been introduced into the standard starting with the 2008 release. Coarrays are much like arrays, as the name implies, except that their elements are distributed along the axis of parallel processes (cores or threads). As such, they provide an intuitive way to copy data between remote processes.

The following listing shows the coarray version of our array copy example.

Listing 1.3   Copying an array from one process to another using coarrays

```fortran
program array_copy_caf

  implicit none

  integer :: array(5)[*] = 0          ⬅ Declares and initializes
  integer, parameter :: sender = 1, receiver = 2    an integer coarray

                                               Throws an error if
                                               we're not running
                                               on two processes
  if (num_images() /= 2) &          ⬅─────────
    stop 'Error: This program must be run on 2 parallel processes'

  if (this_image() == sender) array = [1, 2, 3, 4, 5]    ⬅ Initializes
                                                            array in
  print '(a,i2,a,5(4x,i2))', 'array on proc ', this_image(), &    sender
    ' before copy:', array

                              Waits here for all images;
                              equivalent to mpi_barrier()
  sync all       ⬅────────────

  if (this_image() == receiver) &    Nonblocking copy from sending
    array(:) = array(:)[sender]      image to receiving image

  print '(a,i1,a,5(4x,i2))', 'array on proc ', this_image(), &
    ' after copy: ', array

end program array_copy_caf
```

The output of the program is the same as in the MPI variant:

```
array on proc 1 before copy:    1    2    3    4    5
array on proc 2 before copy:    0    0    0    0    0
array on proc 1 after copy:     1    2    3    4    5
array on proc 2 after copy:     1    2    3    4    5
```

These two programs are thus semantically the same. Let's look at the key differences in the code:

- The number of lines of code (LOC) dropped from 27 in the MPI example to 14 in the coarray example. That's almost a factor of 2 decrease. However, if we look specifically for MPI-related boilerplate code, we can count 15 lines of such code. Compare this to two lines of code related to coarrays! As debugging time is roughly proportional to the LOC, we see how coarrays can be more cost-effective for developing parallel Fortran apps.

- The core of the data copy in the MPI example is quite verbose for such a simple operation

```
if (nproc == 0) then
  call mpi_isend(array, size(array), mpi_int, receiver, 1, &
                 mpi_comm_world, request, ierr)
else if (nproc == 1) then
  call mpi_irecv(array, size(array), mpi_int, sender, 1, &
                 mpi_comm_world, request, ierr)
  call mpi_wait(request, stat, ierr)
end if
```

compared to the intuitive array-indexing and assignment syntax of coarrays:

```
if (this_image() == receiver) array(:) = array(:)[sender]
```

- Finally, MPI needs to be initialized and finalized using `mpi_init()` and `mpi_finalize()` subroutines. Coarrays need no such code. This one is a minor but welcome improvement.

Parallel process indexing

Did you notice that our parallel processes were indexed 0 and 1 in the MPI example and 1 and 2 in the coarray example? MPI is implemented in C, in which array indices begin at 0. In contrast, coarray images start at 1 by default.

As we saw in this example, both MPI and coarrays can be used effectively to copy data between parallel processes. However, MPI code is low-level and verbose, and would soon become tedious and error-prone as your app grows in size and complexity. Coarrays offer an intuitive syntax analogous to the array operations. Furthermore, with MPI, you tell the compiler *what to do*; with coarrays, you tell the compiler *what you want,* and let it decide how best to do it. This lifts a big load of responsibility off your shoulders and lets you focus on your application. I hope this convinces you that Fortran coarrays are the way to go for expressive and intuitive data copy between parallel processes.

A partitioned global address space language

Fortran is a partitioned global address space (PGAS) language. In a nutshell, PGAS abstracts the distributed-memory space and allows you to do the following:

- *View the memory layout as a shared-memory space*—This will give you a tremendous boost in productivity and ease of programming when designing parallel algorithms. When performing data copy, you won't need to translate or transform array indices from one image to another. Memory that belongs to remote images will appear as local, and you'll be able to express your algorithms in such a way.
- *Exploit the locality of reference*—You can design and code your parallel algorithms without foresight about whether a subsection of memory is local to the current image or not. If it is, the compiler will use that information to its advantage. If not, the most efficient data copy pattern available will be performed.

PGAS allows you to use one image to initiate a data copy between two remote images:

```
if (this_image() == 1) array(:)[7] = array(:)[8]
```

The `if` statement ensures that the assignment executes only on image 1. However, the indices inside the square brackets refer to images 7 and 8. Image 1 will thus asynchronously request an array copy from image 8 to image 7. From our point of view, the indices inside the square brackets can be treated just like any other array elements that are local in memory. In practice, these images could be mapped to different cores on the same shared-memory computer, across the server room, or even around the world.

1.8   Running example: A parallel tsunami simulator

Learning happens by doing rather than reading, especially when we're immersed in a longer project. Lessons in this book are thus framed around developing your own, minimal and yet complete, tsunami simulator.

1.8.1   Why tsunami simulator?

A *tsunami* is a sequence of long water waves that are triggered by a displacement in a large body of water. This typically occurs because of earthquakes, underwater volcanoes, or landslides. Once generated, a tsunami propagates radially outward across the ocean surface. It grows in height and steepness as it enters shallow waters. A tsunami simulator is a good running example for this book because tsunamis are the following:

- *Fun*—Speaking strictly as a scientist here! A tsunami is a process that's fun to watch and play with in a numerical sandbox.
- *Dangerous*—Tsunamis are a great threat to low-lying and heavily populated coastal areas. There's a need to better understand and predict them.
- *Simple math*—They can be simulated using a minimal set of equations—*shallow water equations* (SWEs). This will help us not get bogged down by the math and focus on implementation instead.
- *Parallelizable*—They involve a physical process that's suitable for teaching parallel programming, especially considering that it's a nonembarrassingly parallel problem. To make it work, we'll carefully design data copy patterns between images.

To simulate tsunamis, we'll write a solver for the shallow water system of equations.

1.8.2 Shallow water equations

Shallow water equations are a simple system of equations derived from Navier-Stokes equations. They are also known as the Saint-Venant equations, after the French engineer and mathematician A. J. C. Barre de Saint-Venant, who derived them in pursuit of his interest in hydraulic engineering and open-channel flows. SWEs are powerful because they can reproduce many observed motions in the atmosphere and the ocean:

- Large-scale weather, such as cyclones and anticyclones
- Western boundary currents, such as the Gulf Stream in the Atlantic and the Kuroshio in the Pacific
- Long gravity waves, such as tsunamis and tidal bores
- Watershed from rainfall and snow melt over land
- Wind-generated (surf) waves
- Ripples in a pond

This system consists of only a few terms, as shown in figure 1.7.

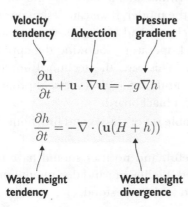

Velocity tendency Advection Pressure gradient

$$\frac{\partial \mathbf{u}}{\partial t} + \mathbf{u} \cdot \nabla \mathbf{u} = -g\nabla h$$

$$\frac{\partial h}{\partial t} = -\nabla \cdot (\mathbf{u}(H + h))$$

Water height tendency   Water height divergence

Figure 1.7 Shallow water equations. The top equation is the momentum (velocity) conservation law, and the bottom is the mass (water level) conservation law. *u* is the 2-d velocity vector, *g* is the gravitational acceleration, *h* is the water elevation, *H* is the unperturbed water depth, and *t* is time. The "nabla" symbol (upside-down triangle) is a vector differentiation operator.

What's the physical interpretation of this system? The top equation states that where there's slope along the water surface, water will accelerate and move toward a region of lower water level because of the pressure gradient. The advection term is nonlinear and causes chaotic behavior in fluids (turbulence). The bottom equation states that where there's convergence (water coming together), the water level will increase. This is because water has to go somewhere, and it's why we also call it conservation of mass. Similarly, if water is diverging, its level will decrease in response.

> **Comfortable with math?**
> If you're experienced with calculus and partial differential equations, great! There's more for you in appendix B. Otherwise, don't worry! This book won't dwell on math much more than this; it will focus on programming.

Shallow water equations are dear to me because I first learned Fortran programming by modeling these equations in my undergraduate meteorology program at the University of Belgrade. In a way, I go back to my roots as I write this book. Despite my Fortran code looking (and working) much differently now than back then, I still find this example an ideal case study for teaching parallel Fortran programming. I hope you enjoy the process as much as I did.

1.8.3   *What we want our app to do*

Let's narrow down on the specification for our tsunami simulator:

- *Parallel*—The model will scale to hundreds of processors with nothing but pure Fortran code. This is not only important for speeding up the program and reducing compute time, but also for enabling very large simulations that otherwise wouldn't fit into the memory of a single computer. With most modern laptops having at least four cores, you should be able to enjoy the fruits of your (parallel programming) labor.
- *Extensible*—Physics terms can be easily formulated and added to the solver. This is important for the general usability of the model. If we can design our computational kernel in the form of reusable classes and functions, we can easily add new physics terms as functional, parallel operators, following the approach by Damian Rouson (http://mng.bz/vxPq). This way, the technical implementation is abstracted inside these functions, and on a high level we'd program our equations much like we'd write them on a blackboard.
- *Software library*—This will provide a reusable set of classes and functions that can be used to build other parallel models.
- *Documented*—All software should be useful, and no user should have to guess what the author of the program intended. We'll write and document our app in such way that the code can be easily read and understood.

- *Discoverable online*—Writing a program just for yourself is great for learning and discovery. However, software becomes truly useful when you can share it with others to solve their problems. The tsunami simulator and other projects developed in this book are all online at https://github.com/modern-fortran. Feel free to explore them and poke around, and we'll dive together into the details as we work through this book.

By working through this book chapter by chapter, you'll gain the experience of developing a fully featured parallel app from scratch. If it's your first software project, I hope it excites your inner software developer and inspires you to go make something on your own. We'll start the next chapter by setting up the development environment so that you can compile and run the minimal working version of the tsunami simulator.

> **Visualizing tsunami output**
>
> As we build and run our simulator, we'll mostly look at raw numbers and time step counts that it logs to the terminal. However, it's both helpful and satisfying to be able to visualize the output of the model. We'll do so every time we add a new piece to the simulator, which makes the solution different and more interesting. I provide Python scripts in the GitHub repository of the project so you can visualize the output yourself. Although it's possible to create high-quality graphics directly from Fortran, it's not as easy to do as it is with Python.

1.9 Further reading

- Fortran website: https://fortran-lang.org
- The history of Fortran on Wikipedia: https://en.wikipedia.org/wiki/Fortran
- Partitioned global address space: http://mng.bz/4A6g
- Companion blog to this book: https://medium.com/modern-fortran

Summary

- Fortran is the oldest high-level programming language still in use today.
- It's the dominant language used for many applications in science and engineering.
- Fortran isn't suitable for programming video games or web browsers but excels at numerical, parallel computation over large multidimensional arrays.
- It's the only standardized natively parallel programming language.
- Coarrays provide a cleaner and more expressive syntax for parallel data exchange compared to traditional Message Passing Interface (MPI) programming.
- Fortran compilers and libraries are mature and battle-tested.

Getting started: Minimal working app

This chapter covers

- Compiling and running your first Fortran program
- Data types, declaration, arithmetic, and control flow
- Building and running your first simulation app

In this chapter, we'll implement the minimal working version of the tsunami simulator. For simplicity, we'll start by simulating the movement of water in space due to background flow, without changing its shape. This problem is sufficiently complex to introduce basic elements of Fortran: numeric data types, declaration, arithmetic expressions and assignment, and control flow. Once we successfully simulate the movement of an object in this chapter, we'll refactor the code to add other physics processes in chapters 3 and 4, which will allow the simulated water to flow more realistically. Implementing the other processes will be easier because we'll be able to reuse much of the code that we'll write in this chapter.

We'll start off by compiling, linking, and running your first Fortran program. Then I'll introduce the physical problem that we want to solve and show you how to express it in the form of a computer program. We'll then dive into the essential elements of Fortran: data types, declaration, arithmetic, and control flow. At the end of the chapter, you'll have the working knowledge to write basic, yet useful, Fortran programs.

2.1   *Compiling and running your first program*

Let's start by creating, compiling, and running your first Fortran program. I assume you've already installed the GNU Fortran compiler (gfortran) on your system. If you haven't yet, follow the directions in appendix A to get yourself set up.

When you have the compiler installed, test it by compiling and running your first Fortran program, as shown in the following listing.

> **Listing 2.1   Your first Fortran program: hello.f90**

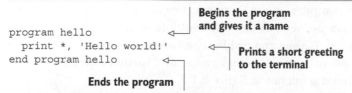

```
program hello
  print *, 'Hello world!'
end program hello
```

Begins the program and gives it a name

Prints a short greeting to the terminal

Ends the program

This program does only one thing—it prints a short greeting message to the terminal—as is common for the first example in most programming books. Let's save it in a file called hello.f90. Compiling is as simple as passing the source file to the compiler and, optionally, specifying the name of the output (-o) executable:

```
gfortran hello.f90 -o hello
```

If you don't specify the name of the output file with -o, the name of the executable defaults to a.out.

Running the program produces the expected output:

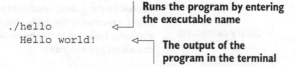

```
./hello
  Hello world!
```

Runs the program by entering the executable name

The output of the program in the terminal

That's it—you wrote and compiled your first Fortran program! Let's take a look at what happens here under the hood. Building a program typically involves two steps:

1. *Compiling*—The compiler parses the source code in a high-level language (here, Fortran) and outputs a corresponding set of machine instructions. In our case, gfortran will read a Fortran source file with a .f90 suffix and output a corresponding binary object file with a .o suffix. Other suffixes for source files, like .f, .f03, or .f08, are acceptable by most compilers; however, I recommend sticking with .f90 for consistency.

2. *Linking*—Binary object files (.o), which are the result of the compilation step, aren't executable on their own. The linker, typically invoked by the compiler under the hood, puts binary object files together into one or more executable programs.

To build our first program, we issued only one command, `gfortran hello.f90 -o hello`, meaning there weren't two separate steps for compiling and linking. This is sufficient when the whole program is contained in a single file, and compiling and linking steps are combined together in one command. That command is equivalent to the following listing.

Listing 2.2   Compilation and linking as separate steps

```
gfortran -c hello.f90          ⟵┐  Compiles only, no linking
gfortran hello.o -o hello      ⟵┐
                                └  Links the object
                                   to an executable
```

In this snippet, the compiler option `-c` means *compile only, do not link*. This procedure is necessary whenever we need to compile multiple source files before linking them into a single program. As your app or library grows in size, you'll find that splitting it into multiple files will make it easier to organize and further develop.

I illustrate the build sequence in figure 2.1.

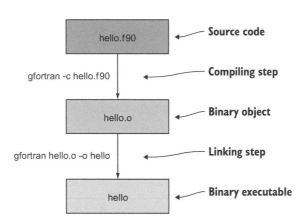

Figure 2.1   Compiling and linking steps that take the input source code and generate binary object and executable files. The source file, hello.f90, is passed to the compiler, which outputs a binary object file, hello.o. The object file is then passed to the linker, which outputs a binary executable file, hello. The linker is implicitly included in the compiler command (`gfortran`).

The GNU Fortran compiler can take many other options that control language rules, warning messages, optimization, and debugging. I encourage you to go ahead and skim through the manual. You can access it by typing `man gfortran` on the command line. If the manual pages aren't available on your system, you can always access the most recent documentation for gfortran at https://gcc.gnu.org/onlinedocs/gfortran.

2.2   *Simulating the motion of an object*

Near the end of the previous chapter, I introduced the shallow water system of equations, which we'll work to solve over the course of this book to produce a realistic simulation of a tsunami. Here we'll start implementing the simulator from scratch, both in terms of the source code and the physics that we'll simulate with it. The first process that we'll simulate is the motion of an object due to background flow. In physics, we call this *linear advection*. Advection means movement through space, and the *linear* property implies that the background flow is independent from the shape and position of the object. Don't worry if you're not a math or physics whiz and this sounds daunting! In the following subsections, I'll illustrate how advection works and show how you can calculate it without having to understand all the math behind it.

> **From calculus to code**
>
> If you want to delve deeper into the math behind this problem, head over to appendix B. There, I explain the *gradient*, which is the key concept behind advection, and how to express it in computer code using *finite differences*. This step is important, as it forms the foundation to express all other terms in the shallow water equations. Otherwise, if you want to skip the math and jump straight to programming, carry on!

In the next subsection, I'll state the problem and set some requirements for our app. Then, I'll guide you through an illustrative example of advection and show how you can calculate it yourself without writing any code. Finally, we'll work together to implement the first version of our app in the remainder of this chapter.

2.2.1 What should our app do?

At this stage, we'll simulate only the movement of an object (or fluid) due to background flow. This will provide the foundation for other physical processes that we'll add to the solver in later chapters. Simulating only one process for now will guide the design of our program structure and its elements: declaration and initialization of data, iterating the simulation forward in time, and writing the results to the terminal. I sketched the result that we expect in figure 2.2.

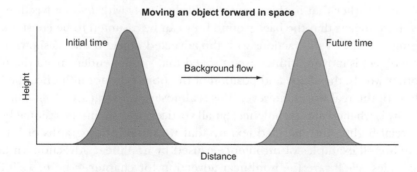

Figure 2.2 Advecting an object in space from left to right. The initial state is on the left. The object is advected from left to right by a background flow and after some time arrives at its final position on the right.

Note that the advected object can be any quantity, such as water height, temperature, or concentration of a pollutant. For now, we'll just refer to it as *the object* for simplicity. The shape of the object is also arbitrary—it can be any continuous or discontinuous function. I chose a smooth bulge for convenience. At the initial time, the object is located near the left edge of the domain. Our goal is to simulate the movement of the object due to background flow and record the state of the object at some future time. Internally, our app will need to perform the following steps:

1 *Initialize*—Define the data structure that will keep the state of the object in computer memory, and initialize its value.

2 *Simulate*—This step will calculate how the position of the object will change over time. At this stage, we expect it only to move from left to right, without change in shape. The simulation is done over many discrete time steps and makes up for most of the compute time spent by the program.

3 *Output*—At each time step, we'll record the state of the object so that we can visualize it with an external program.

As you can guess, the core of our program will revolve around the simulation step. How do we go about simulating the movement of the object? Before writing any code, we need to understand how advection works.

2.2.2 *What is advection?*

Wikipedia defines advection as "the transport of a substance or quantity by bulk motion." Advection is a fundamental process in physics, engineering, and earth sciences. It governs how a solid object or a fluid moves in space because of background flow. When a swimmer is swimming against the current, they're advected by the current, and their speed relative to the ground is lower than if there were no current at all. Advection is also why we find Saharan dust in the atmosphere over the Caribbean, Brazil, or northern Europe, or why garbage patches converge in the middle of ocean basins.

I mentioned earlier that in this chapter we'll deal only with *linear* advection. The word *linear* here means that the background flow can be assumed to be constant, and not changing because of interactions with the advected object itself. As shown in figure 2.2, the object is moving with constant speed that's independent from the object itself. In other words, the shape and position of the object do not influence the background flow. In the real world, however, this is almost never the case! *Nonlinear advection* of velocity is what creates turbulence. Small vortices in a stream, occasional bumps on commercial flights, and marbled texture that we see in photographs of Jupiter's atmosphere are all examples of turbulence caused by nonlinear advection on different spatial scales. We'll save the nonlinear advection for chapter 4; here, we'll focus only on the linear part.

To better understand how advection works, consider a cold front moving across the southeast United States (figure 2.3). A cold front is a large-scale weather phenomenon

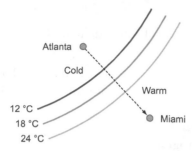

Figure 2.3   An illustration of a cold front moving from Atlanta toward Miami. Curved lines are contours of constant temperature. The dashed arrow shows the direction of front propagation.

associated with mid-latitude cyclones. It typically moves from northwest to southeast in the Northern Hemisphere (southwest to northeast in the Southern Hemisphere) and brings cool and dry air in its wake. Where I live in South Florida, passages of cold fronts are eagerly anticipated because they bring refreshingly cool and dry air from the north.

Now I have a little exercise for you. Consider the following:

- The temperature is 12 °C in Atlanta and 24 °C in Miami.
- The distance between Atlanta and Miami is 960 kilometers.
- The front is moving toward Miami at a constant speed of 20 kilometers per hour (km/h).

Assume there are no other processes at play, and the change of temperature is uniform in space:

1 What is the *temperature gradient* between Atlanta and Miami? Gradient is the difference of a quantity (here, temperature) between two locations, divided by the distance between them. In this case, the temperature gradient has units of °C/km.
2 How many hours will it take for the temperature in Miami to fall to 12 °C?
3 Finally, what will the temperature in Miami be after 24 hours? How did you arrive at this result?

Try to solve this problem with pen and paper. After you've worked through the exercise, you'll have solved the linear advection equation, even if you didn't realize it. The advection equation predicts the change of any quantity due to the spatial gradient of that quantity and the background flow. We'll do the exact same calculation to predict the motion of the object in our simulator. You can find the solution to this exercise in the "Answer key" section near the end of this chapter.

2.3   *Implementing the minimal working app*

Having set the problem to solve, we'll soon be able to dive into Fortran coding. But first we'll go over the implementation strategy (you should always have one) in the next subsection. Then, we'll go over the core elements of the language and apply them to implement the first version of the tsunami simulator.

2.3.1 *Implementation strategy*

Before we do any coding, it will be helpful to sketch out our tentative strategy for implementing the first version of our app:

1 *Define the main program.* This will define the program name and scope. The main program unit provides a skeleton to hold the declaration of data and the executable code, such as arithmetic, loops, and so on.

2 *Declare and initialize variables and constants.* We need to declare all variables and constants that we intend to use in our program:
   - Integer counters i and n, for space and time, respectively, and corresponding loop dimensions grid_size and num_time_steps. The spatial dimension size, grid_size, will determine the length of the arrays, whereas the time dimension size, num_time_steps, will determine for how many iterations we'll calculate the solution.
   - Physical constants for background flow speed, c, time step, dt, and grid spacing, dx.
   - Arrays with real values for water height, h, and its finite difference, dh, such that dh(i) = h(i) - h(i-1) for each i. The array dh is necessary for computing the solution without keeping multiple time levels in memory.

3 *Calculate the equation solution for a set number of time steps.* This step consists of three distinct parts:
   - Loop for a set number of time steps (num_time_steps).
   - At each step, calculate the new value for water height, h, based on the value from the previous time step.
   - Because our domain is limited in size (grid_size), we need to define the boundary conditions. What happens to the object when it reaches the far right edge of the domain (figure 2.4)?

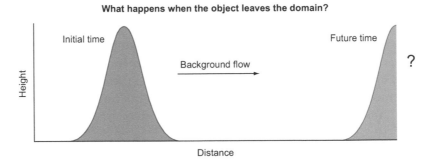

Figure 2.4   Boundary conditions determine what happens to the object when it reaches an edge of the domain. Should it just leave? Reflect back into the domain like a ball bouncing off a wall? Or perhaps cycle and reappear on the left side?

We have a few choices here. The object could be absorbed by the boundary and completely leave the domain without a trace, or it could be reflected back into the domain like a ball bouncing off a wall. Another option is a periodic (or cyclical) boundary condition that connects the right and left edges of the domain. In this case, the object would pass through on the right and reappear on the left. This is a common choice in global atmosphere and ocean prediction because of how our planet is represented in the computational domain. If you go far enough east, you end up in the west! For this reason, we'll implement the periodic boundary condition in our app.

4 *Print the solution to the terminal at each step.* To start, we don't need fancy or specially formatted output. Let's just output our solution in a default text format to the screen. If we want to store the output in a file for analysis or plotting, we can easily direct the output into a file.

Sound good? Let's dive in and tackle these one at a time.

2.3.2 *Defining the main program*

The main program is the fundamental program unit in Fortran. It allows you to assign a name to your program and defines the program scope, as shown in the following listing.

> **Listing 2.3 Defining the program unit and scope**

Begins the new program and gives it a name

```
program tsunami
end program tsunami
```

Ends the program

Assigning a name to a program doesn't do anything in practice, but it can help you stay organized when you start working with dozens of different programs.

Compiling and linking a main program source file results in an executable file that you can invoke from the host operating system (see figure 2.1). You can't invoke a main program from other program units.

> ### What other program units are there?
>
> Here, I give you a sneak peek of what's coming in chapters 3 and 4. Different program units can together form an executable program or a nonexecutable library:
>
> - *Main program*—Top-level unit that can be invoked only from the operating system
> - *Function*—An executable subprogram that is invoked from expressions and always returns a single result
> - *Subroutine*—An executable subprogram that can modify multiple arguments in-place but can't be used in expressions

(continued)
- *Module*—A nonexecutable collection of variable, function, and subroutine definitions
- *Submodule*—Extends an existing module and is used for defining variable and procedure definitions that only that module can access; useful for more complex apps and libraries

For now, we can work with only the main program. We'll dive deep into functions and subroutines in chapter 3, and modules in chapter 4.

The `program` statement is not mandatory. It can be useful to omit it for short test programs. However, it's good practice to include it and pair it with a matching `end program` statement. Technically, `end` is the only required statement for any Fortran program. That statement also makes the shortest possible, though useless, Fortran program.

TIP   Always pair the `program` statement with a matching `end program` statement.

2.3.3 *Declaring and initializing variables*

Explicit is better than implicit.

—Tim Peters

The first part of any program unit is the declaration section. Fortran employs a *static, manifest, strong* typing system:

- *Static*—Every variable has a data type at compile time, and that type remains the same throughout the life of the program.
- *Manifest*—All variables must be explicitly declared in the declaration section before their use. An exception and caveat is *implicit typing*, described in the sidebar.
- *Strong*—Variables must be type-compatible when they're passed between a program and functions or subroutines.

Implicit typing

Fortran has a historical feature called implicit typing, which allows variable types to be inferred by the compiler based on the first letter of the variable. Yes, you read that right.

Implicit typing comes from the early days of Fortran (ahem, FORTRAN), before type declarations were introduced to the language. Any variable that began with I, J, K, L, M, or N was an integer, and it was a real (floating point) otherwise. FORTRAN 66 introduced data types, and FORTRAN 77 introduced the IMPLICIT statement to override the default implicit typing rules. It wasn't until Fortran 90 that the language allowed completely disabling the implicit typing behavior by using the statement `implicit none` before the declaration.

The `implicit none` statement will instruct the compiler to report an error if you try to use a variable that hasn't been declared. Always use `implicit none`!

Intrinsic types are defined by the language standard and are immediately available for use. Fortran has three numeric types:

- `integer`—Whole numbers, such as `42` or `-17`
- `real`—Floating point numbers, such as `3.141` or `1.82e4`
- `complex`—A pair of numbers: one for the real part and one for the imaginary part of the complex number; for example, `(0.12, -1.33)`

Numeric types also come in different *kinds*. A Fortran *kind* refers to the memory size that's reserved for a variable. It determines the permissible range of values and, in the case of `real` and `complex` numbers, the precision. In general, higher integer kinds allow a wider range of values. Higher real and complex kinds yield a higher allowed range and a higher precision of values. You'll learn more about numeric type kinds in chapter 4.

Besides the numerical intrinsic types, Fortran also has the `logical` type to represent Boolean (true or false) states and `character` for text data. These five intrinsic types (`integer`, `real`, `complex`, `logical`, and `character`) are the basis for all variables in Fortran programs. You also can use them to create compound types of any complexity, called derived types, which are analogous to `struct` in C and `class` in Python. We'll dive deep into derived types in chapter 8.

> **TIP** Always use `implicit none`. This statement enforces explicit declaration of all variables, which both serves as documentation for the programmer and allows the compiler to find and report type errors for you.

2.3.4 Numeric data types

Fortran provides three numerical data types out of the box: `integer`, `real`, and `complex`.

INTEGER NUMBERS

The integer is the simplest numeric type in Fortran. Here are some examples of integer literals:

```
0   1   42   100   -500   +1234567
```

You declare one or more integers like this:

```
integer :: i, n
```

This statement instructs the compiler to reserve the space in memory for integer variables `i` and `n`. It's made of the type statement (`integer`) on the left, double colons (`::`) in the middle, and a list of variables separated by commas.

General rules for integers:

- Integers are always signed—they can be both negative and positive, as well as zero.
- They have a limited range that's determined by their type kind. Larger type kinds result in a wider range.

- Exceeding the permissible range of a variable results in an *overflow*. In that event, the value of the variable will wrap around its range limits.
- The default integer size in memory isn't defined by the Fortran standard and is system dependent. However, on most systems, the default integer size is 4 bytes.

REAL NUMBERS

Real numbers, also known as floating-point numbers, describe any number that has a value along a continuous (nondiscrete) axis. Here are some examples of real numbers:

```
0.0    1.000    42.    3.14159256    -5e2    +1.234567e5
```

The first four of these are intuitive enough—the decimal point separates the whole part of the number on the left and the fractional part of the number on the right. The last two may seem strange, as they're written using *exponential* notation. They consist of an integer or real number on the left side of the character e, and an integer on its right side that denotes the decimal exponent. -5e2 thus corresponds to -5×10^2, and +1.234567e5 corresponds to 1.234567×10^5. For positive numbers, the unary plus symbol is optional. We'll talk more about formatting real numbers in chapter 6.

> ### Be mindful about the decimal point!
> When writing literal constants, there's a fine line between what the compiler will understand as an integer or a real. A single period after the number makes the difference. For example, 42 is an integer, but 42. is a real. This is the same behavior as in C or Python.

We declare real numbers using the keyword real:

```
real :: x
```

This declaration statement is analogous to the one for integers, except for the type and variable names.

COMPLEX NUMBERS

A complex number is simply a pair of real numbers, one for the real component and one for the imaginary component. They're declared and initialized like this:

```
complex :: c = (1.1, 0.8)
```

The complex intrinsic type was introduced into Fortran to make arithmetic with complex numbers easier to program. Depending on your application, you'll either use them often or not at all.

2.3.5   Declaring the data to use in our app

Now that you have an idea of how to declare a variable of a specific numeric type, let's declare some variables, constants, and arrays that we'll use in the tsunami simulator.

DECLARING VARIABLES

What kinds of variables will we need? As a reminder, based on our implementation strategy in section 2.3.1, we'll need the following:

- Spatial array size, grid_size, and number of time steps, num_time_steps
- Physical constants, such as time step, dt, grid size, dx, and background flow speed, c
- One-dimensional arrays to carry the values of water height, h, and its difference in space, dh
- An integer index, i, to reference individual array elements, h(i), and another to loop through time, n

Since we need to first specify grid_size before we declare the array h, let's first declare scalar variables and constants, and declare the arrays afterward, as shown in the following listing.

Listing 2.4   Declaring and initializing integer and real variables

```
program tsunami

    implicit none          ⟵⎤  Enforces
                              ⎦  explicit typing

    integer :: i, n              ⎤ Integer
    integer :: grid_size         ⎦ declarations
    integer :: num_time_steps

    real :: dt ! time step [s]        ⎤ Real (floating point)
    real :: dx ! grid spacing [m]     ⎦ declarations
    real :: c  ! phase speed [m/s]

    grid_size = 100         ⎤ Initializes
    num_time_steps = 100    ⎦ integers

    dt = 1.      ⎤ Initializes
    dx = 1.      ⎦ reals
    c = 1.

end program tsunami
```

The declaration section begins with implicit none and ends immediately before the first executable line of code (grid_size = 100). All declarations are done in one place, at the beginning of the program.

Commenting the code

Fortran comments begin with an exclamation mark (!). They can start at the beginning of the line, or they can follow any valid statement.

Ideally, your code should be clear enough that it doesn't need any comments. However, this is often not possible, and most programs need at least some comments. Use your best judgment. If the intent isn't obvious from the code itself, describe it in comments.

Finally, having no comment is *always* better than having an inaccurate or outdated comment.

For variables that won't change value for the duration of the program, it's useful to declare them as constants. This allows the compiler to better optimize the code and prevents you from accidentally changing the value of a constant. We'll declare constants in the next section.

Our program won't do much for now, as we only have the data declarations in it. However, feel free to tweak it, recompile it, and, even better, try to break it! See if the compiler complains.

DECLARING CONSTANTS

Some of the variables will be constant, and Fortran allows you to declare them as such explicitly. Doing so will help you write correct code by triggering a compiler error if you try to change the value of a constant, and will help the compiler optimize the code. You can declare a constant (also known as *immutable*) using the `parameter` attribute, as shown in the following listing.

Listing 2.5   Declaring and initializing constants

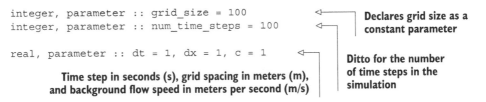

```
integer, parameter :: grid_size = 100
integer, parameter :: num_time_steps = 100

real, parameter :: dt = 1, dx = 1, c = 1
```

Declares grid size as a constant parameter

Ditto for the number of time steps in the simulation

Time step in seconds (s), grid spacing in meters (m), and background flow speed in meters per second (m/s)

Using the `parameter` attribute requires us to initialize the variable on the same line.

> **TIP**   If the value of a variable is known at compile time and won't change for the duration of the program, declare it as a parameter.

DECLARING ARRAYS

Arrays are among Fortran's most powerful features. They have several useful properties:

- *Contiguous*—Array elements are contiguous in memory. Indexing them and performing element-wise arithmetic on arrays is extremely efficient on modern processors.

- *Multidimensional*—The Fortran standard allows up to 15 dimensions for arrays. In contrast, in C you have to emulate multiple dimensions by defining arrays of arrays.
- *Static or dynamic*—Fortran arrays can be static, with dimensions set at compile time, or dynamic, with dimensions set at runtime.
- *Whole-array arithmetic*—You can use the usual scalar arithmetic operators and mathematical functions with arrays as well.
- *Column-major indexing*—Fortran arrays use column-major indexing, like MAT-LAB or R, and unlike C or Python, which are row-major. The first (leftmost) index thus varies fastest. For example, a(1,1), a(2,1), a(3,1), and so on, are consecutive elements of array a. Keep this in mind when you loop over elements of a multidimensional array.

Having declared the integer grid size as a parameter, we can use it to set the size of the array, h, that holds the water height values. You can declare a fixed-length (static) real array using the dimension attribute, and an integer parameter for the array size:

```
real, dimension(grid_size) :: h
```
◁—| **Declares h as a real array with the number of elements equal to grid_size**

The argument to dimension is the integer length of the array—in our case, the parameter grid_size.

Shorthand syntax for declaring arrays

You can declare arrays in an even shorter form by omitting the dimension attribute and specifying the array length in parentheses immediately after the array name:

```
real :: h(grid_size)
```

Whether you use the dimension attribute or the more concise form is completely up to you. However, to conserve space in code listings, I'll use the shorthand syntax throughout this book.

As I mentioned earlier, one of Fortran's strengths is its intrinsic support for multidimensional arrays. You can define an array of up to 15 dimensions by specifying it in the declaration statement, for example:

```
real, dimension(10, 5, 2) :: h
```

Here, h is declared as a three-dimensional array, with a total of 100 elements (10 * 5 * 2).

How about dynamic arrays?

You may have noticed that in both array declarations, we used integer literals to set the size and shape of the array. However, what if our array dimensions are not known until runtime? Fortran provides excellent support for dynamic arrays, also known as *allocatable* arrays. When you declare an allocatable array, you only specify the rank (number of dimensions) of the array in the declaration, not the size of the dimensions. Once the size is known, the `allocate` statement is used to allocate the array with specified dimensions. Allocatable arrays can also be reallocated dynamically any number of times. You'll see more on allocatable arrays in chapter 5, where we'll put them to good use in our app.

For now, we need two arrays in our app—one for water height, h, and another for its finite difference, dh:

```
real :: h(grid_size), dh(grid_size)
```

Now that we have our data structures declared and ready for action, let's see what we can do with them.

2.3.6 *Branching with an if block*

One of the key elements of almost every computer program is taking different execution paths (branches) depending on some criterion. Take, for example, a program that parses a bank account registration form for a customer. If one of the input fields isn't entered correctly, such as a Social Security number having letters or a name having numbers, the program should alert the user and ask for correct input rather than proceeding. You can define this program behavior using an if block. In our tsunami simulator, for now we'll use an if block to check the values of the input grid and physics parameters, as shown in the following listing.

Listing 2.6   Checking for values of input parameters

```
if (grid_size <= 0) stop 'grid_size must be > 0'
if (dt <= 0) stop 'time step dt must be > 0'
if (dx <= 0) stop 'grid spacing dx must be > 0'
if (c <= 0) stop 'background flow speed c must be > 0'
```

Here, we check the values of the parameters to make sure the program can carry out a meaningful simulation. Specifically, we need a grid with at least one element, although this won't make for a particularly interesting simulation. We also need time step, grid spacing, and background flow speed to all have positive values. The conditions are stated in parentheses, immediately after if. On the right side, we specify the statement to be executed if the condition in parentheses evaluates as true. In this case, we use the stop statement to abort the program execution and print a helpful message for the user.

This is only the simplest kind of use case for an `if` statement. Here's its general syntax:

```
if (condition) ...
```

You can use a more verbose `if` block if you need to execute multiple statements on a condition, as shown in the following listing.

Listing 2.7   General syntax of an `if` block with one condition and one branch

```
if (condition) then
    ...                        This branch will execute
end if                         if condition is true.
```

So far, the statements inside this `if` block execute only on a condition that evaluates as true, and nothing happens otherwise. If we need our program to do something in either case, we can use a more general `if/else/end if` block, as shown in the following listing.

Listing 2.8   General syntax of an `if` block with one condition and two branches

```
if (condition) then
    ...                        This branch will execute
else                           if condition is true.

    ...                        This branch will
end if                         execute otherwise.
```

Unlike the single-liner `if` and the `if/end if` block, this one allows for two branches of execution: one if `condition` is true, and another if it's false. It's also possible to test for multiple specific conditions in a single `if` block, as shown in the following listing.

Listing 2.9   The most general syntax of an `if` block

```
if (condition) then
    ...
else if (other_condition) then
    ...                        You can have as many
else                           of these as you want.
    ...
end if
```

The conditions are expressions of the `logical` type. The comparison operators, like the ones we used to check the values of the input parameters, work just like the comparison operators in general arithmetic we learned in elementary school. There are a few other edge cases and logical operators that I'll put on the back burner for now, and that we'll explore later as we encounter them.

In summary, we have a few different forms of an `if`-block:

1 `if` *single-liner*—Useful for simple checks and statements that fit on a single line; for example, zeroing a variable if negative: `if (a < 0) a = 0`

  2 `if/end if`—A more verbose form of the single-line `if`; useful when you have a single condition but multiple statements to execute

  3 `if/else/end if`—Allows executing a statement for either the true or false value of the condition

  4 `if/else if/else/end if`—Like `if/else/end if`, but allows checking the values of multiple specific conditions

That's all you need to know about branching for now. We'll apply these more complex `if` blocks in the following chapters.

2.3.7   *Using a do loop to iterate*

We need to implement looping in our app to do two things:

  1 Loop over array elements to set initial values of water height and calculate the solution at the next time step.

  2 Loop for a number of time steps to iterate the numerical solution forward in time.

The main construct for looping or iterating in Fortran is the `do` loop:

```
do n = start, end          ⊲──|  Increment n from
   ...            ⊲──┐              start to end.
end do                └──  Code inside the loop will execute
                          end - start + 1 times.
```

Here, n is the integer index that changes value with each iteration. In the first iteration, n equals `start`. When the program reaches the `end do` line, n is incremented by one. Internally, the program then checks if n is larger than `end`. If yes, the program breaks out of the loop and proceeds to the code that follows the loop. Otherwise, the control is returned to the beginning of the loop and another iteration is done. The process repeats until the program exits the loop.

By default, `do` loops increment the counter by one. However, you can specify a custom integer increment immediately after the end index:

```
do n = start, end, increment   ⊲──|  Increment n from start
   ...            ⊲──┐                  to end by increment.
end do               └──  Code inside the do loop will execute
                         (end - start) / increment + 1 times.
```

In this case, the loop begins with n equal to `start` and is incremented by the value of `increment` with each iteration.

There are several rules to remember when coding do loops:

- The loop index (n) must be an integer variable (not a `parameter`).
- `start`, `end`, and `increment` must be integers of either sign. They can be variables, parameters, or expressions that evaluate to integer values.

- If start equals end, the loop body will execute only once.
- If start is greater than end and increment is positive, the loop body will not execute.
- If start is less than end and increment is negative, the loop body will not execute.
- A bare do statement without the counter and start and end indices is an infinite do loop that has to be broken out of by other means, such as the exit statement.
- Loops can be nested (loops inside loops).
- Loops can be named. This is useful for nested loops where you want to associate an end do with its matching do, as shown in the following listing.

Listing 2.10 Using names with nested do loops

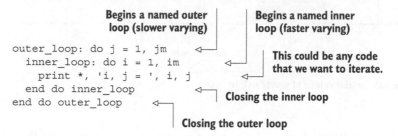

Although naming loops may at first seem unnecessarily verbose, the names become useful in larger programs with multiple levels of nesting. Furthermore, you can use loop names to break out of a specific do loop from any level using the exit statement.

Finally, the general syntax form of a do loop is shown in figure 2.5.

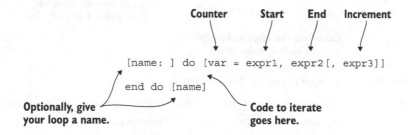

Figure 2.5 General syntax of a Fortran do loop. Optional syntax elements are in square brackets.

In the figure, *expr1*, *expr2*, and *expr3* are start and end indices (inclusive), and the increment, respectively. *name* can be any given name.

2.3.8   *Setting the initial water height values*

Before iterating the solution forward in time, we need to specify the initial state of the water height. In other words, we need to set the initial values of the array h. A common choice in toy models like ours is a Gaussian (bell) shape (figure 2.6).

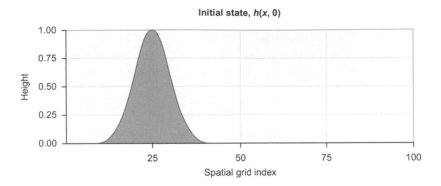

Figure 2.6   Initial values of water height

This is a well-defined, smooth function that we can calculate using the exponential, as shown in the following listing.

Listing 2.11   Initializing the water height with a Gaussian shape

```
integer, parameter :: icenter = 25        Central index and decay
real, parameter :: decay = 0.02           factor of the shape

do i = 1, grid_size                       Loops over all elements,
  h(i) = exp(-decay * (i - icenter)**2)   from index 1 to grid_size
end do
            Calculates the value and assigns it
            to each element of the array
```

Here, we have the first practical use of the following:

- A do-loop to iterate over array elements. Since we've declared h as an array of size grid_size, this loop will iterate over all elements of the array.
- Arithmetic operators -, *, and ** (power).
- An intrinsic mathematical function exp (exponential). This and other intrinsic math functions are readily available to use in Fortran programs and don't need to be imported in any special way.
- Arithmetic assignment (=) of the result of the expression on the right side to the variable on the left side. The value of the left side is updated only after the whole expression on the right side has been evaluated.

Parameters icenter and decay control the position and width of the water height perturbation, respectively. The integer icenter is the array index at which the perturbation is centered. For example, when i equals icenter, the exponent argument reduces to zero, and h(i) equals 1. The real parameter decay determines the rate of exponential decay. Larger values yield a thinner perturbation.

Can our array assignment be done in parallel?

Recall our discussion of embarrassingly parallel problems in the previous chapter. We said that a problem is embarrassingly parallel if there's no data dependency between individual iterations. Take a look at our expression for the initial value of h. Could we distribute this workload among multiple processors?

Begin the practice of asking that question for every computational problem, formula, or equation that you encounter. Over time, you'll find more opportunity to distribute the computation, or at least mark sections of the code that are safe for the compiler to vectorize. Fortran offers a special do loop for this purpose, called do concurrent. It guarantees to the compiler that there's no dependency between individual iterations and that they can be executed out of order, as we'll see in the next subsection.

2.3.9 *Predicting the movement of the object*

We initialized the values of water height and are ready to get to the core of our simulation—iterating forward in time and calculating the solution at each time step. This consists of two steps:

1 Calculate the spatial difference of water height (dh), including the periodic boundary condition.
2 Use dh to calculate the new values of water height h.

The following listing provides the core of the solver.

Listing 2.12 Iterating the solution forward in time

```
time_loop: do n = 1, num_time_steps        ← Iterates over num_time_steps
                                              time steps
  dh(1) = h(1) - h(grid_size)    ←           Applies the periodic boundary
                                             condition on the left
  do i = 2, grid_size
    dh(i) = h(i) - h(i-1)     ←
  end do                                     Calculates the finite
                                             difference of h in space
  do i = 1, grid_size
    h(i) = h(i) - c * dh(i) / dx * dt    ←   Evaluates h at the
  end do                                     next time step

end do time_loop
```

The outer loop, what we call time_loop, increments the integer n from 1 to num_time_steps. Although we're not using n anywhere inside the body of the loop, we use this loop to repeat the body for num_time_steps times. Inside the time_loop, we perform two calculations:

1 We calculate the difference of `h` in space and store it in the array `dh`. We do this in two separate steps:

    a We calculate the value of `dh(1)`, which corresponds to the element on the left edge of the domain. Because we're applying periodic (cyclic) boundary conditions, `dh(1)` depends on the value of `h` from the right edge of the domain.

    b We loop over the remaining elements (from 2 to `grid_size`) and set `dh(i)` to the difference of `h` in space (`h(i) - h(i-1)`).

2 Once we have the array `dh` computed, we use it to compute the new value of `h` and update it. Here we don't need to store the value of `h` for every time step, and we overwrite the old values with new ones.

Fortran follows the same operator precedence rules as general arithmetic:

- Exponentiation (`**`) is evaluated first.
- Multiplication (`*`) and division (`/`) are evaluated second.
- Addition (`+`) and subtraction (`-`) are evaluated last.
- Finally, the precedence can be overridden with parentheses.

Furthermore, Fortran operations of equal precedence are evaluated left to right. For example, this expression

```
h(i) = h(i) - c * dh(i) / dx * dt
```

is equivalent to this one:

```
h(i) = h(i) - (((c * dh(i)) / dx) * dt)
```

A few pages back, I asked you if it's possible to parallelize this loop in a trivial way:

```
do i = 1, grid_size
  h(i) = exp(-decay * (i - icenter)**2)
end do
```

What you should look for is whether any iteration depends on data calculated in any other iteration. Here, the right side depends only on the loop counter `i` and parameters `decay` and `icenter`, whereas the variable on the left side (`h(i)`) is not used on the right side. Could every iteration be carried out in any order without changing the final result? If yes, the computation can be easily parallelized.

The first step is to inform the compiler that this section of the code can be executed in any order it finds most optimal. Fortran 2008 introduced the `do concurrent` construct for this purpose. This construct uses a slightly modified syntax, as shown in the following listing.

> **Listing 2.13 Using `do concurrent` for embarrassingly parallel calculations**

```
do concurrent (i = 1:grid_size)
  h(i) = exp( decay * (i - icenter)**2)
end do
```

Here, we use a `(i = 1:grid_size)` syntax instead of `i = 1, grid_size`. We'll cover this in more detail in chapter 6, but for now we'll use this syntax to promote all our parallelizable loops to do concurrent.

What `do concurrent` is and what it isn't

What does `do concurrent` do exactly? It's a promise from programmer to compiler that the code inside the loop can be safely vectorized or parallelized. In practice, a good compiler would do this using a system threading library or SIMD machine instructions if available.

`do concurrent` by no means guarantees that the loop will run in parallel! In cases such as short loops with simple computations, the compiler may determine that serial execution would be more efficient. We'll study explicit, distributed-memory parallelism with coarrays in chapter 7. For now, we use `do concurrent` as a note for both ourselves and the compiler that some regions of the code are safe to parallelize.

Inside of `time_loop`, can you find any other loops that could be expressed using do concurrent? If yes, use the modified syntax to rewrite them as do concurrent loops.

2.3.10 *Printing results to the screen*

We now have the time loop that iterates the solver for exactly `num_time_steps` time steps. The last remaining step in this chapter is to print the results to screen. The simplest approach is to print the results to the terminal, from where we can redirect the output to a file for later use, such as plotting. For this, you can use the `print` statement, which you already encountered in chapter 1:

```
print *, n, h        ◁—— Prints values n and h to the
                        terminal using default formatting
```

`print` is the simplest output statement in Fortran. The `*` symbol that's placed immediately after `print` signifies default formatting, which tells the compiler to use any format for the data it finds convenient. In most cases, the default format will be reasonable. As noted, here we're printing the values of n (integer scalar) and h (real array with 100 elements) to the screen. This statement will thus output exactly 101 values to the terminal in a single line.

We'll explore Fortran input/output in more detail in chapter 6. For now, `print *` is all we need.

2.3.11 *Putting it all together*

Finally, we've gotten to the exciting part: taking the pieces that we've learned and putting them together into a complete and working program. We'll first look at the solution of our program, visualized with a Python script, and then go through the complete code.

The numerical solution of our simple app is shown in figure 2.7. From top to bottom, each panel shows the state of water height at increments of 25 time steps. The top panel corresponds to the initial condition, as in figure 2.6. The position of the water

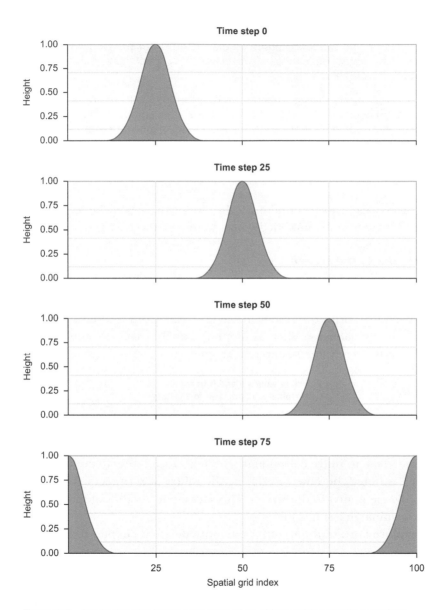

Figure 2.7   **Predicting the linear advection of an object, with periodic boundary conditions. The water height perturbation is advected from left to right with a constant speed of 1 m/s. When the water reaches the boundary on the right, it reenters the domain from the left.**

height peak in each panel is consistent with the configuration of the physical parameters of the simulation: background flow speed (c = 1), grid spacing (dx = 1), and time step (dt = 1). In the bottom panel, we can see the water height peak moving out on the right and reentering on the left. This confirms that our periodic boundary condition works as intended.

Although Fortran is great for high-performance numerical work, it's less elegant for graphics and visualization of data. For brevity and simplicity, I use Python scripts for visualization of the tsunami results. You can find the visualization code in the tsunami repository on GitHub (https://github.com/modern-fortran/tsunami), alongside the Fortran source code in each chapter directory.

COMPLETE CODE

The complete code for the first version of our tsunami simulator is given in the following listing.

Listing 2.14　Complete code of the minimal working tsunami simulator

```fortran
program tsunami          ← Beginning of the program

  implicit none          ← Enforces explicit declaration of variables

  integer :: i, n

  integer, parameter :: grid_size = 100
  integer, parameter :: num_time_steps = 100

  real, parameter :: dt = 1 ! time step [s]
  real, parameter :: dx = 1 ! grid spacing [m]           Declaration of data
  real, parameter :: c = 1 ! background flow speed [m/s]

  real :: h(grid_size), dh(grid_size)

  integer, parameter :: icenter = 25
  real, parameter :: decay = 0.02

  if (grid_size <= 0) stop 'grid_size must be > 0'       Checks input
  if (dt <= 0) stop 'time step dt must be > 0'           parameter values
  if (dx <= 0) stop 'grid spacing dx must be > 0'        and aborts if invalid
  if (c <= 0) stop 'background flow speed c must be > 0'

  do concurrent(i = 1:grid_size)
    h(i) = exp(-decay * (i - icenter)**2)    ← Loops over array elements and initializes values
  end do

  print *, 0, h    ← Writes the initial water height values to the terminal

  time_loop: do n = 1, num_time_steps                    Begins the time loop

    dh(1) = h(1) - h(grid_size)   ← Applies the periodic boundary condition at the left edge of the domain
```

```
do concurrent (i = 2:grid_size)
  dh(i) = h(i) - h(i-1)                    ◁──┐  Calculates the finite difference
end do                                          of water height in space


do concurrent (i = 1:grid_size)
  h(i) = h(i) - c * dh(i) / dx * dt        ◁──┐  Integrates the solution
end do                                          forward; this is the
                                                core of our solver

  print *, n, h          ◁──┐  Prints current values
                             to the terminal
  end do time_loop

end program tsunami
```

With only 30 lines of code, this is a useful little solver! If you compile and run this program, you'll get a long series of numbers as text output on the screen, as shown in the following listing.

Listing 2.15   Text output of the current version of the tsunami simulator

Initial water height output

```
0    9.92950936E-06    2.54193492E-05    6.25215471E-05    ...   ◁──┐  Output after
1    0.00000000        9.92950845E-06    2.54193510E-05    ...   ◁──   first time
2    0.00000000        0.00000000        9.92950845E-06    ...   ◁──┘  step
...
```

Output after second time step

Although it may look like nonsense, these are our predicted water height values (in meters). However, the output is long and will flood your terminal window. You'll be able to explore the output more easily if you redirect it to a file, as the following listing demonstrates.

Listing 2.16   Building, running, and visualizing the output from the tsunami simulator

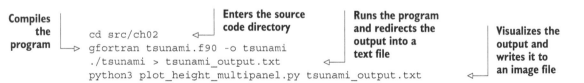

Compiles the program

Enters the source code directory

Runs the program and redirects the output into a text file

Visualizes the output and writes it to an image file

```
cd src/ch02                      ◁──
gfortran tsunami.f90 -o tsunami
./tsunami > tsunami_output.txt                ◁──
python3 plot_height_multipanel.py tsunami_output.txt                  ◁──
```

Alternatively, the source code repository on GitHub also comes with a Makefile to streamline the build process, and you can type make ch02 from the top-level directory. This also assumes that you've set up the Python virtual environment following the instructions in the README.md file in the repository.

Go ahead and play with it. Some ideas that come to mind:

- Tweak the initial conditions, perhaps by changing the shape and position of the initial perturbation. For example, you can change the values of the `decay` and `icenter` parameters, or use a different function when initializing the h array. Try a sine wave (intrinsic function `sin`).
- Change the grid size and number of time steps parameters.

Remember that Fortran is a compiled language. Every time you change the code, you'll need to recompile it before running it.

2.4 *Going forward with the tsunami simulator*

Looking back at this chapter and what we've made so far, it's helpful to summarize what we don't have yet and how we'll get there in the second part of the book:

- In chapter 3, you'll learn about functions and subroutines, and refactor some of the calculations in our simulator as reusable procedures.
- In chapter 4, you'll use Fortran modules to reorganize our app, and you'll implement more realistic physics.
- In chapter 5, you'll learn all about arrays and whole-array arithmetic.
- In chapter 6, we'll dive deeper into input and output, and you'll learn how to output your data in a portable way, format it, and write it to files on disk.

Beyond that, in part 3 of this book we'll explore parallel computing with coarrays, as well as advanced data structures and procedures.

A note on abstractions

As we work through this book, we'll come across new layers of abstraction in each chapter. Here, an abstraction is a programming mechanism that aims to black-box the internal implementation away from the programmer. For example, in the next chapter, functions and subroutines are an abstraction over explicit, imperative code. In chapter 8, you'll learn about derived types, which can contain any number of variables and procedures attached to them, and this is yet another layer of abstraction.

Each layer of abstraction introduces a benefit and a cost. The benefit usually boils down to having to write less boilerplate code, especially when programming repetitive tasks. The cost is that abstractions hide not only the implementation details, but also meaning and side effects if they're not used conservatively and with care. I'll warn you each time we come across a new abstraction in this book. Consider each abstraction carefully, and use them only if the benefits outweigh the perceived costs.

2.5   Answer key

This section contains the solution to the exercise in this chapter. Skip ahead if you haven't worked through the exercise yet.

2.5.1   Exercise: Cold front propagation

1 What is the temperature gradient between Atlanta and Miami? Here, the gradient will be the difference in temperature between the two locations, divided by the distance between them. The answer is thus 24 °C minus 12 °C, divided by 960 km: 0.0125 °C/km.

2 How many hours will it take for the temperature in Miami to reach 12 °C? Let's first get the rate of cooling in Miami. The front is moving with the speed of 20 km/h, and we know that the gradient is 0.0125 °C/km. The cooling rate is then 20 km/h times 0.0125 °C/km: 0.25 °C/hour. The Miami temperature starts at 24 °C, so it will reach 12 °C in 24 °C minus 12 °C, divided by the cooling rate 0.25 °C/hour. The result is 48 hours.

3 What will be the temperature in Miami after 24 hours? We know that the Miami temperature starts at 24 °C and that its cooling rate is 0.25 °C/hour. The answer is then 24 °C - 0.25 °C/hour times 24 hours. The result is 18 °C.

2.6   New Fortran elements, at a glance

- `program`/`end program` statements to define a main program
- Intrinsic numeric types `integer`, `real`, and `complex`
- `dimension` attribute to declare an array
- Arithmetic operators `+`, `-`, `*`, `/`, and `**`, and assignment `=`
- `if` statement and `if` blocks for branching
- `stop` statement to abort the program and print a message to the terminal
- `do`/`end do` construct to iterate over any executable section of the code
- `do concurrent` to mark embarrassingly parallel sections of the code
- `print *` statement as the simplest way to print text and variable values to the terminal

2.7   Further reading

- GNU Fortran compiler documentation: https://gcc.gnu.org/onlinedocs/gfortran
- Wikipedia article on advection: https://en.wikipedia.org/wiki/Advection
- Wikipedia article on finite differences: https://en.wikipedia.org/wiki/Finite_difference

Summary

- Building an executable Fortran program consists of the compilation and linking steps.
- There are five program units in Fortran: main program, function, subroutine, module, and submodule.
- A program begins with a `program` statement and ends with an `end program` statement.
- In every program, we first declare the data, and executable code comes after.
- Use `implicit none` at the top of your declarative code to enforce explicit declaration of all variables.
- There are five built-in data types in Fortran: `integer`, `real`, `complex`, `character`, and `logical`.
- `if` blocks are used to test for conditions and take different execution branches depending on their values.
- Use the `stop` statement to abort the program immediately and print a helpful message to the terminal.
- `do` loops are used to iterate over sections of the code a specified number of times.
- Start, end, and increment values of a `do` loop counter can have any integer value.
- Fortran's arithmetic rules are the same as those we learn in school: exponentiation is evaluated first, then multiplication and division are evaluated, and finally addition and subtraction go last; this order can be overruled with parentheses.
- `print *` is an easy way to print the values of any variable or literal constant to the terminal.

Part 2

Core elements of Fortran

This part covers the core elements of Fortran: procedures, modules, arrays, and I/O.

In chapter 3, you'll learn the most important things to know about functions and subroutines (collectively called procedures). They'll allow you to abstract away any piece of code that you need to run many times. Functions and subroutines are fundamental building blocks that will allow you to write reusable, composable, and complex (but not complicated) code. You'll apply this knowledge to refactor the tsunami simulator we started in chapter 2.

In chapter 4, you'll learn about modules and how to use them to organize your data and procedures in reusable and portable components.

Chapter 5 covers arrays, the fundamental Fortran data structure. You'll learn how to declare, initialize, and use arrays, as well as how to leverage whole-array arithmetic to greatly simplify your code. You'll use arrays for the analysis of stock price time series.

Finally, chapter 6 covers I/O. You'll learn how to read and write data from the standard input, output, and error streams, as well as how to read from and write to files on disk. You'll also learn how to format numerical data as text. You'll practice these skills by writing a minimal note-taking app for the command line.

After you've worked through this part of the book, and with some practice, you'll be a functional and independent Fortran programmer. You'll be able to write Fortran programs and libraries from scratch to solve real-world problems.

Writing reusable code with functions and subroutines

3

This chapter covers

- What procedures are and why we use them
- How procedures break down into two kinds: functions and subroutines
- Writing procedures that don't cause side effects
- Writing procedures that work on both scalars and arrays

In the previous chapter, you learned about the core elements of Fortran: declaration of scalar and array variables, do loops to iterate parts of the code a desired number of times, and arithmetic expressions and assignments. We used them to write a simple simulator that predicts the motion of an object in space and time due to background flow. As we learn new Fortran features, we'll continuously expand and improve our app to produce more realistic simulations. This chapter introduces functions and subroutines, which will help us manage the complexity of our growing app.

This chapter is all about scaling a growing app while maintaining simplicity through code reuse. Our minimal working app has so far been organized as a single program, with a number of statements that the program executes top to bottom.

This is the *imperative* style of programming—you're telling the computer what to do, one statement after another. This approach worked well because we tackled a relatively simple problem. However, we'll now prepare for a more realistic fluid dynamics simulation, which will require more moving parts and complexity.

This is where functions and subroutines, collectively called *procedures*, come in. They'll allow us to define self-contained and reusable nuggets of code that we can invoke whenever needed and using different input data. Procedures are the fundamental building blocks that we'll reuse over and over as we work our way through this book.

3.1   *Toward higher app complexity*

Simple is better than complex. Complex is better than complicated.

—Tim Peters, *The Zen of Python*

Although a mantra of Python, the opening quote applies well to Fortran and programming in general. We always aim for simple, whenever possible. This is especially true in software design, where we often deal with increasingly complex systems. Simple is easy to read, understand, and explain to our friends and colleagues. However, it's a challenge to maintain simplicity as we build an app, a library, or a framework. The more features we add and corner cases we handle, the more bloated our app seems, and we worry that the project will spin out of control. It inevitably becomes more complex. Does that also mean it has to become more complicated?

I don't have a traditional computer science background. I first learned to program so I could solve physics problems, much like the one we worked on in the previous chapter. Programming for me was more a tool to accomplish a given task than an art in itself. Some of my programs could easily grow to thousands of lines of code, consisting of inscrutable reads and writes to binary files, multiply-nested loops, and endless lists of imperative expressions and assignments. No function calls, no code reuse. Abstracting data with object-oriented classes and methods? Forget about it! It was a programmer's nightmare.

Over time, I learned about Fortran features designed specifically to make programming easier. For example, rather than repeating the same calculation on different data, you can write it as a *function* and call it many times with different inputs. You can use modules, introduced by the Fortran 90 standard, to define variables and procedures, which can then be accessed from elsewhere in the program or library. Carefully put together, these elements will make your life easier, whether you prefer an object-oriented, functional, or plain procedural programming approach to your problem.

3.1.1   *Refactoring the tsunami simulator*

In the previous chapter, we made the first working version of what will become a realistic water wave simulator. Contained in a single program, it included data declaration and initialization, arithmetic expressions and assignment to calculate the solution, a do loop to advance the solution forward in time, and a print statement to output the results to screen. With 26 lines of code, this is a simple program that does simple things: it initializes the water height, simulates its movement forward due to background flow, and writes its state to the screen at each time step (figure 3.1).

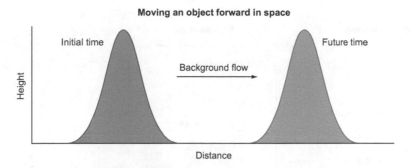

Moving an object forward in space

Figure 3.1 Advecting a Gaussian shape in space from left to right. We worked on this problem in the previous chapter.

In this chapter, we'll refactor the simulator to use a set of common building blocks, such as the finite difference calculation that I introduced in chapter 2. This will allow us to more easily expand the simulator in the following chapters as we move toward a more realistic water wave motion. Recall the core of our solver from the previous chapter, shown in the following listing.

> Listing 3.1 Time integration loop from the minimal working tsunami simulator

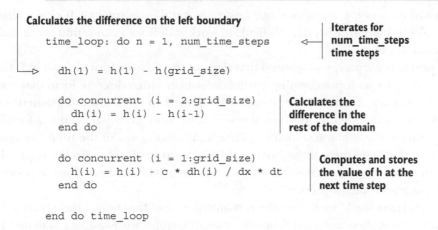

The body of the main loop (time_loop) consists of two steps: calculating the difference of water height h in space, and using that difference to predict and store its new value at the next time step. This solves for only one equation for water height, which features one physics term, namely the linear advection.

To add more terms and another equation, we'll define a new array, u, for the water velocity and add any calculations inside time_loop to make the solver complete. Without assuming anything about what the equations or the code should look like, figure 3.2 illustrates the tentative update of our app.

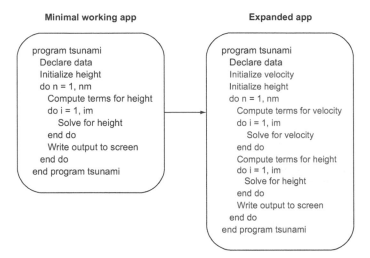

Minimal working app

```
program tsunami
  Declare data
  Initialize height
  do n = 1, nm
    Compute terms for height
    do i = 1, im
      Solve for height
    end do
    Write output to screen
  end do
end program tsunami
```

Expanded app

```
program tsunami
  Declare data
  Initialize velocity
  Initialize height
  do n = 1, nm
    Compute terms for velocity
    do i = 1, im
      Solve for velocity
    end do
    Compute terms for height
    do i = 1, im
      Solve for height
    end do
    Write output to screen
  end do
end program tsunami
```

Figure 3.2   Expanding the minimal working app to a more realistic simulator

The key operations we were doing to simulate the evolution of water height—initialization, calculating the change in time, and solving the equation—we'd now be doing for both water height *and* velocity. It looks like our program would at least double in size if we added code to solve for another variable. Furthermore, if we added more terms to each of the equations, our program would grow further. It's clear that our program will inevitably become difficult to work with if we keep piling more and more code on top of it.

In the previous chapter, you learned that most of the computational work in fluid dynamics boils down to approximating partial derivatives with a discrete form that can be expressed as code. Finite differences, which we used to calculate the gradient of the water surface to predict its movement due to advection, are what we'll use for all the other terms in the tsunami simulator. Since we'll spend most of the time (human and computer time!) on these terms, we should find a way to abstract this low-level calculation and make it reusable from the main solver loop. This is where Fortran procedures and modules come in (figure 3.3).

In this new framework, we define the reusable data and functions inside the module. The module is then accessed from the main program with the use statement. We'll first refactor our minimal working app to compute the finite difference in a function, while exactly reproducing the existing results. Then, in the next chapter, we'll define our new custom module to host our functions, and we'll expand our app to produce more realistic simulations.

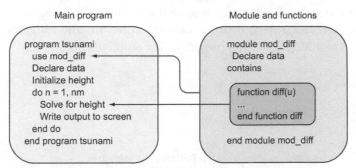

Figure 3.3 Using a module and a function to reuse and simplify code. Module mod_diff, which defines the difference function diff, is accessed from the main program with the use statement (top arrow). Through use association, the function diff can be used within the scope of the main program (bottom arrow).

3.1.2 Revisiting the cold front problem

In the previous chapter (section 2.2.2), I introduced the example of a cold front to illustrate the concepts of temperature *gradient* (change in space) and *tendency* (change in time). There, I asked you to calculate the change of temperature in Miami, considering the temperatures in Atlanta and Miami, the distance between them, and the speed of the front (figure 3.4).

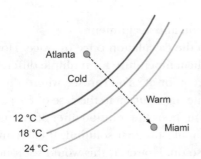

Figure 3.4 An illustration of a cold front moving from Atlanta toward Miami. Curved lines are contours of constant temperature. The dashed arrow shows the direction of front propagation. We used this example in the previous chapter to illustrate the concept of spatial gradients and advection.

What would the program that solves this problem look like? For simplicity, let's assume the same initial parameters as in the example:

- The temperature is 12 °C in Atlanta, and 24 °C in Miami.
- The distance between Atlanta and Miami is 960 kilometers.
- The front is moving toward Miami at a constant speed of 20 km/h.

The compiled program should yield

```
Temperature after    24.0000000    hours is    18.0000000    degrees.
```

If you worked through the exercise of building the minimal working app in the previous chapter, then you have all the ingredients to solve this problem: defining the program unit, declaring and initializing data, basic arithmetic expression and assignment, and printing to screen. The following listing provides the complete code.

Listing 3.2 Solving for temperature due to passage of a cold front

```
program cold_front
                              All declarations
   implicit none              will be explicit.

   real :: temp1 = 12, temp2 = 24      Declares and initializes
   real :: dx = 960, c = 20, dt = 24   the variables
   real :: res ! result in deg. C
                                        The variable to
   res = temp2 - c * (temp2 - temp1) / dx * dt    store the result in

   print *, 'Temperature after ', dt, &    Writes the
              'hours is ', res, 'degrees'    solution to screen

end program cold_front
```

Computes the solution

We first declared and initialized all the input parameters:

1 Origin and destination temperatures, temp1 and temp2, respectively
2 Distance in kilometers, dx
3 Front speed in kilometers per hour, c
4 Time interval in hours, dt
5 The variable res to store the result in

The calculation itself fits into a single expression and assignment.

This program works well if you need to do the calculation once or twice. However, what if the exercise required you to calculate the temperature for multiple different values of input parameters, be it temp1, temp2, dx, c, or dt? You can see where I'm going with this. Specifically, I could ask you to calculate the solution in the case of temp1 being 0 °C, another solution for a front speed of 28 km/h, or the solution after 36 hours. How would you solve this problem? You could compute the first solution, then reinitialize variables and compute another solution, and so on. However, this would soon become quite tedious and result in repetition of code. More problematically, how would you implement a solution that had to work with a continuous stream of input parameters in real time, such as those measured at real-world weather stations?

Experiment a bit

Try plugging in different values for input parameters and rerunning the program. (You'll have to recompile it as well.) Do the results look reasonable? Also, can you find a value of any input parameter that breaks the program? Try it!

3.1.3 An overview of Fortran program units

When I introduced `program` as the main Fortran program unit in the previous chapter, I also mentioned a few others: functions, subroutines, and modules. Functions and subroutines, which are the focus of this chapter, are both kinds of procedures. A procedure is a miniprogram that can be called any number of times from the main program, or from another procedure. Like the main program, procedures have executable code, the code that *does* things. Figure 3.5 illustrates functions and subroutines.

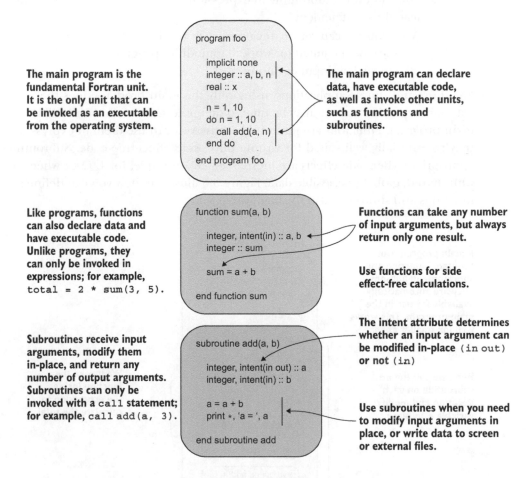

The main program is the fundamental Fortran unit. It is the only unit that can be invoked as an executable from the operating system.

```
program foo

    implicit none
    integer :: a, b, n
    real :: x

    n = 1, 10
    do n = 1, 10
        call add(a, n)
    end do

end program foo
```

The main program can declare data, have executable code, as well as invoke other units, such as functions and subroutines.

Like programs, functions can also declare data and have executable code. Unlike programs, they can only be invoked in expressions; for example, `total = 2 * sum(3, 5)`.

```
function sum(a, b)

    integer, intent(in) :: a, b
    integer :: sum

    sum = a + b

end function sum
```

Functions can take any number of input arguments, but always return only one result.

Use functions for side effect-free calculations.

Subroutines receive input arguments, modify them in-place, and return any number of output arguments. Subroutines can only be invoked with a `call` statement; for example, `call add(a, 3)`.

```
subroutine add(a, b)

    integer, intent(in out) :: a
    integer, intent(in) :: b

    a = a + b
    print *, 'a = ', a

end subroutine add
```

The intent attribute determines whether an input argument can be modified in-place (`in out`) or not (`in`)

Use subroutines when you need to modify input arguments in place, or write data to screen or external files.

Figure 3.5 Overview of a function and a subroutine, and how they're invoked from the main program

Each of these units has different properties and a unique purpose:

- *Main program*—Every Fortran application must have one, and only one, main program. The main program can contain declarative and executable code, as well as definitions of procedures. The main program is the only program unit that you can invoke as its own executable program.

- *Function*—A function is a kind of procedure. Like the main program, it can contain declarative and executable code, but you can't invoke it on its own, and you can only call it from the main program or another procedure. A function always returns only one variable as a result and can only be invoked in expressions. Functions are thus best suited for minimal computational tasks that don't cause side effects.
- *Subroutine*—A subroutine is another kind of procedure. In many respects, it's similar to a function, with two notable differences:
  a You can't use a subroutine in expressions, and you have to call it using a dedicated `call` statement.
  b A subroutine can return any number of results in the argument list. Subroutines are better suited for work that modifies program state or has other side effects, such as input or output.

For short and simple applications, using only the main program does the job. Once you start repeating code, it may be time to define it in a function and call it from the main program. Functions are powerful because you can use them in expressions, and they're especially well suited for writing pure, side effect-free code. Subroutines are appropriate when side effects are inevitable—for example, for I/O or when working with shared, globally accessible data. Figure 3.6 illustrates how you can define and call functions and subroutines in the main program.

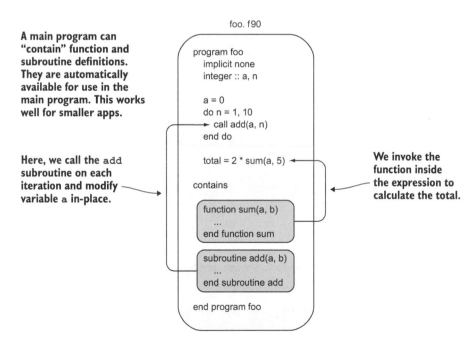

A main program can "contain" function and subroutine definitions. They are automatically available for use in the main program. This works well for smaller apps.

Here, we call the add subroutine on each iteration and modify variable a in-place.

```
foo. f90

program foo
  implicit none
  integer :: a, n

  a = 0
  do n = 1, 10
    call add(a, n)
  end do

  total = 2 * sum(a, 5)

  contains

    function sum(a, b)
      ...
    end function sum

    subroutine add(a, b)
      ...
    end subroutine add

end program foo
```

We invoke the function inside the expression to calculate the total.

Compile it like this: `gfortran foo.f90 -o foo`

Figure 3.6   Defining and accessing an external function and subroutine in the main program

Overall, these are general rules of thumb as best practice, and not hard rules. You'll discover the best way to use functions and subroutines yourself by applying them in practice.

3.2 Don't repeat yourself, use procedures

Like I mentioned earlier, procedures allow you to define snippets of code as their own self-contained units of functionality. You can then use them and reuse them as much as you need, by passing different values of input parameters and getting the results back. They're similar to the main program, in that they can include any declarative and executable code. Unlike the main program, you have to call a procedure from a parent program or another procedure. In other words, you can't just compile a procedure on its own and run it from the command line. Procedures give you the power to define some piece of functionality once, then reuse it as many times as you need by invoking that procedure.

As a general rule of thumb, we'll write any reusable code as functions and resort to subroutines only when we must. This simple principle will help us write simpler programs that are easier to understand and debug.

> **TIP** If you find yourself writing the same piece of code more than a few times, consider making it a procedure.

3.2.1 Your first function

Let's jump straight into it and write our first custom function. We'll take our cold front program from listing 3.2 and rewrite it to delegate the temperature calculation to an external function. This will allow us to easily compute the solution for a series of different input values. Specifically, we'll iterate over several values of time interval dt, ranging from 6 to 48 hours at 6-hourly increments, while holding the other input parameters constant. This will tell us how the temperature in Miami drops over time as the cold front moves through:

```
Temperature after    6.00000000    hours is    22.5000000    degrees.
Temperature after    12.0000000    hours is    21.0000000    degrees.
Temperature after    18.0000000    hours is    19.5000000    degrees.
Temperature after    24.0000000    hours is    18.0000000    degrees.
Temperature after    30.0000000    hours is    16.5000000    degrees.
Temperature after    36.0000000    hours is    15.0000000    degrees.
Temperature after    42.0000000    hours is    13.5000000    degrees.
Temperature after    48.0000000    hours is    12.0000000    degrees.
```

I'll first go over the complete program, as shown in the following listing, and then go more in-depth into the function definition syntax and its rules.

Listing 3.3   Calculating the cold front temperature using an external function

Time interval that we pass to
the function as a real number

```
program cold_front

  implicit none
  integer :: n
  real :: nhours

  do n = 6, 48, 6
    nhours = real(n)
    print *, 'Temperature after ', &
      nhours, ' hours is ', &
      cold_front_temperature(12., 24., 20., 960., nhours), ' degrees.'
  end do

contains

  real function cold_front_temperature( &
    temp1, temp2, c, dx, dt) result(res)
    real, intent(in) :: temp1, temp2, c, dx, dt
    res = temp2 - c * (temp2 - temp1) / dx * dt
  end function cold_front_temperature

end program cold_front
```

Explicit declarations apply to the
whole program scope, including
the contained function.

Loops from 6 to 48 hours
with a 6-hourly increment

Converts the integer counter
to a real number of hours

Prints the
function
result

Separates the program code
and the function definition

Specifies function type,
name, and arguments

Inputs
arguments

Computes the
function result

Closes the
function scope

In this program, we loop over several values of time interval in hours. Inside the loop, we invoke the cold_front_temperature function, using four input arguments that have fixed values, with the fifth input argument being the time interval that varies. The function is invoked on the right side of the print statement, so the result is broadcast directly to the screen. Finally, the function is defined in a special section at the end of the program, marked by the contains statement. In summary, we have three new language elements in this program: how the function is defined, where it's defined, and how it's called from the main program. I'll explain how each element works, one at a time.

DEFINING A FUNCTION

For brevity, I'll go over the function definition by using a simpler example, such as calculating the sum of two integers, as shown in the following listing.

Listing 3.4   A function that returns a sum of two integers

Declares the function result

Specifies the name of the
function and input arguments

```
function sum(a, b)
  integer, intent(in) :: a
  integer, intent(in) :: b
  integer :: sum
```

Declares input arguments
and specifies intent

```
sum = a + b
end function sum
```
Computes the
function result

Closes the function scope

Let's break this down. We open the function body with a `function` statement and specify its name. This is analogous to defining a main program, except for one important difference. With a function, we also list all the arguments in parentheses, immediately following the function name. Like the `program` statement, the `function` statement must have a matching `end function` statement.

Next, we declare the arguments much like we did for the main program, except that here we also have an additional attribute, `intent(in)`. This attribute indicates to the compiler—and to the programmer reading the code—what the intent of the argument is. Here, `intent(in)` means that the variables a and b are to be provided by the calling program or procedure, and their values won't change inside this function.

Like when declaring variables in the main program, you can specify input arguments of the same data type on the same line. Furthermore, you can specify the data type of the function result immediately in front of the word `function`, as shown in the following listing. Notice that we use both of these features in the cold front program as well.

Listing 3.5   Specifying the data type of the function result in the `function` statement

```
integer function sum(a, b)
  integer, intent(in) :: a, b
  sum = a + b
end function sum
```
We specified the data type
of the function result here.

You can put multiple arguments of the
same type and intent on the same line.

It's also possible, for convenience, to specify a different name for the function result, other than the name of the function, using the `result` attribute, as the following listing demonstrates.

Listing 3.6   Specifying the function result as different from the function name

```
integer function sum(a, b) result(res)
  integer, intent(in) :: a, b
  res = a + b
end function sum
```
Specifies a different name
for the function result

The function result is now res.

The advantage to using the `result` attribute may not be obvious from this example because the name of the function (sum) is already quite short, but it comes in handy for longer function names. Note that Fortran comes with an intrinsic (built-in) function sum that returns the sum of all elements in an input array. Because of this, some compilers may warn you if you compile this function, and that's okay. I used the same name for the example in this section only for convenience.

In listing 3.6, the function returns a single scalar as a result. In general, functions can return a scalar, an array, or a more complex data structure, but it's always a single entity.

You may be wondering why I omitted the `implicit none` statement in the declaration section in listing 3.6. In this case, I did it for brevity, and it wouldn't do much here because we use only the input arguments and no other variables in the calculation of the result. However, I omitted it in the `cold_front_temperature` function definition (listing 3.3) as well because the function is defined in the scope of the main program, and `implicit none` then propagates into all procedures defined therein.

As functions always return a single result and can only be invoked from expressions, they're best suited for minimal bits of functionality. A function that does more than one thing is harder to understand. What happens when you start chaining multiple function calls in a single expression, as I'll show you in the next subsection? Well, you should be able to tell what a function does simply based on its name. You can see that it'd be difficult to do so if the function was doing many things. When defining a function, consider the result and the smallest set of inputs required to calculate it. If your function does only that and no more, congratulations—you're on a good track toward clean and maintainable code.

TIP   A function should do one and only one thing.

INVOKING THE FUNCTION

A Fortran function is invoked in the same way as in C, Python, or JavaScript. To call the function `sum` defined in listing 3.6 and print the result to the screen, you'd simply say

```
print *, sum(3, 5)
```

You can also use a function in expressions or output statements, or pass the function result as an argument to another function. All of the statements in the following listing are valid.

Listing 3.7 Examples of invoking an external function

```
six = 2 * sum(1, 2)          ←── Invokes a function in an
                                  arithmetic expression
print *, '2 plus 4 equals', sum(2, 4)   ←── Invokes a function as part
                                             of an output statement
six = sum(sum(1, 2), 3)      ←── Passes a function result as an
                                  argument to another function call
```

You can thus chain functions into more complex expressions, which you can use to write concise and elegant code if used with moderation. In the cold front program in listing 3.3, we invoked the `cold_front_temperature` function directly on the `print` statement.

> **Actual and dummy arguments**
>
> The Fortran Standard uses specific terminology to differentiate between arguments defined inside the procedure and those that are passed in the call. *Actual* arguments are the ones that you pass when invoking the procedure. *Dummy* arguments are the ones declared in the procedure definition. In the previous example of `sum(3, 5)`, the integer literals `3` and `5` are the actual arguments, and integers `a` and `b` in the function definition are dummy arguments. Being aware of this distinction and terminology will prove to be useful later when we tease out more advanced procedure concepts, as well as if you read Fortran Standard documents or other Fortran books.

SPECIFYING THE INTENT OF THE ARGUMENTS

If you look closely at the declaration statements for arguments a and b in listings 3.4 to 3.6, you'll notice the `intent` attribute—something that we haven't used in our programs so far. This attribute informs the compiler about the semantic purpose of the arguments, and it can take three different values:

- `intent(in)`—The argument is an *input* argument. It will be provided to the procedure by the calling program or procedure, and its value won't change inside the procedure.
- `intent(out)`—The argument is an *output* argument. Its value is assigned inside the procedure and returned back to the calling program or procedure.
- `intent(in out)`—The argument is an *input* and *output* argument. It's provided to the procedure by the calling program or procedure, its value can be modified inside the procedure, and its value is returned to the calling program or procedure.

Like `implicit none`, specifying the intent is optional but strongly recommended. First, an intent specification clearly indicates to the programmer (especially if they're not the original author of the code) what the role of each argument is, which helps with both understanding and debugging the code. Second, specifying intent can help the compiler raise errors if the actual code is in violation of the intent specification. For example, if you declare an argument as an `intent(in)` variable, the compiler won't let you use it on the left side of an assignment. Being explicit regarding the intent of all arguments will help you write transparent and correct programs.

TIP Always specify `intent` for all arguments.

I mentioned earlier that functions are best suited for calculations that don't cause side effects, whereas subroutines are more appropriate when we need to modify variables in-place. These are best practices, rather than hard rules: Fortran allows `intent(in out)` and `intent(out)` arguments for functions as well as subroutines, which means that functions could be used to modify variables in-place.

WHERE TO DEFINE A FUNCTION

Before modules were introduced by the Fortran 90 standard, it was common for functions to be defined in their own file. State-of-the-art linear algebra libraries like BLAS (Basic Linear Algebra Subprograms, https://www.openblas.net) or LAPACK (Linear Algebra PACKage, http://www.netlib.org/lapack) are still organized in the one-procedure-per-file model. For larger programs and libraries, it's best practice to define functions in a module and have one module per source file. For short and simple programs, you can place the function definition within the scope of the main program. As we won't go into more details on modules until the next chapter, we'll define all our procedures in the main program for now.

To define a function in the main program, place it near the end of the program, immediately following the `contains` statement and before the `end program` statement. The `contains` statement separates the main program code above it from the procedure definitions beneath it, as the following listing demonstrates.

Listing 3.8   Defining a function inside the program scope

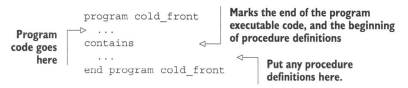

This rule will also apply to defining functions in a module, as you'll learn in the next chapter.

3.2.2   *Expressing finite difference as a function in the tsunami simulator*

You now understand how to define a function and how to call it from the main program. Finally, we get to the fun part—applying our new knowledge about functions to refactor our tsunami simulator. Let's look back at the main time loop in our program, as reprised in the following listing.

Listing 3.9   The time integration loop from the minimal working tsunami simulator

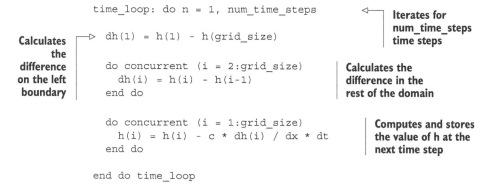

At the beginning of this chapter, I mentioned that we'll use the finite difference calculation quite a bit as we move toward a more realistic wave simulator. A good first step, then, may be to replace the following

```
dh(1) = h(1) - h(grid_size)

do concurrent (i = 2:grid_size)
  dh(i) = h(i) - h(i-1)
end do
```

with a function call like this:

```
dh = diff(h)
```

In a nutshell, we'll pack both the finite difference calculation (`dh(i) = h(i) - h(i-1)`) and the handling of the boundary condition (`dh(1) = h(1) - h(grid_size)`) into a single function `diff` that we can reuse whenever needed. This will be quite useful down the road as we add more physics terms to our solver. If coded correctly, the new program will output exactly the same results as the original version. Our `time_loop` in the main program should now look like the following listing.

Listing 3.10 Delegating the finite differencing to a function

```
time_loop: do n = 1, num_time_steps

  dh = diff(h)            ◁──┤ Calculates the difference
                              │ in a function

  do concurrent (i = 1:grid_size)
    h(i) = h(i) - c * dh(i) / dx * dt    │ Computes and stores
  end do                                 │ the new value of h

  print *, n, h          ◁──┐ Write the values
                            │ to screen
end do time_loop
```

And the following listing shows the definition of the `diff` function.

Listing 3.11 Finite difference calculation expressed as a function

```
function diff(x) result(dx)         │ Assumed-shape real array
  real, intent(in) :: x(:)      ◁───┤ as input argument
  real :: dx(size(x))        ◁──┐ The result will be a real
  integer :: im                 │ array of the same size as x.
  im = size(x)
  dx(1) = x(1) - x(im)            ◁──┐ Calculates the
  dx(2:im) = x(2:im) - x(1:im-1) ◁──┤ boundary value
end function diff
```

Calculates the finite difference
for all other elements of x

We're now calculating the difference in space in the function and are down to only one do loop inside the main time loop. Before we move on to subroutines, I'll give you a sneak peek into one of Fortran's most powerful features—its array-oriented syntax. While I only mentioned this briefly in chapter 1 when discussing the strengths and weaknesses of Fortran, we haven't had the opportunity yet to cast arithmetic operations on whole arrays. We'll go into more depth with everything about arrays in chapter 5, but for now, let's rewrite the main time loop to greatly simplify it, as the following listing demonstrates.

> **Listing 3.12   Solving the advection equation with a single expression**

```
time_loop: do n = 1, num_time_steps
  h = h - c * diff(h) / dx * dt          ⟵   Invokes diff(h) directly to
                                              update the new value of h
  print *, n, h            ⟵   Writes the values
end do time_loop               to screen
```

Now this is pretty sweet! We have a solver that not only fits in a single line of code, but also appears almost exactly the same as our original math equation. The internal details of the finite difference calculation are now hidden in the implementation of the function diff, and here we simply call it to calculate the difference when we need it. Substituting a whole loop with an array operation is possible because h and diff(h) are of the same shape (one-dimensional) and size. Notice also that c, dx, and dt are all scalar variables, and they're compatible with array operations. Stay tuned for more in chapter 5.

3.3   *Modifying program state with subroutines*

I mentioned earlier that Fortran has two kinds of procedures: functions and subroutines. Many rules that we covered for functions apply to subroutines as well. They're both designed to be reused many times, and both may have input and output arguments. Unlike functions, subroutines can't be used in expressions and can only be invoked in a dedicated call statement. They're more suitable for operations with side effects, such as modifying variables in-place and I/O. In this section, I'll show you how subroutines are different from functions and when you should use them instead.

3.3.1   *Defining and calling a subroutine*

Let's see the difference between a subroutine and a function in an example. The following listing defines a subroutine add that's equivalent to our function sum from the previous subsection.

> **Listing 3.13   A subroutine that calculates the sum of two integers**

```
subroutine add(a, b, res)
  integer, intent(in) :: a, b          ⟵   Inputs arguments like before
  integer, intent(out) :: res     ⟵   Outputs argument that's
  res = a + b                          returned to the caller
end subroutine add
```

Here, a and b are input arguments—notice the intent(in) attribute just like in the sum function—and res is the output argument, with the intent(out) attribute. This subroutine calculates the sum of integers a and b and stores the resulting value into res. These arguments need to be matched in type by the arguments passed in the calling program or procedure.

You invoke a subroutine with a call statement:

```
call add(3, 5, res)          ◁── Calculates the sum of 3 and
                                  5 and stores it into res
```

As you can see, it's impossible to invoke a subroutine from an expression, like we did with a function, because Fortran requires a dedicated call statement. Another oddity is that the subroutine itself doesn't have any value on return, but any result must be returned as an argument with an intent(out) or intent(in out) attribute. This is analogous to void-typed functions in C, or any Python function that doesn't have a return statement. This is why, as you'll see in chapter 12, we'll use subroutines and not functions to interface void-typed C functions in a portable way.

It's also possible to declare arguments as intent(in out), which would make them both input and output. For an everyday real-world analogy, consider a toaster:

- Your inputs are electric power, a slice of bread, and a setting, such as toasting time and temperature, and you get a toasted slice of bread as a result.
- The electric power and the toaster setting are intent(in) arguments here—they're not modified or returned by the toaster.
- The slice of bread, however, is an intent(in out) argument.
- The bread goes in untoasted, and comes out toasted, warm, and crispy.
- The bread is thus modified in-place by the toaster.

Simulating a toaster is thus more appropriate with a subroutine than a function. Figure 3.7 illustrates this scenario. type(bread_type) here is an example of a derived type, which we'll explore in detail in chapter 8.

Practice some intent(in out) arguments by modifying a global variable with a subroutine in the "Exercise 1" sidebar.

Exercise 1: Modifying state with a subroutine

I discussed earlier the use of the intent attribute in the declaration specification of arguments. You can use the intent(in out) attribute to modify a variable in-place. Can you rewrite the subroutine add (listing 3.13) such that it adds b to a and returns a so that its value is updated in the calling program? For example, the expected behavior should be as shown in listing 3.14.

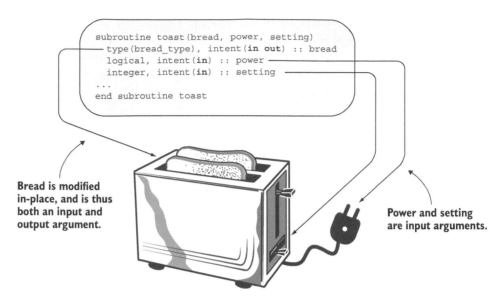

Figure 3.7   An illustration of a subroutine that takes an input/output argument

Listing 3.14   Invoking a subroutine that modifies an input argument in-place

```
program subroutine_example
  implicit none
  integer :: a              Should print 1
  a = 0                     to the screen
  call add(a, 1)
  print *, a            ←   Should print 3
  call add(a, 2)            to the screen
  print *, a            ←
contains                    Define the subroutine
  ...                       "add" here.
end program subroutine_example
```

You can find the solution to this exercise in the "Answer key" section near the end of this chapter.

3.3.2   *When do you use a subroutine over a function?*

Whenever I write a new procedure, I use the rules of thumb shown in figure 3.8 to decide whether to make it a function or a subroutine.

This is a simple decision-making process that you can follow. If you know your procedure will cause side effects, such as I/O or modifying a variable declared outside of the procedure, use a subroutine. Also, if you need your procedure to return more than one variable as a result, you have no choice but to use a subroutine. However, these are all special cases. The general rule from figure 3.8 boils down to always using a function unless a subroutine is necessary.

TIP Always use a function, unless you have to use a subroutine.

Technically, Fortran allows you to have `intent(out)` and `intent(in out)` arguments in functions. This kind of function would both return its normal result and modify one or more of its arguments in place. This inevitably creates side effects that are difficult to debug, and it hinders the compiler from optimizing the program. There's even a feature of the language designed to prevent side effects: *pure procedures*. In practice, pure procedures allow you to write code that the compiler can safely optimize, and that potentially can even be executed out of order.

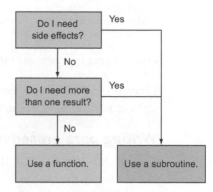

Figure 3.8 Deciding when to use a subroutine over a function

3.3.3 *Initializing water height in the tsunami simulator*

Recall the initialization part of our tsunami simulator from listing 2.13, which is repeated in the following listing for your convenience, where we set the initial conditions.

Listing 3.15 Initializing the tsunami simulator

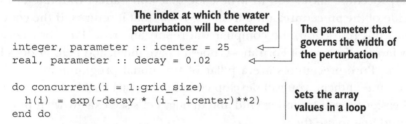

The index at which the water perturbation will be centered

The parameter that governs the width of the perturbation

```
integer, parameter :: icenter = 25
real, parameter :: decay = 0.02

do concurrent(i = 1:grid_size)
  h(i) = exp(-decay * (i - icenter)**2)
end do
```

Sets the array values in a loop

The second part of our refactor involves defining the initialization in an external procedure so that the initial state can be set and changed more easily, by just doing

```
call set_gaussian(h, icenter, decay)
```

Now isn't this much nicer? The algorithm is abstracted away, and if we want to change the initial parameters, we just change the values that we pass as input arguments. This subroutine will need to modify h in-place, so we'll declare it as an `intent(in out)` argument, as in the "Exercise 1" sidebar. The following listing provides the complete subroutine.

Listing 3.16 A subroutine to initialize an array with a Gaussian shape

```
subroutine set_gaussian(x, icenter, decay)
  real, intent(in out) :: x(:)
```

One-dimensional array as input (and output) argument

```
    integer, intent(in) :: icenter          Input parameters for the
    real, intent(in) :: decay               perturbation position and shape
    integer :: i
    do concurrent(i = 1:size(x))
      x(i) = exp(-decay * (i - icenter)**2)    Loops over array elements
    end do                                      and sets their values
end subroutine set_gaussian
```

Like the `diff` function we implemented earlier, we'll place this subroutine after the `contains` statement in the main program.

3.4 Writing pure procedures to avoid side effects

Fortran lets you define a function or a subroutine in a way that prevents side effects. What exactly do I mean here by *side effects*? For a concrete example, consider the traffic grid in a major city. Roadwork on a busy road during rush hour will soon slow down the incoming traffic, causing a traffic jam miles away. This is a side effect of the roadwork; on its own, it's a local effect, but because it impacts the incoming traffic, it causes a ripple effect in a remote part of the system. As a result, we get the repair and the hour-long traffic jam. In contrast, if the roadwork were to be scheduled in the middle of the night when there's no or little traffic, its effects would be isolated from the rest of the system. In that case, we'd only get the repair as intended, without any adverse side effects.

A pure procedure allows you to write code that won't affect the state of the program outside of the procedure, aside from the result that it returns. If the code somehow violates this restriction, the compiler will report an error. Pure procedures are among my favorite features of Fortran—C doesn't have them, and neither does Python or JavaScript. Pure procedures are a pillar of functional programming, and if you make liberal use of them, you will develop code that's easier for the compiler to optimize, and easier for you to understand and debug. Let's see exactly what pure procedures are and how to use them.

3.4.1 What is a pure procedure?

A Fortran procedure is *pure* when it doesn't cause any observable side effects, such as I/O or modifying the value of a variable declared outside of the procedure. To define a procedure as pure, simply add the `pure` attribute to its `function` or `subroutine` statement, as shown in the following listing.

Listing 3.17   Defining a pure, side effect-free function

```
pure integer function sum(a, b)
  integer, intent(in) :: a, b       The pure attribute
  sum = a + b                        asserts that the function
end function sum                     is free of side effects.
```

You can call a pure function in the same way as any other function, and ditto for subroutines.

3.4.2 Some restrictions on pure procedures

A pure procedure, while advantageous from both program design and compiler optimization perspectives, does come with a number of restrictions:

- If it's a function, it can't alter its input arguments. This implies that all dummy arguments must be declared with the intent(in) attribute.
- It can read global variables (for the main program or module), but it can't alter them.
- It can invoke only pure procedures.
- It can't contain the stop statement—this would stop the execution of the whole program, and is thus a side effect.

There are several more restrictions on pure procedures that are more situational and that you're less likely to encounter. We'll revisit this topic later in the book as we encounter these edge cases.

3.4.3 Why are pure functions important?

Including a pure attribute in your function and subroutine statements forces you to write side effect-free code. This has two principal benefits:

- Side effect-free code is easier to debug. It comes with a guarantee that the code isn't changing the state of the program anywhere outside of the procedure, and any effects are localized.
- It allows the compiler to execute the procedure in the most efficient way. A good compiler on a multicore system can even execute a pure procedure in parallel, if that would be more efficient.

> **TIP** Write pure procedures whenever possible.

As I'll show you later in the book, using the pure attribute can get you a long way toward functional programming with Fortran.

3.5 Writing procedures that operate on both scalars and arrays

When a procedure is defined to operate on scalar arguments, it's relatively straightforward to make it work with array arguments as well. For example, recall our pure function sum from the previous subsection:

```
pure integer function sum(a, b)
  integer, intent(in) :: a, b
  sum = a + b
end function sum
```

Invoking this function as, say, sum(3, 5) will evaluate to 8. Is there a way to pass array arguments to this function such that it returns an array as a result? For example, if we called sum([1, 2, 3], [2, 3, 4]), we'd get [3, 5, 7] as a result. One approach would be to declare another function that receives arrays as arguments, and we'd invoke that function instead. Fortran offers a much more elegant approach to this. You can declare the procedure as elemental, which automatically allows the scalar dummy arguments to be treated as arrays, if the arguments passed in are arrays. The result of the procedure then takes the same shape as the input arrays.

Consider the following definition:

```
pure elemental integer function sum(a, b)          ◁─┐   The elemental attribute allows
  integer, intent(in) :: a, b                          receiving array arguments in
  sum = a + b                                          place of scalars.
end function sum
```

With the function defined in this way, you can pass an array as an argument to either a or b, or both. If more than one argument passed is an array, then all the array arguments have to be of the same shape.

Specifically, you can call the function like this:

Both arguments are scalars; evaluates to 8. **Only the first argument is an array; evaluates to [4, 5].**

```
print *, sum(3, 5)          ◁─┘
print *, sum([1, 2], 3)     ◁─
print *, sum(1, [2, 3, 4])      ◁─
print *, sum([1, 2, 3], [2, 3, 4])    ◁─
print *, sum([1, 2], [2, 3, 4])   ◁─┐
```

Only the second argument is an array; evaluates to [3, 4, 5].

Both arguments are arrays; evaluates to [3, 5, 7].

Arrays are not of the same shape—this is illegal!

These elemental snippets demonstrate different ways you can invoke an elemental function. If you try to compile the program with the last line in there (sum([1, 2], [2, 3, 4])), the compiler will raise an error. For example, gfortran reports

```
sum_function_elemental.f90:9:23:

  print *, sum([1, 2], [2, 3, 4])
                      1
Error: Different shape for elemental procedure at (1) on dimension 1 (3 and 2)
```

This is an important restriction of elemental procedures to keep in mind. If you pass multiple arrays as arguments to an elemental procedure, they all have to be of conforming shape.

The cold front function that we worked on earlier in this chapter is the perfect candidate for an elemental function. Try doing the exercise in the sidebar to redefine that function with the elemental attribute, and call it by passing arrays to it.

Exercise 2: Writing an elemental function that operates on both scalars and arrays

In subsection 3.2.1 we wrote a function that calculates the cold front temperature given five real scalar arguments as input (see listing 3.3). In the main program of that same listing, we used a do loop to iterate over different values of time increment to invoke the cold front temperature function at different times.

Can you use the elemental feature to redefine that function, and call it from the main program with an array of times (instead of a do loop)? For example, you could invoke the function like this:

```
real :: dt(8)

dt = [6, 12, 18, 24, 30, 36, 42, 48]
cold_front_temperature(12., 24., 20., 960., dt)
```

As a result, the function should return an array of the same length as dt:

```
22.5000000      21.0000000      19.5000000      18.0000000
  16.5000000      15.0000000      13.5000000      12.0000000
```

You can find the solution to this exercise in the "Answer key" section near the end of this chapter.

When you use the elemental attribute to define a procedure, it's automatically defined as pure, even if pure is not explicitly specified. It is, however, good practice to specify both attributes for clarity.

Impure elemental?

I mentioned that an elemental procedure is automatically promoted to a pure procedure, even if the pure attribute is omitted from the procedure definition. Is the pure attribute really necessary for elemental properties? Since the Fortran 2008 standard, you can define the procedure as impure elemental. This feature is specifically designed to allow elemental behavior for nonpure procedures. In practice, you'd want to use impure elemental whenever you have a function that operates on both scalars and arrays but needs functionality that's not permitted in pure procedures. These include I/O to and from screen or external files, calling C functions, or exchanging data with other parallel processors.

3.6 *Procedures with optional arguments*

Both functions and subroutines can accept optional arguments. These are arguments that may be omitted by the caller, even if they're specified in the procedure definition. To see optional arguments in action, let's take our subroutine add from listing 3.13 and add an optional debug input parameter, as shown in listing 3.18. If this parameter is passed by the caller as the logical `.true.` value, we'll print some debug statements to the screen, which can be helpful in diagnosing unexpected behavior in more complex programs.

Listing 3.18   Example of a subroutine using an optional input argument

```
subroutine add(a, b, res, debug)

  integer, intent(in) :: a, b
  integer, intent(out) :: res
  logical, intent(in), optional :: debug

  if (present(debug)) then
    if (debug) then
      print *, 'DEBUG: subroutine add, a = ', a
      print *, 'DEBUG: subroutine add, b = ', b
    end if
  end if

  res = a + b

  if (present(debug)) then
    if (debug) print *, &
      'DEBUG: subroutine add, res = ', res
  end if

end subroutine add
```

Marks the argument as optional using the "optional" attribute

If debug is both present and .true., prints helpful diagnostics to the screen

The new argument to this subroutine, `debug`, is now declared with the `optional` attribute. Inside, we need to check whether the argument is passed or not. We do so by using an `if` block and `present`, a built-in function. This function returns `.true.` if its argument is present (passed in by the caller), and `.false.` otherwise. If not present, an optional argument must not be referenced inside the procedure in any way other than as an argument to `present`, or as an optional argument to another procedure. Because of this restriction, you now understand why I needed to make separate `if` tests for the presence of `debug` and for its value.

We can now invoke this subroutine in any of the following ways:

```
call add(3, 5, res)
call add(3, 5, res, .true.)
call add(3, 5, res, debug=.true.)
```

If invoked with the `debug` argument set to `.true.`, the subroutine will emit the following to the screen:

```
DEBUG: subroutine add, a =            3
DEBUG: subroutine add, b =            5
DEBUG: subroutine add, res =            8
```

Although this kind of diagnostic printing may seem like overkill in this simple case, it can be a lifesaver when your programs become more complex.

3.7   *Tsunami simulator: Putting it all together*

Finally, we get to put together the new function (from subsection 3.2.2) and subroutine (from subsection 3.3.3) in the main program of the tsunami simulator. In a nutshell, this program has the same functionality and behavior as the previous version from chapter 2. The key difference is that now we've abstracted away the code to set the initial conditions and to calculate the finite difference of an array, as you can see in the following listing.

Listing 3.19   The updated complete code of the tsunami simulator

```fortran
program tsunami

  implicit none

  integer :: n

  integer, parameter :: grid_size = 100
  integer, parameter :: num_time_steps = 100
  real, parameter :: dt = 1, dx = 1, c = 1

  real :: h(grid_size)

  integer, parameter :: icenter = 25
  real, parameter :: decay = 0.02

  if (grid_size <= 0) stop 'grid_size must be > 0'      Checks input
  if (dt <= 0) stop 'time step dt must be > 0'          values and
  if (dx <= 0) stop 'grid spacing dx must be > 0'       aborts if invalid
  if (c <= 0) stop 'background flow speed c must be > 0'

  call set_gaussian(h, icenter, decay)        Calls the subroutine to
                                              initialize water height
  print *, 0, h
  time_loop: do n = 1, num_time_steps
    h = h - c * diff(h) / dx * dt             Computes the finite
    print *, n, h                            difference of water height
  end do time_loop                            on the fly by calling the
                                              diff function
contains

  pure function diff(x) result(dx)           Function to compute
    real, intent(in) :: x(:)                 the finite difference
    real :: dx(size(x))                      of an input array
    integer :: im
    im = size(x)
    dx(1) = x(1) - x(im)
    dx(2:im) = x(2:im) - x(1:im-1)
  end function diff
                                              Subroutine to initialize
                                              the input array to a
  pure subroutine set_gaussian(x, icenter, decay)    Gaussian shape
    real, intent(in out) :: x(:)
    integer, intent(in) :: icenter
    real, intent(in) :: decay
```

```
   integer :: i
   do concurrent(i = 1:size(x))
     x(i) = exp(-decay * (i - icenter)**2)
   end do
  end subroutine set_gaussian

end program tsunami
```

At this point, our simulator produces exactly the same results as its previous version from chapter 2, and this is intended! The goal of this chapter was to refactor our code from a purely imperative to a more procedural style. If you check out the code from GitHub, you can test the correctness of the output by comparing the output from the two versions. The following listing shows what you should use to compare that output.

Listing 3.20   Comparing tsunami simulator results

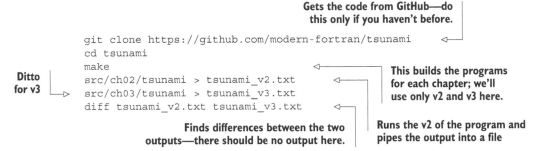

This listing shows all the steps to get the code, compile it, run the chapter 2 and 3 versions of the tsunami simulator, and store the outputs of each version in their own file. It then compares the files to make sure they're exactly the same.

3.8   Answer key

This section contains solutions to exercises in this chapter. Skip ahead if you haven't worked through the exercises yet.

3.8.1   Exercise 1: Modifying state with a subroutine

To modify an input argument in-place, define it with the intent(in out) attribute, as shown in the following listing.

Listing 3.21   A subroutine that modifies an input argument in-place

```
subroutine add(a, b)                  Uses intent(in out) to indicate that
  integer, intent(in out) :: a        a is both an input and an output
  integer, intent(in) :: b
  a = a + b                           We can modify a directly; it will be returned
end subroutine add                    to the calling program or procedure.
```

You can think of the intent attribute as a filter. intent(in) says that the arguments with this attribute can only come in, but not leave. Likewise, intent(out) allows the argument to be emitted to the calling program or procedure, but it can't be used as an input to this procedure. intent(in out) removes these restrictions and allows an argument to be passed as an input, modified within the procedure, and then emitted back to the calling program or procedure.

3.8.2 Exercise 2: Writing an elemental function that operates on both scalars and arrays

The solution is to add the pure elemental attributes to our previous version of the cold front program, as shown in the following listing.

> **Listing 3.22 Cold front temperature function that works with scalars and arrays**

```
real pure elemental function cold_front_temperature( &
    temp1, temp2, c, dx, dt) result(r)
    real, intent(in) :: temp1, temp2, c, dx, dt    ◁──┐  The elemental attribute makes
    r = temp2 - c * (temp2 - temp1) / dx * dt           the function compatible with
end function cold_front_temperature                     both scalars and arrays.
```

You can now invoke this function with one or more input arguments being arrays of any number of dimensions; for example

```
print *, cold_front_temperature(12., 24., [15., 20., 25.], 960., 24.)
```

Keep in mind that if more than one of the input arguments are arrays, they have to be of the same shape and size. The pure attribute isn't required because elemental implies pure by default; however, I included it for clarity. Either of these attributes must appear after the type attribute (real) and before the function or subroutine statement.

3.9 New Fortran elements, at a glance

- function, end function for defining a function.
- subroutine, end subroutine for defining a subroutine.
- contains statement, used to define procedures within the body of a program.
- call statement for invoking a subroutine.
- intent attribute to specify the intention of each procedure argument. (Possible values are intent(in) for an input argument, intent(out) for an output argument, and intent(in out) for an input-output argument.)
- pure attribute can be used to prohibit side effects in procedures.
- elemental attribute allows procedures to operate on both scalars and arrays of any rank and size. (By default, elemental procedures are also pure.) impure elemental can be used when you need an elemental procedure that can't be defined as pure.

- `optional` attribute allows you to declare a procedure argument as optional (keyword).
- Built-in functions:
  - `real`—Converts a numerical value to a real value. (This function is distinct from the `real` data type used in declarations.)
  - `size`—Returns the integer size of an array.
  - `present`—Checks for the presence of an optional argument inside the procedure.

3.10   *Further reading*

functional-fortran: http://mng.bz/nP18

Summary

- Procedures allow you to organize code into self-contained units of functionality, which you can then reuse whenever needed.
- Fortran has two kinds of procedures: functions and subroutines.
- Functions are invoked from expressions and return only one value as a result. They're thus best suited for minimal bits of calculation that don't cause any side effects.
- Subroutines are invoked using a `call` statement; they can't be invoked in expressions but can return any number of arguments as a result. In contrast to functions, subroutines are appropriate whenever you need to return more than one variable as a result, or for operations that cause side effects, such as modifying variables in-place and I/O.
- You can define functions or subroutines as `pure` to prevent side effects. In general, this will allow you to write code that's easier to understand and debug, as well as easier for the compiler to optimize.
- You can also define functions or subroutines as `elemental`, which allows them to operate on both scalars and arrays of any rank and size.
- Functions and subroutines are your first layer of abstraction—design them carefully and use them only if they make your program easier to read and understand.

Organizing your Fortran code using modules

This chapter covers
- Accessing variables and procedures in modules
- Writing your own custom module
- Refactoring the tsunami simulator with modules

So far, we've covered the essential building blocks of Fortran: built-in types and declaration, arithmetic, control flow, and procedures. In theory, this is all you need to write correct and powerful Fortran programs. In practice, however, as your app or library grows in size, organization of your source code becomes ever more important. This is where modules come to the rescue.

Modules allow you to organize variable and procedure definitions in a meaningful way, and make them accessible for use in programs, procedures, or other modules. Modern Fortran libraries are typically organized in one or more modules. Large applications define most functionality in modules, with only the top-level code being defined in the main program. In this chapter, we'll write a few modules to define variables and functions. We'll then access the modules from the main program of our tsunami simulator.

Fortran comes with a few built-in modules, so you'll first learn how to access them in your programs. Then, you'll write your first custom module, place it in its own source file, and compile it. As we refactor our tsunami simulator to use modules, we'll use that opportunity to expand it with more physics terms. Specifically, we'll allow the simulated water to respond to gravity, and we'll make sure that the volume of water is conserved. Considering these factors will allow for more realistic fluid-flow simulations. In the process, you'll learn how to control what variables and procedures get imported from modules, as well as how to avoid potential name conflicts. At the end of the chapter, you'll come out with the practical knowledge you need to organize your app or library in modules.

4.1   Accessing a module

Before we venture into writing our own custom modules, let's first get familiar by accessing a built-in module that comes with Fortran out of the box. Fortran has a few built-in modules. The most commonly used one is iso_fortran_env, which, among other things, provides constants and procedures that allow you to write more portable programs. Another commonly used module is iso_c_binding, which allows you to interface functions and data in C and other languages. We'll dig into that further in chapter 12.

In this section, you'll learn how to import from Fortran modules by tackling two tasks: getting the compiler version and options, and accessing type kind parameters for declaring variables in a portable way. Why would you care about these things in practice? They'll both become important if you ever develop your code in multiple environments (computers, operating systems, or compiler vendors), if you need your code to produce exactly the same results no matter where you run it, or if you distribute your compiled code to your colleagues or customers. Once you understand how to work with a built-in module, you'll be ready to learn how to write your own.

4.1.1   Getting compiler version and options

Once you have a compiled program executable, it's not obvious how it was compiled. Specifically, what compiler was used, and were any compiler options used—for example, for debugging or optimization? Fortran's iso_fortran_env module provides two functions that allow you to get this information at runtime: compiler_version and compiler_options. You get the idea what each of these functions does. Let's write a program that imports these functions from the iso_fortran_env module, then call them to print this information to the screen. Figure 4.1 illustrates how accessing a module from a main program works, with the new syntax marked in bold.

Once you've accessed the module via the use statement, you can use directly in the program any variables or procedures that the module makes available. You also can do this from a function, a subroutine, or another module. (We'll get to this in a bit.) Listing 4.1 provides the complete program that imports two functions from the iso_fortran_env module and calls them on two print statements.

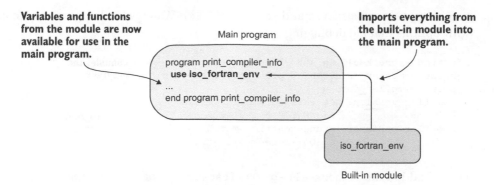

Variables and functions from the module are now available for use in the main program.

Main program

Imports everything from the built-in module into the main program.

```
program print_compiler_info
  use iso_fortran_env
  ...
end program print_compiler_info
```

iso_fortran_env

Built-in module

Figure 4.1 Importing variables and procedures from a module into a main program

Listing 4.1 Printing the compiler version and options at runtime

```
program print_compiler_info
  use iso_fortran_env
  implicit none
  print *, 'Compiler version: ', compiler_version()
  print *, 'Compiler options: ', compiler_options()
end program print_compiler_info
```

Imports everything from the iso_fortran_env module

Prints the compiler version to the screen

Prints the compiler options to the screen

On the second line of this program, we access the built-in iso_fortran_env module with the use statement. This module is available in Fortran out of the box. The use statement means that we want to access entities—variables and/or procedures—from the module. This statement imports *every* entity that's defined in the module, including the two functions that we're looking for.

You must place the use statement *after* the program statement (or the function or subroutine statement) and *before* the implicit none statement, or any other declarative statements. The implicit none statement isn't necessary here because we didn't declare any variables; however, it's a good habit to always include it.

Let's compile and run this program and see the results:

```
gfortran print_compiler_info.f90 -o print_compiler_info
./print_compiler_info
  Compiler version: GCC version 8.3.1 20190223
                    (Red Hat 8.3.1-2)
  Compiler options: -mtune=generic -march=x86-64
```

Compiles the program

Runs the program

Program output

The first line of output tells us the compiler name (GCC), its version (8.3.1), the build date (the date when the compiler was built, 20190223), and the operating system that the compiler was built on (Red Hat). The second line of output gives us the compiler options used at the time we built the program. In this case, we didn't use any options explicitly, and the compiler automatically inserted options that are specific to the computer (-mtune=generic and -march=x86-64). Watch what happens if we compile with options that aid debugging:

Runs the program ⌐

Compiles the program

Program output

```
gfortran -fcheck=all -g -O0 -fbacktrace \
   print_compiler_info.f90 -o print_compiler_info
./print_compiler_info
  Compiler version: GCC version 8.3.1 20190223
                      (Red Hat 8.3.1-2)
  Compiler options: -mtune=generic -march=x86-64
                      -g -O0 -fcheck=all -fbacktrace
```

Here, I added the -fcheck=all -g -O0 -fbacktrace option to compile the program:

- -fcheck=all enables all runtime checks, such as exceeding array bounds.
- -g compiles the program with additional instructions that allow it to be run by a debugger.
- -O0 disables any optimizations by setting the optimization level to zero.
- -fbacktrace will cause the program to print a useful traceback in case of a runtime failure, telling you where in the program the error occurred.

These options are specific to gfortran and vary between compiler vendors. The key point is that printing the result of compiler_version and compiler_options functions allows you to get this information at runtime, without having to keep track of this information otherwise. If you rewrite this program as a subroutine, you can easily invoke it at the beginning of your programs so you'll always know exactly how your program was compiled.

You may be wondering, Why would I care about the compiler information at runtime? First, if you're evaluating multiple compiler vendors for production performance, it's helpful to not have to keep track of this information by some other means. Second, you'll likely use different compiler options between development and production. Specifically, you'll likely keep optimization off and have extra diagnostic options enabled in development, whereas in production you'll want full optimization and minimal diagnostics to maximize performance. Allowing your program to carry this information thus helps you to more easily manage your software stack, in development and production.

In this section, we accessed the iso_fortran_env module, which made the built-in functions compiler_version and compiler_options available for use. However, with the general use statement, we don't know what else may have been imported from that module. In the following subsection, you'll learn how to import only those variables or procedures that you need, and nothing else.

> **Built-in Fortran modules**
>
> Fortran provides five built-in modules: iso_fortran_env, iso_c_binding, ieee_
> arithmetic, ieee_exceptions, and ieee_features. iso_fortran_env provides
> useful procedures and parameters that we'll explore in this chapter, as well as a few
> others we'll explore in chapter 11. iso_c_binding provides facilities to interface C
> functions and data structures. We'll explore that in detail in chapter 12. The latter
> three modules provide facilities specific to floating-point arithmetic and aren't gener-
> ally as useful as the first two.

4.1.2 Using portable data types

In chapter 2, I mentioned that variables of built-in types can be explicitly and portably declared using specific type kinds. Type kind parameters determine the space that numeric variables occupy in memory, which in turn limits the range for integers, and the range and precision for real and complex numbers. Most Fortran compilers by default declare 4-byte-long integers and reals, equivalent to int and float in C, respectively. However, the standard doesn't guarantee that the size will be the same between different systems and compilers. This is where the iso_fortran_env module comes in. It provides, among other things, a set of parameters you can use to specify the size of numeric data types (table 4.1).

Table 4.1 A summary of Fortran's built-in numeric type kinds in `iso_fortran_env`

Type kind	Type	Size (bytes)	C-equivalent
int8	integer	1	None
int16	integer	2	short
int32	integer	4	int
int64	integer	8	long
real32	real, complex	4	float
real64	real, complex	8	double
real128	real, complex	16	long double

These type kinds are defined in the standard and are guaranteed to have a specified size in memory. Most commonly used Fortran compilers, such as GNU and Intel, fully support these type kinds. If your compiler doesn't implement a standard-defined type kind, it will raise a compile-time error. The standard guarantees portability of data types in terms of the memory that they occupy (32 bits, 64 bits, and so on) but not in terms of their range (minimum and maximum values) and precision (how many significant digits can be represented). Unlike C, Fortran doesn't have unsigned integer types. More on Fortran interoperability with C in chapter 11.

To declare a variable with a specific type kind parameter, provide it as a `kind` argument:

```
use iso_fortran_env        ◄─┐  Accesses only the specified
                                 constants from a built-in module

integer(kind=int32) :: n   ◄─┐
real(kind=real32) :: dt    ◄─┐   Declares n as a 4-byte
                                 (32-bit) integer
                           Declares dt as a 4-
                           byte (32-bit) real
```

In the first line, we access the `iso_fortran_env` module, like we did in the previous example of printing the compiler version and options. Then, we use the built-in parameters `int32` and `real32` to declare portable integer and real variables. In doing so, we ensure that both n and dt have a size of 4 bytes, across platforms and compiler vendors. The `kind` keyword is optional, so you can declare these more concisely as

```
integer(int32) :: n
real(real32) :: dt
```

In this shorter syntax, you specify the type kind in parentheses. From here on, I'll omit the `kind` keyword in declarations for brevity. I'll also use `integer` and `integer(int32)` interchangeably, because on all compilers and platforms I'm aware of, they're one and the same in practice. Thus, if you prefer less verbose code and don't need to use long integers like `int64`, it's okay to declare them with just `integer`.

TIP   Always use the portable type kind parameters provided by `iso_fortran _env` to declare your variables, at least for your `real` and `complex` variables.

I mentioned in the previous section that when you use `iso_fortran_env`, you import all the variables and procedures from that module, not just those that you intend to use in your program. There are two issues with this. First, if your program (or procedure) declares a variable with the same name as some entity that's declared in the module, you may end up with a name conflict. I'll describe in a bit how this occurs and how to prevent it, but for now, let's just assume that you don't want it to happen. Second, if your program (or procedure) references many different procedures and variables that were imported from a module, it's difficult to see where the procedures and variables are defined just by looking at the code. This makes a program more difficult to understand and debug. However, if you import only specific variables and/or procedures from a module, it'll be much easier to avoid name conflicts with your own variables, and the code will be more readable.

Back to our example of portable type kind parameters; let's import only the ones that we want to use: `int32` and `real32`. We'll do so with the special variant of the use statement:

```
                                        ┌─  Imports only these
                                            entities from the module
use iso_fortran_env, only: int32, real32  ◄─┘
```

In this example, we imported two integer constants, `int32` and `real32`, from the built-in module `iso_fortran_env`. We used the keyword `use` to access the module, and the keyword `only` to explicitly list only the items that we needed. This is analogous to Python's `from numpy import ndarray`.

> **TIP** Always use the `use …, only: …` syntax to import specific entities from a module. This will help you avoid name conflicts and will make your code easier to read and understand.

Now you know how to import variables from modules, and also how type kind parameters work. Can you help improve the variable declarations in the tsunami simulator by using the portable type kind parameters?

Exercise 1: Using portable type kinds in the tsunami simulator

You now know how to access `iso_fortran_env` for portable type kinds, as well as how to use them to declare your variables with portable types. Can you take our latest version of the tsunami simulator (listing 3.19), and make all declarations use portable type kinds?

You can find the solution to this exercise in the "Answer key" section near the end of this chapter.

4.2 Creating your first module

You're now ready to tackle the next big item—writing your own custom module. Let's do so by implementing it directly in the tsunami simulator. Recall that in the previous chapter we created two procedures:

- A function, `diff`, that computes the finite difference of an input array. The result of this function tells us at what rate the values in an array change from one element to the next.
- A subroutine, `set_gaussian`, that initializes an input array to a Gaussian shape.

We defined both of these procedures in the main program. This worked well because our simulator was still rather simple. However, now we have the perfect opportunity to define some modules and define these procedures there. We'll do that in this section by defining the `diff` finite difference function in its own module and source file.

How will this shift concretely affect our tsunami simulator? It'll allow us to break up and organize the code in a few small building blocks that we'll then reuse in different places. Figure 4.2, which you first saw in chapter 3, illustrates the new code organization.

We'll access the finite difference function, `diff`, in the main program by importing it from the `mod_diff` module with the `use` statement. This reorganization of the code won't semantically change the program. And if we implement our new module correctly, the output will be exactly the same as before. However, splitting the code

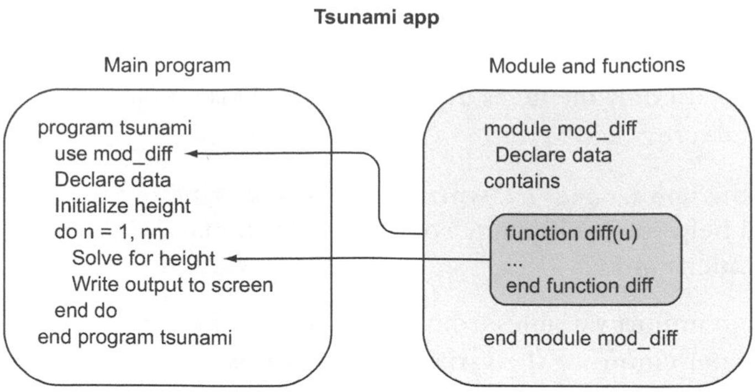

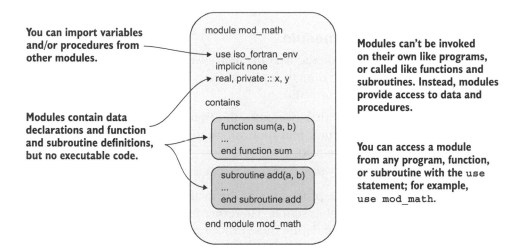

Figure 4.2   **Using a module and a function to reuse and simplify code**

into the main program and modules will allow us to more easily expand the simulator and make it more realistic.

4.2.1   *The structure of a custom module*

Before we begin, let's see what a custom module may look like on the inside, and how its building blocks work (figure 4.3).

Figure 4.3   **Structure of a custom Fortran module**

Every Fortran module is defined with a pair of `module`/`end module` statements. Modules can't have any executable code on their own. Instead, they're used to declare data and define functions and subroutines. Like in the main program, the variable declaration and procedure definition sections are separated with a `contains` statement. Modules can also import variables and procedures from other modules. Finally, you can make any entities defined in a module be public or private, which determines whether they can be imported elsewhere or are meant to be hidden and for internal use only.

That's it in a nutshell! In the rest of this section, we'll work step-by-step toward building our first custom Fortran module.

4.2.2 Defining a module

Here, we'll focus on writing a brand new module, and defining the finite difference function in it. When we're done, we'll be able to import this function from the module and use it in the main program. Start by opening a brand-new source file, mod_diff.f90. Once you're in the file, you can define the module scope with `module` and `end module` statements:

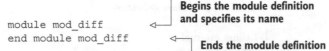

```
module mod_diff
end module mod_diff
```

Begins the module definition and specifies its name

Ends the module definition

Nothing exciting here so far—we defined a module and gave it a name. Like `program`, `function`, and `subroutine` statements, a `module` statement must be matched with a corresponding `end module` statement. Anything that we define between the `module` and `end module` statements will belong to the module.

I mentioned earlier that we'll define our new module in its own Fortran source file. How to name your source files is a matter of style. I like to name my module files starting with `mod_`. This tells me that the file defines a module, and the following word or words in the file name tell me what the module is about. For the finite difference functions, I'll just use mod_diff.f90, as I said before, and for the `set_gaussian`, I'll use mod_initial.f90 because a Gaussian shape is a kind of initial condition. Although multiple modules in a single file are allowed, I recommend keeping one module per source file.

TIP   Define one module per source file.

Our `mod_diff` module isn't useful at all yet because we didn't define any variables or procedures in it. Let's do that now. Recall from the previous chapter how we used the `contains` statement to define our new procedures in the body of the main program, as shown in the following listing.

Listing 4.2   Procedure definitions follow the `contains` statement

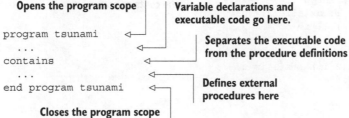

Opens the program scope

Variable declarations and executable code go here.

```
program tsunami
   ...
contains
   ...
end program tsunami
```

Separates the executable code from the procedure definitions

Defines external procedures here

Closes the program scope

Defining them in the main program is a reasonable solution while our tsunami simulator is still rather simple. However, the code will soon become hard to manage as we define more and more procedures. This is where modules come in to help us organize our code in a meaningful way.

Defining variables and procedures in a module works the same way as for the main program, as shown in the following listing.

Listing 4.3 Using the `contains` statement to define procedures in the body of a module

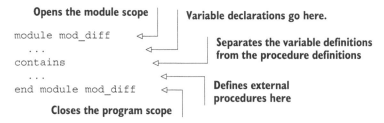

```
module mod_diff
    ...
contains
    ...
end module mod_diff
```

Opens the module scope
Variable declarations go here.
Separates the variable definitions from the procedure definitions
Defines external procedures here
Closes the program scope

If you compare this bare-bones snippet to the one from listing 4.2, you'll see that I only replaced the `program`/`end program` with `module`/`end module` (and their names, of course). One important difference from the main program, functions, and subroutines, is that the module can only contain declarative code, not executable code. This means that you can't run a module like a program, or call it like you can a function or subroutine. What you can do is access any *public* entity, be it a variable, a function, or a subroutine, that's made accessible by the module. I'll get into what I mean by *public* in a little bit.

Let's go ahead and define our `diff` function inside the module. While we're at it, we'll also use the portable type kinds that we learned about earlier in this chapter. The complete code listing is as follows.

Listing 4.4 Custom module that defines the finite difference function

```
module mod_diff

    use iso_fortran_env, only: int32, real32
    implicit none

contains

    pure function diff(x) result(dx)
        real(real32), intent(in) :: x(:)
        real(real32) :: dx(size(x))
        integer(int32) :: im
        im = size(x)
        dx(1) = x(1) - x(im)
        dx(2:im) = x(2:im) - x(1:im-1)
    end function diff

end module mod_diff
```

Imports portable type kinds from the built-in module
The explicit declaration applies to the entire module.
Defines the function after the contains statement

And that's it, your first custom Fortran module. In the first part, before the `contains` statement, we import the type kinds from the `iso_fortran_env` module, and require explicit declaration using `implicit none`. When `implicit none` is used in the module scope, it applies to everything within the `module` and `end module` statements, so we don't need to specify it again in functions or subroutines. Finally, after the `contains` statement, we include our function definition, which I copy-pasted from the main program.

To access the `diff` function in the main program, we need to add one line at the beginning, immediately before the `implicit none`:

```
program tsunami

    use mod_diff, only: diff      ←┐  Imports the diff function
    implicit none                  │  from the mod_diff module
    ...
```

Now that we have a module in its own source file, and a main program in another, let's see how we can compile these two together into a single executable program.

4.2.3 Compiling Fortran modules

The tsunami simulator source code is now made of two source files: the main program (tsunami.f90), which defines the top-level simulation loop, and the finite difference module (mod_diff.f90). In all our work so far, we've always compiled our Fortran programs from single-source files. How do you compile a program that's defined across multiple files? Easy! Compile and link all of them at once in a single line, or compile each file individually and link them all at the end. Let's try the former first, as shown in the following listing.

> **Listing 4.5 Compiling and linking multiple source files in a single step**

Command to compile and link both source files at once

Compiler output showing file name, source line, and column where the error occurred

```
gfortran tsunami.f90 mod_diff.f90 -o tsunami
tsunami.f90:11:6:         ←┘
```

```
    use mod_diff, only: diff      ←┐  Part of the source code
    1                              │  where the error occurred
Fatal Error: Can't open module file 'mod_diff.mod' for reading at (1):
    No such file or directory
compilation terminated.          ←———  Error message
```

Ouch! This doesn't seem to work, and the compiler suggests that the mod_diff.mod file couldn't be found. We'll get to the .mod file in a bit, but for now, let's try something else. Perhaps we need to compile the module first before we compile the program. We can test this by flipping the order of the source files in the compile command:

```
gfortran mod_diff.f90 tsunami.f90 -o tsunami
```

Great, this compiles without error. Note that the compiler will emit only warning and error messages; if you see no output in the terminal, that indicates success.

So, what happened here? In the first attempt, I listed the main program source file (tsunami.f90) first, and the module source file (mod_diff.f90) second. The compiler took that and went from left to right. However, since the module source file came after the program file, the compiler couldn't find the compiled module file that was needed by the main program. This means we have a dependency here—the main program depending on the module—which dictates the compilation order.

To confirm that it works as expected, run the program and compare the output with that of the previous tsunami version from the end of chapter 3. The output should be exactly the same between the two programs, because the only thing we did here is move the function to a module, and import it in the main program. The program only changes in terms of source code organization and is otherwise semantically equivalent. See listing 3.20 for how to exactly compare the output of two programs.

Recall that we have two ways we can compile Fortran programs that are defined across multiple source files. We just compiled the new tsunami simulator by listing all source files on a single line, and in a specific order. As you can imagine, this would be quite challenging if we had many source files to compile. That's where the alternative approach of compiling files individually, and linking them all at the end, is a more sane approach. To compile files individually, use the -c compiler option, where "c" stands for compile only—do not link:

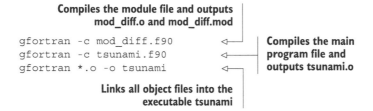

Like before, here the module file needs to be compiled before the source file that uses it. For any nontrivial project, the dependency tree and the order of compilation are typically handled by a build system, such as Make or CMake. Example Makefiles for the tsunami simulator are provided in the GitHub repository, and I encourage you to take a look at how they work. In addition to the compiled object file (.o), building a module also outputs a compiled module file (.mod). The compiler uses these files for optimization. They're not portable across compilers, and sometimes even across compiler versions.

> **Exercise 2: Define the** `set_gaussian` **subroutine in a module**
>
> Like we did with the `diff` function and `mod_diff` module, let's now define the `set_gaussian` subroutine in its own module. As this subroutine sets the initial conditions for the quantity that our simulator predicts, it's appropriate to call this module `mod_initial` and place it in a file called mod_initial.f90. You've got all the ingredients for the solution. If implemented correctly, you'll be able to import the `set_gaussian` subroutine from `mod_initial` into the main program and use it there like we did before.
>
> You can find the solution to this exercise in the "Answer key" section near the end of this chapter.

4.2.4 *Controlling access to variables and procedures*

Modules allow you to specify the visibility of variables and procedures defined in them. All entities in a module can be either public or private:

- *Public*—A public variable or procedure is accessible from within the module and can be accessed from any other program unit. You can declare a variable or procedure public by using the `public` attribute. This is the default behavior if not specified.
- *Private*—A private variable or procedure is accessible only from within the module; it can't be accessed from any other program unit. It's automatically accessible from any procedure defined inside that module. You can declare a variable or procedure private by using the `private` attribute.

For example, let's take a look at a module that defines a function to calculate the area of a circle, given an input radius. The following listing shows how that's done.

Listing 4.6 Accessing a private variable from within the module procedure

```
module mod_circle

  implicit none
  private :: pi                          Defines pi as a
  real, parameter :: pi = 3.14159256     private parameter

contains

  real pure elemental function circle_area(r) result(a)
    real, intent(in) :: r
    a = r**2 * pi          ◁——  Function circle_area can
  end function circle_area        access pi because it's defined
                                  in the module scope.
end module mod_circle
```

This module defines a parameter `pi` and a function `circle_area`. The `pi` constant is only meant to be used by `circle_area`, and is thus marked as `private`. This removes the possibility of pi being imported from outside of the module. You can also just use the private or public words as a statement on their own, which will declare all entities in the module as private or public, respectively. If neither is present, then all entities are assumed public, unless explicitly declared private. For example, if we declare the module for calculating the area of a circle with the private and public statements in the following listing, we'll ensure that only the procedure we want to give to the user can be accessed.

Listing 4.7   Declaring all entities private, except for one

```
module mod_circle
  ...
  private                            Declares everything
  public :: circle_area              as private
  ...
end module mod_circle                Only this function
                                     will be public.
```

You can use the private attribute to hide variables and procedures that are internal to the library and that the user shouldn't access. In general, it's good programming practice to declare everything as private and explicitly declare the public variables and procedures as such.

TIP   Declare all entities as private, and explicitly list those that are meant to be public.

4.2.5   *Putting it all together in the tsunami simulator*

You now know how to import variables and procedures from modules, and also how to write your own modules. Finally, we get to put this all together to refactor, improve, and expand our wave simulator. If you've followed the lessons in this section, and if you've worked through both exercises in this chapter, you now have two modules and one main program that imports procedures from them. The following listing shows the complete code for the main program.

Listing 4.8   Full code for the main program of the tsunami simulator

```
program tsunami
                                          Imports type kind parameters
                                          for numeric data
  use iso_fortran_env, only: int32, real32
  use mod_diff, only: diff                Imports the finite difference
  use mod_initial, only: set_gaussian     function from the mod_diff module

  implicit none                           Imports the set_gaussian subroutine
                                          from the mod_initial module
  integer(int32) :: n
```

Sets time step, grid spacing, and gravitational acceleration

Declares arrays to use in the simulation

```fortran
integer(int32), parameter :: grid_size = 100
integer(int32), parameter :: num_time_steps = 100
real(real32), parameter :: dt = 1, dx = 1, c = 1

real(real32) :: h(grid_size)

integer(int32), parameter :: icenter = 25
real(real32), parameter :: decay = 0.02

if (grid_size <= 0) stop 'grid_size must be > 0'
if (dt <= 0) stop 'time step dt must be > 0'
if (dx <= 0) stop 'grid spacing dx must be > 0'

call set_gaussian(h, icenter, decay)

print *, 0, h
time_loop: do n = 1, num_time_steps
  h = h - c * diff(h) / dx * dt
  print *, n, h
end do time_loop

end program tsunami
```

Sets grid size and number of time steps

Parameters to use to set the initial condition for water height

Checks input values and aborts if invalid

Initializes water height and velocity arrays

Loops for num_time_steps time steps

Computes the water velocity in next step and updates

Prints the values of the time step and water height

At this time, you can compile this program, and the one from the end of the previous chapter, and run each of them to confirm that they produce exactly the same result. They should, as the only thing we changed here was moving the set_gaussian and diff functions from the main program to external modules.

4.3 Toward realistic wave simulations

I promised in the previous chapter that we'd finally get to some more realistic wave simulations in this chapter. With the additions to the simulator in the final section of this chapter, our water will finally start to move and slosh like real water would (figure 4.4).

As in the previous chapter, we'll run our simulation for 100 s. We initialize the water height h (this is the perturbation from resting water depth) as a blob with the same shape and amplitude as in the advection example. At time zero (top panel in figure 4.4), the water level is completely flat, except for where we initialized it as a Gaussian shape. So far, so good. A little bit over a second into the simulation, the initial shape splits into two wave packets, which begin propagating in opposite directions (second panel from the top). This is expected! Imagine throwing a pebble into a pond, triggering a series of ripples that radiate away from where the pebble fell in. Our initial perturbation is emulating that pebble. Periodic boundary conditions allow the waves to move past either edge of the domain and reenter from the other side. We thus produce "perpetual" sloshing of water in our small domain.

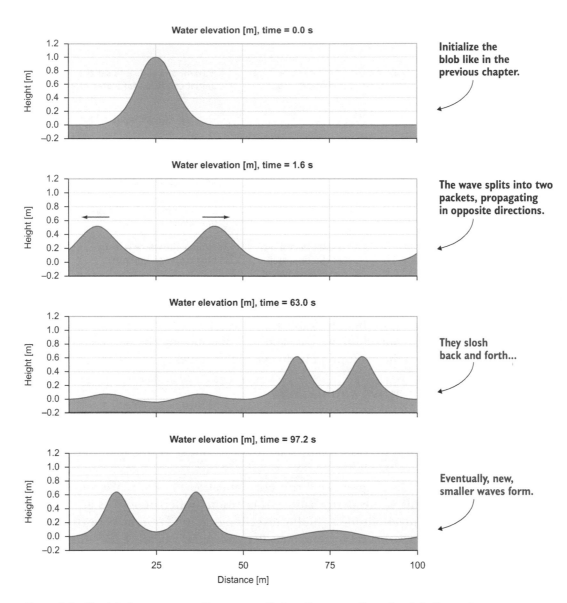

Figure 4.4 Simulated wave propagation as a result of nonlinear one-dimensional shallow water equations. A water basin with a uniform depth of 10 m is perturbed with a 1 m high blob. The water height and velocity are then simulated forward in time for 100 seconds, allowing the wave to propagate and slosh back and forth.

4.3.1 *A brief look at the physics*

To go from uniform motion to a more realistic fluid flow, we need to add a few terms to the equations in our simulation code. Let's briefly look at the shallow water equations that I first introduced in chapter 1 (figure 4.5). If you don't care for the math, don't worry about it; you can skip ahead to the next section, where we delve into the implementation.

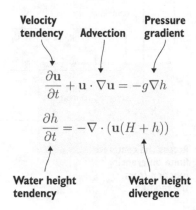

Figure 4.5   Shallow water equations revisited. The top equation is for water velocity, and the bottom for water height. We've already solved for the (linear) advection term.

We're almost there! We already have the advection calculation, which allows the shape to move due to background flow. However, our water is currently moving like a solid object, and that's what advection does—it simply moves things around in space. For the water to flow and slosh in response to gravity, much like real water would in a bathtub, we need to add the pressure gradient term. This term is proportional to gravitational acceleration multiplied by the slope of the water surface. The steeper the surface, the more it will accelerate in the horizontal direction. If the water rushes in from both sides, the water level will go up, and that's what the water height divergence term does. The upside-down triangle symbol is called *nabla* and is the vector calculus symbol for the spatial gradient (difference in space). All the terms other than the tendency terms use this same operator! With some forethought, we designed our module so that we can reuse the finite difference function `diff` to add the remaining terms:

- The pressure gradient can now be expressed as `-g * diff(h) / dx`. When the water surface is steep, this term makes the water rush forward, like in a breaking wave. We'll add this term to our equation for velocity.
- The water height divergence, which we can now write as `-diff(u * (hmean + h)) / dx`, acts to decrease the water height when the water mass is diverging (moving apart) or increase it when the water mass is converging (coming together). Think of a leaky bucket and the water level in it going down as the water comes out the bottom.

The structure of the new version of our app is illustrated in figure 4.6.

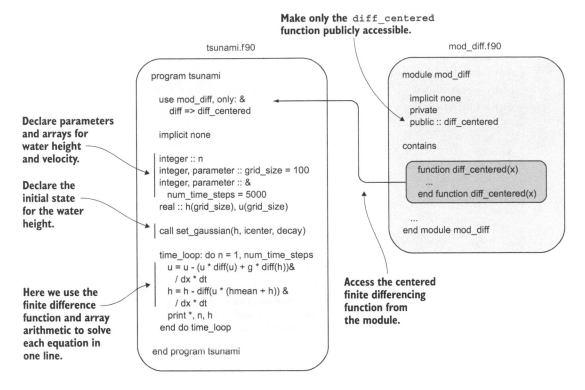

Figure 4.6   A diagram summarizing the structure of the one-dimensional tsunami simulator. The main program is shown on the left, and the supporting module is shown on the right. Only the key parts of the code are shown.

4.3.2   *Updating the finite difference calculation*

As you probably noticed in the previous subsection, in the new version of the tsunami simulator we'll get to apply the `diff` function not once, but three times. It looks like our work with procedures and modules will finally pay off. There's just one more thing we need to do, and that is make our finite difference function a tad more general. Recall that our original finite difference function calculated the upwind difference between the current and previous element:

```
dx(2:im) = x(2:im) - x(1:im-1)          ⟵──── Whole-array difference
```

It turns out that this difference pattern works well only if the motion in the system is moving from left to right—that is, from lower to higher array indices. This is also why it worked well for our simple advection simulator, where the constant background flow was configured from left to right.

However, in a more realistic configuration, where water velocity is coupled with water height and water is allowed to move in both directions, we need a centered finite difference that can account for changes coming from either direction:

```
dx(2:im-1) = 0.5 * (x(3:im) - x(1:im-2))
```

In contrast to the original finite difference, here we're calculating the difference between the next and previous element and dividing by 2 to account for the fact that we're calculating the difference over two increments. Figure 4.7 illustrates the difference in calculating these differences.

Upwind finite difference: `dx(2:im) = x(2:im) - x(1:im-1)`

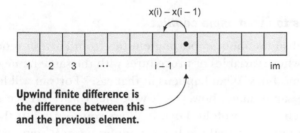

Upwind finite difference is the difference between this and the previous element.

Centered finite difference: `dx(2:im-1) = 0.5 * (x(3:im) - x(1:im-2))`

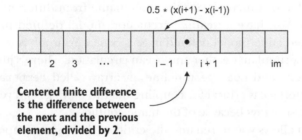

Centered finite difference is the difference between the next and the previous element, divided by 2.

Figure 4.7 Illustration of upwind and centered finite difference calculations

The following listing provides the complete finite difference function, centered in space.

Listing 4.9   Finite difference of a one-dimensional array, centered in space

```
pure function diff_centered(x) result(dx)
  real(real32), intent(in) :: x(:)
  real(real32) :: dx(size(x))
  integer(int32) :: im
  im = size(x)
  dx(1) = x(2) - x(im)
  dx(im) = x(1) - x(im-1)
  dx(2:im-1) = x(3:im) - x(1:im-2)
```

Calculates the boundary value on the left

Calculates the boundary value on the right

Calculates the difference in the interior

```
  dx = 0.5 * dx                      ◁─┐  Divides all
end function diff_centered             │  elements by 2
```

We now have two different versions of the finite difference function: one for the centered difference in space, and another for the upstream difference in space. They both receive the same input, a one-dimensional array x, and they each return a result that has the same meaning—it's just calculated differently. However, it's important to use the centered difference function now to allow the water to move in both directions. Notice that in listing 4.9, I multiply dx by 0.5 rather than dividing it by 2. In theory, this is preferred, because for floating-point (real) numbers, multiplication is a much faster operation than division. In practice, however, a good compiler is typically able to optimize floating-point division for you, so this becomes a matter of style.

4.3.3 *Renaming imported entities to avoid name conflict*

Based on what we've covered so far about importing entities from Fortran modules, you can imagine a situation where variables or procedures with the same name could be imported from different modules. What happens in that case? Fortran will let you import two entities with the same name; however, it won't let you reference them. The purpose of this design choice is twofold: First, it allows you to use just the use (without only) statement to import everything from modules, even if some entities may have conflicting names. Second, it doesn't allow you to mistake one entity for another by accident.

What if you need a variable or function with the same name from different modules? Consider this scenario: You have a weather prediction model defined in mod_atmosphere and an ocean prediction model defined in mod_ocean. Your job is to make them talk to each other as they simulate weather and ocean circulation. There's just one problem: both mod_atmosphere and mod_ocean define an array called temperature. Having both arrays in your interface is critical for coupling the two models, and yet, you won't be able to reference these arrays because of the name conflict.

As a workaround, Fortran allows you to rename the entity at the time of import:

```
                                                  ┌─ Imports temperature as is
use mod_atmosphere, only: temperature       ◁────┘
use mod_ocean, only: temperature_ocean => temperature   ◁───┐
          Imports temperature as temperature_ocean          │
```

The key element here is the => operator on the second line. It allows you to import a variable or procedure under a different name. The first line in the snippet is analogous to Python's from numpy import sqrt. The second line is analogous to Python's from numpy import sqrt as np_sqrt. The operator => means "points to" rather than "is renamed as." The name on the left side is the new name we want to use, whereas the one on the right side is the original name as defined in the module. (This may not be intuitive at first.)

If you need to rename multiple entities, separate them with a comma:

```
use mod_ocean, only: temperature_ocean => temperature, &
                     velocity_ocean => velocity
```

In summary, the easiest way to access a module is to import everything from it. use …, only: … lets you list explicitly the variables that you want to import. Finally, to resolve any name conflicts, you can use the => operator to rename the imported variables or procedures. Keep in mind that unlike Python, Fortran doesn't have namespaces. As your application and library grow in size, and you import all entities from all modules implicitly, it becomes difficult to keep track of what came from what module, and there's no way to find out until you look inside the modules for the declarations.

Let's return to our finite difference functions in the mod_diff module. To avoid naming conflicts between the two functions, let's call the old function diff_upwind and add the new function diff_centered. We can then import the centered difference function as diff in the main program:

```
use mod_diff, only: diff => diff_centered
```

At this point, you should have a mod_diff module that defines both the diff_upwind and diff_centered functions.

4.3.4 The complete code

Finally, we get to the end! The complete code for the main application is shown in the following listing.

> **Listing 4.10   Complete code of the main program of the tsunami simulator**

```
program tsunami

    use iso_fortran_env, only: int32, real32       ←  Imports type kind parameters
    use mod_diff, only: diff => diff_centered       ←      for numeric data
    use mod_initial, only: set_gaussian       ←   Imports the diff_centered
                                                    function from the mod_diff
    implicit none                                   module and renames it as diff

    integer(int32) :: n       Imports the set_gaussian procedure
                              from the mod_initial module

    integer(int32), parameter :: grid_size = 100       Sets grid size and
    integer(int32), parameter :: num_time_steps = 5000   number of time steps

    real(real32), parameter :: dt = 0.02, dx = 1, g = 9.8   ←  Sets time step,
    real(real32), parameter :: hmean = 10                       grid spacing, and
                                                                gravitational
    real(real32) :: h(grid_size), u(grid_size)                  acceleration

    integer(int32), parameter :: icenter = 25       Parameters to use to set the initial
    real(real32), parameter :: decay = 0.02         condition for water height
```

Declares arrays to use in the simulation

```
if (grid_size <= 0) stop 'grid_size must be > 0'        Checks input
if (dt <= 0) stop 'time step dt must be > 0'            parameter
if (dx <= 0) stop 'grid spacing dx must be > 0'         values

call set_gaussian(h, icenter, decay)        Initializes water height
u = 0                                        and velocity arrays

print *, 0, h                                                    Loops for
time_loop: do n = 1, num_time_steps              ◄────          num_time_steps
  u = u - (u * diff(u) + g * diff(h)) / dx * dt     ◄──         time steps
  h = h - diff(u * (hmean + h)) / dx * dt    ◄──┐
  print *, n, h                                  │     Computes the water
end do time_loop             Computes the water   │    velocity in the next
                             height in the next   │    step and updates
                             step and updates
end program tsunami
```

There are quite a few changes in this program relative to our previous version.

First, we're now using a new function (`diff_centered`) for the finite difference calculation, which allows us to account for changes coming from either direction. On import, we rename this function to just `diff` so that we don't have to change the existing terms from the previous version of the simulator. The other imports from modules are also new and should be familiar by now, if you've worked through this chapter in order.

Second, our main simulation loop now has two equations instead of one. We're now solving for both water velocity (`u`) and water height (`h`). These two equations are coupled: water velocity appears on the right side of the equation for water height, and vice versa. This coupling is exactly what leads to a more realistic fluid flow. However, more realistic physics requires higher resolution in time, and this is reflected in our time step `dt` now being smaller than before. For an analogy, think about watching an extremely slow-paced video in which not much is going on. You may not even notice if the video is playing at a low frame rate. However, if you're watching a fast-paced video of a car chase or a basketball game, you'll easily notice any lag or drop in frame rate. The same goes for fluid dynamics—a more realistic simulation (more physics terms) and a finer computational grid (level of detail) require a shorter time step, which translates to a higher frame rate.

Congratulations, we made it! If you now compile the simulator, run it, and plot the results, you'll be able to see the flow similar to that in figure 4.4. To account for the shorter time step, I increased the number of time steps (now 5,000) to simulate for a long enough period of time. I encourage you to play with a few of the simulation parameters, such as the grid size, number of time steps, and the initial shape and perturbation of the water.

4.4 Answer key

This section contains solutions to exercises in this chapter. Skip ahead if you haven't worked through the exercises yet.

4.4.1 Exercise 1: Using portable type kinds in the tsunami simulator

The task is to import the portable type kind parameters from the `iso_fortran_env` module and use them in the tsunami simulator. To do this, we'll rewrite only the declaration section, as shown in the following listing.

Listing 4.11　Using portable type kinds in the tsunami simulator

```
program tsunami

    use iso_fortran_env, only: int32, real32
    implicit none

    integer(int32) :: n

    integer(int32), parameter :: grid_size = 100
    integer(int32), parameter :: num_time_steps = 100
    real(real32), parameter :: dt = 1, dx = 1, c = 1

    real(real32) :: u(grid_size)

    ...

end program tsunami
```

Assigns a name to the program → `program tsunami`

Enforces explicit declaration → `implicit none`

Accesses only these two constants from the built-in module ← `use iso_fortran_env, only: int32, real32`

Declares integer variables for loop counters → `integer(int32) :: n`

Declares integer constants for grid size and number of time steps ←

Declares real constants for time step, grid spacing, and phase speed ←

Declares an array → `real(real32) :: u(grid_size)`

Marks the end of the program → `end program tsunami`

We first import the standard type kinds `int32` and `real32` from the `iso_fortran_env` module. We then specify these type kinds in each `integer` and `real` declaration statement, respectively. That's it, we're done! As long as we declare all our variables like this, we ensure that they're always of the same size in memory across different machines and compilers. This is one of many important steps toward reproducibility of results. As always, with any change or addition to the code, make sure it works as expected by recompiling and rerunning it.

4.4.2 Exercise 2: Defining the set_gaussian subroutine in a module

The task is to define the `set_gaussian` subroutine, which sets the values of an input array to a specific shape, in its own module. The solution is analogous to defining the `diff` function in the `mod_diff` module. This time, we're defining the `set_gaussian` procedure in the `mod_initial` module, as shown in the following listing.

Listing 4.12　Defining the `set_gaussian` subroutine in a custom module

```
module mod_initial

    use iso_fortran_env, only: int32, real32
    implicit none
```

Imports standard type kinds ←

Enforces explicit declaration in the whole module ←

```
contains

    pure subroutine set_gaussian(x, icenter, decay)        ⊲──┐  Defines the subroutine
      real(real32), intent(in out) :: x(:)                     │  after the contains
      integer(int32), intent(in) :: icenter                    │  statement
      real(real32), intent(in) :: decay
      integer(int32) :: i
      do concurrent(i = 1:size(x))
        x(i) = exp(-decay * (i - icenter)**2)
      end do
    end subroutine set_gaussian

end module mod_initial
```

Like with the `diff` function and the `mod_diff` module, we'll import this subroutine in the main program, as shown in the following listing.

> **Listing 4.13 Importing the `set_gaussian` subroutine from the `mod_initial` module**

```
program tsunami
                                          ┌─ Imports the diff function
                                          │  from the mod_diff module
    use mod_diff, only: diff        ⊲─────┘
    use mod_initial, only: set_gaussian    ⊲──┐  Imports the set_gaussian
    implicit none                              │  subroutine from the
    ...                                        │  mod_initial module
```

All external procedures that we use in the main program are now defined in their own modules. This will become especially useful as our tsunami simulator grows and becomes more complex.

4.5 *New Fortran elements, at a glance*

- `use` statement for accessing a module
- Built-in `iso_fortran_env` module, which includes
  - portable type kind parameters: `int8`, `int16`, `int32`, `int64`, `real32`, `real64`, `real128`
  - functions to get compiler information: `compiler_info`, `compiler_version`
- `module`/`end module` for defining a module
- `use ..., only: ...` syntax to import specific variables and procedures defined in a module
- The `=>` operator to rename entities on import
- `public` and `private` attributes to allow and restrict access to entities defined in a module, respectively

4.6 *Further reading*

Fortran Wiki article on submodules: http://fortranwiki.org/fortran/show/Submodules

Summary

- Modules are special program units that allow you to define functions, subroutines, and variables in one place.
- Fortran comes with a few built-in modules, such as `iso_fortran_env` and `iso_c_binding`.
- The built-in module `iso_fortran_env` provides, among other things, functions that return information about the compiler and the options used to compile the program, as well as type kind parameters that allow you to declare variables in a portable way.
- Compiling modules produces special `.mod` files, which must be included in the compiler path when building other Fortran code that accesses the modules.
- Accessing a module with just the `use` statement imports all public entities from the module into the current scope. You can use an expanded variant, `use ...,` `only: ...,` to import only specific entities.
- Entities defined in a module can be public or private. Public entities are available for use to any program or procedure that uses that module. Private entities can only be accessed within the module itself.
- You can set public and private properties of module entities using the `public` and `private` attributes, respectively.
- Variables and procedures with conflicting names can be imported from modules but can't be referenced. To work around the name conflict, use the `=>` operator to rename a variable or procedure on import.

Analyzing time series
data with arrays

5

This chapter covers

- Analyzing stock prices with Fortran arrays
- Declaring, allocating, and initializing arrays
- Using whole-array arithmetic to quantify stock performance and risk

An array is a sequence of data elements that are of the same type and contiguous in memory. While this may seem restrictive, it comes with its advantages. First, it allows you to write simpler code using expressive one-liners that work on many elements at once. Whereas arrays have been part of Fortran since its birth, whole-array operators and arithmetic were introduced in Fortran 90, allowing programmers to write cleaner, shorter, and less error-prone code. In a nutshell, arrays allow you to easily work on large datasets and apply functions and arithmetic operators on whole arrays without resorting to loops or other verbose syntax.

Back in section 3.2.2, I gave you a sneak peek into how to replace entire do loops in the tsunami simulator with single-line, whole-array operations. We're now going to take a deep dive into Fortran arrays and learn the mechanics of declaring arrays, allocating them in memory, and using them with familiar arithmetic operators. For this chapter, we'll take a small break from the tsunami simulator and explore Fortran arrays by writing a stock price analysis app. You'll learn how to declare, allocate, and initialize dynamic arrays; read and store data into them; and then perform whole-array arithmetic to quantify stock performance, volatility, and other metrics. This knowledge will give you a solid foundation for what's coming in the next few chapters—parallelizing the tsunami simulator with Fortran coarrays and expanding it into two dimensions for more realistic tsunami prediction.

5.1 Analyzing stock prices with Fortran arrays

We'll learn how Fortran arrays work in a real-world application—analyzing stock price time series. This has been an increasingly popular topic since the early days of computer programming, and Fortran has been used in the bowels of many trading and banking systems, mainly thanks to its robustness, reliability, and efficiency. In this chapter, we'll work with a dataset that's freely available, small enough to be easily downloaded, and yet large enough to demonstrate the power of Fortran arrays.

I'm no trader, and I won't go into the details of true technical stock market analysis. Therefore, I recommend that you don't use this chapter as trading advice. Instead, I'll merely show you how you can leverage the power of Fortran arrays to perform any kind of time series analysis that you can think of, whether it's stock or commodity prices, weather measurements, or signal processing. Let's start by setting objectives for our application, and looking at the data that we'll work with.

5.1.1 Objectives for this exercise

In this section, we'll set tangible goals for this exercise:

- *Find the best and worst performing stocks.* We'll first evaluate which stock grew (or lost value) the most, relative to its starting price. For this, we'll need to know the stock price from the start and the end of the time series, and calculate the difference relative to the initial price. In this challenge, you'll learn how to declare, allocate, and initialize dynamic arrays; calculate the size of an array; and reference individual array elements.
- *Identify risky stocks.* Some stocks are riskier than others. This can be quantified using stock volatility, which is related to the standard deviation of the stock price. Standard deviation is a statistical measure of how much the values deviate from the average value, and it can be defined over arbitrary time periods. In this challenge, you'll learn to slice arrays and perform whole-array arithmetic.
- *Identify good times to buy and sell.* Traders commonly use a technique called the moving-average crossover to decide whether it's a good time to buy or sell shares of a stock. The moving-average crossover tells us when the stock price crosses the moving average (average over a limited time window) and indicates change in the longer term trend of the stock price, regardless of high-frequency fluctuations. In this challenge, you'll learn how to search the arrays for specific values and extract elements that meet any criteria that you want.

Before we dive into implementing the solutions to these challenges, let's get familiar with the data that we'll work with.

5.1.2   *About the data*

In this chapter, we'll work on daily stock price time series from 10 technology companies, including Apple, Amazon, and Intel. The data is stored in the comma-separated value (CSV) format. Here's a sample of the Apple stock daily data:

```
timestamp,open,high,low,close,adjusted_close,volume,dividend_amount,
    split_coefficient
2018-05-14,189.0100,189.5300,187.8600,188.1500,188.1500,20364542,0.0000,1.0000
2018-05-11,189.4900,190.0600,187.4500,188.5900,188.5900,26212221,0.7300,1.0000
2018-05-10,187.7400,190.3700,187.6500,190.0400,189.3072,27989289,0.0000,1.0000
2018-05-09,186.5500,187.4000,185.2200,187.3600,186.6376,23211241,0.0000,1.0000
2018-05-08,184.9900,186.2200,183.6650,186.0500,185.3326,28402777,0.0000,1.0000
...
```

The columns in each CSV file are

- `timestamp`—Date in YYYY-mm-dd format
- `open`—Opening price at the start of the trading day
- `high`—Highest price that the stock reached during the trading day
- `low`—Lowest price that the stock reached during the trading day
- `close`—Closing price at the end of the trading day (reflects the price of the last stock that was traded that day)
- `adjusted_close`—Closing price that has been retroactively adjusted for stock splits (See split coefficient below.)
- `volume`—The total number of shares traded during the day
- `dividend_amount`—The amount of dividend paid per share
- `split_coefficient`—Occasionally, a stock can be split for various reasons, and the split coefficient indicates the factor by which the stock was split. If `split_coefficient` is 1, the stock was not split. If it's 0.5, the stock price is halved because of the split.

For a birds-eye view of how these stocks performed since 2000, I plotted the adjusted close price against time in figure 5.1.

Most of the companies had their stock grow in the overall. We can even spot some trends. For example, IBM grew considerably from 2009 to 2012 following the growth of cloud-based technologies and expanding in that space. Nvidia (NVDA) entered a period of explosive growth in early 2016 thanks to the mass adoption of their GPUs for machine learning.

You may be wondering, why use the adjusted close and not just the closing price? Occasionally, a company splits its stock, resulting in a much different closing price than the day before. We could see this in effect in June of 2014 when Apple split its stock sevenfold:

```
timestamp,open,high,low,close,adjusted_close,volume,dividend_amount,
    split_coefficient
2014-06-09,92.7000,93.8800,91.7500,93.7000,87.1866,75414997,0.0000,7.0000
2014-06-06,649.9000,651.2600,644.4700,645.5700,85.8134,12497800,0.0000,1.0000
```

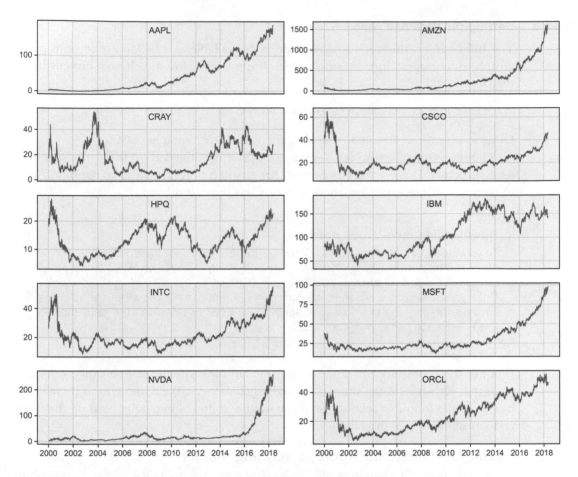

Figure 5.1   Adjusted close stock prices (USD) of 10 technology companies. The y-axis on each panel has a different scale.

On June 6, the closing price was $645.57, whereas on the next trading day, June 9 (exchange markets close on weekends), the opening price was $92.70. Notice that the split coefficient on this day is 7, indicating the factor by which the stock price was divided. If we analyzed long time series of closing prices, we'd also capture occasional large increases or drops due to events that don't reflect the market value of the stock. Adjusted closing price retroactively accounts for all stock splits that occurred, and results in time series that are consistent with stock value. It's thus a useful metric when analyzing the long-term historical performance of a stock.

5.1.3   Getting the data and code

The full code for the stock analysis exercise is available as a GitHub repo at https://github.com/modern-fortran/stock-prices. If you use git, you can clone it directly from the command line:

```
git clone https://github.com/modern-fortran/stock-prices
```

Otherwise, you can download it as a zip file from http://mng.bz/OMZo.

The repository already includes the stock price data needed for this exercise in the data directory. However, if this exercise leaves you hungry for more in-depth analysis or larger stock price datasets, there's an easy way to get more data.

> **Downloading more stock data**
>
> To download the stock data in CSV format for this exercise, I used the free service Alpha Vantage (https://www.alphavantage.co), which provides an HTTP API to obtain data in JSON or CSV format. You'll need to register for the API key at their website. Once you have one, you can make your own API requests to get various stock data. For an example, see the download script that I used to download the daily data for this exercise in data/get_data.sh.

Cloning the repository (or downloading the zip file) will also get you the complete code that implements the three data analysis challenges. We'll implement them step-by-step in the following sections, so if you want to follow along, defer reading the final code until the end of this chapter.

5.2   Finding the best and worst performing stocks

Before we do any data analysis, we need to take care of the logistics. These steps will generally apply to each of the three challenges in this exercise:

1   *Define the arrays to hold the data.* We'll learn how to declare dynamic arrays whose size isn't known at compile time. We'll use built-in types: real for stock prices and character for timestamps.

2   *Read data from the CSV files.* We'll implement a custom subroutine to read the files and store the data into arrays defined in step 1.

3   *Calculate statistics from raw data.* Most of the number crunching described in this chapter will be in relation to this step.

To start, we can estimate the performance of different stocks by calculating their gain over the whole period of the time series data—from January 2000 to May 2018. When we implement the solution to our first challenge, the output of the program will look like this:

```
2000-01-03 through 2018-05-14
Symbol, Gain (USD), Relative gain (%)
------------------------------------
```

```
AAPL    184.594589              5192
AMZN    1512.16003              1692
CRAY    9.60000038                56
CSCO    1.71649933                 4
HPQ     1.55270004                 7
IBM     60.9193039                73
INTC    25.8368015                89
MSFT    59.4120979               154
NVDA    251.745300              6964
ORCL    20.3501987                77
```

For each stock, we'll calculate its gain; that is, the difference between the closing price at the end of the beginning of the time series, and the gain in percent relative to the starting price. The main program (not including the utility functions) looks like the following listing.

Listing 5.1   Calculating stock gains over the whole time series

```fortran
program stock_gain                              ┌─ Function to
                                                │  reverse an array
  use mod_arrays, only: reverse   ←─────────────┘
  use mod_io, only: read_stock    ←─────── Function to read
                                           data from CSV files
  implicit none
                                                      Array to store
  character(len=4), allocatable :: symbols(:)         timestamps
  character(len=:), allocatable :: time(:)   ←──────
  real, allocatable :: open(:), high(:), low(:),&
                  close(:), adjclose(:), volume(:)    Array to store
  integer :: n                                        stock price data
  real :: gain

  symbols = ['AAPL', 'AMZN', 'CRAY', 'CSCO', 'HPQ ',&   List of stocks that
            'IBM ', 'INTC', 'MSFT', 'NVDA', 'ORCL']     we'll analyze

  do n = 1, size(symbols)

    call read_stock(                            &       Uses a custom
      'data/' // trim(symbols(n)) // '.csv', &          subroutine to read the
      time, open, high, low, close, adjclose, volume)   data from CSV files

    adjclose = reverse(adjclose)
    gain = (adjclose(size(adjclose)) - adjclose(1))

    if (n == 1) then
      print *, &
        time(size(time)) // ' through ' // time(1)
      print *, 'Symbol, Gain (USD), Relative gain (%)'     Writes the table
      print *, '-----------------------------------'       header to the screen,
    end if                                                 only in first iteration
```

Array to store stock symbols → points to `character(len=4), allocatable :: symbols(:)`

Reverses the order of adjusted close price → points to `adjclose = reverse(adjclose)`

Calculates the absolute stock gain → points to `gain = (adjclose(size(adjclose)) - adjclose(1))`

```
    print *, symbols(n), gain, &
       nint(gain / adjclose(1) * 100)
```

**Calculates relative gain and
prints results to the screen**

```
   end do

end program stock_gain
```

In this program, we first declare the dynamic (allocatable) arrays to hold the list of
stock symbols and the timestamps and stock price data for each stock. We then loop
over each stock and read the data from the CSV files one at a time. Finally, we calculate the difference between the end and start price and print the results to the screen.
The following subsections go into detail about how dynamic Fortran arrays work. Specifically, we'll examine how to declare them, allocate them in memory, initialize their
values, and finally clear them from memory when done.

5.2.1 *Declaring arrays*

In chapter 2, we covered the basic declaration of arrays when implementing the minimal working version of our tsunami simulator:

```
real :: h(grid_size)
```

**grid_size is the integer
size of array h.**

When you specify the size of the array in the declaration line, you tell the compiler to
declare a static array. The array size is known at compile time, and the compiler can
use this information to generate more efficient machine code. Effectively, when you
declare a static array, it's allocated in memory when you run the program.

However, you won't always know the size of the arrays ahead of time. It just so happens that each stock data CSV file has the same number of records (4,620), but this
may not always be the case, as some companies may have a much longer presence in
the public markets than others. Furthermore, if you chose to later work on a different
or larger stock price dataset, it would be unwieldy to have to hardcode the size of the
arrays every time. This is where dynamic, or, in Fortran lingo, *allocatable*, arrays come
in. Whenever the size of the array is unknown ahead of time, or you anticipate that it
will change at some time during the life of the program, declare it as `allocatable`:

```
real, allocatable :: h(:)
```

**The colon in parentheses indicates
that the size is to be determined.**

Writing more general and flexible apps will also require allocating arrays at runtime.

Notice that there are two key changes here relative to the basic declaration. We
added the `allocatable` attribute, and we used the colon (`:`) as a placeholder for the
array size. At this point in the code, we didn't allocate this array in memory but simply
stated, "We'll use a real, two-dimensional array h, whose size is yet to be determined."

When do we use dynamic over static arrays?

Use dynamic over static arrays whenever you don't know the size of the arrays ahead of time, or know that it will change. A few examples come to mind:

- Storing user-input data, either entered by standard input (keyboard) or read from an input file
- Reading data from multiple files of different lengths
- Arrays that will be reused across datasets
- Arrays that may grow or shrink during the lifetime of the program

Dynamic arrays will help you write more general and flexible code but may carry a performance penalty, as allocation of memory is a slow operation compared to, say, floating-point arithmetic.

It does seem that for our use case we should use dynamic arrays. Following the data description from the previous section, we'll need the following:

- An array of character strings to hold stock symbols (AAPL, AMZN, etc.)
- An array of character strings to hold the timestamps (2018-05-15, 2018-05-14, etc.)
- Arrays of real numbers to hold the actual stock data, such as opening and closing prices and others

We can apply the syntax from the allocatable declaration earlier to declare these arrays, as shown in the following listing.

Listing 5.2   Declaring the arrays for stock symbols, timestamps, and stock price data

```
program stock_gain

  implicit none

  character(len=4), allocatable :: symbols(:)       ←──  Dynamic array of stock symbols
  character(len=:), allocatable :: time(:)           ←──  Dynamic array of timestamps
  real, allocatable :: open(:), high(:), low(:), &        Dynamic arrays for
                       close(:), adjclose(:), volume(:)    stock price data

end program stock_gain
```

Notice that for symbols I declared an array of character strings of length 4, whereas for the time array I didn't specify the length ahead of time (len=:). This is because we'll determine the length of timestamps in the subroutine that's in charge of reading the data files, and we don't need to hardcode the length here. For the rest of the data, I declared real (floating point) arrays. Even though the volume is an integer quantity (number of shares traded), real will work just fine for typical volume values and will help simplify the code. You can compile and run this program, but it won't do anything useful yet, since it only declares the arrays that we'll use. To loop over stock symbols and print each one to the screen, we'll use an array constructor to initialize the array `symbols`.

Specifying the length of character strings

The keyword argument `len` in the `character` data type declaration isn't required, and you can just type `character(4)` instead of `character(len=4)`. Likewise for `character(:)`. The value can also be omitted entirely (`character`), in which case it defaults to `character(1)`, which is a single character. Feel free to type out `len` if you want to help a casual reader of your code, or omit it to make your code less verbose.

5.2.2   Array constructors

Array constructors will come in handy to initialize the stock symbols. If we do it correctly, looping over them and printing each one to the screen, the output will look like this:

```
Working on AAPL
Working on AMZN
Working on CRAY
Working on CSCO
Working on HPQ
Working on IBM
Working on INTC
Working on MSFT
Working on NVDA
Working on ORCL
```

As you can imagine, specific symbols depend on what data we have. Since in this exercise we'll work with only 10 stocks, we can type them directly in the code, as shown in the following listing.

Listing 5.3   Initialize and print stock symbols to screen

```
program stock_gain
  ...
  integer :: n

  symbols = ['AAPL', 'AMZN', 'CRAY', 'CSCO', 'HPQ ', &    ◁─── Initializes stock
            'IBM ', 'INTC', 'MSFT', 'NVDA', 'ORCL']            symbols

  do n = 1, size(symbols)                          ◁─── Loops over stock
    print *, 'Working on ' // symbols(n)                symbols and prints
  end do                                                them to screen

end program stock_gain
```

Here, I use the built-in function `size` to return the integer size of an input array, in this case 10. We used this function already back in chapter 3. Where I initialize the stock symbols, I also introduce a new syntax element, the *array constructor*, to assign the stock symbols to the `symbols` array. Array constructors allow you to create arrays on the fly and assign them to array variables:

```
integer :: a(5) = [1, 2, 3, 4, 5]
```
←⎯ **Initializes from a constant array**

In this example, I used square brackets to enclose a sequence of five integers. Together, this syntax forms a literal constant array that is then assigned to a. For static arrays, the size and shape of the array constructor must match the size and shape of the array variable on the left side.

Alternative syntax for array literals

Besides the square brackets, there's another standard-compliant way to create array literals, using parentheses and forward slashes:

```
integer :: a(5) = (/1, 2, 3, 4, 5/)
```

I mention this because you may encounter it in existing Fortran code. However, since this syntax is more verbose (twice as much, in fact), I recommend using square brackets exclusively, which I'll do throughout this book.

In the array constructor snippet, I initialized a on the declaration line. This makes for an easy and concise declaration and initialization of a small array. However, there's one exception case in which you're not allowed to do this: pure procedures. In that case, you have no choice but to declare and initialize in separate statements:

```
integer :: a(5)
a = [1, 2, 3, 4, 5]
```
←⎯ **Initializes from a constant array**

This is no big deal, but you may rightfully ask, why this restriction? It stems from a historical feature of Fortran called *implicit save* behavior.

Implicit save

Adding a `save` attribute to the declaration statement in a procedure causes the value of the declared variable to be saved between calls. In other words, the procedure would "remember" the value of that saved variable. Now, here's the twist: if you initialize a variable in the declaration statement, this will implicitly add the `save` attribute to the declaration. A variable with the `save` attribute will maintain its value in memory between procedure calls. As this is a side effect, it can't be used in `pure` procedures.

I don't recommend using the `save` attribute or relying on the implicit save feature to maintain state between calls. In main programs and modules, it's harmless, and you can safely initialize on declaration. In procedures, I recommend against using the implicit save behavior, as it leads to bug-prone code.

There's another, more general way of constructing an array. In several examples, I've assigned to a an array of five elements, and they were easy to type in by hand. However, what if you wanted to assign a hundred or a thousand elements? This is where we can use the so-called implied do loop constructor, as shown in the following listing.

Listing 5.4 Initializing an array from an implied do loop constructor

```
integer, allocatable :: a(:)
integer :: i

a = [(i, i = 1, 100)]
```

Elements will range from 1 to 100.

This syntax is called an implied do loop because (i, i = 1, 100) is just syntactic sugar for an explicit do loop:

```
do i = 1, 100
  a(i) = i
end do
```

With an implied do loop array constructor, you aren't restricted to just the loop counter. For example, you can use it to assign array values from arbitrary functions or expressions, as shown in the following listing.

Listing 5.5 Initializing a real array with sines from 0 to 2π, with 1,000 steps

```
real, allocatable :: a(:)
integer :: i
real, parameter :: pi = 3.14159256

a = [(sin(2 * pi * i / 1000.), i = 0, 1000)]
```

Initializes an array with sines from 0 to 2π

Here, I used the integer index i to construct an array of sines with arguments that go from 0 to 2π in 1,000 steps. Although it's almost always useful, i doesn't need to appear in the expression that evaluates array elements.

For example, initializing an array of a thousand zeros is trivial:

```
a = [(0, i = 1, 1000)]
```

Finally, Fortran also lets you create empty arrays using [integer ::] or [real ::]. In practice, these could be useful if invoking a *generator*—a function that appends an element to an array on every call.

Combining different numeric types in expressions
Notice that in listing 5.5 I've mixed integer and real variables in a single expression: sin(2 * pi * i / 1000). What's the type of the result then? Integer or real? Fortran follows two simple rules:

1 The expression is first evaluated to the strongest (most precise) type. For example, multiplying a real with an integer always results in a real, and multiplying a complex number with either a real or an integer always results in a complex number. Same goes for kinds of different precision—adding a `real32` to a `real64` results in a `real64` value.

2 If you're assigning the result of the expression to a variable, its type is automatically promoted (or demoted!) to the type of the variable.

In the specific example of listing 5.5, 2, `i`, and `1000` are integers, and `pi` is a real. The whole expression is thus a real number. This is generally known as *type coercion* or *mixed-mode arithmetic*. We'll use it often in this book.

5.2.3 *Reading stock data from files*

Now that we have the list of stock symbols that we'll work on, let's use this information to load the data from file and store it in our newly declared dynamic arrays. The prototype of our main loop should look like the following listing.

Listing 5.6   Reading stock data from a file using a `read_stock` subroutine

```
do n = 1, size(symbols)
  call read_stock(                              &
    'data/' // trim(symbols(n)) // '.csv', &
    time, open, high, low, close, adjclose, volume)
end do
```

For each symbol, reads stock data from the file and stores it in arrays

However, we haven't implemented the read_stock subroutine yet! Based on the calling signature, we should pass the file name as the first argument, an array of times as the second, and six real arrays to hold the stock data as the remaining arguments. At this point, we're passing arrays that haven't been allocated yet. As we iterate over the stocks, we'll need to explicitly allocate our arrays before loading data from the files. The declaration of data in our read_stock subroutine prototype may thus be rendered as shown in the following listing.

Listing 5.7   Data declaration in the `read_stock` subroutine

```
subroutine read_stock(filename, time, open, high, &
                      low, close, adjclose, volume)
  character(*), intent(in) :: filename
  character(:), allocatable, intent(in out) :: time(:)
  real, allocatable, intent(in out) :: open(:), &
    high(:), low(:), close(:), adjclose(:), volume(:)
  ...
end subroutine read_stock
```

Assumed-length input character string

Dynamic array of character strings of length 10

Dynamic real arrays for stock data; ampersand marks line continuation

This is where the action will happen.

Let's look at our arguments in this subroutine definition. `filename` is declared as `character(*)`. This is an *assumed-length* character string. It says that whatever the length of the string is that's passed to the subroutine, this argument will accept and assume that length. This is useful when you want to pass character strings that are of either varying or unpredictable length. `time`, however, is declared as a `character(:)` allocatable array to match the declaration in the calling program. Finally, the arrays to hold the actual stock data are declared as `real` and `allocatable`.

Recall the `intent` attribute from section 3.2.1? Here, we're using `intent(in out)` for all arrays, which means that they will be passed back and forth between the main program and the subroutine. Notice also that here we've matched the data type and allocatable attributes for the stock data with those declared in the main program. (See listing 5.2.)

In the next subsection, I give a detailed explanation of how explicit allocation and deallocation works and how we can implement it in our app.

5.2.4 *Allocating arrays of a certain size or range*

In the previous few sections, we've learned how to declare and initialize dynamic arrays. However, what if we need to assign values to individual array elements, one by one, in a loop? This will be the case as we load the data from CSV files into arrays—we'll iterate over records in files, and assign values to array elements one at a time. However, we don't really have a way to initialize the data arrays like we did with `stock_symbols` in listing 5.3. Note that implicitly allocating by assigning an empty array `[integer ::]` or `[real ::]` won't work here because we may need to index elements of an array in some order other than just appending values. This calls for a more explicit mechanism to allocate the array without assigning known values to it:

```
real, allocatable :: a(:)        ⟵┤  Declares a real,
integer :: im = 5                     dynamic array a
allocate(a(im))          ⟵┐  Allocates the array
                          │  a with size im
```

This code tells the program to reserve memory for the array a of size `im`, in this case 5. When invoked like this, a will, by default, have a lower bound of 1, and an upper bound of `im`. The lower bound of 1 is the default, similar to what you'll find in Julia, R, or MATLAB. This is unlike C, C++, Python, or JavaScript, where array or list indices begin with 0.

However, Fortran doesn't impose a constraint to the start index being 1, unlike Python, where the first index is always 0. You can specify the lower and upper bounds in the allocation statement:

```
integer :: is = -5, ie = 10      │  Allocates the array a with
allocate(a(is:ie))        ⟵┘  a range from is to ie
```

Notice that I used a colon (`:`) between `is` and `ie` to specify the range. This range is inclusive (unlike in Python!), so the size of a is now `ie - is + 1`—in this case 16.

Inquiring about array bounds

You can use the built-in functions `lbound` and `ubound` to get the lower and upper bound, respectively, of any array.

5.2.5 Allocating an array from another array

It's also possible to dynamically allocate an array based on the size of another array. The `allocate` statement accepts two optional arguments:

- `mold`—A variable or an expression that has the same type as the object being allocated
- `source`—Equivalent to `mold`, except that the values of `source` are used to initialize the object being allocated

For example, allocating a from b using mold will reserve the space in memory for a but won't initialize its elements:

```
real, allocatable :: a(:), b(:)        Allocating from mold
allocate(b(10:20))                     won't initialize a.
allocate(a, mold=b)         <—         Initializes values
a = 0                       <—         separately
```

However, if we allocate a from b using source, it will be allocated and initialized with values of b:

```
real, allocatable :: a(:), b(:)        Allocates and initializes
b = [1.0, 2.0, 3.0]                    a with values of b
allocate(a, source=b)       <—
```

TIP No matter how you choose to allocate your arrays, always initialize them immediately after allocation. This will minimize the chance of accidentally using uninitialized arrays in expressions. Although Fortran will allow you to do this, you'll likely end up with gibberish results.

You may have noticed that when describing the array constructors in section 5.2.2, I initialized arrays without explicitly allocating them with an `allocate` statement (see, for example, listings 5.4 and 5.5). How come? You may rightfully ask, do I need to explicitly allocate arrays or not? Since Fortran 2003, we've had available a convenient feature of the language called *allocation on assignment*.

5.2.6 Automatic allocation on assignment

If you assign an array to an allocatable array variable, the target array variable is automatically allocated with the correct size to match the array on the right side. The array variable can be already allocated or not. If it is, it will be reallocated if its current size differs from that of the source array. For example, try appending elements to an array on the fly, as shown in the following listing.

Listing 5.8   Automatically reallocating an array on assignment

```
integer, allocatable :: a(:)          Initializes an empty array

a = [integer ::]                       Reallocated to [1]
a = [a, 1]
a = [a, 2]                      Then to [1, 2]
a = [a, 2 * a]

             Now [1, 2, 2, 4]
```

This feature is particularly useful when trying to assign an array that is a result of a function, and whose size is not known ahead of time. We'll use this feature often in this book.

There's an important difference between explicit allocation with the `allocate` statement and allocation on assignment. The former will trigger a runtime error if issued twice—that is, if you issue an `allocate` statement on an object that's already allocated. On the other side, the latter will gracefully reallocate the array if already allocated. To be able to effectively reuse dynamic arrays, Fortran gives us a counterpart to the `allocate` statement that allows us to explicitly clear the object from memory.

5.2.7   *Cleaning up after use*

When we're done working with the array, we can clean it from memory like this:

```
deallocate(a)
```

After issuing `deallocate`, you must allocate array a again before using it on the right side of assignments. We'll apply this mechanism to reuse arrays between different stocks.

> **Automatic deallocation**
> An allocatable array is automatically deallocated when it goes out of scope. For example, if you declare and allocate an array inside of a function or subroutine, it will be deallocated on return.

Much like it's an error to allocate an object that's already allocated, it's also an error to deallocate an object that's not allocated! In the next subsection, I explain how you can check the allocation status so you'll never erroneously allocate an object twice or deallocate an object that hasn't even been allocated yet.

Otherwise, there's no restriction with regard to whether the array has been initialized or not. You're free to deallocate an uninitialized array; for example, if you learn that the array is not of the expected size, or similar.

TIP   Deallocate all allocatable variables when you're done working with them.

The diagram in figure 5.2 illustrates a life cycle of a dynamic array.

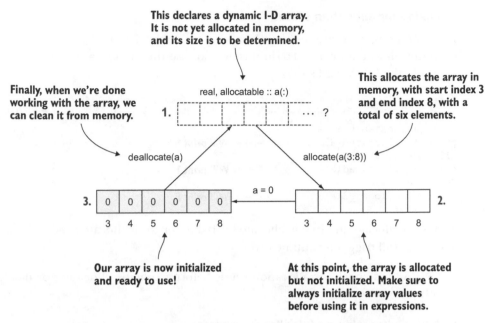

Figure 5.2 A life cycle of a dynamic array

We first declare the array as `allocatable`. At this point, the array isn't yet allocated in memory, and its size is unspecified. When ready, we issue the `allocate` statement to reserve a chunk of memory to hold this array. This is also where we decide the size of the array or the start and end indices (in this example, 3 and 8). If not allocating from another source array, the values will be uninitialized. We thus need to initialize the array before doing anything else with it. Finally, once we're done working with the array, we issue the `deallocate` statement to release the memory that holds the array. The status of the array is now back to unallocated, and it's available for allocation. You can reuse a dynamic array like this any number of times, even with different sizes or start and end indices. This is exactly what we'll do in our stock price analysis app. For each stock, we'll allocate the arrays, use them to load the data from files, work on them, and then deallocate them before passing them on to the next stock.

Careful with frequent allocation!

Arrays are contiguous in memory. This has pros and cons. On one side, indexing an array is a fast operation (constant in time, $O(1)$) because the computer can predict the position in memory of an element solely based on the index. On the other side, inserting, appending, or removing elements always triggers a reallocation of the whole array! The cost of this operation is proportional to the array size (linear in time, $O(n)$). For small arrays, this may be insignificant. However, appending an element to a 100 million-element-long array will trigger reallocation of ~400 MB! This can easily turn into a performance bottleneck in your app if you're not careful.

5.2.8   *Checking for allocation status*

It will, at times, be useful to know the allocation status of a variable; that is, whether it's currently allocated or not. To do this, we can use the built-in `allocated` function, as shown in the following listing.

Listing 5.9   Checking for allocation status

```
real, allocatable :: a(:)
print *, allocated(a)        ◁———————  Will print F
allocate(a(10))
print *, allocated(a)        ◁———————  Will print T
deallocate(a)
print *, allocated(a)        ◁———————  Will print F
```

Trying to allocate an already allocated variable, or to deallocate a variable that's not allocated, will trigger a runtime error.

> **TIP**   Always check for allocation status before explicitly allocating or deallocating a variable.

5.2.9   *Catching allocation and deallocation errors*

Your allocations and deallocations will occasionally fail. This can happen if you try to allocate more memory than available, allocate an object that's already allocated, or free an object that has been freed. When it happens, the program will abort. However, the `allocate` statement also comes with built-in error handling if you want finer control over what happens when the allocation fails. You can use

```
allocate(u(im), stat=stat, errmsg=err)
```

where `stat` and `errmsg` are optional arguments:

- `stat`—An `integer` that indicates the status of the `allocate` statement. `stat` will be zero if allocation was successful; otherwise, it will be a nonzero positive number.
- `errmsg`—A `character` string that contains the error message if an error occurred (such as `stat` being nonzero) and is undefined otherwise.

By using the built-in error handling, you get the opportunity to decide how the program should proceed if the allocation fails. For example, if there isn't enough memory to allocate a large array, perhaps we can split the work into smaller chunks. Even if you want the program to stop on allocation failure, this approach lets you handle things gracefully and print a meaningful error message.

> **TIP**   If you want control over what happens if (de)allocation fails, use `stat` and `errmsg` in your `allocate` and `deallocate` statements to catch any errors that may come up. Of course, you'll still need to tell the program what to do if

an error occurs; for example, stop the program with a custom message, print a warning message and continue running, or try to recover in some other way.

We can use the built-in error handling in our stock analysis app. However, we're going to need this for several arrays. This seems suitable to implement once in a subroutine, and then reuse it as needed. That's the goal of our first exercise for this chapter, as shown in the "Exercise 1" sidebar.

Exercise 1: Convenience (de)allocator subroutines

Explicitly allocating and deallocating arrays can be quite tedious. This is especially true if you decide to make use of the built-in error handling. If you're working with many different arrays at a time, this can quickly build up to a lot of boilerplate code.

For this exercise, write subroutines for allocation and deallocation that handle the allocation status, as well as handling errors:

1 Write a subroutine, `alloc`, that allocates a given array with a given integer size. If the input array is already allocated, free it from memory first. (See #2.)

2 Write a subroutine, `free`, that takes an input allocatable array and deallocates it. If the input array is not allocated, do nothing and return.

Both subroutines should use the `stat` and `errmsg` arguments to catch and report any errors if they occur. Once implemented, you should be able to allocate and free your arrays like this:

```
call alloc(a, 5)
! do work with a
call free(a)
```

You can find the solution in the "Answer key" section near the end of this chapter, or in the stock-prices repository in stock-prices/src/mod_alloc.f90.

We'll use these convenience subroutines to greatly reduce the boilerplate in the `read_stock` subroutine. Be aware, however, that convenience procedures like this add a layer of abstraction over existing code. This can be a blessing and a curse—abstractions help reduce the amount of boilerplate code we need to write, but they also obscure how things are implemented under the hood, which may add to cognitive complexity for a reader who's trying to understand how the code works. Use abstractions carefully and mindfully.

5.2.10 *Implementing the CSV reader subroutine*

Having covered the detailed mechanics of allocating and deallocating arrays, including the built-in error handling, we finally arrive at implementing the CSV file reader subroutine, as shown in the following listing.

Listing 5.10   Reading stock price data from CSV files and storing them into arrays

```
subroutine read_stock(filename, time, open, high,&
                      low, close, adjclose, volume)

  ...
  integer :: fileunit
  integer :: n, nm

  nm = num_records(filename) - 1          ←──┐ Finds the number of
                                              records (lines) in a file

  if (allocated(time)) deallocate(time)        Allocates the array
  allocate(character(10) :: time(nm))          of timestamps
  call alloc(open, nm)
  call alloc(high, nm)
  call alloc(low, nm)              Allocates the
  call alloc(close, nm)           stock price
  call alloc(adjclose, nm)        data arrays
  call alloc(volume, nm)

  open(newunit=fileunit, file=filename)     Skips the data header
  read(fileunit, fmt=*, end=1)         ←──  in the first line
  do n = 1, nm
    read(fileunit, fmt=*, end=1) time(n), open(n),&
      high(n), low(n), close(n), adjclose(n), volume(n)    Reads the data
  end do                                                   line-by-line and stores
1 close(fileunit)        ←──┐ Closes the file              them into arrays
                             when done
end subroutine read_stock
```

Opens the CSV file points to `open(newunit=fileunit, file=filename)`

To find the length of the arrays before I allocate them, I inquire about the length of the CSV file using a custom function num_records, defined in src/mod_io.f90. If you're wondering what the number 1 means in the 1 close(fileunit), it's just a line label that Fortran uses if and when it encounters an exception in the read(fileunit, fmt=*, end=1) statements. If you're interested in how this function works, take a look inside src/mod_io.f90. I won't spend much time on the I/O-specific code here, as we just need it to move forward with the array analysis. We'll explore I/O in more detail in chapter 6.

On every subroutine entry, the arrays time, open, high, low, close, adjclose, and volume will be allocated with size nm. The subroutine alloc now seamlessly reallocates the arrays for us. Notice that we still use the explicit way of allocating and deallocating the array of timestamps. This is because we implemented the convenience subroutines alloc and free that work on real arrays. Because of Fortran's strong typing discipline, we can't just pass an array of strings to a subroutine that expects an array of reals. We'll learn in chapter 9 how to write generic procedures that take arguments of different types. For now, explicitly allocating the array of timestamps will do. Furthermore, we also need to specify the string length when allocating the time array.

Having read the CSV files and loaded the stock price arrays with the data, we can move on to the actual analysis and fun with arrays.

> **Getting the number of lines in a text file**
> If you're curious how the `num_records` function is implemented, take a look at src/mod_io.f90. This function opens a file and counts the number of lines by reading it line-by-line.

5.2.11 *Indexing and slicing arrays*

Did you notice that the stock data in the CSV files are ordered from most recent to oldest? This means that when we read it into arrays from top to bottom, the first element will correspond to the most recent stock price. Let's reverse the arrays so they're oriented in a more natural way, going forward in time with the index number. If we express the reverse operation as a function, we could apply it to any array like this:

```
adjclose = reverse(adjclose)
```

The `reverse` function will prove useful for the other two objectives of the stock-prices app. Before implementing it, we need to understand how array indexing and slicing works.

To select a single element, we enclose an integer index inside the parentheses; for example `adjclose(1)` will refer to the first element of the array, `adjclose(5)` to the fifth, and so on.

To select a range of elements—for example, from fifth to tenth—use the start and end indices inside the parentheses, separated by a colon:

```
real, allocatable :: subset(:)
...
subset = adjclose(5:10)
```

In this case, `subset` will be automatically allocated as an array with six elements, and values corresponding to those of `adjclose` from index 5 to 10.

By default, the slice `adjclose(start:end)` will include all elements between the indices `start` and `end`, inclusive. However, you can specify an arbitrary stride. For example, `adjclose(5:10:2)` will result in a slice with elements 5, 7, and 9. The general syntax for slicing an array a with a custom stride is

```
a(start:end:stride)
```

where `start`, `end`, and `stride` are integer variables, constants, or expressions. `start` and `end` can have any valid integer value, including zero and negative values. `stride` must be a nonzero (positive or negative) integer.

Similar rules apply for `start`, `end`, and `stride` as apply for do loops:

1 If `stride` is not given, its default value is 1.
2 If `start` > end and `stride` > 0, or if `start` < end and `stride` < 0, the slice is an empty array.

3 If `start == end`—for example, `a(5:5)`—the slice is an array with a single element. Be careful not to mistake this for `a(5)`, which is a scalar (nonarray).

Furthermore, if `start` equals the lower bound of an array, it can be omitted, and the same is true if `end` equals the upper bound of an array. For example, if we declare an array as `real :: a(10:20)`, then the following array references and slices all correspond to the same array: `a`, `a(:)`, `a(10:20)`, `a(10:)`, `a(:20)`, `a(::1)`. The last syntax from this list is particularly useful when you need to slice every n-th element of the whole array—it's as simple as `a(::n)`. If you have experience with slicing lists in Python, this will feel familiar.

Exercise 2: Reversing an array

Write a function `reverse` that accepts a real one-dimensional array as an input argument and returns the same array in reverse order. Use array slicing rules to perform the reversal. You can test your new function by reversing the input array twice and comparing it to itself:

```
print *, all(a == reverse(reverse(a)))
```

Here, `all` is the built-in function that takes a `logical` array as input and returns `.true.` if all elements evaluate as `.true.`.

Hint: use the built-in function `size` to determine the end index of the input array.

You can find the solution in the "Answer key" section near the end of this chapter.

Play with different ways to slice arrays. Try different values of start, end, and stride. What happens if you try to create a slice that's bigger than the array itself? In other words, can you reference an array out of bounds?

Referencing array elements out of bounds

Be very careful to not reference array elements that are out of bounds! Fortran itself doesn't forbid this, but you'll end up with either an invalid value or a segmentation fault, which can be particularly difficult to debug.

By default, compilers don't check if an out-of-bounds reference occurs during run-time, but you can enable it with a compiler flag. Use `gfortran -fcheck=bounds` and `ifort -check bounds` for GNU and Intel Fortran compilers, respectively. This can result in significantly slower programs, so it's best if used only during development and debugging.

Now that we understand how array indexing works, it's straightforward to calculate the stock gain over the whole time series. Take the difference between the last and first element of the adjusted close price to calculate the absolute gain in US dollars:

```
adjclose = reverse(adjclose)
gain = (adjclose(size(adjclose)) - adjclose(1))
```

Reverses the array so that the first element refers to the oldest record

Takes the difference between the last and the first element

Here, I'm using the built-in `size` function, which returns the integer total number of elements, to reference the last element of the array. Like everything else we did before, `gain` must be declared, in this case as a `real` scalar. The absolute gain, however, only tells us how much the stock grew over a period of time; it doesn't tell us anything about whether that growth is small or large relative to the stock price itself. For example, a gain from $1 to $10 per share is greater than a gain from $100 to $200 per share, assuming you invest $100 in either stock. In the former case, you'll come out with $1,000, whereas in the latter case, you'll have just $200! To calculate the relative gain in percent, we can divide the absolute gain by the initial stock price, and multiply by 100 to get the percent; that is, `gain / adjclose(1) * 100`. For brevity, I'll also round the relative gain to the nearest integer using the built-in function `nint`:

```
print *, symbols(n), gain, nint(gain / adjclose(1) * 100)
```

The output of the program is

```
2000-01-03 through 2018-05-14
Symbol, Gain (USD), Relative gain (%)
---------------------------------------
AAPL    184.594589           5192
AMZN    1512.16003           1692
CRAY    9.60000038             56
CSCO    1.71649933              4
HPQ     1.55270004              7
IBM     60.9193039             73
INTC    25.8368015             89
MSFT    59.4120979            154
NVDA    251.745300           6964
ORCL    20.3501987             77
```

From this output, we can see that Amazon had the largest absolute gain of $1,512.16 per share, and Hewlett-Packard had the smallest gain of only $1.55 per share. However, the relative gain is more meaningful than the absolute amount per share because it tells how much the stock has gained relative to its starting price. Looking at relative gain, Nvidia had a formidable 6,964% growth, with Apple being the runner up with 5,192%. The worst performing stock was that of Cisco Systems (CSCO), with only 4% growth over this time period.

If you've cloned the stock-prices repo from GitHub, it's straightforward to compile and run this program. From the stock-prices directory, type

```
make
./stock_gain
```

We've now covered a lot of the nitty-gritty of how arrays work. Let's apply this knowledge to the other two challenges we have for the main exercise for this chapter.

5.3 *Identifying risky stocks*

One of the ways to estimate how risky a stock is at some time is by looking at volatility. Stock volatility can be quantified as the standard deviation of the stock price relative to its average. Standard deviation is a statistical measure that tells you how much individual array elements deviate from the average. To estimate volatility, we'll implement functions to compute average and standard deviation given an arbitrary input array. Furthermore, we'll compute these metrics over a limited time window, and we'll slide that window along the whole time series. This is the so-called moving average. For example, figure 5.3 shows the actual price, 30-day moving average, and volatility based on the 30-day moving standard deviation for Nvidia stock.

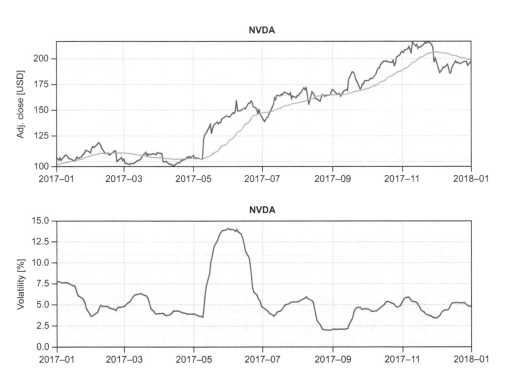

Figure 5.3   Top: Nvidia stock price (black) and a 30-day simple moving average (gray). Bottom: Volatility expressed as standard deviation relative to the 30-day simple moving average, in percent.

While Fortran comes with many built-in mathematical functions, it doesn't include a function to compute the average of an array. That's fairly straightforward to implement using the built-in functions `sum` and `size`, as shown in the following listing.

Listing 5.11 Computing the average value of an array

```
pure real function average(x)
  real, intent(in) :: x(:)
  average = sum(x) / size(x)
end function average
```
◁— **The sum of all elements divided by the number of elements**

We already saw earlier that we can use `size` in a do loop when we want to iterate over all elements of an array, or when we want to reference the last element of an array. `sum` does exactly what you think it does—you pass to it an array, and it returns the sum of all elements.

To calculate the standard deviation of an array x, follow these steps:

1 *Calculate the average of the array*—For this, use the function that we just wrote: `average(x)`. The result is a scalar (nonarray).

2 *Find the difference between each element of the array and its average*—This is where the power of whole-array arithmetic comes in. We can use the subtraction operator `-` that we're familiar with and apply it directly on the whole array, without the need for a loop: `x - average(x)`. When using arithmetic (`+`, `-`, `*`, `/`, `**`), assignment (`=`), or comparison (`>`, `>=`, `<=`, `<`, `==`, `/=`) operators, they're applied element-wise. In this case, x is an array, and `average(x)` is a scalar; `x - average(x)` will subtract `average(x)` from each element of x. The result is an array.

3 *Square the differences*—This operates the same as in step 2, except this time we need to take the power of 2: `(x - average(x)) ** 2`. In this expression, `**` is the power (exponentiation) operator.

4 *Calculate the average of the squared differences*—We can apply the same function again: `average((x - average(x))**2)`.

5 *Finally, take the square root of the result from step 4*—For this, we can use the built-in `sqrt` function, which is also an elemental function—it works on both scalars and arrays.

Here's the complete code for the standard deviation function. Thanks to Fortran's whole-array arithmetic, we can express all five steps as a one-liner, as shown in the following listing.

Listing 5.12 Computing the standard deviation of an array

```
pure real function std(x)
  real, intent(in) :: x(:)
  std = sqrt(average((x - average(x))**2))
end function std
```
◁— **Root of mean squared differences**

To use arithmetic operators on whole arrays, the arrays on either side of the operator must be of the same shape and size. You can also combine an array of any shape and size with a scalar. For example, if a is an array, `2 * a` will be applied element-wise; that is, each element of a will be doubled.

TIP   Use whole-array arithmetic over do loops whenever possible.

We're not done here yet. Rather than just the average and standard deviation of the whole time series, we're curious about the metrics that are relevant to a specific time, and we want to be able to see how they evolve. For this, we can use the average and standard deviation along a moving time window. A commonly used metric in finance is the so-called *simple moving average*, which takes an average of some number of previous points, moving in time. I'll let you tackle this one in the "Exercise 3" sidebar, and will meet you on the other side.

Exercise 3: Calculating moving average and standard deviation

Our current implementations for average and standard deviation are great, but they don't let us specify a narrow time period that would give us more useful information about stock volatility at a certain time.

Write a function, `moving_average`, that takes an input real array, `x`, and integer window, `w`, and returns an array that has the same size as `x`, but with each element being an average of `w` previous elements of `x`. For example, for `w = 10`, the moving average at element i would be the average of `x(i-10:i)`. In finance, this is often referred to as the *simple moving average*.

Hint: You can use the built-in function `max` to limit the indices near the edges of `x` to prevent going out of bounds. For example, `max(i, 1)` results in `i` if greater than 1, and 1 otherwise. Note that you'll need to use a combination of looping and whole-array arithmetic to implement the solution.

You can find the solution in the "Answer key" section near the end of the chapter.

The main program of this challenge is very similar to the previous one (`stock_gain`). However, besides printing the total time series average and volatility on the screen, now we also write the 30-day moving average and standard deviation into text files, as shown in the following listing.

Listing 5.13   Calculating stock volatility using moving average and standard deviation

```
program stock_volatility

  use mod_arrays, only: average, std, moving_average,&         Accesses custom
                   moving_std, reverse                          functions from
  use mod_io, only: read_stock, write_stock                    modules
  ...
  do n = 1, size(symbols)
    ...
    im = size(time)
    adjclose = reverse(adjclose)
    ...
```

```
    call write_stock(                               &
      trim(symbols(n)) // '_volatility.txt',  &
      time(im:1:-1), adjclose,                 &
      moving_average(adjclose, 30),            &
      moving_std(adjclose, 30))
```

Writes the 30-day moving average and standard deviation to files

```
  end do

end program stock_volatility
```

Look inside src/mod_io.f90 to see how the `write_stock` subroutine is implemented. The full program is located in src/stock_volatility.f90.

5.4 Finding good times to buy and sell

Can we use historical stock market data to determine a good time to buy or sell shares of a stock? One of the commonly used indicators by traders is the *moving average crossover*. Consider that the simple moving average is a general indicator of whether the stock is going up or down. For example, a 30-day simple moving average would tell you about the overall stock price trend. You can think of it as a smoother and delayed stock price, without the high-frequency fluctuations. Combined with the actual stock price, we can use this information to decide whether we should buy or sell, or do nothing—see figure 5.4.

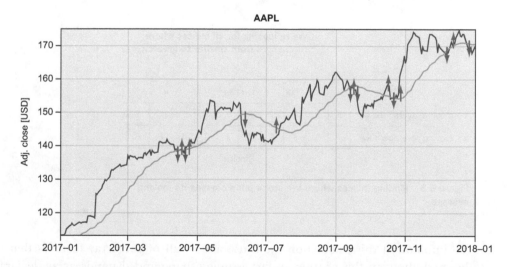

Figure 5.4 Moving average crossover indicators for Apple. Black is the adjusted daily closing price, gray is the 30-day simple moving average, and up and down arrows are the positive and negative crossover markers, respectively.

In this figure, I've marked with an up arrow every point in time when the actual price crossed the moving average line from low to high, and with a down arrow when crossing from high to low. The rule of thumb is this: sell when the actual price drops below the moving average line, buy when it rises above the moving average line.

Let's employ Fortran arrays and arithmetic to compute the moving average crossover. The calculation has two steps:

1 Compute the moving average over some time period. It can be any period of time, depending on the trends that you're interested in (intra-day, short-term, long-term, etc.) and the frequency of the data that you have. We're working with daily data, so we'll work with a 30-day moving average. Hopefully, you worked through exercise 3 in the previous subsection and implemented the `moving_average` function. Otherwise, you can find it in src/mod_arrays.f90.

2 Once we have the moving average, we can follow the actual stock price and find times when it crosses the moving average line. If the actual price crosses the moving average from below going up, it's an indicator of a potentially good time to buy. Otherwise, if it crosses from above going down, it's likely a good time to sell.

The main trick we'll use for this challenge is to determine all array indices where the stock price is greater than its moving average, as well as those where the stock price is smaller than its moving average. We can then combine these two conditions and find all the indices where the stock price changes from smaller to greater, and vice versa. Figure 5.5 illustrates this algorithm.

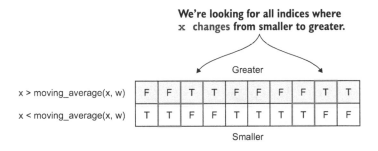

Figure 5.5   Finding indices where the stock price crosses its moving average

To implement this calculation, we'll use almost all of the array features that we've learned about in this chapter so far: assumed-shape and dynamic array declaration, array constructor, and invoking a custom array function (`moving_average`). Furthermore, we'll create logical (Boolean) arrays to handle the conditions I described in figure 5.5. Finally, we'll employ a built-in function, `pack`, to select only those indices that satisfy our criteria.

We can write all this in about a dozen lines of code, as the following listing demonstrates.

Listing 5.14 Computing the moving-average crossover, low to high

Array to
store the
moving
average
of x

Computes
the
moving
average

```
pure function crosspos(x, w) result(res)        We don't know the size ahead
  real, intent(in) :: x(:)                       of time, so we'll declare this
  integer, intent(in) :: w                        as a dynamic array.
  integer, allocatable :: res(:)        ←
  real, allocatable :: xavg(:)                         Logical (Boolean)
  logical, allocatable :: greater(:), smaller(:)  ←    arrays to mask x
  integer :: i
  res = [(i, i = 2, size(x))]        ←        First guess result, all
  xavg = moving_average(x, w)                  indices but the first
  greater = x > xavg                   Logical arrays to tell us where
  smaller = x < xavg                   x is greater or smaller
  res = pack(res, greater(2:) &                  Uses built-in function
                  .and. smaller(:size(x)-1))     pack to subset an array
end function crosspos                             according to a condition
```

We first initialize our result array, res, as an integer sequence from 2 to size(x). This is our first guess from which we'll subset only those elements that satisfy our criteria. The crux is in the last executable line, where we invoke the pack function. How does pack work? When you have an array x that you want to subset according to some condition mask, invoking pack(x, mask) will, as a result, return only those elements of x where mask is true. mask doesn't have to be a logical array variable—it can be an expression as well, which is how we used it in our function in the listing. Recall the automatic reallocation on assignment from section 5.2.5? This is exactly where it comes in handy—we pass the original array, res, and a conditional mask to pack, and it returns a smaller, reallocated array, res, according to the mask.

This function only returns the crossover from low to high value, thus named crosspos. However, we also need the crossover from high to low so that we know when the stock price is going to drop below the moving average curve. How would we implement the negative variant of the crossover function, crossneg? We can reuse all the code from crosspos except for the last criterion—we need to look for elements that are going from higher to lower, instead of lower to higher:

```
pure function crossneg(x, w) result(res)
  ...
  res = pack(res, smaller(2:) .and. greater(:size(x)-1))     Different criterion
end function crossneg+                                         for the mask
```

The main program will use these functions to find the indices from the time series, and write the matching timestamps into files, as shown in the following listing.

Listing 5.15 Finding the moving average crossover times and writing them into files

```
program stock_crossover
  ...                                                  Accesses new functions
  use mod_arrays, only: crossneg, crosspos, reverse  ←  from a module
  ...
  integer, allocatable :: buy(:), sell(:)     ←   Integer indices for
                                                   storing the crossovers
```

```
...
do n = 1, size(symbols)
  ...
  time = time(size(time):1:-1)        ◁         Time is an array of strings,
  adjclose = reverse(adjclose)        ◁         so we have to use the slice.
                                                Reverses using our
                                                custom function

  buy = crosspos(adjclose, 30)        │         Finds the positive and
  sell = crossneg(adjclose, 30)       │         negative crossover

  open(newunit=fileunit, &                      Opens the file to
      file=trim(symbols(n)) // '_crossover.txt')   store the results
  do i = 1, size(buy)
    write(fileunit, fmt=*) 'Buy ', time(buy(i))   ◁   Writes the positive
  end do                                              crossover timestamps
  do i = 1, size(sell)
    write(fileunit, fmt=*) 'Sell ', time(sell(i))  ◁   Writes the negative
  end do                                               crossover timestamps
  close(fileunit)     ◁    Closes
                           the file
end do

end program stock_crossover
```

I included only the relevant new code in listing 5.15. The full program is located in src/stock_crossover.f90. The program itself doesn't do much new stuff. For each stock, it calls the moving average crossover functions, stores the results into arrays (buy and sell), and writes the timestamps with these indices into a text file. I plotted the results for Apple (AAPL) for 2017 in figure 5.4. You can use the Python scripts included in the repository to plot the results for other stocks and time periods.

Plotting the results

Both the second and third challenge in this chapter produce results that I've plotted and showed in this section. The Python plotting scripts that I used are included in the stock-prices/plotting directory. Follow the directions in README.md to set up your own Python plotting environment. If you decide to further explore the stock prices data, you can use and modify these scripts for your own application.

And that's it, we made it! Following only a few rules for array declaration, initialization, indexing, and slicing, we wrote a nifty little stock analysis app that tells us some useful things about the longer term trends and risk of individual stock prices. The skills that you learned in this chapter will form a foundation for what's coming in chapter 7.

5.5 Answer key

This section contains solutions to exercises in this chapter. Skip ahead if you haven't worked through the exercises yet.

5.5.1 Exercise 1: Convenience (de)allocator subroutines

Start with the allocator subroutine `alloc`. For the key functionality to work, our subroutine needs to do the following:

1. Check if the input array is already allocated and, if yes, deallocate it before proceeding.
2. Allocate the array with input size n.
3. If an exception occurs during allocation, abort the program and print the error message to screen.

The following listing demonstrates the implementation.

Listing 5.16   Allocating an array with error handling

```
subroutine alloc(a, n)                                          Array to allocate
  real, allocatable, intent(in out) :: a(:)
  integer, intent(in) :: n
  integer :: stat
  character(100) :: errmsg                    Character string to store
  if (allocated(a)) call free(a)              the error message
  allocate(a(n), stat=stat, errmsg=errmsg)               Free if already
  if (stat > 0) error stop errmsg                        allocated
end subroutine alloc
```

- **Array size** → `integer, intent(in) :: n`
- **Integer status code** → `integer :: stat`
- **Allocates with error handling** → `allocate(a(n), stat=stat, errmsg=errmsg)`
- **If nonzero status, aborts and prints error message** → `if (stat > 0) error stop errmsg`

Now, take a look at the implementation of the `free` subroutine shown in the following listing.

Listing 5.17   Freeing an array with error handling

```
subroutine free(a)                                             Array to deallocate
  real, allocatable, intent(in out) :: a(:)
  integer :: stat
  character(100) :: errmsg                    If already freed, return
  if (.not. allocated(a)) return
  deallocate(a, stat=stat, errmsg=errmsg)               Deallocates with
  if (stat > 0) error stop errmsg                       error handling
end subroutine free
```

- **Integer status code** → `integer :: stat`
- **Character string to store the error message** → `character(100) :: errmsg`
- **If nonzero status, aborts and prints error message** → `if (stat > 0) error stop errmsg`

The code is very similar to `alloc` except that here, at the start of the executable section of the code, we check if a is already allocated. If not, our job here is done, and we can return immediately.

These subroutines are also part of the stock-prices repository. You can find them in src/mod_alloc.f90, and they are used by the CSV reader in src/mod_io.f90.

5.5.2   *Exercise 2: Reversing an array*

The solution to this exercise has only two steps and you can write it as a single-line function (not counting the declaration code). First, we know that since we're just reversing the order of elements, the resulting array will always be of the same size as the input array. The size will also correspond to the end index of the array. Second, once we know the size, we can slice the input from last to first and use the negative stride to go backward. The following listing provides the full code.

Listing 5.18   Reversing an input array

```
pure function reverse(x)
  real, intent(in) :: x(:)          ◁——  Assumed-shape array—
  real :: reverse(size(x))          ◁——  no need for allocatable!
  reverse = x(size(x):1:-1)         ◁——  The result will be the
end function reverse                        same size as the input.

                                    Slice with negative stride
                                    to reverse order
```

Notice that our input array doesn't need to be declared allocatable. This is the so-called assumed-shape array, which takes whatever size array is passed by the caller. We can use the information about the size directly when declaring the result array.

You may be wondering why we'd make this a separate function at all when we can just do x(size(x):1:-1) to reverse any array. There are two advantages to making this a dedicated reverse function. First, if you need to reverse an array more than a few times, the one-liner slicing syntax soon becomes unwieldy. Every time you read it, there's an extra step in the thought process to understand the intention behind the syntax. Second, the slicing syntax is allowed only when referencing an array variable, and you can't use it on expressions, array constructors, or function results. In contrast, you can pass any of those as an argument to reverse. This is why we can make a test like all(x == reverse(reverse(x))). Try it!

I use this function in our stock-prices app, so if you've cloned the repo from GitHub, you can find it in src/mod_arrays.f90.

5.5.3   *Exercise 3: Calculating moving average and standard deviation*

You can implement the moving average by iterating over each element of the input array, slicing that array over a subrange determined by the input window parameter, and applying the general average function to that slice, as shown in the following listing.

Listing 5.19   Calculating moving average of a real array x over window w

```
pure function moving_average(x, w) result(res)
  real, intent(in) :: x(:)
  integer, intent(in) :: w
```

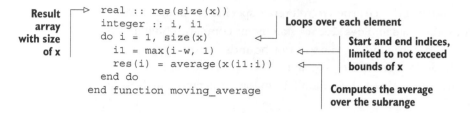

```
real :: res(size(x))
integer :: i, i1
do i = 1, size(x)
  i1 = max(i-w, 1)
  res(i) = average(x(i1:i))
end do
end function moving_average
```

Result array with size of x

Loops over each element

Start and end indices, limited to not exceed bounds of x

Computes the average over the subrange

Notice that inside the loop, I use the built-in functions `min` and `max` to limit the subrange from exceeding the bounds of the array x. For a standard deviation function over an equivalent window, we'd just replace `average(x(i1:i))` with `std(x(i1:i))`. You can find these functions in src/mod_arrays.f90.

5.6   New Fortran elements, at a glance

- `allocatable` attribute to declare a dynamic array whose size is unknown at compile time
- Bracket syntax for array constructors; for example, `[1, 2, 3]`
- Implied do loop array constructor; for example, `[(i, i = 1, 3)]`
- Type coercion, or mixed mode arithmetic, where the values of lower kinds get implicitly promoted when used in expressions with higher kinds
- `allocate` and `deallocate` statements to explicitly allocate or free arrays from memory
- Indexing and slicing arrays
- Built-in functions:
  - `sum`, which returns the sum of all elements of a numeric array
  - `lbound` and `ubound` to return the lower and upper bounds, respectively, of an array
  - `pack`, which returns array elements that meet a condition
  - `min` and `max` to return the minimum or maximum, respectively, from any number of values
  - `nint`, which returns the nearest integer of an input real number
  - `all`, which returns `.true.` if all elements of an input logical array are `.true.`

5.7   Further reading

Best practices with arrays: http://mng.bz/pBp2

Summary

- An array is a sequence of values of the same type that is contiguous in memory.
- Arrays are Fortran's only built-in data structure.
- Fortran arrays can be statically or dynamically allocated, and support up to 15 dimensions.

- You can index and slice arrays to reference specific elements or sections of them.
- Fortran's `allocate` and `deallocate` statements come with built-in error handling.
- Take care to never index arrays out of bounds, or you'll get undesired results and perhaps even crash the program.
- Arrays are the basis of their parallel analog, coarrays, which we'll explore in chapter 7.

Reading, writing, and formatting your data

6

This chapter covers

- Reading from the keyboard and writing to the screen
- Standard input, output, and error streams
- Formatting numbers and text
- Writing data to files on disk

One of the pillars of every useful program is its input and output (I/O). Almost every program reads some input data from the keyboard, file, or network; does some calculation or processing on it; and outputs the result to the screen, a file on disk, or some other device. If the program is designed to be used directly by a human user (rather than being a piece of some intricate pipeline), I/O becomes even more important. Specifically, inputting data to the program should be as easy as possible, with minimum effort for the user. The output should be easy to parse and not surprising. Some of the best end-user software out there is intuitive on the first try, without the need to refer to dense user manuals.

In what kind of real-world scenarios are you most likely to work with I/O? First, reading and parsing input from the keyboard is likely in any program that needs some initial configuration from the user; for example, a program that calibrates an instrument to measure the flow through water lines. Second, formatting and writing data to the screen will come up for any program that periodically outputs results for the user (or another program) to consume. Such output needs to be easy to read and of predictable format. Think financial metrics of a market, weather data logs, or a dashboard in the control room of a power plant. Finally, many programs, and especially large simulation software, need to write their output data to files on disk for later processing and analysis. This is true of all weather, ocean, and climate prediction models today.

In this chapter, you'll learn how to read data from user input (such as the keyboard or another program) and how to format and write data to screen. We'll cover standard streams, such as standard input, output, and error units, and why they matter. Then, you'll learn how to explicitly format numerical, logical, and text values for readable and portable output. Finally, we'll explore Fortran's I/O capabilities for writing to files on disk by building a minimal note-taking app for the command line.

6.1 Your first I/O: Input from the keyboard and output to the screen

So far, we've read data and written it to screen and/or files in almost every chapter in this book. For brevity, and to stay focused on other features of the language, I only briefly mentioned what we did and why, so I haven't explained in much detail about how it works. Before we jump into a more concrete miniproject (a note-taking app), we'll first spend some time getting familiar with the basics. In this section, we'll start with the most basic I/O tasks—reading user input from the keyboard, and writing data to the screen.

6.1.1 The simplest I/O

Let's start with the simplest I/O imaginable. In this subsection, we'll program a simple robot called Echo. This robot can't do many things. He can't move, ask questions, or even think. In fact, Echo can do only two things—listen to what we say, and say it back to us. This is actually more powerful than it seems at first. Echo can hear us, and he can also speak. He doesn't seem to do much internally with what we tell him, but let's worry about that later. The important part for now is that we can *communicate* with Echo.

To make Echo the robot, we'll write a program that will receive our input from the keyboard and emit that data to the screen. If you're familiar with Linux command-line tools, this functionality is similar to that of `tee`, a GNU core utility. The program should work like this: when invoked, it will wait for the user to enter some message into the terminal. Once received, the program will print the same message to the screen, as shown in the following listing.

Listing 6.1   Compiling and running your first I/O program

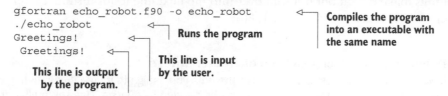

```
gfortran echo_robot.f90 -o echo_robot                    ◁──   Compiles the program
./echo_robot               ◁─────┐  Runs the program            into an executable with
Greetings!              ◁─────┐  └─                             the same name
 Greetings!   ◁──┐      └─
```

This line is output   **This line is input**
by the program.   **by the user.**

The first output of the message ("Greetings!") isn't output by the program, but is typed in by the user and emitted to the terminal at the same time. Only after the user presses the Enter key will the program read this message and write it back to the screen. The message thus appears twice.

To accomplish this task, we'll engage the `read` and `print` statements in their basic form. The following listing provides the complete program.

Listing 6.2   Reading user input from the keyboard and writing it to the screen

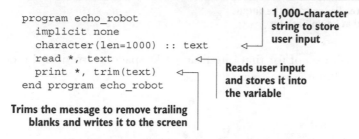

```
program echo_robot                                    1,000-character
  implicit none                                       string to store
  character(len=1000) :: text        ◁──┘             user input
  read *, text              ◁──┐
  print *, trim(text)    ◁──┐  └─    Reads user input
end program echo_robot     │         and stores it into
                           │         the variable
```

Trims the message to remove trailing
blanks and writes it to the screen

This program consists of essentially three statements: one declaration and two built-in I/O statements. We first declare a character string `text` that will hold the data input from the keyboard. Recall that when declaring a character variable, we need to give it a fixed length a priori, or declare it as a dynamic (allocatable) string. While using the allocatable string would be a more elegant solution here, it would complicate the code quite a bit because Fortran doesn't allow us to automatically allocate a string on a `read` statement. Instead, we'd need to somehow find out the length of the input, allocate the string, and then use the `read` statement to store the data into the variable. To keep this example simple, we'll stick with a fixed-length string. There's nothing special about the number 1000 here—we're just making this character variable long enough to hold an unusually large text input. The first I/O statement is `read *, text`. It instructs the computer to read the data from the *standard input* (more on this in a bit), using default formatting (`*`), and store it into `text`. The second I/O statement, `print *, trim(text)`, does the same, but the other way around. It takes the value of `trim(text)` and prints it to the screen (terminal) using default formatting (`*`).

`trim` is the built-in function that removes any trailing blanks. It takes care of the fact that `text` is 1,000 characters long, and anything beyond the text input by the user is padded by spaces. What would happen if we didn't do this? Since `text` is declared as `character(len=1000)`, only the first 10 characters will be occupied by "Greetings!", and the rest will remain blank. Trimming the blank characters off the end of `message` will thus make the output not spill over into the next line if our terminal screen is less than 1,000 characters wide (mine is 80).

> **Removing trailing blanks from character strings**
> If your character variable is longer than the data you assign to it, like it is in listing 6.2, the unused part of the variable will always be padded by spaces. Use the built-in function `trim` whenever you need to remove such trailing spaces on the fly. For example, `trim('run-017.dat ')` returns just `'run-017.dat'`. This is useful in any situation in which you can't predict the length of the string you're working with; for example, a user inputting the name of the file to be read by the program.

Compile and run this program a few times. Play around with it. Does it work as expected? Almost, but not quite:

```
./echo_robot
Hello!
 Hello!
```
Leading space in the output that I didn't ask for

This is what I expected, except for that one little pesky space in front of the output. OK, I can swallow this. But it gets worse:

```
./echo_robot
Hi, there, Echo! :)
 Hi
./echo_robot
Wait, what just happened?
 Wait
```

Oh no! Now whole parts of my input are gone—our poor robot is broken. This is not at all what we intended. What's going on here? Based on our experiments so far, the program seems to read input only up to a comma and writes a spurious leading space in the output.

It turns out that the culprit is the default formatting, specified by the asterisk (*) in the `read` and `print` statements. This is also what's known in the Fortran lingo as *list-directed I/O*, which allows you to read or write multiple variables on the same line, separated by spaces or commas. It's a feature, not a bug! When we use default formatting and try to enter a message with spaces or commas in it, the program will interpret these as separate variables. However, we provide only one variable on the right side of the `read` statement, so the rest of the message is discarded. Fortunately, there's an easy fix, and that is to specify a text formatting string in place of the asterisk:

```
read '(a)', text
print '(a)', trim(text)
```
Reads text from the keyboard using text formatting

Writes trim(text) to the screen using text formatting

Immediately after typing `read`, we provide the format string for text data (`'(a)'`). This statement will thus read any data that's input on the keyboard, format it with `'(a)'`, and print it to the screen.

The formatting strings are instructions for the program on how to format data. We'll get into the specifics of number and text formatting soon. For now, all you need to know is that you can use `'(a)'` as a format string to read data as character strings, no matter if the data is plain text or numbers.

This program is not terribly useful in the real world, but it illustrates how `read` and `print` statements work in their most basic form.

Passing data from other programs

Typing the data using the keyboard isn't the only way to get data into the program through standard input. For example, with the bash shell on Linux or macOS, you could also input data straight from the command line when executing the program

```
./echo_robot <<< "Hi, there, Echo! :)"
```

or pipe it from another program:

```
echo "Hi, there, Echo! :)" | ./echo_robot
```

6.1.2 *Reading and writing multiple variables at once*

While implementing a simple echo program in the previous subsection, we accidentally stumbled on *list-directed I/O*, which allows you to read or write multiple variables on the same line. It's called list-directed because of its functionality to consume and emit an arbitrary list of variables. For example, if you input a character string, an integer, and a real number on a single line, our next program will write out "'User typed:'", and print the variables on the remainder of the line:

```
Hello 42 3.14159
   User typed: Hello      42    3.14159012
```

Values for each variable typed in by the user

The output of the program

We'll modify our program from listing 6.2 to accommodate all the variables, as shown in the following listing.

Listing 6.3   Using list-directed I/O to read and write an arbitrary number of variables

```
program read_write_list
  implicit none
  character(len=1000) :: text
  integer :: a
  real :: x
  read *, text, a, x
  print *, 'User typed: ', trim(text), a, x
end program read_write_list
```

Reads a string, an integer, and a real from the terminal

Writes the variables to the screen

What's new here relative to listing 6.2 are the declarations for integer a and real x, and also that we are now using the default formatting in the read and print statements, indicated by a single asterisk (*). This does two things:

- The output will be written in a format that is compiler- and system-dependent. This means arbitrary leading and trailing spaces, and nonportable output precision for real numbers.
- It allows you to list any number of variables in the read and print statements, including arrays or derived type components. For example, if you read an array of five elements, it would work the same as if you were to read five separate scalar variables. Likewise, writing out a derived type instance would write out each of its public components.

Using list-directed I/O is convenient for easy printing of values in your program. However, the form of the output isn't portable across compilers and operating systems, and is thus not predictable. For these reasons, I only recommend using list-directed I/O during development, for quick and easy diagnosis or manual debugging.

Now run the read_write_list program again, and input data of different types (text, integer, or real) in a different order. What happens if you pass text to a variable that's typed as an integer or a real? How about if you pass more than three items? Play with different inputs and explore what makes the program break and why.

> **TIP** Use list-directed I/O only for quick-and-dirty tasks, such as manual debugging.

So far, we've assumed that the input data is coming from the keyboard, and the output data is going to the screen. Is this always the case, and how does the Fortran program know where the data comes from, and where it should go? By default, and in their basic form that we used in listings 6.2 and 6.3, the read statement will receive data from the *standard input*, and the print statement will send the data to the *standard output*. Let's go into more detail about what they are and how we can use them for good.

> **NOTE** When working with plain text data, read, print, and write statements always process one line at a time. To read or write multiple lines of data, invoke these statements as many times as needed.

6.1.3   *Standard input, output, and error*

If you've done any programming before picking up this book, you've likely heard of standard input (stdin), output (stdout), and error (stderr). They're collectively known as *standard streams* and were introduced in the early days of the Unix operating system to allow easier interaction with the local file system and hardware, such as keyboards, printers, and, later, screens. Today, standard streams are ubiquitous on all mainstream operating systems, including Linux, macOS, and Windows.

In the context of Fortran, standard streams matter when you want to read and write data in a portable manner. Using read * and print * is likely to access standard input and output but isn't guaranteed by the Fortran standard. Furthermore, if your program encounters an exception and you want to send the error message to the user, the least surprising place to put it is the standard error stream. Fortran 2003 introduced the following named constants with the `iso_fortran_env` module to allow the programmer to specify standard I/O units in a portable way:

```
use iso_fortran_env, only: input_unit, output_unit, error_unit
```

I prefer to rename them to their widely used shorthands. The following listing shows an expanded variant of the program in listing 6.2 that will read user input in a portable way, write the message back to standard output, and print a dummy error message (for demonstration) to the standard error.

> **Listing 6.4 Reading from stdin and writing to stdout and stderr**

Waits for and reads user input

```
program standard_streams
   use iso_fortran_env, only: stdin => input_unit, &      Imports standard
                              stdout => output_unit, &    units as their
                              stderr => error_unit        shorthands
   implicit none
   character(len=1000) :: text          ◁──  Declares the character string variable
   read(stdin, '(a)') text                   in which we'll store user input
   write(stdout, '(a)') trim(text)
   write(stderr, '(a)') 'This is an error message'   ◁──  Emits an error
end program standard_streams                               message to the
                                                           standard error
```

**Emits the user-input message
to the standard output**

This is a rather simple program. We first import standard input, output, and error units from the `iso_fortran_env` module, renaming them on import so that we can use their shorter names, stdin, stdout, and stderr, respectively. We then use the `read` statement to read the user-input data from stdin and store it into text. Finally, we emit messages to stdout and stderr using the `write` statement. `write` is a more general and versatile variant of `print`, and we'll use it almost exclusively from here on.

What's an I/O unit?

Since we're talking about standard streams, it's a good time to introduce Fortran I/O units, as they'll be relevant to the rest of this chapter. An I/O unit is like a file handle in other programming languages. It's a unique identifier that's assigned to a file when you open it. This number can then be used to reference the file in a unique way until the file is closed. Standard streams also come with I/O units preassigned to them— the `input_unit`, `output_unit`, and `error_unit` constants from the `iso_fortran _env` module. Internally, I/O units are represented as integer numbers; however, in most cases, you won't need to worry about their values.

The `read` and `write` statements shown in listing 6.4 take two arguments: the first being the I/O unit to read from (or write to), and the second being the format to use to read and write data. These arguments are called `unit` and `fmt`, respectively, as illustrated on figure 6.1. In general, you can omit spelling out these keywords in your code if you find them to be too verbose. `read` and `write` statements can take quite a few more optional arguments than this. We'll take a look at some of them a bit later in this chapter.

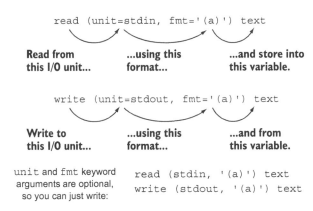

Figure 6.1   The relationship between the `read` and `write` statements. In this example, the `read` statement reads data from the standard input and writes it into a character variable, `text`. Similarly, the `write` statement writes data from the `text` variable to standard output (screen).

To see it in action, compile and run the program in listing 6.4 while redirecting the standard error to a file, as shown here:

```
./standard_streams 2> log.err       ⟵─┤  This will redirect stderr
Hi, there! :)                             to the log.err file.
Hi, there! :)
cat log.err
This is an error message   ⟵─┤  Contents of the file stderr
                                 was redirected to
```

You may ask, when should I use standard error over standard output? Standard output and error streams are typically used to differentiate the output between normal and erroneous operation of a program. You can follow a simple rule of thumb: if the program should report an error or a warning to the user, write it to stderr. Any other output of the program, such as a log or progress bar, should be written to stdout.

Better logging

If you're looking for more serious logging capability for your Fortran application, check out the `flogging` (Fortran logging) library by Chris MacMackin at https://github.com/cmacmackin/flogging. It features easy logging to file and/or standard output and error streams, built-in log timestamps, colored output, and more! (See figure 6.2.)

```
[Dec 18 2016 23:55:26][logger_example] <info> Found result of calculation
[Dec 18 2016 23:55:26][logger_example] <error> Calculation failed due to error
```

Figure 6.2   Example output from the flogging library

6.2   *Formatting numbers and text*

In this section, you'll learn how to explicitly format numbers and text for output to screen or files on disk. You've probably noticed that in most cases when we used `print` or `write` statements to display values on the screen, they produced output with somewhat awkward formatting and wide empty spaces between values. For example, in the previous section, we used list-directed I/O to read a few text and numerical variables from standard input and write them back to the screen:

```
Hello 42 3.14159         ⟵┘ Values for each variable
    User typed: Hello        typed in by the user        The output of
                          42    3.14159012    ⟵┘ the program
```

Notice the odd empty space between "Hello" and 42. Worse, when writing the number 3.14159 back to the screen, the program output "3.14159012," which is a similar but nevertheless different number. What the heck is going on here?

These inconsistencies are due to the default formatting that's compiler- and system-dependent. Anytime that we use `read *`, `print *`, or `write(*,*)` statements, we instruct the compiler to use any format it sees fit. Default formatting is fine for quick and dirty printing of values from your program. However, if you want your app to produce human-readable output, or write results in a portable format, you'll need to explicitly format your output. In this section, you'll learn how to compose the format strings (or, in Fortran terminology, *edit descriptors*) to control how the values of variables should be converted to text data for output to screen or files. Formatting your output will prove important in any production app or system where the output of your program is either directly consumed by your users or used as input to some other program.

6.2.1   *Designing the aircraft dashboard*

Fortran's formatting rules are quite tedious, so let's learn them by tackling a practical problem. Consider the following scenario. You're an aircraft flight instruments engineer, and you're tasked with implementing the on-screen display of several key parameters related to the aircraft's in-flight state. The design team has instructed you to display only certain parameters and to a limited precision:

- *Latitude and longitude (real)*—With a precision up to 0.00001 degree (about a meter on the equator)
- *Altitude in meters*—With a precision up to 0.1 m
- *Engine load in percentage*—Represented with integer values between 0 and 100 (There are four engines total, so this parameter is an array of four elements. It should always be displayed with all three digits.)
- *Airborne (logical) status*—To show whether the aircraft is airborne. (This parameter will be displayed as `T` or `F` depending on the aircraft state.)

Furthermore, each parameter should be separated by at least two empty spaces to make them easier to read. Note that this is a much simplified version of flight instruments, even for the most rudimentary aircraft. However, it's all we need from an example to learn how formatting data works.

In our implementation, we'll assume that the plane is flying over Stockholm, Sweden, at an altitude of close to 12 km, with a velocity of 267.5 m/s. We'll hardcode the example values in the declaration for simplicity. In the production code, the data would come from some external subroutine, like `get_aircraft_parameters` or something similar. We don't have to worry about how that works, and we'll focus on just formatting the data for readable display. Let's begin with the full program, as shown in the following listing, which we'll break down step by step.

> **Listing 6.5   Formatting airplane state parameters for display on the dashboard**

```
program dashboard
  use iso_fortran_env, only: dash => output_unit    ⬅─┤ Imports standard
  implicit none                                          output unit as dash

  real :: lat = 59.329444, lon = 18.068611, alt = 11678.3   ⎤ Sets parameter
  integer :: eng(4) = [96, 96, 95, 97]                      ⎬ values
  logical :: airborne = .true.                              ⎦

  character(len=:), allocatable :: dashfmt

  dashfmt = '(2(f9.5, 2x), f7.1, 2x, 4(i3.3, 2x), 1)'   ⬅─┘ Assigns the format
  write (dash, dashfmt) lat, lon, alt, eng, airborne    ⬅─┐ string value
                                                           Writes parameter
end program dashboard                                      values to the
                                                           dashboard using
                                                           given format
```

Declares the format string as an allocatable character variable

This program is quite simple. We first declare and initialize the aircraft parameters, then we assign the formatting string to `dashfmt`, and finally we apply `dashfmt` in the `write` statement to format the data to our liking. The key question we seek to answer is, What value of `dashfmt` will correctly display the flight parameters as per the design specification sheet? The result will look like this:

```
59.32944   18.06861   11678.3   096   096   095   097   T
```

Though I've already given you the answer in listing 6.5, we don't yet understand how this formatting string works. We'll dive into the details of its syntax in the following subsection.

6.2.2   *Formatting strings, broken down*

If you're familiar with any C-style language, you've likely had some experience with formatting numbers and text there. In Python, for example, if you wanted to display the number pi as "3.14," you'd type `'%4.2f' % pi`—four characters total, two of which are used for the fractional part, with the character `f` denoting a floating-point number. This is part of the C-style format specification syntax. Fortran's formatting rules are similar, but with plenty of differences that will take some time getting used to. Otherwise, if you're new to formatting text and numbers, it may be even easier for you to learn Fortran's format strings from scratch.

Let's take a look again at the crux of our formatting code from listing 6.5:

```
dashfmt = '(2(f9.5, 2x), f7.1, 2x, 4(i3.3, 2x), l)'
write (dash, dashfmt) lat, lon, alt, eng, airborne
```

The formatting string consists of comma-separated substrings that are each made of different letters and numbers. Letters will denote different data types, and numbers will instruct how many spaces to provide for output, or how many times to repeat the formatting instruction. This is a quite tedious part of the language, so don't worry if it feels overwhelming at first. You don't have to learn the complete syntax at once, and you can come back to it at any time when you need it. Let's see how it works, step by step.

FORMATTING REAL NUMBERS

A formatting string consists of one or more substrings, each made of a letter and one or more numbers. We'll start by formatting the latitude, longitude, and altitude parameters:

```
real :: lat = 59.329444, lon = 18.068611, alt = 11678.3
```

Their values fall in the range of (–90, 90) degrees, (–180, 180) degrees, and (0, 99999) meters, respectively. This means that we need to reserve at least three characters for the integer part of the value (left of the decimal point) for `lat` and `lon`. We also need to display the coordinates with the precision down to 0.00001 degree, so we'll reserve five characters for the fractional part. In total, this will require nine characters (including the decimal point).

To format a real or complex number, use `f` (floating-point; for example, 523.11) or `e` (exponential; for example, 5.2311×10^2) edit descriptors. These descriptors must be followed by an integer number representing the total width, a period, and an integer number representing the fractional (in the case of `f`) or the exponential (in the case of `e`) part. For example, the number pi formatted with `f8.3` will be displayed as `"   3.142"` (three leading blanks), whereas the same number formatted with `e8.3` will be displayed as `.314E+01`. These are illustrated in figure 6.3. In general, use the exponential format for very small (< 0.01) or very large (> 1000) numbers, and the floating-point format otherwise. The exponential format allows two additional flavors, namely the engineering one (`en`) and the scientific one (`es`). I leave it to you as an exercise to explore how these two work.

Back to latitude and longitude. We'll format them as floating-point (`f`) numbers having a total of nine digits (including the decimal point), with five digits for the fractional part: `f9.5`.

To format two values using the same formatting string, we can add a number to the front of the string: `2f9.5`. Not so fast, though. As is, this format string will yield

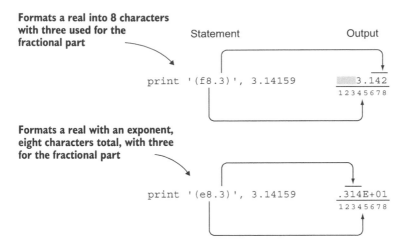

Formats a real into 8 characters with three used for the fractional part

Statement

Output

`print '(f8.3)', 3.14159`

`    3.142`
`12345678`

Formats a real with an exponent, eight characters total, with three for the fractional part

`print '(e8.3)', 3.14159`

`.314E+01`
`12345678`

Figure 6.3 **Example of formatting a real number for output. The gray spaces represent empty spaces or blanks. The numbers underneath each output indicate character positions.**

"59.3294418.06861" as output. These are our latitude and longitude values, but without any blank spaces between them. To add two empty spaces after each value, we'll compose our format string as 2(f9.5, 2x). We now get " 59.32944 18.06861 ". Much better! The leading space in this string is due to the fact that our integer part is three characters wide (9 minus 5 minus 1 for the decimal point). You can use the edit descriptor, x, to insert one or more empty spaces in combination with any other format string. For example, 5x will insert five empty spaces, and 100x will insert a hundred.

Now that we've formatted the latitude and longitude values, formatting the altitude is easy. From the design spec, we have the requirement to display up to a 0.1 m precision, and we can safely assume that this aircraft won't fly above 100 kilometers in altitude. So our formatting string will be f7.1—five digits for the integer part, and one digit for the fractional part. Our formatting string so far is 2(f9.5, 2x), f7.1, and our output is

```
59.32944   18.06861   11678.3
```

FORMATTING INTEGERS

Now we can tackle the display of our integer values—the four-element array of values describing engine load, one for each engine:

```
integer :: eng(4) = [96, 96, 95, 97]
```

To format an integer, we'll use the letter i followed by the number of characters that will be reserved to display the value. For example, 34 formatted with i5 will be output as "   34" (three leading blanks, for a total of five characters). Optionally, you can specify the number of digits that must be output, even if they're leading zeros. For example, i5.5 applied to 34 will output 00034.

Formatting an integer is illustrated in figure 6.4. With print '(i4)', 42, we make sure that the number 42 will be output using exactly four characters, no more and no less. As a result, we get 42 (two leading blanks) in the output. If the number we output was a three-digit number, such as 123, we'd end up with one leading blank. In the second example, print '(i4.3)', 42, we specify that we want four characters, with at least three of them being nonblank. Thus, for any one- or two-digit number, the compiler will add leading zeros to satisfy this requirement.

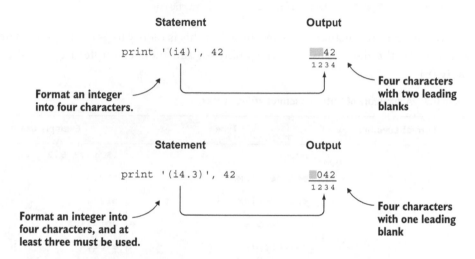

Figure 6.4 Example of formatting an integer for output. The gray spaces represent empty spaces or blanks. The numbers above each output indicate character positions.

Back to our task. The engine load is an array of four integers that go from 0 to 100. We'll display any leading zeros (rather than blanks), so the format string will be 4(i3.3, 2x), and it will yield:

```
096  096  095  097
```

Both i and f edit descriptors allow a field width of zero; for example, i0 or f0.2. This instructs the compiler to use the minimum width necessary to display the variable. This is useful when you want to format your numbers just wide enough that they can be properly output, but don't care about the total width of your output changing from line to line.

FORMATTING LOGICAL AND TEXT VALUES

To format character and logical variables, use a and l, respectively. These can stand on their own, and the compiler will use exactly the number of characters needed to display them entirely. Alternatively, you can limit the number of characters used by appending an integer width to them. For example, applying a7 to "Hello world" will print "Hello w." You can use edit descriptor g in place of any built-in type (i, f, e, a, or l), as long as you properly set the total width and the width of the fractional part (in the case of f). Note that while both g and * will match any data type, g gives you explicit control over formatting, whereas * will allow the compiler to format values the way it sees fit.

Finally, as the airborne status is a logical scalar, we'll use just l to format it. This brings us to our final form of dashfmt:

```
dashfmt = '(2(f9.5, 2x), f7.1, 2x, 4(i3.3, 2x), l)'
write (dash, dashfmt) lat, lon, alt, eng, airborne
```

There's a bit more nuance to formatting, but this is plenty to get you going. The edit descriptors, the data types that they apply to, and their example uses are shown in table 6.1.

Table 6.1   A summary of Fortran's format string syntax

Format specifier	Type	Example use
i	integer	i3, i3.3, 5i2
f	real, complex	f12.4
e	real, complex	e12.4
en	real, complex	en12.4
es	real, complex	es12.4
a	character	a,
l	logical	l, l5
g	Any	g5, g8.3
x	character (blank)	1x, 5x
*	Any (system dependent)	*

In read or write statements with parentheses, the format string is specified as the second positional or keyword argument. All of these statements are thus equivalent:

```
print fmt_string, 'User typed: ', trim(text), a, x
write (*, fmt=fmt_string) 'User typed: ', trim(text), a, x
write (*, fmt_string) 'User typed: ', trim(text), a, x
```

Whichever form you use is completely a matter of style. Pick one that's easiest on your eyes and be consistent throughout your code.

6.2.3 *Format statements in legacy Fortran code*

If you find yourself working with a legacy Fortran program or library for some time, you'll eventually run into labeled `format` statements that look like this:

```
write (*, fmt=1022) x, y, z          ◁──┐  Refers to the format
...                                       │  statement via a
1022 format(3(f6.3, 2x))    ◁─────────────┘  numbered label

     Label and format statement
```

Here, the format string is specified not with a character variable or string literal, but with an integer number that directs the compiler to a labeled line elsewhere in the program. This line then specifies the format string using the `format` statement. It can be placed anywhere in the local scope—before or after the I/O statement that refers to it. This is a historical, although correct, alternative approach to formatting variables for I/O. Although I don't recommend that you use the `format` statement in any new code, I think it's important that you be aware of its use and meaning, as you may encounter it in existing Fortran code.

> **TIP** Avoid labeled `format` statements in new code. They break the structure of the code and can make it harder to read and understand. Instead, use literal format strings or character variables in `read` and `write` statements directly.

6.3 *Writing to files on disk: A minimal note-taking app*

You now know how to read from standard input and write to standard output. You also know how to format the data for pretty printing, or for reading specially formatted records. Sooner or later, you'll need to read data from and write data to files on disk. In this section, we'll implement a minimal, yet surprisingly useful, note-taking app for the command line. The app should do the following:

- Take a filename to write notes into a command-line argument.
- Read user input from the standard input stream and write it into a file.
- If the file exists, prompt the user about whether to overwrite the file, append to it (continue writing), or quit.

Figure 6.5 illustrates the workflow of our note-taking app.

What does it take to write some text to a file? For example, here's what my mini-journal entry looks like this morning:

```
Fresh cup of coffee
Wrote a small note-taking app
Hope readers like it
```

Nothing fancy, just some text, spread across a few lines. It's also a Haiku poem, but that's not crucial for this exercise. To write this note, while considering the specifications above, my command-line experience with the app (let's call it qn, short for quicknote) will look like listing 6.6.

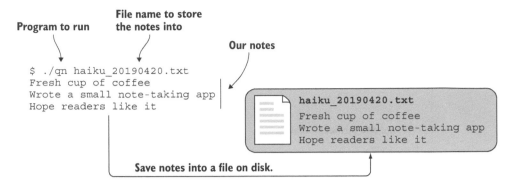

Figure 6.5 Illustration of a simple workflow for our note-taking app

Listing 6.6 Writing a short note with the `qn` **app**

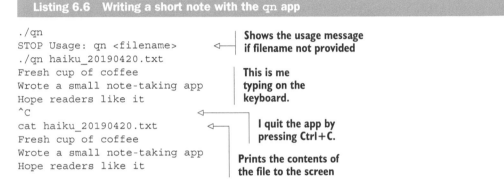

In summary, we want an app to quickly jot down some notes in the file of our choice, stored as a plain text file that can be easily read. The ability to resume writing to an existing file, though not shown in listing 6.6, would also be a nice feature. Finally, we should have some protection from accidentally overwriting an existing file. By implementing these features, you'll learn the most important elements of Fortran for working with files. Ready? All right, then, let's get started.

6.3.1 Opening a file and writing to it

The first step involves getting the filename as a command-line argument, opening the file for writing, and allowing the user to write into it. To implement this is relatively straightforward but will require quite a few new language elements. Let's take a look at the complete program first, as shown in the following listing.

Listing 6.7 First version of the `qn` **app**

```
program qn
  use iso_fortran_env, only: stdin => input_unit
  implicit none
  integer :: fileunit                              I/O unit number used
  character(len=9999) :: filename, text            to connect to a file
```

Long character strings

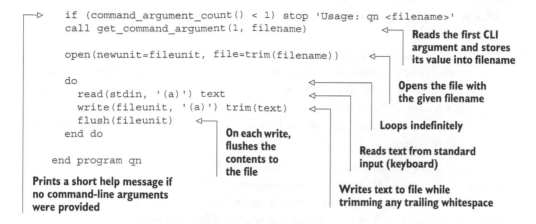

```
if (command_argument_count() < 1) stop 'Usage: qn <filename>'
call get_command_argument(1, filename)          ◁    Reads the first CLI
                                                      argument and stores
open(newunit=fileunit, file=trim(filename))     ◁     its value into filename

do                                              ◁    Opens the file with
  read(stdin, '(a)') text                       ◁    the given filename
  write(fileunit, '(a)') trim(text)             ◁
  flush(fileunit)        ◁                            Loops indefinitely
end do
                              On each write,          Reads text from standard
end program qn                flushes the             input (keyboard)
                              contents to
Prints a short help message if the file              Writes text to file while
no command-line arguments                            trimming any trailing whitespace
were provided
```

The first step is to parse the command line for an argument, and its value will be the name of the file to write notes into. Here we use the built-in `command_argument_count` function and the `get_command_argument` subroutine to check for the number of arguments, and to store the value of the first argument into the character variable `filename`. Note that we declared `filename` as `character(len=9999)`. There's no special meaning behind this number—we're simply declaring a character variable long enough to store strings of arbitrary length. On most Linux file systems, maximum path length is 4,096, but this should be handled elsewhere. You'll learn in more detail how `command _argument_count` and `get_command_argument` work in chapter 10.

> ### Fixed-length or allocatable character variables?
> If you're thinking that using fixed-length character variables is awkward, you're absolutely right! Why would I not use allocatable character strings instead? This situation is due to Fortran's inability to implicitly allocate a dynamic character variable on a `read` statement. In other words, the character variable must be allocated before using it on the right side of a `read` statement, which would require us to somehow know what the length of the input data would be.
>
> The choice to use fixed-length strings that are just long enough to hold most input data is thus a pragmatic one, though not too elegant.

6.3.2 Opening a file

Once we have the desired filename stored in the `filename` variable, our next step is to open the file for writing. Opening a file means creating a connection between the program and some file on disk. We can do this using the `open` statement:

```
open(newunit=fileunit, file=trim(filename))     ◁    Opens a file with a given
                                                      filename, assigning its I/O
                                                      unit to fileunit
```

This is one of the most basic forms of the `open` statement. It takes two keyword arguments:

- `newunit`—An integer variable whose value will be set to an available I/O unit number. This number is system-dependent and not known ahead of time, but is guaranteed to be available and not conflict with any other units, be it other open files or standard streams such as stdout or stderr.
- `file`—A character variable or literal constant whose value is the name of the file to open.

On successful execution of this `open` statement, the new file is now open and ready for use, with a unique I/O unit number assigned to `fileunit`. Once a file is opened and attached to a unit, it can't be opened again before it's closed and its I/O unit is released. Alternatively, you can pass the unit number to the `open` statement yourself, but you have to make sure that I/O unit is available for use:

```
open(unit=2112, file=trim(filename))
```

With this statement, a file is opened, and the unit number 2112 is assigned to it. Note that spelling out `unit=` is optional but `file=` is not, so you can just write `open(2112, file=trim(filename))` for brevity. Historically, a Fortran programmer was expected to keep track of the I/O units being used. It's important to be aware of this form of the `open` statement because you're likely to encounter it in Fortran code in the wild, as the `newunit` functionality was added to the language only recently (Fortran 2008). If your compiler supports it, and a recent version of any mainstream compiler should, I recommend that you use `newunit` exclusively.

> **TIP** Use `newunit` in your `open` statements rather than specifying the unit number yourself. It will spare you from having to keep track of available I/O units.

There may be exceptional situations where you'd need to specify an I/O unit in the open statement, rather than getting a new one from the system. One such situation is if you wanted to redirect standard output and error channels to files. Let's do this one as an exercise. (See "Exercise" sidebar.)

Exercise: Redirect stdout and stderr to files

You now know how to access standard output and error I/O units, and you know how to open files with a specific I/O unit number. Write a program that redirects its standard output and error into files; for example, `log.out` and `log.err`, respectively.

You can find the solution to this exercise in the "Answer key" section near the end of this chapter.

6.3.3   Writing to a file

OK, so we've parsed the command line for a filename as the argument, and we've opened the file as requested by the user. Let's write some notes to it. To do this, we'll need to parse user input from the keyboard, and write the data to the file on each new line—that is, every time the user presses the Enter or Return key. The following listing demonstrates this.

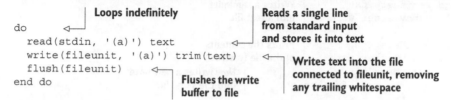

Listing 6.8   Reading user input and writing to a file in a loop

```
        Loops indefinitely               Reads a single line
                                         from standard input
do      ◄──┘                             and stores it into text
  read(stdin, '(a)') text        ◄──┘
  write(fileunit, '(a)') trim(text)     ◄──
  flush(fileunit)        ◄──┐           Writes text into the file
end do                      Flushes the write   connected to fileunit, removing
                           buffer to file       any trailing whitespace
```

We use a plain do statement to loop indefinitely. Within each iteration, the program reads the user's input from the console, trims any trailing whitespace (because text is 9,999 characters long), and writes it to the file. On each write, we use the flush statement to make sure that any data from the buffer is written to disk. The program doesn't have any way to exit the loop, except by hitting an exception in one of the I/O statements (for example, running out of disk space), or by the user quitting the program with a keyboard interrupt (Ctrl+C). For our little app, this is good enough.

> **Flushing the output buffer to a file**
>
> For efficiency, some compilers and operating systems may use a buffer as an intermediate storage of output before dumping it into a file. The motivation for using buffers is that writing to a file too often may keep the disk busier than necessary. By using a buffer, the program writes to disk only when the data exceeds the buffer size. For a more responsive behavior, you may want to explicitly write to disk whatever is currently stored in the buffer, using the flush statement.
>
> Furthermore, the program will write to a file only after the user presses Enter to make a new line in the note. This is the case because the read statement won't execute until the user enters the whole line. Thus, if you exit the program by pressing Ctrl+C halfway through the note, the line in progress will be lost.

Let's now see how we can add more nuanced functionality to the quick-note app. First, we'll allow our app to write to existing files by appending notes to them. Second, we'll add a prompt to ask the user what action to take if the file for writing notes to already exists. In doing so, we'll cover some optional parameters to the open statement. We'll also learn about the inquire statement and how to use it to get information about a file without opening it.

6.3.4   *Appending to a file*

Our little note-taking app is simple and neat and does what it promised. However, one of the first issues we may run into is that if we specify an existing file to write our notes into, the program will overwrite the previous contents of the file with our new notes. The following listing shows an example of what that could look like.

Listing 6.9   Overwriting previous notes if writing to an existing file

```
./qn reminders.txt            Writes a reminder
Call Jenny after work         into a text file
^C
cat reminders.txt             Prints the contents
Call Jenny after work         of the file to screen
./qn reminders.txt                 Now writes a new note
Pick up groceries for tonight      into the same file
^C
cat reminders.txt                  Prints the
Pick up groceries for tonight      contents again
```

Oh no! The reminder to call Jenny is gone. What happened? Let's take a look again at how we're opening the file:

```
open(newunit=fileunit, file=trim(filename))
```

Without other keyword parameters specified, Fortran will default to opening a file at its beginning. If you write anything to it, the program will write from the beginning, and any contents that were already there will be overwritten. It doesn't matter if you had a thousand lines of data and you're writing only one line—the entire contents of the previous file will be gone.

What we really want our app to do is to keep writing to an existing file, continuing from the end and preserving existing notes:

```
./qn groceries.txt
Toast
^C
./qn groceries.txt
Avocadoes
^C
cat groceries.txt
Toast
Avocadoes
```

Fortunately, Fortran provides an easy way to open a file in the append mode, allowing you to continue where you left off:

```
open(newunit=fileunit, file=trim(filename), position='append')
```

(Note in margin, pointing to `^C`:) **Ctrl+C to exit the program**

Here, we added a third keyword parameter, `position`. It can take one of three values:

- `append`—The file will be opened at its final position, preserving any previously written data.
- `asis`—The file will be opened "as is." This is the default value if the `position` parameter is not specified and matters only if the file is already opened and pre-connected to an I/O unit. (It must be the same unit!) In that case, the file will be opened at the same position. Otherwise, the file is opened at the beginning.
- `rewind`—The file will be opened at the beginning, without exception.

In general, if your app will always write from the beginning, whether to old or new files, you don't have to specify `position`. Use `position='append'` only if you need to continue writing to an existing file, while preserving its original content. `position='asis'` and `position='rewind'` may only be useful in some special cases where you're opening a file that's already connected to an I/O unit and you need to change its position. Use this with caution, as rewinding the file and writing to it will truncate any existing content.

The `position='append'` setting in the `open` statement is convenient because it won't change the behavior of writing to new files. If you're appending to a new (empty) file, the result is the same as if you were writing from scratch. You can add this now to the `open` statement in listing 6.7. Does it work as expected? Great! The quick-note app is now more versatile, as it can add notes to existing files.

> **Rewinding a file**
>
> You can also rewind a file (set the read or write position to the start) at any time using the `rewind` statement:
>
> ```
> rewind(fileunit)
> ```

6.3.5 Opening files in read-only or write-only mode

Sooner or later, you'll run across files that are meant to be used as read-only; for example, important satellite data that shouldn't be overwritten. Similarly, some files will be useful only in write-only mode, such as the quick notes that we've been working on in this section. Fortran allows you to open a file in a mode that restricts certain operations to a file. Here's an example of opening a file in read-only mode:

```
open(newunit=fileunit, file=trim(filename), action='read')
```

The read/write behavior is controlled with the `action` keyword parameter. It can take one of three values:

- `read`—The file will be opened in read-only mode, and `write` and `print` statements can't be used on this file. Furthermore, the file will be assumed to be existing, so it's impossible to open new files when using `action='read'`.

- write—The file will be opened in write-only mode, and the read statement can't be used in connection with this file.
- readwrite—The file is opened without restriction. This is also the default behavior (if action is not specified) on all the systems that I'm aware of; however, the Fortran Standard allows this to be system-dependent.

Why do this? If the file is supposed to be read-only, can we simply not issue any write statements and be done with it? Likewise for write-only files. You don't ever have to use the action parameter to write correct Fortran programs. However, it may be beneficial to do so for at least two reasons. First, if you're working with a read-only file, specifying action='read' in the open statement will prevent you from accidentally writing to it elsewhere in the program, either because of a typo or by confusing two different I/O units. Second, your code will be easier to read and understand. This is analogous to my advice from chapter 3 about always specifying intent for procedure arguments. It's easier to understand what the program is doing to a file if the open statement says it loud and clear.

> **TIP** Always specify action in your open statements. It will make your code easier to understand and can prevent you from accidentally overwriting important files.

You can go ahead and update the open statement in our quick-note program to read

```
open(newunit=fileunit, file=trim(filename),&
    action='write', position='append')
```

While not strictly necessary, it's good practice and will help future readers of your code (including yourself).

6.3.6 *Checking whether a file exists*

With the upgrade to the open statement that allows our program to open an existing file in the append mode, we can now continue writing notes to an old file. This is a useful feature, but it assumes that the user would want to continue writing. There are situations where I'd want to start writing from the beginning; that is, overwrite the file. To allow for more general behavior, and to not surprise the user, it may be a good idea to allow them to choose whether to keep writing to an existing file, or start over, as shown in the following listing.

Listing 6.10 Prompting the user if a file exists

```
./qn daily_todo.txt
Finish chapter draft                Tries to write to
Email Jerry                         an existing file
neural-fortran pull request
^C                                  Prints warning
./qn daily_todo.txt                 message
File daily_todo.txt already exists!
[O]verwrite, [A]ppend, [Q]uit:      Prompts and lets
                                    user decide
```

How can we know programmatically whether or not a file exists? This is where the inquire statement comes in, as shown in the following listing.

Listing 6.11 Checking whether a file exists without opening it

```
logical :: file_exists          ◄──┤  Declares a logical variable to store
...                                    the existence status of the file
inquire(file=trim(filename), exist=file_exists)        ◄──┐  Inquires by filename
                                                           whether it exists or not
```

You can inquire about a file by its name or its I/O unit number (inquire(fileunit, ...)). Of course, the latter is possible only if you've already opened the file and its I/O unit number has been assigned. Here, we're inquiring by filename, which is necessary because the file hasn't been opened yet. The exist keyword parameter takes a logical variable whose value will be either .true. or .false. on successful completion of the inquire statement. Whenever you open a new file, the file will be present and detectable by inquire, even if you haven't written to it yet.

The following listing shows the new version of the program that checks for the presence of the file, and prompts the user if the file exists.

Listing 6.12 Updated program that prompts the user if the file exists

```
program qn
  use iso_fortran_env, only: stdin => input_unit, &
                             stdout => output_unit
  implicit none
  integer :: fileunit
  character(len=9999) :: filename, text
  character(len=6) :: pos
  logical :: file_exists

  if (command_argument_count() < 1) stop 'Usage: qn <filename>'
  call get_command_argument(1, filename)

  inquire(file=trim(filename), exist=file_exists)    ◄──┐  Checks for presence
  pos = 'rewind'                        ◄──┐              of the file
                                          Assumes writing
                                          from scratch
  if (file_exists) then
    write(stdout, '(a)') &                                   Prints warning
      'File ' // trim(filename) // ' already exists!'        message if file exists
    do
      write(*, '(a)', advance='no') &
        '[O]verwrite, [A]ppend, [Q]uit: '          Prompts the user and
      read(stdin, '(a)') text                      awaits their response
      if (any(trim(text) == ['O', 'o'])) then
        write(stdout, '(a)') &                            Leaves loop if user
          'Overwriting ' // trim(filename)               chose "overwrite"
        exit
      else if (any(trim(text) == ['A', 'a'])) then
```

```
        pos = 'append'
        write(stdout, '(a)') &
          'Appending to ' // trim(filename)
        exit
      else if (any(trim(text) == ['Q', 'q'])) then
        stop
      end if
    end do
  end if


  open(newunit=fileunit, file=trim(filename), &
      action='write', position=pos)


  do
    read(stdin, '(a)') text
    write(fileunit, '(a)') trim(text)
    flush(fileunit)
  end do


end program qn
```

Annotation (top right): Sets the position parameter and leaves loop if user chose "append"

Annotation (middle): Stops the program if user chose "quit"

The code added to the program starts with the inquire statement and ends immediately before the open statement. Its purpose is to determine whether the position parameter in the open statement should have the value rewind or append. We start by assuming that the file will be opened in rewind mode, which is the case if the file is not present (start a new file) or the user chooses to overwrite an existing file. If the requested file is present, the program will warn the user and prompt them regarding whether to overwrite ("O" or "o") or append ("A" or "a") to the file. At this point, the user can also choose to quit ("Q" or "q") the program without committing any changes to the file. Note that if the user input doesn't match any of the coded options (overwrite, append, or quit), no if branch is matched, and we'll prompt the user again for input.

If you look carefully, you'll notice that the first write statement in the program has advance='no' as a keyword parameter. This makes the position in the file not move to the next record (line) after printing the message. As a result, the user will be entering their choice on the same line:

```
./qn daily_todo.txt
File daily_todo.txt already exists!
[O]verwrite, [A]ppend, [Q]uit: a
```

Annotation: The user's choice appears on the same line.

If omitted, advance has the value yes by default, so any such write statement will move the position to the next line after executing, and likewise for the read statement.

> **Nonadvancing I/O**
>
> It's possible to use the `read` and `write` statement without advancing the file position to the next record. Although this may seem like a purely aesthetic feature, there are cases where it can be quite useful. A common example that comes to mind is progress bars in the terminal. If you're interested in fancy progress bars for your Fortran app, check out the forbear library by Stefano Zaghi on GitHub: https://github.com/szaghi/forbear. It uses nonadvancing I/O in combination with the Unicode character set to display some impressive, dynamic progress bars.

6.3.7 *Error handling and closing the file*

In our quick-note app, we haven't had an explicit need to close the file because we're prompting the user for input and writing to the file in an infinite loop. The only way for the program to quit is by the user pressing Ctrl+C. However, if any of the I/O statements encounters an error (such as no space on disk, for example), the program should be able to print a helpful error message and close the file gracefully. The changes needed to enable error handling in the quick-note app are shown in the following listing.

> **Listing 6.13 Catching and recovering from errors in I/O statements**

```
integer :: stat
...
do
  read(stdin, '(a)', iostat=stat, err=100) text
  write(fileunit, '(a)', iostat=stat, err=100) &          Gets the status number
    trim(text)                                             and jumps to the label if
  flush(fileunit, iostat=stat, err=100)                    an error is encountered
end do
                                     The program will jump
100 close(fileunit)    ←┘             to this point on error.
if (stat > 0) then
  write(stderr, '(a, i3)') &
    'Error encountered, code = ', stat          Prints the message
  stop                                          with the error code
end if
...
```

The main additions to the code are the `iostat` and `err` keyword parameters to each of the `read`, `write`, and `flush` statements. They enable Fortran's built-in error handling for I/O statements. Each of the `read`, `write`, `open`, `close`, `inquire`, `flush`, and `rewind` statements allows passing the `iostat` and `err` keyword parameters:

- `iostat`—The integer status code, which evaluates to 0 if no error is encountered, and a positive number otherwise
- `err`—An integer error label to which the program will jump if the error is encountered

For brevity and demonstration, we're only checking for errors on read, write, and flush statements. If an error is encountered in any of them, the program control is transferred to the label (the line of code that begins with a number, in this case 100) and the program continues from there. It will first use the close statement to close the file, then print the error message with the error code if the code is nonzero. The meaning of each error code isn't defined by the Standard and is specific to each compiler, so you'd need to consult the compiler documentation for details. Note that without error handling, I/O errors are always nonrecoverable, meaning that the program will stop, usually with a descriptive error message, although this is also compiler-specific.

It's good practice to close the file when we're done working with it. This ensures that any data left over in the I/O buffer gets written to disk before the program ends.

With error handling and closing the file, this concludes our minimal note-taking app. For your reference, you can find the complete code in the listings repository on GitHub (https://github.com/modern-fortran/listings) in src/ch06/qn.f90.

6.4   *Answer key*

This section contains the solution to the exercise in this chapter. Skip ahead if you haven't worked through the exercises yet.

6.4.1   *Exercise: Redirect stdout and stderr to files*

Let's redirect output to standard output and error channels into their respective files from within the Fortran program. Why would you want to do this? For some applications that run for a long time, such as large weather and ocean prediction models that can run for days, it's useful to write standard output and error streams into files by default. More critically, if you're running your program in parallel, a convenient way to differentiate the output from different images is to redirect standard output and error streams from each image into their own respective files.

Recall from section 6.1 how we write text to standard output and error channels, as shown in the following listing.

Listing 6.14 Writing to standard output and error streams

```
program redirect_stdout_to_file

  use iso_fortran_env, only: stdout => output_unit, &    ⟵ Gets standard output and
                             stderr => error_unit           error unit constants from
  implicit none                                             the built-in module

  write(stdout, *) 'This goes to stdout.'    ⟵  Writes some text
  write(stderr, *) 'This goes to stderr.'    ⟵  to standard output
                                             ⟵  Writes some text
end program redirect_stdout_to_file            to standard error
```

If you compile and run this program as is, both messages will be printed to screen:

```
./redirect_stdout_to_file
 This goes to stdout.
 This goes to stderr.
```

However, with shell redirection, we can confirm that each of these messages indeed goes to its respective standard stream:

```
./redirect_stdout_to_file 1> log.out 2> log.err
cat log.out
 This goes to stdout.
cat log.err
 This goes to stderr.
```

Now, how do we redirect the output within our Fortran program such that log.out and log.err files are written without the help of shell redirection? The solution is simple, though perhaps not immediately obvious. Open a file log.out while assigning it an I/O unit number of stdout, and likewise for stderr. The following listing provides the complete program.

> **Listing 6.15 Redirecting standard output and error streams to their own files**

```
program redirect_stdout_to_file

  use iso_fortran_env, only: stdout => output_unit, &
                             stderr => error_unit
  implicit none

  open(stdout, file='log.out')
  open(stderr, file='log.err')

  write(stdout, *) 'This goes to stdout.'
  write(stderr, *) 'This goes to stderr.'

  close(stdout)
  close(stderr)

end program redirect_stdout_to_file
```

Gets standard output and error unit constants from the built-in module

Opens a file for each of the stdout and stderr I/O units

Writes some text to standard output, now redirected to log.out

Closes the files when done

Writes some text to standard error, now redirected to log.err

And voilà, we're done! By opening files and assigning them reserved stdout and stderr I/O units, you're effectively instructing the compiler to send any output intended for standard streams into these files. This will apply to print statements as well! For example, if you type print *, 'where will this go?', the text will be written to log.out rather than the screen.

6.5 *New Fortran elements, at a glance*

- read, print, and write—Statements for reading and writing data to files on disk or standard streams, such as standard input, output, or error
- *Format strings*—For formatting values of any built-in data type into text.

- open, close, and inquire—Statements to open, close, and get information about a file, respectively
- trim—A built-in function that returns the input character string without any trailing blanks

Summary

- Six core syntax elements provide most of Fortran's I/O functionality: read, print, write, open, close, and inquire.
- Use read and write for input and output of any data, respectively.
- You can access standard input, output, and error streams from the iso_fortran _env module as input_unit, output_unit, and error_unit.
- Fortran I/O units are unique integer identifiers that let you access standard streams and files on disk that you work with, akin to file handles in other programming languages. Use them in your code to write to standard streams in a portable way.
- Use format strings to convert numbers and other non-text data into text. For example, i3 formats an integer into text with width 3, whereas f5.2 will format a real number into text with a total width of 5 and a width of 2 for the fractional part.
- You can use the open statement to open existing or new files, as well as to redirect output from standard streams to files on disk.
- You can use the inquire statement to get information about a file, including whether the file is open or not.

Part 3

Advanced Fortran use

In this part, you'll get an introduction to parallelism and working with advanced data structures.

Chapter 7 introduces images and coarrays for parallel programming. This is the parallel programming model that's built into Fortran. In this chapter, you'll write your first program to analyze weather buoy data in parallel. Here, we'll also implement the parallel version of the tsunami simulator.

Chapter 8 covers derived types, which is the Fortran concept of classes in object-oriented programming. Derived types will allow you to create your own custom data types that can have other data as components and procedures as bound methods. In this chapter, we'll transition the tsunami simulator from a one-dimensional to a two-dimensional solver.

In chapter 9, you'll learn how to write generic procedures that can work on arguments with any data type. This will be important in any scenario where input data can come in more than one data type. You'll also have your first encounter with custom operators, beyond the built-in ones that we've been working with so far.

Finally, chapter 10 will teach you how to define your own operators for your derived types and override the existing arithmetic or logical operators with your own. You'll see that this is quite powerful—it will allow you to create your own data structures and your own rules to govern them. We'll use these capabilities in the tsunami simulator to make our parallel variables synchronize automatically on assignment. At this point, we'll have mostly completed our journey with the tsunami simulator.

This is the heaviest part of the book. Approach it with patience and an open mind. At the end, you'll be able to understand, reuse, and extend most of the existing Fortran code in the wild. For the first time, you'll also be able to write your own parallel programs from scratch.

Going parallel
with Fortran coarrays

7

This chapter covers

- Processing weather buoy data in parallel
- Decomposing a problem between parallel processors
- Using coarrays to exchange data between processors
- The first parallel version of the tsunami simulator

Parallel programming became more commonly used in the early 1990s when the need for larger and faster solutions in physical sciences and engineering exceeded what could be done with individual existing computers. Scientists and engineers began connecting computers in intricate, dense networks and exchanging packets of data between them. What used to be one impossibly large computational problem became feasible because each computer could work on a small subset of the problem, and only communicate the data needed by other computers to proceed with their calculations. This gave rise to the message-passing style of parallel programming, later implemented as the Message Passing Interface (MPI) library. To date, MPI remains the de facto standard for parallel programming in Fortran, C, and C++ applications.

Unfortunately, MPI programming is hard, to the point that the developers of parallel applications dubbed it "the assembly of parallel programming." This is where Fortran *coarrays* come in. Coarrays were introduced in the 2008 revision of the Standard as a minimal extension to Fortran syntax that would allow an efficient and robust parallel model. Coarrays are very much like arrays, and use a similar indexing mechanism to reference individual elements. In chapter 1, I strongly advocated for the use of parallel programming to take advantage of modern CPU and interconnect architectures, and contrasted a simple data exchange program implemented using MPI and more recent Fortran coarrays. There, I emphasized that coarrays offer a much more elegant and concise way of expressing parallel algorithms compared to MPI. Although parallel Fortran initially became known as *Coarray Fortran*, there's much more to it than coarrays, as I will explain later in this chapter. I believe that parallel Fortran will make you rethink how to build high-performance applications from the ground up.

By now, you're probably warmed up and ready to dive deep into parallel programming. We'll first build an application to process and analyze real-world weather buoy data. In that exercise, you'll learn how to break down the data and distribute it between processors. You'll also use coarrays for the first time to gather the distributed data to a single processor. Finally, you'll apply these skills to parallelizing the tsunami simulator that we've been building since chapter 2.

7.1   Why write parallel programs?

The way the processor industry is going, is to add more and more cores, but nobody knows how to program those things. I mean, two, yeah; four, not really; eight, forget it.

—Steve Jobs (2008)

You may be asking, Why write parallel programs? It seems like an unnecessary complication. In general, you'll want to write parallel programs for two reasons:

- *Too big to fit into memory*—Some programs are too big to fit into a single computer's memory. For example, if you want to calculate statistics such as average and variance on a data file that's 20 GB, but your computer's RAM can only fit 8 GB, you may be stuck. The parallel programming solution to this problem is to load only a fraction of the file in each parallel computer, compute the statistics, and only share the intermediate data required to compute the final results.

- *Too slow to be useful*—Even if your program can fit into memory, it may be too computationally expensive to run on a single CPU. Consider this weather prediction problem: If the forecast for the next day takes 12 hours to compute, it has already lost a lot of its value by the time the program is done. Today's operational forecast centers are able to deliver forecasts for a week ahead with only a few hours of compute time by distributing the computational workload across hundreds of CPUs.

Figure 7.1 illustrates these challenges.

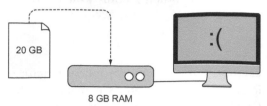

Some problems are too big to fit
into a single computer's memory.

20 GB

8 GB RAM

Parallel processing is one solution.

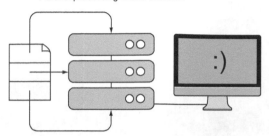

**Figure 7.1 When a problem is too big to fit
into a single computer's memory, one solution
is to split the input data and process it in
parallel. Because each computer will work on
only a fraction of the calculation, this program
will also finish in a fraction of the time.**

You'll find that most problems that take very long to compute are also too big to fit
into the memory of a single computer. Computational fluid dynamics problems like
the tsunami simulator definitely fall into both of these categories. So far, we've been
solving the shallow water equations over only 100 grid cells. But as we go to 1,000 or
10,000 grid cells for more realistic simulations, we'll inevitably increase the memory
and computational footprint. We'll soon tackle problem sizes for which parallel programming will significantly reduce compute time.

7.2 *Processing real-world weather buoy data*

For a gentle entry into parallel programming, we'll process and analyze a real-world
weather buoy dataset. This is a miniature example of the big data challenge: how to
process a large amount of data that may be too big to fit into memory, or may take too
long to process sequentially. The crux of the problem is in the sheer volume of data;
however, the computation itself can typically be carried out on subsets of the data
independently from one another. For this exercise to be tenable and easily repro-
duced on personal computers, I created a sample of a real weather dataset that's small
enough to be easily downloaded, but large enough to demonstrate the application of
parallel data processing with Fortran.

In this exercise, you'll learn the following:

- How to distribute the data and workload between parallel processes
- How to exchange intermediate results between parallel processes using Fortran
  coarrays

I'll first describe the data and show you how to get it, and then we'll dive straight into the serial implementation of the program. We'll then identify which parts of the program we can parallelize and how.

7.2.1   *About the data*

The dataset that we'll use in this exercise consists of hourly measurements of several weather, ocean, and wave parameters, recorded by buoys managed by the NOAA National Data Buoy Center (NDBC). One such buoy is shown in figure 7.2.

Figure 7.2   A weather and wave buoy operated by the NDBC. Instruments that measure wind, temperature, humidity, and pressure are located on the mast from top to bottom. Accelerometers inside the hull record the wave-induced motion of the buoy, which is used to derive wave height and other properties. Photograph courtesy of NDBC (http://www.ndbc.noaa.gov).

Why are these buoys so important? There are a few big reasons:

- They report real-time weather, wave, and ocean conditions and help provide guidance and safety warnings to mariners.
- The data is fed in real time into weather and ocean prediction models, making them more accurate.
- Most buoys now accrue measured data for at least a few decades. These records allow for unprecedented insights into the change of climate in the recent past.

There are hundreds of these buoys located throughout the world's oceans, but in this exercise, we'll focus on nine buoys located in the Gulf of Mexico (figure 7.3).

The dataset contains hourly measurements of wind speed, air pressure, air temperature and humidity, water temperature, and ocean wave height and period, in the comma-separated value (CSV) format, for the years 2005 through 2017. Data from

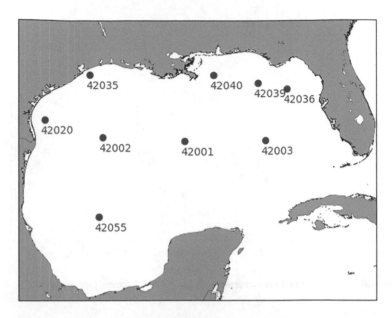

Figure 7.3   Locations of the nine weather buoys in the Gulf of Mexico used in this exercise

each buoy are stored in their own respective file, so we have a total of nine data files, one for each buoy:

```
2005-01-01_00:00:00,  9.4, 1020.9, 24.2, 20.5, 24.6,   2.22,   6.11
2005-01-01_01:00:00,  8.6, 1021.5, 24.0, 20.6, 24.5,   2.41,   6.44
2005-01-01_02:00:00,  7.3, 1021.8, 24.3, 20.9, 24.5,   2.16,   5.97
2005-01-01_03:00:00,  7.6, 1022.0, 24.5, 20.6, 24.5,   2.26,   6.38
2005-01-01_04:00:00,  7.8, 1022.4, 24.6, 20.1, 24.5,   2.03,   5.98
...
```

This is a sample of weather data that we'll use in this exercise. From left to right, the columns are: Timestamp (UTC), wind speed (m/s), pressure (mbar), air temperature (deg. C), dew point (deg. C), water temperature (deg. C), wave height (m), and wave period (s).

To give you an idea of what the data look like through time, I plotted the wind speed measured by buoy 42002 during January of 2017 in figure 7.4. The peaks on January 8 and January 24 are associated with the passage of cold fronts through the Gulf of Mexico, much like the one that we used in exercises in chapters 2 and 3. This is also just a small subset of the data. The full dataset for this exercise contains 13 years of hourly measurements of several weather, ocean, and wave parameters, for each of the nine buoys. I use 13 years here to keep the problem small enough. However, if you're feeling adventurous, I encourage you to explore longer time series and process more buoys available from NDBC. Some of the buoy measurements go as far back as the early 1970s!

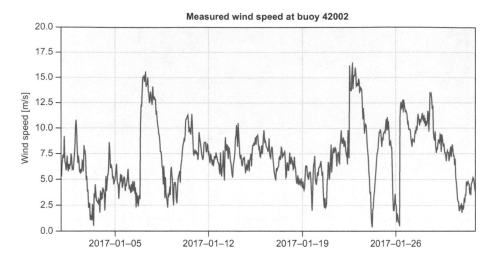

Figure 7.4   Time series of wind speed measurements at buoy 42002 during January of 2017

7.2.2   *Getting the data and code*

The complete source code for the weather buoy exercise is available on GitHub at https://github.com/modern-fortran/weather-buoys. If you use git, clone it directly from the command line:

```
git clone https://github.com/modern-fortran/weather-buoys
```

Otherwise, you can download it as a zip file from http://mng.bz/aRVo.

The CSV data files are located in the weather-buoys/data directory. I encourage you to explore the data files from your favorite text editor. The repository also contains full code for this exercise. I suggest that you defer looking at the parallel code until the end of this exercise.

7.2.3   *Objectives*

Let's set some simple objectives for our data analysis exercise. This should be challenging enough to require data decomposition and communication in parallel mode, but simple enough to not get bogged down in the details of math or statistics. To that end, I'd like to know

1 What was the maximum measured wind speed in the Gulf of Mexico in the 2005-2017 period? Which buoy recorded the maximum value?

2 Which buoys had the strongest average winds, and which had the lowest average winds? What were their respective values?

To find the answers, we'll need our program to have a few elements:

- Reading each CSV file and storing the wind speed data in arrays
- Finding the maximum and mean (average) wind speed values for each buoy
- Comparing the maximum and mean wind speed between all buoys

You could program each of these tasks without parallel considerations. However, if we execute this program serially, each file will be processed in order, one at a time. For many large files, this approach can become infeasible or even impossible. This is where parallel data decomposition will come to our aid!

If we implement our program correctly, we should get output like this:

```
Maximum wind speed measured is    40.9000015       at station 42001
Highest mean wind speed is     6.47883749     at station 42020
Lowest mean wind speed is      5.43456125     at station 42036
```

7.2.4 *Serial implementation of the program*

Before we devise our parallelization strategy, let's first go over the serial program, as shown in the following listing, so we understand how each step works.

Listing 7.1   Serial implementation of the weather buoy processing program

```fortran
program weather_stats

  use mod_arrays, only: denan, mean          ⟵ Helper functions for working with arrays
  use mod_io, only: read_buoy               ⟵ Subroutine to read the buoy CSV data

  implicit none

  character(5), allocatable :: ids(:)        ⟵ Dynamic arrays for timestamps and wind speed
  character(20), allocatable :: time(:)
  real, allocatable :: wind_speed(:)
  real, allocatable :: max_wind(:), mean_wind(:)   ⟵ Temporary arrays for maximum and mean wind speed
  integer :: i

  ids = ['42001', '42002', '42003', '42020', '42035', &     ⟵ Buoy IDs to process
    '42036', '42039', '42040', '42055']

  allocate(max_wind(size(ids)), mean_wind(size(ids)))       ⟵ Allocates maximum and mean wind speeds

  do i = 1, size(ids)                        ⟵ Loops over buoys
    call read_buoy('data/buoy_' // ids(i) // '.csv', &      ⟵ Reads buoy file and stores timestamps and wind speed in arrays
                   time, wind_speed)
    wind_speed = denan(wind_speed)           ⟵ Removes missing values
    max_wind(i) = maxval(wind_speed)         ⟵ Calculate maximum and mean values for this buoy
    mean_wind(i) = mean(wind_speed)
  end do

  print *, 'Maximum wind speed measured is ', &             ⟵ Writes the results to screen
    maxval(max_wind), 'at station ', ids(maxloc(max_wind))
  print *, 'Highest mean wind speed is ', &
    maxval(mean_wind), 'at station ', ids(maxloc(mean_wind))
  print *, 'Lowest mean wind speed is ',
```

```
          minval(mean_wind), 'at station ', ids(minloc(mean_wind))

end program weather_stats
```

We use this array to determine both the number of buoys to process and the data file names. We allocate the dynamic arrays `max_wind` and `min_wind` to be of the same length as `ids`. We'll use these arrays to store intermediate results: maximum and mean values for each buoy. The bulk of the work happens within the do loop and consists of the following:

1 Reading the data using the `read_buoy` subroutine, and storing it into the `wind_speed` array
2 Removing missing values (nan) using the `denan` function
3 Calculating the maximum wind speed using the `maxval` built-in function
4 Calculating the mean wind speed using the `mean` function

Finally, we use the `minval`, `maxval`, `minloc`, and `maxloc` built-in functions to find the minimum and maximum values, and their respective indices, of the arrays `max_wind` and `min_wind`. Whereas inside the do loop we were evaluating maxima in time for each buoy, at this step we compare the values between buoys. Figure 7.5 illustrates the program flow.

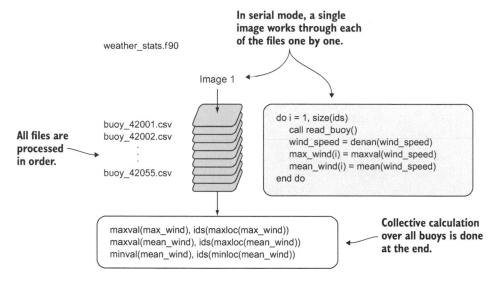

Figure 7.5   The flow of the serial `weather_stats` program. "Image 1" here refers to a single serial core or CPU.

Note that for removing missing data (not a number (NaN)) and calculating the mean value of the arrays, we defer to the external functions `denan` and `mean`, respectively. To scc how they're implemented, take a peek inside src/mod_arrays.f90. If you're

interested in how the CSV data reader (read_buoy) works, it's defined in src/mod
_io.f90. The main program is defined in src/weather_stats.f90.

> **Run it yourself!**
> If you cloned the repository from GitHub and installed OpenCoarrays (see appendix
> A), you're good to go! Inside the weather-buoys directory, type make weather_stats
> to build the serial program, and run it by typing ./weather_stats.
>
> Note that the weather_stats program doesn't use any coarrays or other parallel fea-
> tures at this point. However, for simplicity, the repository is configured to build using
> the OpenCoarrays wrapper caf, which can be used to build both serial and parallel
> programs.

How can we parallelize the program in listing 7.1 in the most straightforward way?
What you need to look for is what region of the program repeats over different inputs.
Recall the discussion about embarrassingly parallel problems in chapter 1. They're
the kind of problems where you can break the input data down into pieces and work
on each piece independently, regardless of the rest of the data. In the weather_stats
program, the do loop over the buoy data files is like that:

```
do i = 1, size(ids)
  call read_buoy('data/buoy_' // ids(i) //  '.csv', time, wind_speed)
  wind_speed = denan(wind_speed)
  max_wind(i) = maxval(wind_speed)
  mean_wind(i) = mean(wind_speed)
end do
```

If I loop over the buoys in any order, I'll still end up with the same result for max_wind
and mean_wind. This means that I can safely dispatch the processing of each buoy file
to a different processing core or thread. However, this also means that the elements of
max_wind and mean_wind will be scattered across the parallel processes. To calculate
the global minima and maxima across all buoys, we'll need to gather the data on one
processor. This is where Fortran coarrays come in.

7.3 Parallel processing with images and coarrays

> *What is the smallest change required to convert Fortran into a robust and efficient
> parallel language? Our answer is a simple syntactic extension. It looks and feels like
> Fortran and requires Fortran programmers to learn only a few new rules.*
>
> —John Reid, *Coarrays in the next Fortran Standard*

You need to grasp two concepts to get started with parallel Fortran programming:
images and *coarrays*. A Fortran image refers to a parallel process, be it a thread or a
core. Each image exists with its own copy of the program and its local memory. Images
execute the program independently from one another, until instructed otherwise.
You can tell the images to wait for each other; that is, *synchronize* them. You can also

order the images to send or receive data between one another. Coarrays are the main mechanics for doing this, and I'll spend most of the time explaining how they work.

7.3.1   *Fortran images*

When writing a parallel Fortran program, you don't have to worry about whether you're writing a multithreaded concurrent application that's meant to run on a single core, a shared-memory multicore application, or a distributed memory application. The code that you write is independent of the underlying architecture. Fortran introduces the concept of *image*, which identifies parallel processes and can map to one or more threads in a single core, or multiple cores in a shared- or distributed-memory system. For example, if you ran multiple images on a single core, the application would behave very much like a threaded application in some other language, like C or Python. This would give you concurrency without necessarily cutting down on the compute time. On the other hand, if a separate core was available for each image, the application would speed up significantly. This way, you focus on the parallel algorithm and let the compiler do the dirty work when it comes to executing the program on different architectures, using the Single Program, Multiple Data (SPMD) model (see sidebar).

Single Program, Multiple Data

Fortran parallelism follows the so-called Single Program, Multiple Data (SPMD) model. With SPMD, a single program is replicated on each invoked parallel process, with its own independent set of data objects. In a nutshell, this means that if we invoke the program on, say, four parallel images, each processor will run an exact copy of the same program and will have an independent copy of the working data in local memory. This is true regardless of whether the program is running on a shared-memory or distributed-memory system. The logic inside the program then determines and assigns a different workload for each image and, if necessary, exchanges data between images. SPMD is the most common style of parallel programming.

The implication of the SPMD paradigm is that you can invoke any serial program in parallel, without modifications! It's easiest to illustrate this with the simplest meaningful program (figure 7.6).

Now go ahead and try running the `weather_stats` program in parallel using, for example, two images:

```
cafrun -n 2 ./weather_stats
```

The output is the same as when we ran this program, but repeated twice:

```
Maximum wind speed measured is    40.9000015      at station 42001
Highest mean wind speed is     6.47883749      at station 42020
Lowest mean wind speed is    5.43456125      at station 42036
Maximum wind speed measured is    40.9000015      at station 42001
Highest mean wind speed is     6.47883749      at station 42020
Lowest mean wind speed is    5.43456125      at station 42036
```

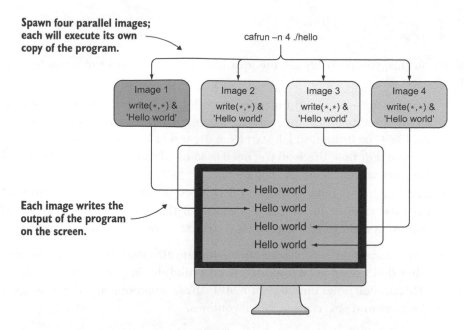

Figure 7.6 A serial "Hello, World!" program executed in parallel on four images

If you look at figure 7.6, this is not surprising at all. What you did is load a copy of the `weather_stats` program on two images, and each of them ran it and wrote their respective output to the screen. Now you must be thinking, This can't be super useful, can it? This is where inquiring about the images within the program comes in! You, the programmer, have to tell the images what to do differently. Looking back at the diagram in figure 7.5, we should tell each image to work on a different subset of the data. Let's see how we can do that by inquiring about the images themselves.

7.3.2 Getting information about the images

To tell the images what to work on, we first need to know more about the images themselves, specifically how many there are and who they are. Fortran provides the functions `this_image` and `num_images` to do exactly this. Here's how we write the image number and total number of images to screen:

```
program hello_images
  print *, 'I am image', this_image(), 'of', num_images()
end program hello_images
```

Let's store this into a file, hello_images.f90, compile it, and run it:

```
caf hello_images.f90 -o hello_images
cafrun -n 4 hello_images
 I am image            1 of            4
 I am image            2 of            4
```

```
I am image          3 of          4
I am image          4 of          4
```

Based on this, you probably get the idea how these functions work, but let's go over the details:

- this_image—A built-in function that, when called without arguments, returns an integer index of the current image. Fortran array indices start from 1 (unlike C or Python, which start from 0), and this_image follows the same convention. For now, this is all you need to know about this_image. We'll explore a bit more advanced use in chapter 12.
- num_images—A built-in function that takes no arguments and returns an integer total number of images. The result of this function will always match the argument number of images passed to cafrun -n.

Both this_image and num_images are automatically available in any Fortran program—they don't need to be imported from a module. In case you have some experience with parallel programming with MPI, these functions are the analogs of the mpi_comm_rank and mpi_comm_size subroutines.

7.3.3 *Telling images what to do*

So far, we've used this_image and num_images to instruct each image to tell us who it is and how many total images there are. This is useful information, but we still haven't done anything with it yet. How can we use this information to split the weather buoy data between images? Recall from listing 7.1 that we define the list of data files by specifying the array of buoy IDs:

```
ids = ['42001', '42002', '42003', '42020', '42035',&
  '42036', '42039', '42040', '42055']
```

To break down the data, we need to split this array into nearly equal pieces and assign each piece to an image. For example, if we work with two images, image 1 should have ids = ['42001', '42002', '42003', '42020', '42035'], and image 2 should have ids = ['42036', '42039', '42040', '42055']. For three images, each should have three buoy IDs total. You get the idea.

For exercise, let's implement this as an external function. (See the "Exercise 1" sidebar.) You have all the ingredients: declaring arrays like we did in chapter 2, defining a function and input arguments like we did in chapter 3, and the built-in functions this_image and num_images that we just covered.

If you got the exercise right, great! Otherwise, no worries; you can take a look at my implementation in the "Answer key" section near the end of the chapter. This function is also a necessary ingredient for the parallel tsunami simulator, so we'll reuse it there. Right now, let's see how we can use it to distribute the buoy data between images, as listing 7.2 demonstrates.

> ### Exercise 1: Finding the array subranges on each image
>
> Write a function `tile_indices` that does the following:
>
> - Takes an integer size of a global array. In our example, this corresponds to `size(ids)`, or 9.
> - Returns an integer array of size 2, which contains a start and end index that define the subset of the array on each image, or the so-called *tile*.
>
> For example:
>
> - `tile_indices(9)` invoked on one image should return `[1, 9]`.
> - `tile_indices(9)` invoked on two images should return `[1, 5]` and `[6, 9]` on images 1 and 2, respectively.
> - `tile_indices(9)` invoked on three images should return `[1, 3]`, `[4, 6]`, and `[7, 9]`, on images 1, 2, and 3, respectively.
>
> Hints:
>
> - Use `integer :: tile_indices(2)` to declare the result of the function.
> - Use the built-in function `mod(a, b)` that returns the remainder of a divided by b.
>
> For bonus points: Can this function be declared as `pure`?
>
> You can find the solution to this exercise in the "Answer key" section near the end of this chapter.

Listing 7.2   Finding a subrange for buoy IDs on each image

```
program weather_stats_parallel
  ...
  use mod_parallel, only: tile_indices        ⟵  Imports the function from
  ...                                              the external module
  integer :: is, ie, indices(2)        ⟵┤  Declares subrange
                                           indices
  ids = ['42001', '42002', '42003', '42020', '42035',&
    '42036', '42039', '42040', '42055']

  indices = tile_indices(size(ids))     │ Calculates and
  is = indices(1)                       │ stores subrange
  ie = indices(2)                       │ indices
                                                    │ Allocates arrays over
                                                    │ the local subranges
  allocate(max_wind(is:ie), mean_wind(is:ie))   ⟵
                                              │ Each image loops over its
  do i = is, ie                          ⟵──┘ own unique subrange.
    call read_buoy('data/buoy_' // ids(i) //  '.csv', time, wind_speed)
    wind_speed = denan(wind_speed)
    max_wind(i) = maxval(wind_speed)
    mean_wind(i) = mean(wind_speed)
  end do
  ...
end program weather_stats_parallel
```

In listing 7.2, I only included relevant additions to the serial version of the program. How does the data distribution work here? The key line is in the invocation of `tile_indices(size(ids))`. Even though each image invokes the same code, this function will return different start and end indices for each image! This is exactly the point at which our parallel universes start to bifurcate. At the end of the do loop, each image will have processed a subset of data files. However, our work is not done yet. Take a look at figure 7.5 again. We have one last step, which is to do a collective calculation over all nine elements of `max_wind` and `mean_wind`. But this may be trickier now that we've scattered the data across images. Enter coarrays!

7.3.4 Gathering all data to a single image

Let's look at how the data gathering pattern is implemented in code, as shown in the following listing.

Listing 7.3   Gathering distributed data to image 1

```
program weather_stats_parallel
  ...
  real, allocatable :: gather(:)[:]
  ...
  allocate(gather(size(ids))[*])

  gather(is:ie)[1] = max_wind
  sync all
  if (this_image() == 1) then
    print *, 'Maximum wind speed measured is ', maxval(gather),&
      'at station ', ids(maxloc(gather))
  end if
  ...
end program weather_stats_parallel
```

Allocates a full-size coarray →

Sends max_wind from each image into a subrange of gather on image 1

This forces all images to wait for each other.

Only image 1 will enter this if block and write the results to screen.

This listing includes only the added code relevant for gathering data to image 1. There are five new elements here:

1. Declaring a coarray with `real, allocatable :: gather(:)[:]`. Notice the square brackets! With regular arrays, we used only parentheses.
2. Allocating a coarray with `allocate(gather(size(ids))[*])`.
3. Sending the data (`max_wind`) from *each image* to image 1 with `gather(is:ie)[1] = max_wind`.
4. Synchronizing all images with `sync all`. This will make all images wait for each other at this point. This ensures that image 1 doesn't calculate and print the collective results *before* it receives data from all other images.
5. Use `this_image()` in the `if` statement to allow only image 1 to enter and do the collective calculation and printing to screen.

Figure 7.7 illustrates this pattern.

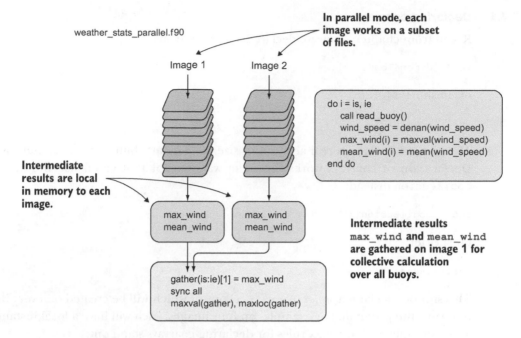

In parallel mode, each image works on a subset of files.

weather_stats_parallel.f90

Image 1   Image 2

```
do i = is, ie
    call read_buoy()
    wind_speed = denan(wind_speed)
    max_wind(i) = maxval(wind_speed)
    mean_wind(i) = mean(wind_speed)
end do
```

Intermediate results are local in memory to each image.

max_wind
mean_wind

max_wind
mean_wind

Intermediate results
max_wind **and** mean_wind
are gathered on image 1 for collective calculation over all buoys.

```
gather(is:ie)[1] = max_wind
sync all
maxval(gather), maxloc(gather)
```

Figure 7.7 **The flow of the parallel buoy processing program**

The full parallel program is defined in src/weather_stats_parallel.f90. You can build it by typing make weather_stats_parallel from the weather-buoys directory. To run it in parallel, use the cafrun command:

```
cafrun -n 4 ./weather_stats_parallel
```

Does it produce the same results as the serial program? Try to run it with different numbers of images. How does the runtime change between running the program with one, two, three, four, or five images?

7.4 *Coarrays and synchronization, explained*

In the previous section, you learned how to decompose the input data and parallelize a simple data processing and analysis program. However, parallelizing the tsunami simulator will present us with a unique challenge, because there we'll need to send and receive data between images at every time step, and carefully synchronize the images as we iterate the solution in time. This is where things become interesting (and challenging!) for the parallel programmer.

7.4.1 Declaring coarrays

Recall from chapter 2 how we declared a regular array:

```
real, dimension(10) :: a
```

or, in shorter form:

```
real :: a(10)
```

The snippet declares a real array, a, of size 10. The attribute `dimension` here is key. Declaration of coarrays works the same way, except that you'll use the attribute `codimension` instead:

```
real, codimension[*] :: a
```

Or shorter:

```
real :: a[*]
```

This snippet declares a *scalar coarray*, a, a copy of which will be created on every image that runs the program. For example, on four images, each will have a local instance of a real variable a. Two syntax rules for declaring coarrays stand out:

1 The `codimension` attribute uses square brackets, not parentheses. This rule applies to indexing the elements of a coarray, as we'll see in a bit.
2 The coarray size, indicated in square brackets, must be *, not any other literal constant or parameter, because the total number of images is determined when loading the program on the OS-level, and not programmatically.

Notice how I emphasized that the most recent snippets declare a scalar coarray, not an array coarray. This may confuse you at first because arrays and coarrays have such similar names. However, it helps to think about coarrays as completely separate entities from arrays that share some of their characteristics. To declare a coarray that's also an array, combine the rules for declaring each of them:

```
real, dimension(10), codimension[*] :: a
```

or, in shorter form:

```
real :: a(10)[*]
```

This snippet will declare a real array a with 10 elements on each image.

7.4.2 Allocating dynamic coarrays

Like with regular (noncoarray) variables, coarrays can be made allocatable, which is necessary whenever we don't know the size or shape of the variable at compile time.

For example, you'd declare an allocatable array coarray like this:

```
real, dimension(:), codimension[:], allocatable :: a
```

Or, in shorter form:

```
real, allocatable :: a(:)[:]
```

The same rules apply as with allocating regular variables. The following snippet will allocate a with 10 elements on each image:

```
allocate(a(10)[*])
```

Like any other allocatable variables, coarrays can also be deallocated:

```
deallocate(a)
```

This frees the memory used by a on all images.

> **Synchronization on `allocate` and `deallocate`**
> Allocating or deallocating a coarray always triggers a synchronization of images. Think of it as there always being an implicit `sync all` anytime you allocate or deallocate a coarray.

7.4.3 Sending and receiving data

The key to sending or receiving data with coarrays is understanding how to reference values on remote images. There are two ways to do this:

1 *Without square brackets*—The reference is that of the local image; for example, the following will assign a value to coarray a on the current image:

```
a = 3.141
```

2 *With square brackets*—The image is indicated with a scalar integer inside the brackets; for example:

```
a[2] = 3.141
```

When indexing a coarray, the number inside the square brackets is called a *coindex*. A coindex must be within the bounds of existing images. If we run a program with images [1, 2, 3, 4], a coarray must not be coindexed outside of that range.

You are allowed to use a coindex that matches the local image. For example, this snippet

```
if (this_image() == 1) a[1] = 3.141
```

is semantically equivalent to

```
if (this_image() == 1) a = 3.141
```

Let's look at a program that demonstrates various ways you can reference and copy data between remote images. We'll first use an integer coarray a to send the value of a variable from image 1 to image 2, assign a new value to it on image 2, and then send it back from image 2 to image 1. Finally, we'll confirm from image 2 that image 1 has updated its value of a:

```
caf coarrays.f90 -o coarrays
cafrun -n 2 ./coarrays
 Image          1  has value                 1
 Image          1  sending new value to image 2
 Image          2  has value                 2
 Image          2  sending new value to image 1
 Image          2  sees that image 1 now has value          4
```

The following listing provides the complete code of the program.

Listing 7.4   Sending and receiving data between two images

```
program coarrays

  implicit none

  integer :: a[*]          ◁──── Declares an integer
                                  scalar coarray

  if (num_images() /= 2) &
    error stop 'Error: This program must be run on 2 images'

  a = 0                    Initializes to zero on all images

  if (this_image() == 1) then    ◁──── Only image 1 will enter this if block.
    a = 1                  Assigns a value on this image
    print *, 'Image ', this_image(), ' has value ', a
    print *, 'Image ', this_image(), ' sending new value to image 2.'
    a[2] = 2 * a           ◁──── Sends a value from this image to image 2
  end if

  sync all                 All images wait for each other here.

  if (this_image() == 2) then    ◁──── Only image 2 will enter this if block.
    print *, 'Image ', this_image(), ' now has value ', a
    print *, 'Image ', this_image(), ' sending new value to image 1.'
    a[1] = 2 * a           ◁──── Sends a value from this image to image 1
  end if

  sync all

  if (this_image() == 2) &
    print *, 'Image ', this_image(), &
      ' sees that image 1 now has value ', a[1]

end program coarrays
```

Compiling and running the program in listing 7.4 confirms that the sending and receiving of data between two images works as expected.

With this program, we exercised both assigning a value on all images using familiar syntax and assigning a local value to a remote coarray. Notice that I also used the `sync all` statement in this example. This ensures that image 2 doesn't proceed into its `if` block before it receives the coarray from image 1. Let's see in more detail how synchronization of images works.

7.4.4 Controlling the order of image execution

When executing the program on multiple images, there's no imposed order in which the images execute—they all run at their own pace and independently from each other.

Any program that requires an exchange of data between processors will also require synchronization at one or more times during the calculation. This is true of the tsunami simulator as well! If image 2 needs data from image 1, it's important that image 1 send that data *before* it updates it with the solution in the next iteration. This is where Fortran's `sync` statement comes in. `sync` is used to request synchronization between any or all parallel images. The most basic form of the `sync` statement is `sync all`—synchronize all images. `sync all` basically states that no image will go past this point until all other images have arrived (figure 7.8).

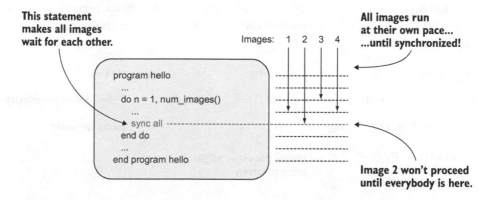

Figure 7.8 Using the `sync all` statement to make images wait for each other

For those of you who have experience with parallel programming with MPI, the `sync all` statement is equivalent to `call mpi_barrier()`.

To illustrate using synchronization to enforce order, the following listing demonstrates the coarray "Hello, World!" program from before, but with a slight twist.

Listing 7.5 Synchronizing the images to enforce order

```
program hello_images_ordered
  implicit none
```

```
            integer :: n
            do n = 1, num_images()        ⟵    Loops over the
If it's    ┌→   if (this_image() == n) &          images in order
my turn,   │       print *, 'Hello from image', this_image(), 'of', num_images()
print to   │     sync all                  ⟵
the screen.│   end do                          ⌐ Synchronizes with everybody
         ⎣ end program hello_images_ordered   └ before moving on
```

The output of this program will be the same as what you saw in subsection 7.3.2, except that here the images are guaranteed to report in ascending order.

7.5   *Toward the parallel tsunami simulator*

If you're reading this book in order, you know that we've been building a tsunami simulator from scratch, and adding more to it in each chapter. In this chapter, we'll still refactor the tsunami code and apply what we've just learned. However, unlike in previous chapters, this time our simulation results will be exactly the same, because the only change that we'll make will be to go from serial to parallel!

7.5.1   *Implementation strategy*

Before we start refactoring the solver for parallel execution, let's refresh our memory about where we left off.

Relative to the top-level directory of the project, the main program is located in src/ch04/tsunami.f90. The core of our solver is the do loop to integrate the solution in time:

```
time_loop: do n = 1, num_time_steps        ⟵——— Iterates in time

    u = u - (u * diff(u) + g * diff(h)) / dx * dt    ⟵——— Solves for velocity

    h = h - diff(u * (hmean + h)) / dx * dt        ⟵——— Solves for water

    print *, n, h        ⟵⌐ Writes the water height
                          └ array to screen
end do time_loop
```

As we saw in chapter 3, assignments for velocity u and water height h are whole-array operations, and we don't need to loop over the elements. Hopefully, we should be able to do the same in parallel mode, except that each image will work on its own section of the array. Now, recall what we did in section 7.3 where we parallelized the weather buoy program. We divided the input array into a number of equal parts, a number that matched the total number of images. Then we did the core calculation in the same way as we did in the serial version of the program. Let's apply the same strategy here, keeping in mind that we need to send, receive, and synchronize data at every step of the time_loop. This is because at each time step, the spatial difference function diff will need nonlocal data that belong to neighbor images, as shown in figure 7.9.

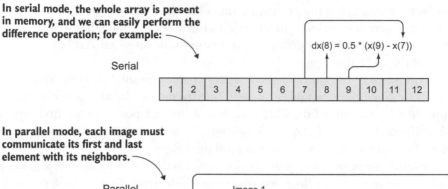

In serial mode, the whole array is present in memory, and we can easily perform the difference operation; for example:

In parallel mode, each image must communicate its first and last element with its neighbors.

Dashed boxes are halo cells. They are needed for calculation and must be received from neighbor images.

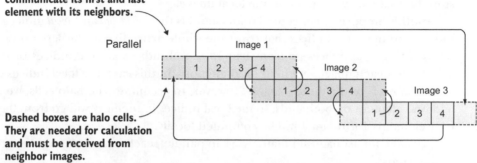

Figure 7.9 Communicating data between neighbor images. The numbers in each box are array indices. Each image computes the solution for the elements in solid boxes; however, values from dashed boxes are needed for the computation and must be received from neighbor processors. The far-end communication between images 1 and 3 is to satisfy the periodic boundary condition.

Recall from src/ch04/mod_diff.f90 how our difference function works:

```
do concurrent(i = 2:im-1)
  dx(i) = 0.5 * (x(i+1) - x(i-1))
end do
```

Loops over all elements except first and last

Takes centered difference in space

Each element of the result of the `diff` function depends on the elements immediately next to it. This is a classic example of a nonembarrassingly parallel (or communication-intensive) function, in which we have to send and receive data between neighbor images before doing the calculation. To better understand why, see figure 7.9.

In serial mode (figure 7.9, top), array indices go from 1 to the total size of the array (12, in this case), and there's no distinction between global and local indices. In parallel mode (figure 7.9, bottom), each image holds a subsection of the array, with local indices going from 1 to the total size of the subsection of the array (4, in this case). Each local index maps to a unique global index: local indices 1–4 on images 1, 2, and 3 map to global indices 1–4, 5–8, and 9–12, respectively.

When invoking the `diff(x)` function, the calculation of each array element `x(i)` depends on the two elements immediately next to it: `x(i-1)` and `x(i+1)`. What happens on image 2 when we try to calculate the difference for element 5? We need elements 4 and 6, but the problem is that element 4 is computed by image 1, so image 2 doesn't have it in its local memory! This is a new challenge that we didn't encounter before, and it requires performing the communication pattern before each invocation of the `diff` function.

This is where the concept of *halo* cells becomes useful. Halo cells refer to array elements that belong to neighbor images, but are needed locally to perform the calculation. In the example of the `diff` function, if index `i` points to the first array element on the local image, `x(i-1)`, which belongs to a neighbor image, must be received and stored into an array element on the local image.

Another important concept to understand is that of *global* and *local* indices. Global indices are the array indices that cover the whole array, like in the serial program. In figure 7.9, global indices go from 1 to 12. Local indices are the indices of the array subsets that each image sees in its local memory. In this case, the local indices go from 1 to 4 on each of the three images. However, to accommodate halo cells, we need to add one element on both ends, so the local indices in memory will go from 0 to 5, but only elements 1 through 4 will be computed locally.

To make the tsunami simulator work in parallel, each image must carry out the following steps:

1 Determine neighbor images.
2 Determine start and end indices on each image, and allocate the coarrays accordingly.
3 Update the halo cells and compute the solution.

Let's go over these steps one at a time. You can follow the next few subsections and build the parallel code together with me if you want.

7.5.2 *Finding the indices of neighbor images*

Looking back at figure 7.9, it's obvious who the neighbors are for each image. For image 1, the left and right neighbors are images 3 and 2, respectively. For image 2, they're images 1 and 3. And for image 3, they're images 2 and 1. Let's generalize this rule so that it works for any number of images. Try to implement it as an external function! It's a necessary ingredient for getting the parallel tsunami simulator to work, so you can also skip ahead and use it out of the box. I defined it in the `mod_parallel` module in src/ch07/mod_parallel.f90.

> **Exercise 2: Writing a function that returns the indices of neighbor images**
> To exchange data with the neighbors, we need to know who they are! Write a function that can be invoked on any image and that returns the image numbers of the neighbors to the left and to the right. The right neighbor of the last image should be the first image, and the left neighbor of the first image should be the last image, to satisfy the periodic boundary condition.

Hints:

- The function should take no input arguments.
- All you need is the `this_image` and `num_images` functions to work out the logic.
- Use `integer :: tile_neighbors(2)` to store the results into a single variable.

The solution is given in the "Answer key" section near the end of this chapter, and is included in src/ch07/mod_parallel.f90.

In the the main program, each image will invoke this function and store the neighbor image indices in local variables:

```fortran
integer(int32) :: neighbors(2)    ⟵ Temporary array to store
integer(int32) :: left, right     ⟵ results of tile_neighbors()
                                     Variables that will
                                     hold the indices
neighbors = tile_neighbors()
left = neighbors(1)               Copies from the temporary
right = neighbors(2)              array into target variables
```

Invokes the function and stores the result into a temporary array

Now that we know who our neighbors are, the next step is to determine the start and end indices on each image and to allocate the coarrays.

7.5.3 Allocating the coarrays

To allocate the water height and velocity as coarrays over appropriate sections, we need to know their start and end indices on each image. Sounds familiar? We already did this in section 7.3 and exercise 1! All we have to do here is properly call that function and store the start and end indices in local variables. I called the function `tile_indices`, and you can find it both in the "Answer key" for Exercise 1 near the end of this chapter and in the tsunami repository in src/lib/mod_parallel.f90.

The following listing provides the relevant section of src/app/tsunami.f90 that calculates the start and end indices on each image and allocates the coarrays accordingly.

Listing 7.6 Allocating the coarrays with the correct start and end indices

```fortran
integer(int32), parameter :: grid_size = 100    ⟵ Global array size
...
real(real32), allocatable :: h(:)[:], u(:)[:]   ⟵ Declares water height
real(real32), allocatable :: gather(:)[:]          and velocity as
real(real32), allocatable :: hmean(:)              allocatable coarrays
...
integer(int32) :: indices(2)                    Will be used to gather
integer(int32) :: is, ie                        and write water height
integer(int32) :: ils, ile                      data to screen
```

Labels (left margin): **Global array size**, **Global indices**

Labels (right margin): Declares water height and velocity as allocatable coarrays; Will be used to gather and write water height data to screen; Temporary array to store tile indices; Local indices, excluding halo

Local memory indices, including halo

```
integer(int32) :: ims, ime
...
indices = tile_indices(grid_size)
is = indices(1)
ie = indices(2)
```
Calculates global indices

```
tile_size = grid_size / num_images()
ils = 1
ile = tile_size
```
Calculates local indices

```
ims = ils - 1
ime = ile + 1
```
Calculates memory indices, including halo cells

```
allocate(h(ims:ime)[*])
allocate(u(ims:ime)[*])
```
Allocates water height and velocity over local memory indices

```
allocate(hmean(ims:ime))
```

```
allocate(gather(grid_size)[*])
```
Allocates over full domain size

There's an important distinction between local start and end indices `ils` and `ile` and memory indices `ims` and `ime`. The former are the indices over each image that will compute and update the solution at each step. The latter include the halo points and are the indices that each image must have in memory to do the computation over the `ils:ile` range. Let's see how exactly that works out in the implementation of our main time loop.

7.5.4   *The main time loop*

We're now ready to apply the parallel skills we learned in this chapter: referencing coarray elements from other images to exchange data, and synchronizing the images. Following the halo exchange pattern in figure 7.9, for both the water height and velocity arrays, we'll copy the elements from each end into the halo cells of each of our neighbors. An example of sending the first element from the local image to the left neighbor's halo cell is illustrated in figure 7.10.

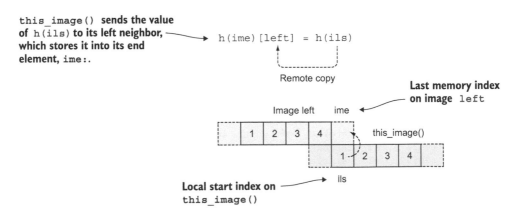

Figure 7.10   Sending a value from the local image to our left neighbor's halo cell

This pattern is the main addition to the existing code to make it run in parallel. The sequence is

1 Update halo cells.
2 Synchronize images.
3 Solve the equation.

Since we've been solving for both water height and velocity, we need to repeat this sequence twice, once for each equation (figure 7.11).

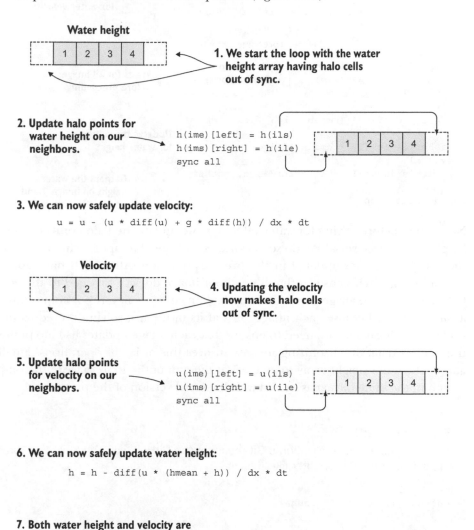

Figure 7.11 Tsunami time integration loop from the perspective of `this_image`

The following listing shows what this looks like in actual code.

Listing 7.7   The main time loop of the parallel tsunami simulator

```
time_loop: do n = 1, num_time_steps

    h(ime)[left] = h(ils)
    h(ims)[right] = h(ile)
    sync all

    u = u - (u * diff(u) + g * diff(h)) / dx * dt

    sync all

    u(ime)[left] = u(ils)
    u(ims)[right] = u(ile)
    sync all

    h = h - diff(u * (hmean + h)) / dx * dt

    gather(is:ie)[1] = h(ils:ile)
    sync all
    if (this_image() == 1) print *, n, gather

end do time_loop
```

- Updates halo cells for water height
- Waits for all images before proceeding
- Updates the solution for water velocity
- Waits for all images before proceeding
- Updates halo cells for velocity
- Waits for all images before proceeding
- Updates the solution for water height
- Gathers the water height on image 1 and prints it to screen

Notice that before solving for water velocity, u, we update the halo points for the water height, h, and vice versa! We do so because we only need to update the halo points for the variable that was updated in the previous iteration. After each halo update, we sync all images. This ensures that a neighbor image doesn't proceed to the equation before the current image gets its halo update. In concurrency, this is commonly called a *race condition*. Because each image runs at its own pace, solving the equations and updating its local data, we need to ensure that each image updates its halo points with the correct data. Synchronizing images ensures this order of operations. Finally, we gather the water height array to image 1 at the end of the loop to write the output to screen in the same format as we did with the serial version of the program.

> **Run it yourself!**
> If you've cloned the application's Git repository on GitHub, you can build and run the application from this chapter like this:
>
> ```
> make ch07
> cafrun -n 4 src/ch07/tsunami
> ```

That's it; we made it! Our tsunami simulator now runs in parallel and produces bit-for-bit the same results as the serial version. This means that if you run the program on different numbers of images, you'll get the exact same results every time. This is an important milestone for the development of our app. In the next chapter, we can expand the solver from one to two dimensions and visualize the tsunami from a top-down view, like when you throw a pebble into a pond. Because expanding to two dimensions will demand much higher processing power, parallelism will prove to be crucial in getting to our results faster.

At this point, you have the working knowledge to parallelize simple programs. For problems that require communication between images to get to the final solution, coarrays provide a familiar array-like syntax for sending and receiving data between remote images. For many problems, clever synchronization is key to avoid race conditions. On their own, each of these concepts is relatively simple, but, to be honest, parallel programming is hard! The main difficulty comes from the fact that many things are happening all at once, and they're often difficult to keep track of. Practicing these patterns on various problems will get you a long way.

In the next chapter, we'll dive into derived types, which is Fortran's concept of classes. Derived types will allow you to make high-level abstractions of your data, beyond the basic numeric, logical, and character types. In the context of the tsunami simulator, we'll use derived types to cast our variables in a form that can be easily expanded to two dimensions, while maintaining the same arithmetic operators and writing code that looks like math on a chalkboard. Having refactored the tsunami simulator into a parallel version, we'll move forward in parallel and won't look back!

7.6 Answer key

This section contains solutions to exercises in this chapter. Skip ahead if you haven't worked through the exercises yet.

7.6.1 Exercise 1: Finding the array subranges on each image

We need a function that returns a start and end index for each image, given the integer size of the global array to be decomposed. For example, for an input 100 and total number of images 2, the result should be [1, 50] on image 1 and [51, 100] on image 2. When the input is divisible by `num_images()`, the solution is straightforward. However, we also need to handle a special case when the input isn't divisible by `num_images()`; for example, if input is 100 and `num_images() == 3`. The following listing provides the solution.

Listing 7.8 Calculating start and end indices on each image

```
pure function tile_indices(dims)       ◁── Input integer scalar, size
                                            of array to decompose
    integer, intent(in) :: dims       ◁──┘
    integer :: tile_indices(2)            ◁── Array to store the result in
    integer :: offset, tile_size

    tile_size = dims / num_images()    ◁── First guess for tile size;
                                           correct only if dims is
                                           divisible by num_images()

    tile_indices(1) = (this_image() - 1) * tile_size + 1   ◁── First guess for start index
    tile_indices(2) = tile_indices(1) + tile_size - 1      ◁── First guess for end index
```

```
      offset = num_images() - mod(dims, num_images())
      if (this_image() > offset) then
        tile_indices(1) = tile_indices(1) &
                        + this_image() - offset - 1
        tile_indices(2) = tile_indices(2) &
                        + this_image() - offset
      end if

    end function tile_indices
```

> **If dims is not divisible by num_images(), distribute the remainder accordingly.**

This function is also an important piece of the parallel tsunami simulator and is available there as a function in src/ch07/mod_parallel.f90.

7.6.2 Exercise 2: Writing a function that returns the indices of neighbor images

If you've practiced using the `this_image` and `num_images` built-in functions long enough, the solution will be straightforward. For any image that calls this function, its left neighbor will be `this_image() - 1`, and its right neighbor `this_image() + 1`. (Except when `this_image()` is at the boundary, that is, `this_image() == 1` or `this_image() == num_images()`.) The following listing provides the solution.

Listing 7.9 Calculating the index of neighbor images

```
pure function tile_neighbors()

  integer :: tile_neighbors(2)           Two-element integer
  integer :: left, right                 array to store the result

  if (num_images() > 1) then
    left = this_image() - 1
    right = this_image() + 1             General case
    if (this_image() == 1) then
      left = num_images()
    else if (this_image() == num_images()) then
      right = 1                          Special case for
    end if                               the last image
  else
    left = 1                   Special case if we're working
    right = 1                  with only one image
  end if

  tile_neighbors(1) = left    Stores the indices
  tile_neighbors(2) = right   in the result array

end function tile_neighbors
```

Neighbor indices

Special case for the first image

This is also a function that's essential for the tsunami simulator and is defined in src/ch07/mod_parallel.f90.

7.7 New Fortran elements, at a glance

- `this_image` and `num_images` built-in functions that return the current image number and the total number of images, respectively
- `codimension[]` attribute for declaring coarrays
- Bracket syntax `[]` for indexing coarrays
- `sync all` statement to synchronize all images

7.8 Further reading

- Chapter 17 ("Coarrays") of *Modern Fortran Explained: Incorporating Fortran 2018*, by Michael Metcalf, John Reid, and Malcolm Cohen, Oxford University Press.
- *Parallel Programming with Co-arrays*, by Robert W. Numrich, Chapman and Hall/CRC.

Summary

- Fortran refers to any parallel process as an *image*, whether it's a physical core or an operating system thread.
- All images execute the same copy of the program in parallel, independent from one another.
- The built-in functions `this_image` and `num_images` allow you to identify different images.
- Use these functions in `if` branches to control the flow of the program for each image.
- Coarrays are the key mechanism for copying data between images.
- Use the `sync all` statement to synchronize all images.
- The higher the ratio of computation versus communication between images, the more efficient your parallel program will be.

Working with abstract data using derived types

This chapter covers

- Using derived types to create new collections and data types
- Binding procedures to derived types
- Refactoring the tsunami simulator to two dimensions using derived types

So far in this book we've worked only with the core Fortran data types: integer, real, complex, logical, and character. Although even with just these data types we've been able to do quite a few useful things, such as analyze time series of stock prices or buoy measurements, or write a parallel tsunami simulator, we're still somewhat limited in what we can do. This becomes more obvious as we encounter more complex problems with abstract and unstructured data that are ubiquitous in real-world applications. So far, all of the examples we've worked on have been structured and thus easy to tackle with the core numeric types and arrays alone. However, this is just a small subset of problems, and real-world applications and data will require more complex and abstract data structures in our code. Such applications include machine learning, web and mobile apps, and more sophisticated physics simulations.

In this chapter, we'll get our feet wet with a new kind of data type—a *derived type*. In its most basic form, a derived type is nothing more than a collection of variables. As you may guess from its name, it allows you to design and build arbitrary data types of any level of complexity, using core data types (or other derived types) as components. You'll be able to create different instances of the same derived type, and even attach functions and subroutines to operate on their state. If you have prior experience with object-oriented programming, you'll recognize that I'm really talking about classes. That's exactly right—a derived type is a Fortran term for what's widely known as a class in many programming languages. The features that we'll cover in this chapter will thus form a basis for object-oriented programming techniques.

To learn how derived types work at a basic level, we'll first look into a simple example of modeling a person, a kind of data entry that you'd find in applications that deal with user data, civic or school records, contact books, and similar. I'll show you how you can define completely new data types from scratch, access and modify their components, and even assign functions and subroutines to them. We'll gently transition to applying derived types to model physical fields, and see how this will help us write more clear and expressive simulation apps. We'll apply this knowledge to the tsunami simulator to abstract away much of the low-level boilerplate we've built up over the past few chapters. This will open new doors and greatly simplify more advanced features of the tsunami simulator that we'll develop in the remainder of the book.

8.1 *Recasting the tsunami simulator with derived types*

The main goal of this chapter is to apply derived types toward refactoring our parallel tsunami simulator. Specifically, we'll use them to abstract away the low-level code to allocate and manipulate data arrays, as well as to black-box much of the tedious code used for setting up the data structures. Derived types will help us write more expressive and concise code, which will be ever more important as we work toward making it more general and user-friendly. They'll also allow us to expand the solver from one to two dimensions without compromising the simplicity of the main program.

At the end of the previous chapter, we left off with the core of the tsunami simulator as shown in the following listing.

Listing 8.1 The main time loop of the parallel tsunami simulator

```
time_loop: do n = 1, num_time_steps

  h(ime)[left] = h(ils)          Updates halo cells
  h(ims)[right] = h(ile)         for water height
  sync all          ←——  Waits for all images
                          before proceeding

  u = u - (u * diff(u) + g * diff(h)) / dx * dt     ←——  Updates the solution
                                                          for water velocity

  sync all     ←——  Waits for all images
                     before proceeding
```

```
u(ime)[left] = u(ils)          Updates halo
u(ims)[right] = u(ile)         cells for velocity
sync all                       Waits for all images
                               before proceeding

h = h - diff(u * (hmean + h)) / dx * dt        Updates the solution
                                               for water height

gather(is:ie)[1] = h(ils:ile)                  Gathers the
sync all                                       water height
if (this_image() == 1) write(unit=output_unit, fmt=*) n, gather    on image 1
                                                                   and prints it
                                                                   to the screen
end do time_loop
```

In each iteration of the time loop, this code computed new values for water velocity, u, and height, h; synchronized the data with the neighboring parallel images; and wrote the water height data to the screen. This solver produced a fairly realistic-looking simulation of a propagating water wave (figure 8.1).

Although working directly with coarrays has served us well so far, and helped us learn how they work, this approach may not be ideal in the long run. That's the case because each piece that we needed for the solver to work led to quite a bit of boiler-plate code, specifically

- Calculating start and end indices on each parallel image
- Explicitly allocating coarrays
- Updating the halo points between neighboring images
- Synchronizing images to prevent race conditions
- Gathering and writing data into a file

This is bound to get worse as we extend the solver from one to two dimensions. We'll go from two to three equations (two for each of the *x*- and *y*-velocity components and one for water height), and each of the equations will have additional terms in the *y* dimension. Since most of these operations are the same for each of the variables, we can express most of this code as derived type components and methods once, and reuse it whenever we need it.

Here are the main advantages of formulating our fields as derived type instances instead of bare multidimensional coarrays:

- We can use type-bound procedures for operations that are common to all fields.
- We can abstract away a lot of the low-level code, such as partitioning the computational domain, calculating start and end indices, setting initial conditions, and synchronizing the tiles in parallel mode.
- If we decide to implement more features in the future, we can write them directly in the definition of the type and its methods, keeping the main program concise and clean.

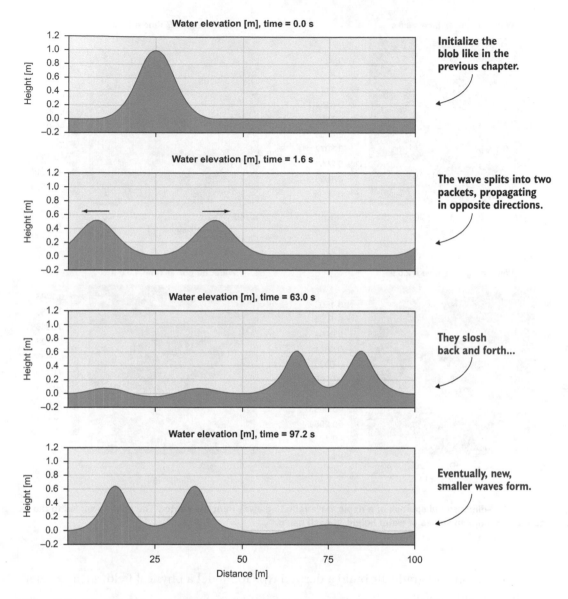

Figure 8.1 Simulation of water height initialized as a bell-shape 1 m high and about 20 m wide

At the end of this chapter, the tsunami simulator will produce a solution of a water wave radiating outward from the center of the domain, just as if we threw a pebble in a pond (figure 8.2).

In the next section, we'll go over the basic syntax and rules for defining, declaring, and initializing derived types. At each step, we'll tie the new knowledge into the tsunami

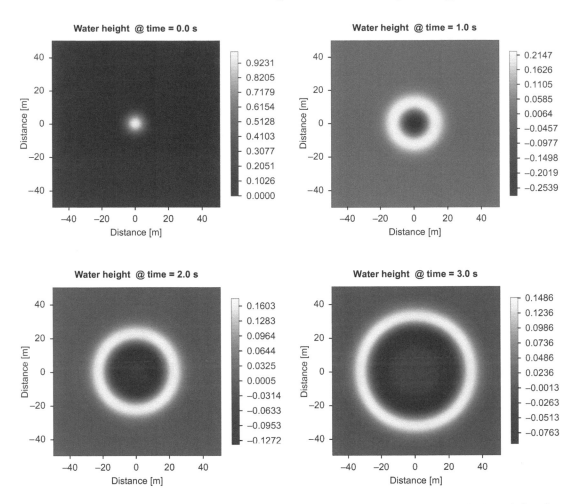

Figure 8.2   Two-dimensional solution of a ripple wave radiating away from the center. The color is scaled to the minimum and maximum values of water height in each panel.

application and gradually build a derived type to model a physical field, such as water height and velocity.

8.2   *Defining, declaring, and initializing derived types*

Perhaps the greatest strength of an object-oriented approach to development is that it offers a mechanism that captures a model of the real world.

—Grady Booch (1986)

Let's start with a small program that makes use of a derived type. We'll define a `Person` type and assign to it a greeting subroutine, which will do nothing more than print the greeting message to the screen. We'll then declare an instance of the new type and call the greeting method. Compiling and running this program will yield

```
gfortran hello_derived_types.f90 -o hello_derived_types
./hello_derived_types
 Hello, my name is Jill!
```

Let's dive straight in. The following listing provides the complete code for the hello_ derived_types program.

Listing 8.2   A hello world program expressed using a derived type

```
module mod_person                    ← Opens a new
  type :: Person                       type definition
    character(len=20) :: name
  contains
    procedure, pass(self) :: greet
  end type Person
contains
  subroutine greet(self)
    class(Person), intent(in) :: self
    print *, 'Hello, my name is ' // trim(self % name) // '!'
  end subroutine greet
end module mod_person

program hello_derived_types
  use mod_person, only: Person
  implicit none
  type(Person) :: some_person = Person('Jill')
  call some_person % greet()
end program hello_derived_types
```

Annotations:
- **Separates components from methods**
- **Closes the type definition block**
- **Opens a new type definition**
- **Type will have only this component (a variable)**
- **Type will have only this method (a procedure)**
- **Type-bound procedure has the type itself as input argument**
- **Imports the type from the module**
- **Declares and instantiates the type**
- **Invokes the greet method**

Quite a few new things are going on in this program:

1. We defined a simple Person type, with a character(len=20) name as a component.
2. We also specified that a Person type contains a procedure, greet, defined in the same module. This way, we effectively bound (attached) this procedure to the Person type.
3. In the main program, we imported the Person type from the module, declared a new instance, some_person, and initialized it as Person('Jill').
4. Finally, we called this instance's greeting method, some_person % greet().

Each of these steps includes at least one new language or syntax element, so let's take it slowly as we go over each one. The first thing to get used to is some new terminology. I'll be talking a lot about classes, instances, components, and methods. These are all closely related to the so-called *object-oriented programming* (OOP) style. If you're familiar with OOP from some other language, feel free to skim through, or jump straight ahead to the next section.

These are the specific terms that we'll adopt in this chapter:

- *Class*—I'll use the terms *class* and *derived type* interchangeably. The word *class* is commonly used in general programming and computer science lingo, while *derived type* is a Fortran-specific term. In OOP terminology, a class is a recipe for creating objects.
- *Instance*—Once you define a class (or import its definition from a module), you can declare as many different instances of that class as you want. The word *instance* thus always refers to a concrete realization of a class in the program, an object.
- *Component*—What's unique about classes is that they can have any number of variables of any type, be it numeric types, such as integer or real, scalar or array, or even an instance of the same or some other class. I'll refer to all these as *class components*. In short, a component is what a class *has*.
- *Method*—Much like we can define variables as components of a class, we can bind procedures (functions or subroutines) to a class to two great effects. First, they always come with the class instance and don't need to be imported separately. Second, methods have access to all of a class's components and methods. In simple terms, a method is what a class *does*.

At first, if you look at listing 8.2, you may protest and say, "Hey, this is so much code and complexity for just a simple greeting message!" I hear you, and I agree that this is a trivial example. However, a simple example like this will help us understand how derived types work at their core, and for what kind of problems they may be useful. Bear with me, and soon you'll see some of the powerful capabilities of this approach. As we work through this chapter, we'll use these tools to refactor the tsunami solver and extend it to two dimensions.

At the same time, notice that a derived type is yet another layer of abstraction over fundamental data types. Introducing it can be justified only if its benefits outweigh the cost. In this case, the benefit is that if a more complex data structure will be used often, using a derived type can do away with much of the boilerplate code. The cost is associated with added complexity and opaqueness. A casual reader may ask, "What's inside this `Person` instance?" or, "Does `Person % greet()` really just print a message to the terminal, or does it have other side effects?" You get the idea. Figure 8.3 illustrates the most basic use of a derived type.

NOTE A Fortran derived type is analogous to a C `struct` or a Python or JavaScript `class`.

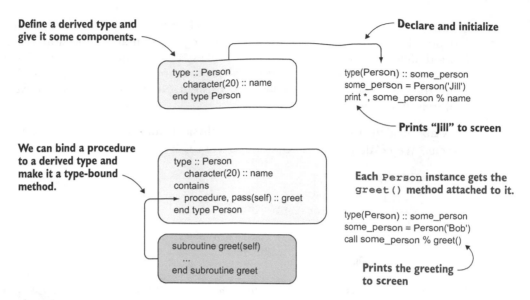

Define a derived type and give it some components.

```
type :: Person
    character(20) :: name
end type Person
```

Declare and initialize

```
type(Person) :: some_person
some_person = Person('Jill')
print *, some_person % name
```

Prints "Jill" to screen

We can bind a procedure to a derived type and make it a type-bound method.

```
type :: Person
    character(20) :: name
contains
    procedure, pass(self) :: greet
end type Person
```

```
subroutine greet(self)
    ...
end subroutine greet
```

Each `Person` instance gets the `greet()` method attached to it.

```
type(Person) :: some_person
some_person = Person('Bob')
call some_person % greet()
```

Prints the greeting to screen

Figure 8.3 Defining, declaring, initializing, and invoking a method of a derived type

8.2.1 Defining a derived type

Now that you see where we're going, let's take a few steps back and start simple and slow. The following snippet demonstrates the syntax to define a new derived type:

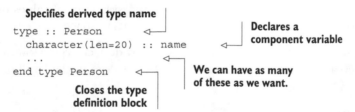

Specifies derived type name

```
type :: Person
    character(len=20) :: name
    ...
end type Person
```

Declares a component variable

We can have as many of these as we want.

Closes the type definition block

The type definition block always opens with `type :: <type-name>` and closes with `end type <type-name>`, akin to `program/end program`, `function/end function`, and others. All the component declarations go inside the type definition block, and you can have as many as you want. Components aren't limited to built-in numeric, character, or logical types. You can include components that are instances of derived types, and, in some special cases, even those of the same type. Specifically, having derived types with pointers to components of the same type is a popular pattern used to build a linked list.

Like with all other variable declarations we've covered so far, you must place a derived type definition within the declarative section of the code; that is, before the executable section.

TIP Define a new derived type in a dedicated module, in a dedicated source file. It will keep you organized and will help maintain a mental map of where different types are defined. For example, if I want to define a `Field` derived type, I'll define it and all its methods in a `mod_field` module, and store it in a mod_field.f90 file. In some cases, it makes sense to define closely related derived types in the same module. There are no hard rules here—do what makes the most sense to you, and be consistent. No matter what your convention is, it's good to have one.

How about a derived type to represent a physical quantity, such as water height or velocity? We could define this type simply as `Field`:

Begins Field type definition

```
type :: Field
  character(len=:), allocatable :: name
  integer :: dims(2)
end type Field
```

Field name; for example, "water_height" or "velocity"

Domain dimensions in x and y

Ends Field type definition

For now, our `Field` type can be as simple as just the name and an integer array of two elements that will contain the size of the domain for this field. In the previous version of tsunami, we specified these dimensions as `im` and `jm`, so the `dims` component will correspond to [im, jm]:

```
integer(int32), parameter :: im = 101, jm = 101
```

Domain sizes in x and y

> **DEFINITION**   In math or physics, a *field* represents an assignment of values of some quantity (such as water height or velocity) to points in space.

We're now getting more comfortable with defining a new derived type. However, this is just a recipe for creating data structures. Let's see how we can declare and initialize an instance of a brand new derived type.

8.2.2 Instantiating a derived type

Defining a derived type was the first necessary step, but to actually use it, we need to *instantiate* one. Instantiating means nothing more than creating a new instance. It's kind of an unwieldy word, but the more you use it, the more natural it becomes. In listing 8.2, I used a shortcut to declare and initialize a derived type instance in a single statement:

```
type(Person) :: some_person = Person('Jill')
```

This is equivalent to a more explicit, two-step process:

```
type(Person) :: some_person
some_person = Person('Jill')
```

Declares an instance of the Person type

Initializes the new instance

Now we get to our second new syntax element for this chapter—initializing a derived type instance by invoking the name of the type, and passing the values of its components in parentheses: `Person('Jill')`. This is the default way to initialize a derived type, which requires all components to be passed to the type constructor as arguments, much like we did in procedure calls. For a refresher on invoking Fortran procedures, see section 3.2.1.

Take, for example, a slightly richer type with three components, as shown in the following listing.

Listing 8.3   Attempting to initialize a derived type instance

```
type :: Person
  character(len=20) :: name            This type has
  integer :: age                       three components.
  character(len=20) :: occupation
end type Person

                                       Declares a new
type(Person) :: some_person      ←     Person instance

                                       Tries to initialize with
some_person = Person('Bob')      ←     just the name argument
```

If you try to initialize this type with just the name, like in listing 8.3, the compiler will yell back at you:

```
$ gfortran derived_type_init.f90
derived_type_init.f90:20:16:

    some_person = Person('Bob')
                1
Error: No initializer for component 'age' given in the structure constructor
    at (1)
```

Here, the compiler expected to receive parameters for all three type components, not just the name. This means that the code won't compile until we provide all input parameters to match all derived type components:

```
some_person = Person('Bob', 32, 'Engineer')
```

Back in the tsunami app, our `Field` type could be initialized as

```
                     Grid size in x and y directions
integer(int32), parameter :: im = 101, jm = 101   ←
type(Field) :: h                            ←       Declares a
h = Field('Water height', [im, jm])         ←       field instance
     Instantiates using default constructor
```

Currently, our new `Field` type still doesn't do anything interesting, nor does it contain much useful data. We just gave it a name and assigned it a size in each of the two dimensions. However, we'll be able to use this information for all the setup work, such as decomposition of the domain into parallel tiles, determining start and end indices of data arrays, and allocating the arrays.

Now that we've created new instances of the `Person` and `Field` types, let's see how we can access their components.

8.2.3 *Accessing derived type components*

Once we have a class instance declared and initialized, in most cases we'll want to access its components, often to read their values, sometimes to modify them. After all, if we use type components to store data that's specific to the instance, there's no use for it unless we can access it in some way.

To access derived type components, we'll place a `%` symbol immediately after the type instance name, and before specifying the component name: `some_person % name`. The type instance name acts a lot like a namespace. If you had a regular variable declared as `name`, `some_person % name` wouldn't conflict with it because it's specific to the `some_person` instance.

Let's say you want Bob from listing 8.3 to tell us more about himself; for example

```
Hi, I am Bob, a          32 year old Engineer
```

To print this to screen, you'd access the type components using the `%` syntax, and connect them with a few character string literals using the string concatenation operator `//`:

```
print *, 'Hi, I am ' // trim(some_person % name) // ', a ', &
  some_person % age, 'year old ' // some_person % occupation
```

Don't worry about the awkward blank space in the middle of the greeting message. This is due to default formatting when mixing strings and integers in the `print` statement, like we saw back in chapter 6.

Similarly, we can access the 'Field' instance we initialized before using

```
print *, 'Initialized field ' // trim(h % name) // &
  ' with size ', h % dims
```

> **NOTE** The Fortran derived type component access operator `%` is analogous to the dot operator (`.`) in C, Python, or JavaScript.

8.2.4 *Positional vs. keyword arguments in derived type constructors*

As you'll recall from chapter 3, we can invoke a procedure by passing either positional or keyword arguments, or a combination of the two. The same rules apply here. If you use strictly positional arguments, you must provide them in the order of their declaration in the derived type definition (thus the name *positional*). However, if you use keyword arguments, you can specify them in any order, as long as they appear after any positional arguments. Several of the following examples illustrate this rule:

```
⟶▷  some_person = Person('Bob')
⟶▷  some_person = Person('Bob', 'Engineer', 32)
⟶▷  some_person = Person(occupation='Engineer', age=32, 'Bob')
    some_person = Person('Bob', 32, 'Engineer')                      ◁⟵
    some_person = Person(occupation='Engineer', name='Bob', age=32)  ◁
    some_person = Person('Bob', 32, occupation='Engineer')           ◁
```

Illegal: keyword arguments
before positional

Illegal: occupation
given before age

Illegal: missing input arguments
'age' before occupation

Legal: Positional arguments
first, keyword argument last

Legal: All keyword
arguments in any order

Legal: All positional
arguments given in order

In summary, these are the rules for default type constructor parameters:

- If a component doesn't have a default value (more details to come), it must be passed as an argument in the constructor.
- Any positional arguments in the type constructor must be listed in the same order as they're defined in the type definition and must appear before any keyword arguments.
- Any keyword arguments can appear in any order.

Caution when passing positional arguments

Be careful of the order of positional arguments. The only way the compiler can tell that `32` isn't a valid occupation, or `Engineer` isn't a valid age, is based on their data types being distinct. However, if the types of conflicting components are the same, and the compiler can't make that distinction, it will happily compile the program, and you can only hope that the error will become apparent at runtime and not much later! This is a common source of errors in heavy numeric and simulation software, where a few of many numeric input parameters could be swapped by mistake. Such errors can go unnoticed by the compiler, the programmer, and the end user of the program for years—and in some cases even decades—before being discovered.

Using the default type constructor is easy for relatively small derived types like the one in this example. However, how would we do this with more complex derived types that may have tens or even hundreds of components of different types? For example, a derived type used to model a bank customer may have a long list of components that hold their personal information, as well as component types holding the data of multiple bank accounts, each of which would hold a list of transactions (figure 8.4). Complex types like this will, more often than not, also have components whose values or size (in the case of arrays) are not known at initialization time, but are determined later, either as user input or based on some calculation.

Figure 8.4 illustrates a few prototype classes that could form the basis for a banking app. The top-level class, `Customer`, nests an array of `Account` instances. Since every

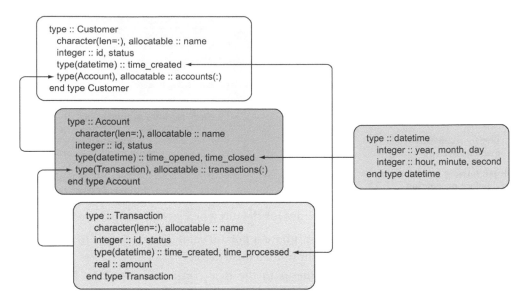

Figure 8.4   A prototype of `Customer`, `Account`, `Transaction`, **and** `datetime` **types as base elements of a banking app**

customer starts without any open accounts, but they can open as many as they want over time, I defined the `accounts` component as an allocatable array. Each account can have any positive number of transactions, which is again modeled using an allocatable array of `Transaction` instances. `Customer`, `Account`, and `Transaction` types each have ID, name, and status components, and one or more components of a `datetime` type. This is an example of a pattern in which one derived type has components of another derived type.

How could we initialize a `Customer` instance if we also needed to provide all its components as arguments to the type constructor, which means all the `Account` instances and all the `Transaction` instances for each account? There are two ways to tackle this. In one approach, we can assign default values for components in the derived type definition, thus removing the requirement to provide these values at initialization. In another approach, we'd write a custom constructor function that would override (which we'll discuss soon) the default one. While the latter is a general solution for derived types of any level of complexity, default values for components will work for the simplest cases, as we'll see in the next subsection.

8.2.5   *Providing default values for derived type components*

Fortran allows you to set a default (initial) value of any component in the derived type definition itself. The following listing provides an example.

```
type :: Person
  character(len-20) :: name
```

```
    integer :: age
    character(len=20) :: occupation = 'Programmer'          Sets the
end type Person                                              default value
```

With the `Person` type defined like this, only the `name` and `age` components are required to be passed to the constructor. If the `occupation` argument is given, it will override the default value:

```
some_person = Person('Allison', 28)                 Will print "Programmer"
print *, some_person % occupation
other_person = Person('Richard', 32, 'Accountant')
print *, other_person % occupation              Will print "Accountant"
```

Obviously, this approach works only for components that have meaningful default values, which is not always the case. For example, if you wanted to have a `Person` type that you could initialize as `some_person = Person()`, and set the component values at a later time, you'd initialize all its components in the type definition block:

```
                    type :: Person
Sets
name                    character(len=20) :: name = ''
to an                   integer :: age = 0              Sets age to an invalid
empty                   character(len=20) :: occupation = ''   value, such as zero
string              end type Person
```

Note that in this case, both the `name` and `occupation` component will be character strings of length 20 but will be initialized to blank characters (empty spaces). For `age`, a zero or a negative number could serve as the default value if an argument isn't provided to the constructor.

As I mentioned earlier, the other, more general approach is to write a custom derived type constructor function to override the default one. This will become important whenever we want to work with the input parameters, such as validate the input, allocate dynamic data, or call any number of other procedures, before returning the new instance to the caller.

8.2.6 *Writing a custom type constructor*

Fortran provides a simple mechanism to override the default type constructor with a user-defined function or subroutine. This gives you the power to do any prep work with type components such as allocation, initialization, input validation, and others.

Let's first define the function that returns an instance of the type whose constructor we're overriding. For example, we could write a custom greeting message that depends on the occupation of the person. Let's say Bob is an engineer, and Davey is a pirate. Their respective greetings could sound something like

```
Bob says Hi, there.
 Davey says Ahoy, matey!
```

We'll write our custom constructor to accept `name`, `age`, and `occupation` as mandatory arguments, and to test for the value of `occupation`. The complete code for this custom constructor is shown in the following listing.

Listing 8.4   Custom constructor for a derived type

```
pure type(Person) function person_constructor( &          The function result must
  name, age, occupation) result(res)                       have the Person type.
  character(len=*), intent(in) :: name
  integer, intent(in) :: age                 Input
  character(len=*), intent(in) :: occupation arguments
  res % name = name                          Setting type components
  res % age = age                            to instance values
  res % occupation = occupation
  if (occupation == 'Pirate') then
    res % greeting_message = 'Ahoy, matey!'  Depending on input,
  else                                       sets custom value
    res % greeting_message = 'Hi, there.'    for a component
  end if
end function person_constructor
```

First, the function that will override the default type constructor must result in that same type, in this case `Person`. It's not required (and sometimes not possible) for the constructor function to be `pure`; however, here it's a reasonable choice, since we don't cause any side effects from within the function. Second, any components that we want to set at the initial time, we can pass as input arguments to this function. In this case, we pass and explicitly assign the `name`, `age`, and `occupation` components. In general, you're not required to initialize any or all components, in which case they'll be left undefined, and you'll need to be careful not to reference them in expressions before first defining them. Also note that here we declare the input character strings as `character(len=*)`, which instructs the compiler to accept character strings of any length as input. Finally, we assign a custom greeting message to the type instance depending on the value of `occupation`.

Now that we have a function that will override the default type constructor, we need to tell the compiler to invoke the `person_constructor` function whenever we use the type instance creation syntax, in this case `Person()`. This is done by specifying the interface to the derived type of the same name:

```
                                    Creates an interface
                                    to the Person type
interface Person
   module procedure :: person_constructor        Points to the
end interface Person                             procedure to be used
                                    Closes the
                                    interface block
```

We use the `module procedure` statement inside the interface block to indicate which procedure to call to create an instance of the derived type `Person`. This interface block must be placed in the declarative section of the module after the definition of the derived type, but before the `contains` statement, as shown in the following listing.

Listing 8.5 Order of type definition, its interface, and the custom constructor function

```
module mod_person

  type :: Person                                    First define
    ...                                             the type.
  end type Person

  interface Person                                  Then specify
    module procedure :: person_constructor          the interface.
  end interface Person

contains

  pure type(Person) function person_constructor()   Finally, define the
    ...                                              custom constructor
  end function person_constructor                    function.

end module mod_person
```

To successfully override the type constructor, you need to make sure of the following:

- The name of the interface matches the name of the derived type.
- The interface points to a valid function defined in the module.
- The function result is of the same type as the derived type.

To see this in action, from the main program, we'd do something like this:

```
type(Person) :: some_person
some_person = Person('Bob', 32, 'Engineer')
print *, trim(some_person % name) // &
  ' says: ' // trim(some_person % greeting_message)
some_person = Person('Davey', 44, 'Pirate')
print *, trim(some_person % name) // &
  ' says: ' // trim(some_person % greeting_message)
```

Note that to be able to assign to the greeting_message component, it needs to have been declared in the derived type definition, which I've omitted here for brevity.

Resolving the constructor interface

When a custom constructor function overrides the default one, the compiler will first try to use the custom function and will check that all the actual arguments (those passed in the function call) match all the dummy arguments (those defined in the function definition) by type and kind. If the arguments are incompatible, the compiler will then attempt to revert to the default type constructor. If the arguments are then incompatible with any of the type components, the compiler will abort with an error message.

This makes Fortran a strongly typed, and a bit more verbose, language, but it also makes it more reliable and robust once compiled and running.

Let's apply the custom constructor technique to our tsunami `Field` derived type. Inside the constructor function, we'll have the chance to do all the necessary prep work, such as calculating start and end indices of the data array, allocating the array in memory, and initializing its values.

8.2.7   *Custom type constructor for the Field type*

Recall that in the previous version of the tsunami simulator, we did quite a lot of prep work before allocating the data arrays. Now that we know how to write a custom constructor, let's apply this technique to initializing the `Field` type. For the time being, let's focus on just finding the start and end indices, allocating the data array, and initializing its values.

Continuing from where we left off in section 8.2.1, we'll now add two more integer components to keep track of the lower and upper bounds of the array, and a real, two-dimensional array to hold the actual values of the field:

```
type :: Field
  character(len=:), allocatable :: name
  integer(int32) :: dims(2), lb(2), ub(2)        Tracks the global array
  real(real32), allocatable :: data(:,:)         size and lower and upper
end type Field                                   bounds of this tile

                                                 Dynamic 2-D array to
                                                 hold the field values
```

Relative to the earlier `Field` definition, we now have three additional components: integer length-2 arrays `lb` and `ub` to represent lower and upper array bounds, respectively, and the data array itself, the allocatable two-dimensional array of real numbers. The goal for our custom constructor is to compute the lower and upper bounds given input dimensions `dims`, use these bounds to allocate the array `data(:,:)` with correct extents (start and end indices), and initialize it to zero. Figure 8.5 illustrates the relationship between the global dimensions `dims = [im, jm]` and lower and upper bounds (`lb` and `ub`, respectively) of the array after the parallel decomposition of the domain.

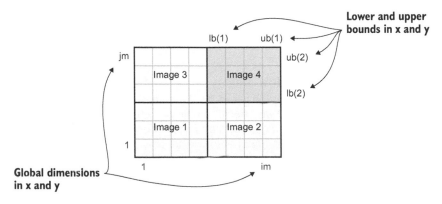

Figure 8.5   Global dimensions and local bounds in a parallel decomposition of a two-dimensional field

The large rectangle in figure 8.5 represents the whole domain that the tsunami simulator is solving for. This domain extends from 1 to `im` in the x direction and from 1 to `jm` in the y direction. When decomposed between four parallel images, each tile extends from `lb(1)` to `ub(1)` in the x direction, and from `lb(2)` to `ub(2)` in the y direction. The following listing shows the first version of our new constructor.

Listing 8.6   Adding lower and upper bound indices and field values to the components

Temporary integer array to store start and end indices

```
type(Field) function field_constructor(name, dims) result(res)
  character(len=*), intent(in) :: name
  integer(int32), intent(in) :: dims(2)
  integer(int32) :: indices(4)
  res % name = name
  res % dims = dims
  indices = tile_indices(dims)
  res % lb = indices([1, 3])
  res % ub = indices([2, 4])
  allocate(res % data(res % lb(1)-1:res % ub(1)+1,&
                      res % lb(2)-1:res % ub(2)+1))
  res % data = 0
end function field_constructor
```

Assigns input name and dimensions to type components

Assigns lower and upper bounds

Allocates the data array

Initializes data to zero

Calculates local tile indices using an external function

This constructor function does a few things. First, we pass the field name and domain dimensions (`dims`) as arguments, and these are assigned to its respective components, `res % name` and `res % dims`. If we left it at this, the constructor would be semantically equivalent to the default constructor from section 8.2.1. However, now that we intend to allocate the data array, we need to do a few more operations.

The second step is to determine the lower and upper bounds for the local image. Recall from the previous chapter that at the beginning of the tsunami program, we break the domain down into pieces and assign each piece to all available images. The local array extents will thus be different for each parallel image, like tiles on a chess board. These extents are calculated in the `tile_indices` function. We've already worked with the one-dimensional variant of this function, and here we apply it for a two-dimensional array. Its implementation is a bit more complex, and you can find it in appendix C.

Finally, once we have the start and end indices computed and stored in `res % lb` (lower bounds) and `res % ub` (upper bounds), respectively, we can use them to allocate the data array, `res % data`. In the `allocate` statement, we give one extra point on each end to account for the halo exchange. Once allocated, we initialize the array to zero to avoid potential undefined behavior due to uninitialized array values.

Notice that we've carefully designed our custom constructor such that we can still create a `Field` instance in the same way as we did at the end of section 8.2.2. Here's an example initialization of fields for water height and velocity with global dimensions of [im, jm]:

```
h = Field('Water height', [im, jm])
u = Field('Water velocity in x', [im, jm])
v = Field('Water velocity in y', [im, jm])
```

If the benefits of derived types for our tsunami simulator haven't been obvious before, they should be now. Whereas before we had to calculate lower and upper bounds and explicitly use them to allocate arrays in memory, this is now all done under the hood for each `Field` instance that we create. This becomes especially powerful once we do significantly more work in the constructor. If you take a look at the code for the `Field` constructor in src/ch08/mod_field.f90, you'll see that we actually need to do a few more things related to the parallel decomposition of the field, which I haven't covered in this section for brevity. Feel free to explore the code, but know that we'll revisit this in chapter 10 when we finish the implementation of the `Field` class.

8.3 Binding procedures to a derived type

Besides storing arbitrary data in type components, we can also *bind* functions and subroutines to the type, making them *type-bound methods*. Similar to the custom constructor procedures, there are two steps to defining a type-bound method. The first is to define the function or subroutine itself, and the second is to specify the binding in the type definition block.

8.3.1 Your first type-bound method

Looking back at our derived-type hello world program from listing 8.2, the subroutine we'll bind to the type is the greeting subroutine, as shown here:

```
subroutine greet(self)                          The input argument will be
  class(Person), intent(in) :: self    ◄──      the type instance itself.
  print *, 'Hello, my name is ' // trim(self % name) // '!'    ◄──
end subroutine greet
                                         We can access type
                                         components from here.
```

Here we have another new syntax element—class. Declaring `class(Person)` instead of `type(Person)` allows any type that's extended (derived) from `Person` to be passed to this subroutine. For now, you don't need to know more about `class` than this. Just think of `class(Person)` as a more general form of `type(Person)`. This argument we'll call `self`, to refer to the type instance itself. This can be any word you want—some people like to use `this`, others prefer some other keyword—it's totally up to you. Once we have the instance passed to the procedure, we can reference any of its components using the `self %` syntax.

The second step involves the actual *binding*—attaching the procedure to the type so that it comes with it wherever the type instance is used. We'll bind the procedure inside the derived type definition, immediately after the `contains` statement:

```
type :: Person
   ...
contains                              ┌─ Separates the components
   procedure, pass(self) :: greet  ◄─┘   and the methods
end type Person                    ◄─┐ Binds this procedure and passes
                                      │ the type as the argument self
```

Notice that binding a procedure to the type is somewhat similar to overriding a default type constructor like we did in section 8.2.6. One key difference is that for a type-bound procedure, the type must be declared as an `intent(in)` (if read-only) or `intent(in out)` argument, rather than being the function result. The other difference is that the method is bound in the `contains` section of the type definition, instead of a separate interface that's used for custom constructors.

8.3.2 Type-bound methods for the Field type

It's now a good time to start planning for the type-bound methods for our `Field` type, as shown in the following listing.

> **Listing 8.7 Type-bound components to be defined for the `Field` type**

```
type :: Field                    Gathers data on        Initializes a
   ...                              one image            bell-shaped
contains                                                 blob
   procedure, pass(self) :: gather        ◄─┐
   procedure, pass(self) :: init_gaussian ◄─┘    Synchronizes data
   procedure, pass(self) :: sync_edges    ◄─┐    between tiles
   procedure, pass(self) :: write  ◄─┐
end type Field                        │ Writes data to file
```

Each of the methods in listing 8.7 has a specific purpose. Recall that in the previous version of the tsunami simulator, we were carrying each of these operations explicitly in the main program. In the derived type approach, these tasks can be defined inside the type-bound methods and invoked when needed, analogous to the setup tasks that we carried out in the custom `Field` constructor. Specifically, here's what each of the methods does:

- `gather`—Applies the `gather` parallel pattern to make the whole array (across all parallel images) available on a single image. We already explored this pattern in chapter 7 when we gathered the whole weather buoy time series array on a single image to find the maximum value. In the tsunami simulator, we'll use this method prior to writing data to a file.
- `init_gaussian`—Sets the values of `Field % data` to a bell-shaped gaussian blob centered at a desired index pair.
- `sync_edges`—Updates the outer edges of `Field % data` to be in sync with the values on neighboring tiles.
- `write`—Writes the data values into a file.

For brevity, I won't go into the implementation details of each of these methods here. However, I encourage you to explore the code and study how they work. These methods are defined in tsunami/src/ch08/mod_field.f90.

Finally, in the next subsection, we'll look into access control for type components and methods.

8.3.3 Controlling access to type components and methods

So far, we've been able to access any type components or methods from the main program without issues. This is also the default behavior: all type components and methods are visible (public), unless otherwise specified. Recall from section 4.2.4 that this is the same behavior as with module variables and procedures, where we used `public` and `private` attributes to explicitly specify which entities can be accessed from outside of the module, and which can't.

The following rules apply:

1 If no `private` or `public` attribute is specified in the declaration, all components and methods are public by default.
2 A single `private` statement inside the derived type definition means that all following components will be declared as `private` by default. The same is true for a single `public` statement.

An interesting caveat to private type components is that they make it impossible to use a default type constructor. Take the type in the next listing, for example.

Listing 8.8 A derived type with a private component

```
type :: Person
  character(len=20) :: name
  integer, private :: age
end type Person
```

If you try to initialize it as

```
type(Person) :: some_person
some_person = Person('Jill', 32)
```

the compiler will yell at you:

```
derived_type_private_error.f90:12:16:

    some_person = Person('Jill', 32)
               1
Error: Component 'age' at (1) is a PRIVATE component of 'person'
```

If, on the other hand, you try `some_person = Person('Jill')`, this happens:

```
derived_type_private_error.f90:12:16:

    some_person = Person('Jill')
               1
Error: No initializer for component 'age' given in the structure constructor
    at (1)
```

The compiler won't budge on this. We can't pass the age parameter because the component is declared as private, and we can't not pass it because the default constructor needs it!

There are two ways to work around this:

- Set a default value for the private component inside the type definition, like we did in section 8.2.5.
- Override the default type constructor with a custom function, like we did in section 8.2.6.

While the first approach is easier to code, it may not be suitable for derived types with many components, and for those components that don't have a meaningful default value. The second approach involves more work but is more generally applicable for anything other than the simplest toy apps. We'll revisit private and public attributes again in chapter 10 when we explore defining built-in operators (such as +, -, etc.) for derived types.

Exercise 1: Working with private components

In some applications, it may be useful to protect certain type components from being directly accessed or modified from the client code; for example, by the user of your software library. Sometimes, you'll want to add some additional instructions or data processing when setting the value of a component. Other times, you may want to validate the value of the component on access.

In this exercise, take the derived type Person with the private age component from listing 8.8, and define methods to get (read) and set (modify) the value of age. Furthermore, raise an error if the input argument to the set method is invalid; for instance, if input age is a negative number.

You can find the solution in the "Answer key" section near the end of this chapter.

Using the so-called getter and setter methods to read to and write from, respectively, a type component is one of the pillars of object-oriented programming: encapsulation. This approach allows you to hide the internal details of the component while allowing access via well-defined methods. It's especially advantageous when writing more complex and robust applications. Here are some cases:

- When the internal implementation of a component changes, your getters and setters will still work as expected without any modifications.
- If you need to check whether a type component is allocated in memory or initialized, you can do so inside the get method.
- If assigning a value to a type component requires any additional calculation or housekeeping, such as counting the number of elements in an array, you could include it in the setter method.

However, whether you'll use encapsulation or not is totally up to you and the app that you build.

8.3.4 *Bringing it all together*

So far in this chapter, we've covered the essentials of Fortran derived types:

- Defining a type and its components
- Declaring and initializing a type instance
- Writing a custom type constructor function
- Turning procedures into type-bound methods
- Accessing components and invoking type-bound methods

Fortran offers much more in this realm, such as extending derived types (known as *inheritance* in object-oriented programming), and abstract types whose methods can do different things depending on the concrete type of the instance. See the "Further reading" section at the end of this chapter to learn more about these concepts.

Before we move on to the final steps in refactoring the tsunami simulator, I have one more exercise for you to complete ("Exercise 2" sidebar), which will tie derived types together with the power of elemental procedures that we learned about in section 3.5.

Exercise 2: Invoking a type-bound method from an array of instances

In section 3.5, you learned about elemental procedures, which you define as if operating strictly on an input scalar (nonarray), but can be readily used on arrays of any size or dimension. Can you rewrite our program from listing 8.2, such that we can define an array of `Person` instances and then invoke the `greet` method on that array? For example

```
call people % greet()
```

should output the following to the screen:

```
Hello, my name is Jill!
Hello, my name is James!
Hello, my name is Allison!
```

You can find the solution in the "Answer key" section near the end of this chapter.

Hint: Recall the use of `impure elemental` attributes from chapter 3.

8.4 *Extending tsunami to two dimensions*

In sections 8.2 and 8.3, we learned the basic syntax of defining a derived type and its components, and binding a method to it. We also began to apply these techniques toward building the `Field` derived type, which we'll use to model the physical quantities that the tsunami simulator predicts, namely water height and velocity. What we haven't quite addressed is the transition from a one-dimensional solver that gave us a profile of a water wave (see figure 8.1), to a two-dimensional solver that will give us a top-down view in an *x-y* plane (figure 8.2).

8.4.1 Going from 1-D to 2-D arrays

Extending the solver from one to two dimensions carries two major implications:

- We'll now be working on 2-D arrays instead of 1-D arrays.
- We'll be solving for two components of velocity (one for each of *x* and *y* axes) and water height, for a total of three equations.

In other words, whereas so far we've been solving for a single velocity u(:) and water height h(:), now we'll be solving for velocities in *x* and *y* axes (u(:,:) and v(:,:), respectively), and for water height h(:,:). This is illustrated in figure 8.6.

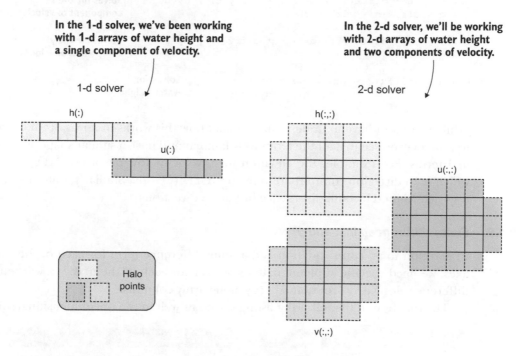

Figure 8.6   Comparison of data arrays for water height and velocity between the 1-D and 2-D tsunami solvers

Also recall the halo points from the previous chapter, which we used to synchronize the array values along the edges with the neighboring tiles. In the 1-D solver, we were exchanging only one value on each side of the tile. However, in the 2-D solver, each data array has four edges and the same number of neighbors. We'll defer this part until chapter 10, where we'll look into it in more detail.

8.4.2   *Updating the equation set*

This is the part that you'll either enjoy very much, if you're into math and physics, or not care for at all, if you're not—expanding our equation set from one to two dimensions. Either way, feel free to read through or skip to the next subsection.

Up to this chapter, our solver consisted of two equations:

```
u = u - (u * diff(u) / dx + g * diff(h) / dx) * dt          ⟵⎤ Solves for water
                                                              ⎦ velocity
h = h - diff(u * (hm + h)) / dx * dt          ⟵⎤ Solves for
                                               ⎦ water height
```

As we saw in the previous subsection, expanding the solver to two dimensions now requires solving three equations, two for each of the velocity components u and v, and one for water height h:

```
u = u - (u * diffx(u) / dx + v * diffy(u) / dy &          ⎤ Solves for the x
    + g * diffx(h) / dx) * dt                              ⎦ component of velocity

v = v - (u * diffx(v) / dx + v * diffy(v) / dy &          ⎤ Solves for the y
    + g * diffy(h) / dy) * dt                              ⎦ component of velocity

h = h - (diffx(u * (hm + h)) / dx &          ⎤ Solves for
        + diffy(v * (hm + h)) / dy) * dt      ⎦ water height
```

While you don't have to understand in detail how this works in terms of fluid dynamics, you may notice that all the terms look familiar and have a similar shape as the original terms. For example, the equation for u velocity now has a v * diffy(u) / dy, which is a *y* direction counterpart to the u * diffx(u) / dx. Similarly, water height h is now determined by both divergence in *x* and *y* directions.

8.4.3   *Finite differences in x and y*

In addition to an extra equation and a finite difference term for each of the *x* and *y* axes, we need specific implementations of diff for each of them. diffx will return a difference along array rows, and diffy along array columns.

The function in the following listing served us well in the one-dimensional solver.

> **Listing 8.9   One-dimensional version of the finite difference function**

```
pure function diff(x) result(dx)
  real(real32), intent(in) :: x(:)          ⟵ Input array
  real(real32) :: dx(size(x))          ⟵⎤ Same size as
  integer(int32) :: i, im                    ⎦ input array
  im = size(x)
  dx = 0
  do concurrent(i = 2:im-1)          ⟵⎤ Can be evaluated
    dx(i) = 0.5 * (x(i+1) - x(i-1))   ⎦ in any order
  end do                          ⟵⎤ Difference between
end function diff                    ⎦ neighboring cells
```

To extend it to two dimensions, we need to adapt the declaration of the input array x and the result dx to both be two-dimensional arrays. Furthermore, for a finite difference in the *x* direction, we'll calculate the difference between i+1 and i-1 elements for each i, applied to the whole-array slice in the *y* direction, as shown in the following listing.

Listing 8.10   Two-dimensional `diff` function for differencing in the *x* direction

```
pure function diffx(x) result(dx)
  real(real32), intent(in) :: x(:,:)          ← The input array is now two-dimensional.
  real(real32) :: dx(size(x, dim=1), size(x, dim=2))   ← Same shape as input array
  integer(int32) :: i, im
  im = size(x, dim=1)        ← Length of the first dimension
  dx = 0
  dx(2:im-1,:) = 0.5 * (x(3:im,:) - x(1:im-2,:))    ← Finite difference with whole-array slices along the y direction
end function diffx
```

In listing 8.10, diffx expects a two-dimensional real array x as the only input argument. This is an assumed-shape array (x(:,:)), so the function will accept a two-dimensional real array of any size. We then use the size built-in function to declare the result dx to have exactly the same size as the input array x. To calculate the difference in x, we apply a whole-array slice in both dimensions. Like before, the result of each element doesn't depend on any other element, so we can evaluate dx in any order by applying a whole-array slice. Note that in the two-dimensional case, diffx only returns the finite difference along the array rows. We'll also need a diffy function to compute the finite difference along the array columns. I leave this to you as an exercise ("Exercise 3" sidebar).

Exercise 3: Computing finite difference in the y direction

We just implemented a two-dimensional variant of the original diff function that we used in the one-dimensional solver, but only for calculating the difference in *x* direction (along rows). Using diffx from listing 8.10 as a template, can you implement the function diffy that will return the finite difference in *y* direction (along columns)? Is either one of these two functions likely to be more efficient than the other, and why?

You can find the solution in the "Answer key" section near the end of this chapter.

If you follow along with the code from GitHub, you can find these functions in tsunami/src/ch08/mod_diff.f90.

However, our job here is not done yet. We still need to be able to pass the Field instance to diffx and diffy, which expect real arrays as input. In the next subsection, I describe how you can make a wrapper function that will accept a Field instance as an input argument and perform a finite difference calculation on its data component.

8.4.4   *Passing a class instance to diffx and diffy functions*

To use finite difference functions directly with our new `Field` instances, we'll make simple wrappers around those functions. First, we'll import the functions and make them available in the `mod_field` module:

```
use mod_diff, only: diffx_real => diffx, &
                    diffy_real => diffy
```
| **Renames on import so we can use the original names**

We want to keep the original names `diffx` and `diffy`, so I've renamed them on import to avoid a name conflict. In the following listing, we define the function `diffx` that takes a `Field` instance as input and calls `diffx_real` under the hood to calculate the finite difference of the input field.

> **Listing 8.11   A wrapper function to pass a `Field` instance to `diffx`**

```
pure function diffx(input_field)
  class(Field), intent(in) :: input_field
  real(real32), allocatable :: diffx(:,:)
  diffx = diffx_real(input_field % data)
end function diffx
```
A Field instance as the input argument

The result is a two-dimensional dynamic array.

Passes the data component to the diff function that operates on real arrays

How about the `diffy` function? Its definition is the same as for `diffx`, except that it invokes `diffy_real` under the hood. I'm omitting its listing here for brevity.

Voilà! We can now import both the `Field` class and the `diffx` and `diffy` wrapper functions from `mod_field`, and use them just like we would plain ol' Fortran arrays, as shown in the following listing.

> **Listing 8.12   Applying a finite difference function to a `Field` instance**

Declares type instances

```
  use mod_field, only: Field, diffx, diffy
  type(Field) :: h, dh_dx, dh_dy
  h = Field('h', [100, 100])
  dh_dx = diffx(h)
  dh_dy = diffy(h)
```
Imports type and functions from a module

Computes finite differences in x and y

Initializes a Field instance with size 100 * 100

In this snippet, I declared two instances of `Field` type, `h` and `dh`. I initialized `h` as a two-dimensional field of 100 by 100 data points, of which I then computed the finite differences using `diffx` and `diffy` and assigned them to `dh_dx` and `dh_dy`, respectively. This technique allows us to use the same solver code as we did with whole-array operations in the previous versions of the tsunami simulator. For example, when computing the value of water height at the next time step, we can write

```
h = h - (diffx(u * (hm + h)) / dx &
       + diffy(v * (hm + h)) / dy) * dt
```

In this snippet, all prognostic variables (that is, variables that we're calculating the solution for) are Field instances—h, hm, u, and v.

> **Compatibility between Field instances and real arrays**
>
> You may have noticed that in listing 8.12, we assigned the result of diffx(h) (a two-dimensional real array) to dh, a Field instance. Normally this shouldn't work, because the compiler on its own doesn't know how to assign a real array to a Field instance. For this to work, we'll need to define the custom assignment operator for the Field class with a special function. We'll explore this and other advanced derived type topics in detail in chapter 10.

8.4.5 Derived type implementation of the tsunami solver

Finally, we're getting close to the home stretch. The following listing provides the (almost) complete code of the derived type implementation of the tsunami simulator. I've omitted the declaration section for brevity.

Listing 8.13 Derived type implementation of the tsunami solver

```
u = Field('u', [im, jm])          Initializes
v = Field('v', [im, jm])          Fields
h = Field('h', [im, jm])
hm = Field('hm', [im, jm])

call h % init_gaussian(decay, ic, jc)   Sets initial water height
call h % sync_edges()                    perturbation and sync

                         Sets a constant
hm = 10.          ◁──┤   mean water depth

call h % write(0)    ◁──┤ Writes the initial
                         height to the file

time_loop: do n = 1, num_time_steps

  if (this_image() == 1) &
    print *, 'Computing time step', n, '/', num_time_steps

  u = u - (u * diffx(u) / dx &
          + v * diffy(u) / dy &       Solves for u
          + g * diffx(h) / dx) * dt   and syncs with
  call u % sync_edges()                neighbors
```

```
v = v - (u * diffx(v) / dx &          Solves for v
        + v * diffy(v) / dy &          and syncs with
        + g * diffy(h) / dy) * dt      neighbors
call v % sync_edges()


h = h - (diffx(u * (hm + h)) / dx &    Solves for h
        + diffy(v * (hm + h)) / dy) * dt   and syncs with
call h % sync_edges()                  neighbors


call h % write(n)

end do time_loop
```

How did we achieve with derived types the same form of the code for evaluating u, v, and h inside the time loop as we did with plain arrays? Before we used familiar arithmetic operators +, -, *, and / and applied them on whole arrays at once. Now, since u, v, and h are derived type instances and not arrays, something else must be going on here. The answer is in user-defined operators for derived types, which we haven't covered yet and will explore in detail in chapter 10.

Why diffx(u) and not u % diffx()?
You may be wondering why we made all external procedures such as init_gaussian, sync_edges, and write type-bound methods of Field, except the finite difference functions diffx and diffy. The answer is simply style preference! Since diffx(u) more closely resembles the mathematical form than u % diffx(), which we certainly could've done, I chose to leave diffx and diffy as regular functions that take an instance of Field as an input argument.

Although I didn't go into detail with the specific implementation of methods such as Field % sync_edges and Field % write, feel free to explore the code in src/ch08/mod_field.f90. You can find the main program in src/ch08/tsunami.f90.

Running the tsunami simulator in two dimensions now produces a circular ripple. (See figure 8.2.) This will be our end result for this chapter. The effect of the initial blob in the center of the domain is the same as if we dropped a pebble in a pond. The perturbation creates a circular ripple that radiates away from the center. If you let the ripple go long enough, it will propagate through the edge and appear on the other side because of the periodic (circular) boundary conditions that are built into the Field % sync_edges method. Like in the one-dimensional case, the pond is 10 meters deep, and the perturbation is about 20 meters wide. After 3 seconds, the wave has propagated about 30 meters.

> **Did you know?**
> The theoretical phase speed of a shallow water wave—that is, the speed at which its crest moves—is equal to the square root of the gravitational acceleration (about 9.8 m/s^2 in most places on Earth) times water depth. For our wave, this gives us a phase speed of 9.9 m/s, consistent with what we saw in figure 8.2. This is just one example of an emerging pattern from basic laws of physics implemented in code. Nowhere in the code did we specify how fast the wave should move, but expressing the physical laws in code on a grid-point level brought up a natural phenomenon on a larger scale. This is exactly how sophisticated dynamic models can predict a hurricane's track days ahead without there even being a concept of a hurricane in the equation set.

That's it for now! In the next chapter, we'll explore generic procedures, which will allow us to use the same procedure with different input data types. We'll also dig into redefining built-in arithmetic operators (+, -, *, /, **) for arbitrary derived types. For example, in the tsunami simulator, this will allow us to treat `Field` instances just like numeric arrays, and do arithmetic operations directly on them.

> **Run it yourself!**
> If you've cloned the application's Git repository on GitHub, you can compile and run it like this:
>
> ```
> make ch08
> cafrun -n 4 src/ch08/tsunami
> ```

8.5 Answer key

This section contains solutions to exercises in this chapter. Skip ahead if you haven't worked through the exercises yet.

8.5.1 Exercise 1: Working with private components

The solution to this exercise involves defining the so-called getter and setter, methods to get and set type components, respectively. Recall our rule of thumb from section 3.3.2 about when to use functions over subroutines. In this case, the get method is read-only and returns a single value, making it a perfect candidate for a pure function. On the other hand, the set method will modify the value of a component, causing a side effect. For this reason, we'll use a subroutine for the setter. The following listing provides the complete solution.

Listing 8.14   Using getters and setters to access a private type component

```
module mod_person

  implicit none

  type :: Person
    character(len=20) :: name
    integer, private :: age = 0          ◄── Sets default
  contains                                    value for brevity
    procedure, pass(self) :: get_age     ◄── Type-bound
    procedure, pass(self) :: set_age     ◄── get method
  end type Person                             Type-bound
                                              set method
contains

  pure integer function get_age(self)
    class(Person), intent(in) :: self
    get_age = self % age                 ◄── Reads age from
  end function get_age                        the component

  subroutine set_age(self, age)
    class(Person), intent(in out) :: self
    integer, intent(in) :: age
    if (age < 0) error stop 'Age must not be negative.'   ◄── Raises an error
    self % age = age                     ◄── Sets the component    if bad input
  end subroutine set_age                      from input

end module mod_person

program derived_type_private
  use mod_person, only: Person
  implicit none
  type(Person) :: some_person = Person('Jill')   ◄── Will return the
  print *, 'Age before set_age():', &                 default value
            some_person % get_age()    ◄──
  call some_person % set_age(33)       ◄── Sets a new
  print *, 'Age after set_age():', &        value for age
            some_person % get_age()    ◄── Will return 33
  print *, 'Setting age to a negative number.'
  call some_person % set_age(-5)       ◄── Bad input will
end program derived_type_private            trigger an error.
```

Note that I've set the default value for age to avoid having to write a custom type constructor function here. Thus, if we try to get its value before setting it to anything else,
it will still have its initial value.

Compiling and running this program yields

```
Age before set_age():           0
Age after set_age():           33
Setting age to a negative number.
ERROR STOP age must not be negative.
```

8.5.2 Exercise 2: Invoking a type-bound method from an array of instances

To allow invoking the `greet()` method on arrays of type instances, the main trick is to declare it as `elemental`. Not so fast, though! Recall from section 3.5 that the `elemental` attribute also implies `pure`, which would be violated in this case because printing a message to the screen is a side effect. To work around this, we have to specify the `impure` attribute alongside `elemental`, as shown in the following listing.

Listing 8.15 Invoking a type-bound method from an array of instances

```
module mod_person
  type :: Person
    character(len=20) :: name
  contains
    procedure, pass(self) :: greet          Declares as elemental
  end type Person                           to work on both
contains                                    scalars and arrays
  impure elemental subroutine greet(self)  ◁─┘
    class(Person), intent(in) :: self
    print *, 'Hello, my name is ' // trim(self % name) // '!'
  end subroutine greet
end module mod_person

program hello_derived_types        Declares and
  use mod_person, only: Person     initializes an array of
  implicit none                    Person instances
  type(Person) :: people(3) = &   ◁─┘
    [Person('Jill'), Person('James'), Person('Allison')]
  call people % greet()
end program hello_derived_types
```

The other necessary change to the program is to declare an array of `Person` instances. Here, I used an array constructor that we learned about back in section 5.2.2.

8.5.3 Exercise 3: Computing finite difference in y direction.

Most of the code for this function is the same as in `diffx`. However, we need to be careful to get the correct loop length, and to calculate the difference over the second index instead of the first, as shown in the following listing.

Listing 8.16 Computing finite difference in y direction

```
pure function diffy(x) result(dx)
  ! Centered finite difference in y.
  real(real32), intent(in) :: x(:,:)
  real(real32) :: dx(size(x, dim=1), size(x, dim=2))   Computes the finite
  integer(int32) :: j, jm                              difference along the
  jm = size(x, dim=2)                                  second dimension
  dx = 0                                               using whole-array
  dx(:,2:jm-1) = 0.5 * (x(:,3:jm) - x(:,1:jm-2))  ◁─   arithmetic
end function diffy
```

Gets the
size of the
second
dimension
└▷

Is one of these two functions likely to be more efficient than the other, and why? Let's take a look at the order of indexing in each case. In diffx we're solving for dx(i,:) for i = 1:im, whereas in diffy we're solving for dx(:,j) for j = 1:jm. Recall from chapter 1 that Fortran arrays are sequentially laid out in memory with the leftmost index varying the fastest (column-major), unlike C or Python, where the rightmost index varies the fastest (row-major). This means that the elements of dx(:,j) are all contiguous in memory, which most CPUs can take advantage of. On the other hand, the elements of dx(i,:) are strided with an equal offset of im, which can cause the CPU to load the values from RAM on each iteration. Figure 8.7 illustrates this situation.

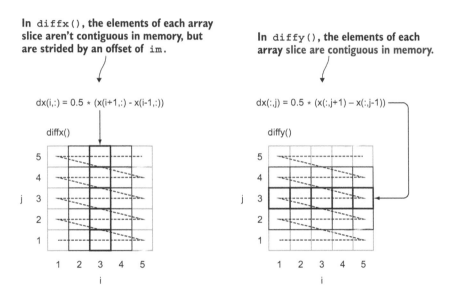

Figure 8.7 Layout of two-dimensional arrays in memory and implications for finite difference functions. The dashed lines indicate the layout of data in memory.

diffy may thus perform better in some cases, depending on the hardware, compiler, and/or size of input array x. You can read more about the implications of column- and row-major ordering here: http://mng.bz/wB5W.

While unrelated to derived types, I hope this exercise served as a refresher on functions, array indexing, and whole-array arithmetic that we covered in chapters 3–5.

8.6   *New Fortran elements, at a glance*

- type/end type—Defining a new derived type.
- type(Person) :: some_person—Declaring a new instance of a derived type.
- some_person = Person('Jill')—Initializing a new instance of a derived type.
- some_person % name—Accessing a type component.

- `call some_person % greeting()`—Invoking a type-bound method.
- `public` and `private`—Attributes to allow or restrict access to a type component or method. (They work the same way as in modules.)

8.7 Further reading

- Chapter 15 ("Object-oriented programming") of *Modern Fortran Explained: Incorporating Fortran 2018*, by Michael Metcalf, John Reid, and Malcolm Cohen, Oxford University Press.
- *Scientific Software Design: The Object-Oriented Way*, by Damian Rouson, Jim Xia, and Xiaofeng Xu, Cambridge University Press, 2011.
- "Object-oriented programming" on *Fortran Wiki*, http://mng.bz/qM0E.

Summary

- Derived types allow you to model complex data structures.
- A derived type is defined inside the `type`/`end type` construct, in the declarative section of the code.
- A derived type can contain any number of variables (called components) and procedures (called methods) bound to it.
- A derived type can contain other derived type instances as components, as well as extend other derived types.
- Derived types are the basic element for object-oriented programming in Fortran.

Generic procedures and operators for any data type

Every useful computer program takes some input data, performs a number of operations on that data, and outputs the results. The data that the program works with is stored in variables of various types. Different languages handle different types with different strictness. Fortran, being a strongly typed language, is quite strict about how you pass input arguments to functions and subroutines. Specifically, the data types of arguments between the procedure invocation and definition must match, or else the compiler will abort with an error message. This strong typing discipline has its pros and cons. On the one hand, it can be tedious to have to write the same procedure for multiple different data types. On the other hand, Fortran's strong typing pushes you to write correct and robust code. Fortunately, Fortran provides a mechanism to use the same procedure name to invoke different specific procedures that operate on different data types. This mechanism is the generic procedure, which is also the main topic of this chapter.

This is where several elements of the language come to work together. In chapter 2, we wrote our first arithmetic expressions with built-in numeric types such as `integer` and `real`. In chapter 3, we learned how to write functions and subroutines to define these expressions as reusable miniprograms that we can invoke as many times as needed. In chapter 5, we worked with arrays, Fortran's fundamental data collection. In chapter 7, we focused mostly on the concept of images and coarrays for parallel processing—we'll take a break from these for this chapter. Finally, in chapter 8, you learned how to define your own custom data types of arbitrary complexity. In this chapter, we'll tie these elements together in a powerful concept called *generic procedures* that will help you write cleaner and more expressive code. Generic procedures allow you to define a function or subroutine that accepts input arguments of different data types or shapes. We'll wrap up the chapter with an intro to custom operators and overriding built-in operators, which will serve as a hook for chapter 10, where we'll explore the power of user-defined operators for derived types.

9.1 Analyzing weather data of different types

Consider the following scenario: You're fresh out of school, or perhaps ready to move on to the next step in your career. You're looking into a number of cities around the world to live in: Seattle, New York City, Miami, London, Mexico City, and a few others. For many people, myself included, weather is an important factor for a place to live, especially if you're looking to settle down and build a nest. In this exercise, we'll process a relatively long weather dataset and look for the most pleasant climate to live in. I know, this is subjective, but bear with me for the sake of this exercise.

What makes a climate pleasant to live in? The answer is different for everybody. Personally, I like it dry, warm, and breezy, with clear skies. I often wonder which city on earth has the ideal climate for me. This question is difficult to answer because of so many different factors that contribute to weather and climate. Some cities are cool and rainy, others are warm and sunny. Some cities have a relatively steady breeze, allowing for good ventilation and clean air, while others can suffer from pollution and smog. For example, Miami (Florida) has gorgeous (warm and dry) winters but gets hot and humid in the summer. On the other hand, Los Angeles (California) is known for its clear and sunny days, but is overall colder throughout the year.

To get to a quantitative and more objective answer, we'll analyze the time series of weather measurements such as air temperature, humidity, wind speed, and number of clear sky days. In other words, we'll quantify the *climate* of different cities around the world.

What is climate?

I often see people confusing weather and climate with each other. Weather is the actual state of the atmosphere at any given time. As I write this sidebar, it's the evening before New Year's Eve, and my wife and I just got back from a walk in one of the

(continued)

wildlife preserves here in South Florida where we live. The weather was clear with few clouds (which made for a beautiful sunset), relatively warm and dry, with a decent breeze. What the atmosphere is like right here and now: that's *weather*.

On the other hand, climate is the weather averaged over long periods of time. It's a statistical concept—you never directly experience climate itself. There are many games you can play or questions you can ask in the context of climate. For example, what were the warmest and coldest temperatures ever measured in New York City on December 31, of all the years on record? Although these are two weather extremes, determining their values requires processing the complete time series of temperatures in that location. You could also ask, Which city on Earth was warmest on average in 2018? The list goes on. In this exercise, we'll focus on the simplest statistical metric used in climate analysis—the arithmetic average.

What's the connection between generic procedures and this exercise? The weather parameters in the dataset will be of different types: temperature and humidity are floating-point values (degrees Fahrenheit), wind speed is an integer (in knots), and clear sky data is indicated as a Boolean `True` or `False`. In this exercise, we'll first implement the function to average an array of each of the different types. Then we'll override these specific functions with a single generic function. Finally, we'll use the same generic function in the main program to average data of different types.

9.1.1   *About the data*

The dataset that we'll work in this chapter is based on weather data collected at automated ground stations all over the world and gathered every hour to a central database. The specific weather parameters, their units, and their data types are summarized in table 9.1.

Table 9.1   Variables and their units and data types in the weather dataset

Column	Variable	Units	Data type	Example value
1	Temperature	Fahrenheit	`real`	57.9
2	Humidity	%	`real`	93.0
3	Wind speed	Knots	`integer`	10
4	Clear sky	None	`logical`	False

The key factor here is that the dataset consists of three different data types: `integer`, `real`, and `logical`. Don't worry about the specific units—since we'll be looking for minimum and maximum values of the averages, the units are irrelevant for the analysis.

Here's a sample of the post-processed data that we'll be working with—the first 10 lines of a post-processed data file for London Heathrow:

```
head data/processed/EGLL.csv
44.6,81.2,16,True
44.6,75.68,16,True
44.6,75.68,14,True
42.8,81.07,13,True
44.6,75.68,17,True
42.8,75.5,12,True
42.8,75.5,11,True
42.8,81.07,12,False
42.8,75.5,13,False
42.8,75.5,9,True
```

⟵ **Lists first 10 lines of a file**

Here I used the Linux utility `head` to print the first 10 columns of the data file EGLL.csv. `EGLL` is the international airport code for Heathrow Airport in London, England. This data is significantly reduced from its original content to minimize the data volume in the source code repository. If you're interested in seeing what the complete dataset looks like, type `make download` from the `data` directory.

In this exercise, we'll work with the weather data for the year 2018. If you want to apply this code to a larger dataset, or data from a different year, you can use the scripts included in the repo to get more data.

> **Getting the code and data**
>
> If you want to download the whole source code to follow along as you read the chapter, you can do so by cloning the repository from GitHub:
>
> ```
> git clone https://github.com/modern-fortran/generic-procedures
> ```
>
> The repository also includes the sample data we'll use in this exercise, as well as scripts to download more data; for example, for different cities and/or time periods.

An example plot of temperature, humidity, and wind speed measured at the Miami International Airport is shown in figure 9.1.

There's a lot of data in this figure—one data point for every five minutes for wind speed, and every hour for temperature and humidity. In this chapter, we'll crunch all of it for 10 different cities around the world. Most of these are from airport weather stations, local or international, but some automated weather stations could be located in city parks or in the countryside.

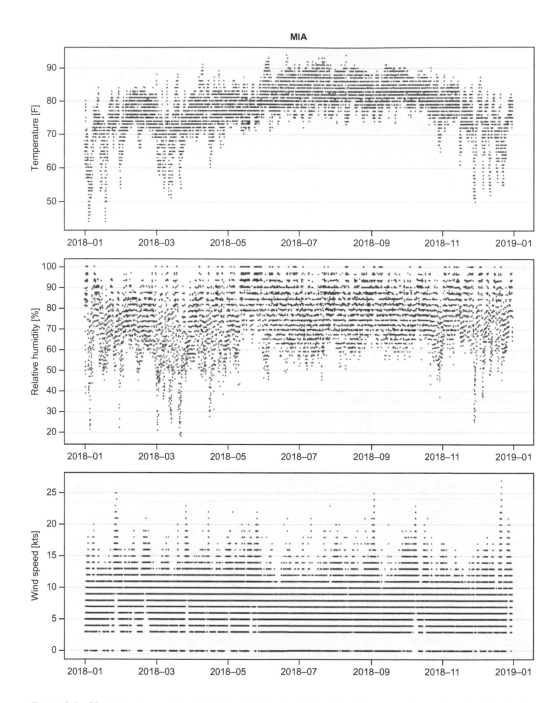

Figure 9.1   Measurements of temperature, relative humidity, and wind speed at the Miami International Airport in 2018

9.1.2 Objectives

As I said earlier, we're looking to parse weather data to identify the city with the most pleasant climate (average weather). What is the most pleasant climate? The answer will likely vary depending on who you ask, but for me, that means

1 *Highest average temperature*—I prefer to avoid cold winters if possible. Of course, high average temperatures would also come from hot summers, which can be unpleasant for many. However, it's a trade I'm willing to make.

2 *Lowest average humidity*—I like it warm but don't like to sweat profusely. Warm and dry weather is my favorite for spending time outdoors.

3 *Highest average wind*—The more wind on average, the better ventilated the area, which reduces the chance of stagnant and polluted air. Large cities with weaker winds on average are known for higher occurrences of smog (a term coined by blending smoke and fog).

4 *Clear days*—The more the better.

To be fair, these are quite crude and arbitrary criteria, but they will do for the sake of this exercise. For each city, we'll calculate the score for each of the four variables: temperature (the higher the better), humidity (the lower the better), wind speed (the higher the better), and the clear sky frequency (the higher the better). The total score is simply an arithmetic average of the four specific scores. I'll defer the interpretation of these scores to the end of the exercise later in this chapter. At the end, we'll end up with a neat little score table like this, showing the results of our final weather averaging program:

```
City | Temp.  | Humidity | Wind  | Clear | Total
Code | Score  | Score    | Score | Score | Score
-----+--------+----------+-------+-------+------
EGLL   0.02     0.04       1.00    0.97    0.51
LAX    0.45     0.14       0.72    1.00    0.58
LYBE   0.15     0.13       0.80    0.05    0.28
MIA    1.00     0.00       0.77    0.86    0.66
MMMX   0.41     0.57       0.68    0.47    0.53
NYC    0.10     0.13       0.00    0.41    0.16
OIII   0.55     1.00       0.63    0.41    0.65
SEA    0.00     0.10       0.86    0.58    0.39
SKBO   0.14     0.01       0.50    0.00    0.16
ZGSZ   0.90     0.03       0.80    0.27    0.50
```

The city code is the unique international code for each weather station. The cities are London, United Kingdom (EGLL); Los Angeles, California (LAX); Belgrade, Serbia (LYBE); Miami, Florida (MIA); Mexico City, Mexico (MMMX); New York City, New York (NYC); Tehran, Iran (OIII); Seattle, Washington (SEA); Bogota, Colombia (SKBO); and Shenzhen, China (ZGSZ). I chose these ten locations for this exercise; however, if you want, you can follow the direction from the previous subsection and download data for your location, or as many other locations as you want.

9.1.3   *Strategy for this exercise*

To find the city with the optimal climate, we'll go through the following steps:

1 For each city, read the time series data of temperature, humidity, wind speed, and clear/cloudy skies.
2 For each city, compute the average value of each weather parameter.
3 Assign scores to each city using the criteria from the previous subsection.
4 Sum up the scores to find the winner.

Sounds easy, right? We covered most of the logistics around reading and processing time series data in chapters 5 and 7. Here, we'll focus on implementing the generic `average` function that can operate on `integer`, `real`, or `logical` data.

9.2   *Type systems and generic procedures*

Before jumping into writing our first generic procedure, let's briefly introduce a few new concepts that will get us there:

- *Strong typing*—As I mentioned earlier, Fortran is a strongly typed language, which means that the variables and expressions you pass as input arguments to procedures must match the data type of arguments declared in the function or subroutine definition.
- *Specific procedure*—A specific procedure is the implementation of a function or subroutine that's specific to the input data type. For example, if you're writing a function to average integer or real numbers, you'd write specific functions—for example, `average_int` and `average_real`.
- *Generic procedure*—A generic procedure is the interface that can refer to a number of different specific procedures. If you define a generic interface `average` that overrides specific `average_int` and `average_real` functions that operate on integers and reals, respectively, then you'll be able to invoke `average` with either data type.

Although Fortran is both statically and strongly typed, don't confuse the two. I'll explain the difference in the following subsection.

9.2.1   *Static versus strong typing*

Static and *strong* typing are often confused and used interchangeably. However, they describe two different properties of a programming language.

A statically typed language assumes that all variables must have either a manifestly declared data type (like in Fortran or C) or a data type inferred from their use (like in Julia, Nim, or Rust) at compile time. The opposite of static typing is dynamic typing, where the types of all variables are evaluated at runtime. Python, JavaScript, and Lisp are a few examples of dynamically typed languages. Static versus dynamic typing is thus about *when* (at compile time or runtime) the types of variables and expressions are determined.

Strong typing refers to the level of type checking that's done when combining variables of different types in expressions, or when passing an argument of one type to a function that expects another type. For example, Fortran allows type coercion, or so-called mixed-mode arithmetic (see section 5.2.2), where lower numeric types such as integers are promoted to real or complex. On the other hand, passing an argument of one type to a procedure that expects another is not allowed. This very property makes Fortran a strongly typed language. The opposite of strong typing is weak (or loose) typing. JavaScript is a typical example of a weakly typed language, since you can pass any variable to any function.

It's worth noting that whereas static and dynamic typing are clearly defined and distinct, the difference between strong and weak typing is more fuzzy. I give a couple of examples in table 9.2.

Table 9.2 Examples of languages and their type systems

Typing	Static	Dynamic
Strong	Fortran	Python
Weak	C	JavaScript

Many other languages would fit in one of the cells in this table. For simplicity, I include only the characteristic languages that a scientist or engineer is likely to have in their arsenal.

To be honest, you don't need generic procedures and custom operators to survive as a Fortran developer. However, they'll make your code easier to understand, use, and extend. This is aligned with our case for functions, modules, or derived types. Although none of these language elements are absolutely necessary to solve any programming problem, they allow you to design elegant solutions to difficult problems.

9.3 Writing your first generic procedure

In this section, you'll learn how generic procedures work, how to implement them, and how to apply them to data of different data types. We'll start by identifying the problem with strong typing, as we attempt to pass data of one type to a procedure that expects a different type.

9.3.1 The problem with strong typing

In the previous section, we learned that Fortran's strong typing discipline prohibits passing arguments of incompatible data types to procedures. This means that when you write a function that expects a real number as input, you can't simply pass an integer as an input argument. This would trigger a compile-time error. You can see this for yourself right now. Start with a basic function to compute the average of a one-dimensional real array:

```
pure real function average(x) result(res)        Real I-D array
  real, intent(in) :: x(:)
  res = sum(x) / size(x)                   Sum of all elements divided
end function average                        by the number of elements
```

Attempting to invoke average with an array of integers—say, average([1, 6, 4])—the compiler will report an error:

```
gfortran mod_average_incompatible.f90        File name, row, and column
mod_average_incompatible.f90:20:10:          where the error occurred

  print *, average([1, 6, 4])            The source code that
          1                              triggered the error
Error: Type mismatch in argument 'x' at (1);
       passed INTEGER(4) to REAL(4)          The error message
```

In this case, the error message is quite helpful. The compiler tells us that there's a type mismatch for argument x, as well as which data type was passed (INTEGER(4)) and which was expected (REAL(4)). Here, the number 4 corresponds to the default type kind of 4 bytes—int32 and real32 literal constants from the iso_fortran_env module. We could do due diligence and make sure that we pass an argument with a matching type to every procedure. However, being able to pass data to a function without having to worry about the type is convenient and will help you write shorter and more correct code.

To implement a generic function to compute an average of arrays of different data types, we'll go through the following steps:

1 Write the specific functions for each data type; these functions must have unique names.
2 Write the interface (generic procedure) that points to the specific functions.
3 Make the interface publicly available in the module.
4 Apply the generic procedures to the data.

9.3.2 *Writing the specific functions*

In this subsection, we'll implement all three specific functions, one for each data type that we intend to parse: integer, real, and logical. We'll need the following specific functions:

- average_real(x)—Returns an average value of a one-dimensional real array x. This function will operate on temperature and humidity time series.
- average_int(x)—Returns a real average value of a one-dimensional integer array x. This function will operate on wind speed time series.

- `average_logical(x)` —Returns a real average value of a one-dimensional logical array x, where `True` values are represented as ones, and `False` values as zeros. This function will operate on time series of clear sky data.

Let's write the first specific function, which will operate on `real` arrays. Note that we already wrote this function in section 5.3, when analyzing stock price time series.

THE REAL IMPLEMENTATION

The implementation of the `average` function for real numbers is the simplest of the three. As noted, it's simple enough that we already implemented one in chapter 5. The following listing reproduces that function.

Listing 9.1 A function to average `real` arrays

```
pure real function average_real(x) result(res)
  real, intent(in) :: x(:)
  res = sum(x) / size(x)
end function average_real
```

Assumed size, one-dimensional real array

Divides the sum by the number of elements

This function takes a real, one-dimensional array x as input, computes the sum of all its elements (`sum(x)`), and divides it by the total number of elements (`size(x)`) to get us to the arithmetic average. Recall the rules about type coercion and mixed mode arithmetic from section 5.2.2. When you mix different numeric types (such as `integer` and `real`) in an expression, a variable or expression of a lower type is always promoted to the higher type (`integer` < `real` < `complex`) before evaluating the operation. Here, `sum(x)` evaluates to a real number because x is a real array, while `size(x)` always returns an integer. However, since here we're dividing a real number by an integer, the integer is promoted to a real before the division operation is evaluated. Unlike before, I've appended the name of the input type (`real`) to the function name so we can set it apart from other specific functions.

THE INTEGER IMPLEMENTATION

The analogous averaging functions on integers should work the same way as for reals, thanks to both `sum` and `size` functions supporting either type. However, unlike with `average_real`, here we have to be careful about integer division when evaluating `sum(x) / size(x)`. For example, if x is `[1., 1., 2.]` (real numbers), `sum(x) / size(x)` will evaluate to `1.66666663`, as expected. However, if x is `[1, 1, 2]` (integers), `sum(x) / size(x)` will evaluate to `1`, because dividing one integer with another always returns an integer. Now that x is an integer array, we can't rely on automatic type coercion to get the correct result. We need to do some extra work to make sure we don't fall prey to unintended integer division, like in the example we just considered.

A dilemma comes up about whether the result should be an integer or a real, considering the integer array as input. Ultimately, this depends on your application and how the result will be used. In certain applications, an integer average result is desired (for example, passing an average age of a population to a function that expects an integer). For our example, we'll just stick to a real-typed result for all specific implementations of the average function, as shown in the following listing.

Listing 9.2   A function to average an array of integers

```
pure real function average_int(x) result(res)
  integer, intent(in) :: x(:)
  res = real(sum(x), kind=kind(res)) / size(x)
end function average_int
```

Assumed size, one-dimensional real array

Explicitly promotes the sum to a real number before dividing

While at its core similar to the average_real implementation, here we need to take special care with the conversion from integer to real. For an integer array x, both sum(x) and size(x) return an integer by definition. As integer division always returns an integer, we'd actually get an incorrect result in any case where sum(x) is not divisible by size(x). We can work around this by explicitly promoting sum(x) to a real number before dividing by size(x).

Here we've used two built-in functions:

- *real*—Given input variable or expression x, real(x) returns its value as a real number. x must be of type integer, real, or complex. This function accepts an optional kind parameter, where you can specify the desired type kind of the result (for example real32, real64, or real128). Note the distinction between the built-in function real() and the real data type.
- *kind*—Given input variable or expression x, kind(x) returns the type kind value of x. Use this whenever you need to make sure that the function real promotes to the kind that you need, rather than the default one (real32 on most compilers and architectures).

In listing 9.2, I used the built-in function real to explicitly promote the integer to a real number. If you remember the type coercion rules from section 5.2.2, I could've done this implicitly:

```
res = (1.0 * sum(x)) / size(x)
```

Here, we implicitly promote sum(x) to a real number by multiplying it by 1.0 (a real number). We carefully enclose this operation in parentheses to ensure that it evaluates before the division with size(x), which would otherwise return an integer—not what we intended. Whether you choose to promote types explicitly or implicitly is a matter of style. Implicit usually leads to more concise code, while explicit clearly communicates the intent. Although it may take a few thought cycles to understand why we're multiplying a number by 1.0, real(sum(x)) is as clear as you can get. This especially makes a difference when the person reading the code is your colleague from the office next door, your open source contributor in Japan, or yourself a few years from now.

TIP We repeat Tim Peters's mantra from the Zen of Python: "Explicit is better than implicit." Explicit type promotion, while more verbose, will almost always be clearer and easier to understand.

This takes care of `integer` and `real` data. On to `logical`.

THE LOGICAL IMPLEMENTATION

For the logical `average` implementation, we need to do something a little bit different. This is because the average value of a logical array is not well defined. The most intuitive interpretation of an average of `True` or `False` values is perhaps the probability of occurrence. If an array has 99 elements that are `False` and one that's `True`, the average value could be interpreted as 0.01 truth probability, or 1%. For our weather average application, where we want to quantify how often the skies are clear or cloudy, this is just the right meaning, as shown in the following listing.

Listing 9.3 A function to average an array of logical values

```fortran
pure real function average_logical(x) result(res)
  logical, intent(in) :: x(:)
  res = real(count(x), kind=kind(res)) / size(x)
end function average_logical
```
⟵ **Counts the number of True elements, casts it to real, then divides by the total number**

Here, we're using the built-in function `count`, which returns the number of elements in a logical array x (whether a variable or an expression) that evaluate as `.true.`. By counting the number of `True` elements and dividing that by the size of the array, we effectively define our average of the logical array as a real number between 0, if all elements are `.false.`, and 1, if all elements are `.true.`.

And that's all as far as specific procedures are concerned. Our next step is to write the generic interface that will override these procedures. If you're following along with the code checked out from the GitHub repo, these functions are implemented in src/mod_average.f90.

9.3.3 *Writing the generic interface*

At this point, we have our specific procedures implemented. Now we need to define the interface such that we can simply invoke `average(temperature)`, `average(wind_speed)`, and so on, rather than having to match the data types, like `average_real(temperature)`, `average_int(wind_speed)`, and so on.

To do so, we'll open an interface block at the top of the module, before the `contains` statement, that will look like the following listing.

Listing 9.4 Defining a generic interface to specific procedures

```fortran
module mod_average
  ...
  private
  public :: average
  ...
```
Declares everything as private by default

⟵ **Makes only the generic function "average" publicly accessible**

Beginning of the interface

```
interface average
    module procedure :: average_int
    module procedure :: average_real
    module procedure :: average_logical
    end interface average
    ...
contains
    ...
end module mod_average
```

Lists all the specific procedures to be accessible by the generic name

End of interface

Specific procedure definitions go here.

The interface specifies the name of our new generic procedure, `average`, and lists the specific procedures that are to be overridden. Recall the interface that we wrote in the previous chapter (section 8.2.6) to override the default type constructor with a custom function:

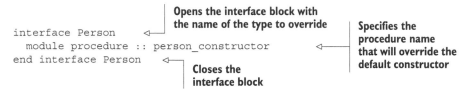

Opens the interface block with the name of the type to override

```
interface Person
    module procedure :: person_constructor
end interface Person
```

Specifies the procedure name that will override the default constructor

Closes the interface block

We opened the `interface` block with the name that we'll use to invoke the constructor (the name of the type, `Person`), and inside we specified the name of the function that will be called whenever we use the type name. Here, we're using the exact same syntax rules, but for a slightly different purpose. We're listing all the specific procedures that can be accessed with a generic name. Note that you can list all your specific procedures inside the `interface` block on the same line or a separate `module procedure` line:

```
interface average
    module procedure :: average_int, average_real, average_logical
end interface average
```

In essence, we're using the same mechanism here as we did for a custom type constructor, this time for a new concept. You could use the same mechanism to define multiple type constructors that could take different sets of input arguments.

Which specific procedure will be invoked?

You may be wondering, If I define my generic interface to point to many different specific procedures, how does the compiler know which specific procedure to invoke? The simple answer is that it has to be obvious! All specific procedures that are overridden by a generic interface must be uniquely distinct. The Fortran standard defines clear rules on this matter. Two functions `f1` and `f2` can be distinguished in the following ways:

- *Number of positional arguments*—`f1(x)` and `f2(x, y)` are distinct because they expect a different number of arguments.
- *Type*—`f1(x)` and `f2(i)`, where `x` and `i` are declared real and integer, respectively, are distinct because their arguments have different types.
- *Rank (number of dimensions)*—`f1(x(:))` and `f2(x(:,:))` are distinct because they expect arrays of different ranks (1 and 2, respectively) as input arguments.
- *Number of optional arguments*—Prior to Fortran 2018, the compiler wasn't expected to distinguish between procedures that expect a different number of optional arguments, but now it is.

At this point, we can import this function in our main program and invoke it with integer, real, or logical data, as shown in the next listing.

Listing 9.5 Importing and applying the generic procedure in the main program

```
program weather_average
  ...
  use mod_average, only: average
  ...
  do n = 1, nm
    dataset = weather_data('data/processed/' &     ← Reads data from the
                       // trim(cities(n)) // '.csv')    file into a custom
                                                        structure
    temperature(n) = &
      average(denan(dataset % temperature))
    humidity(n) = average(denan(dataset % humidity))   ← Removes NaNs
    wind_speed(n) = average(denan(dataset % wind_speed))  from the array
    clear_sky(n) = average(dataset % clear_sky)    ←      and averages it
  end do
  ...                                              Averages
end program weather_average                        the array
```

I'll just touch on two items here for brevity. The first is the `weather_data` derived type that I use to read the data from the post-processed CSV files and store arrays into type components. We covered derived types in chapter 8, and this type is fairly straightforward. I encourage you to take a look at its implementation in src/mod_weather_data.f90. The second item is the `denan` function, which I use to remove any NaN (not a number) values from the arrays before passing them to the `average` function. (See also section 7.2.4 and src/mod_arrays.f90.)

What's a NaN?

A *NaN* is a special value for a real number that can't be represented otherwise. Try doing something naughty like dividing by zero—you'll get a NaN. The square root of a negative real number? NaN!

> **(continued)**
> NaNs were introduced to widespread use by the IEEE 754 standard for floating-point numbers in 1985, along with a few other special values, such as infinities of either sign.

Figure 9.2 illustrates what goes on under the hood when you pass, for example, an array to a generic function that's just an interface to a few different specific functions.

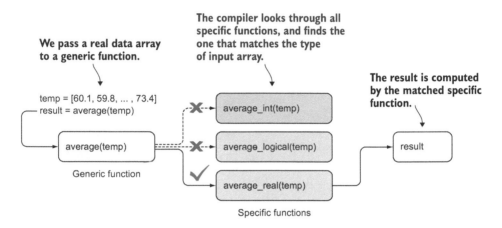

Figure 9.2   From the `real` input array to the result of a generic function

We start with a real array of air temperature values. We pass this array to a generic `average` function. Thanks to static typing, the compiler knows the type of the input array (`real`), and it has a list of specific procedures that the interface `average` overrides:

```
interface average
  module procedure :: average_int
  module procedure :: average_logical
  module procedure :: average_real
end interface average
```

The compiler then goes in order and checks whether the type, rank, and number of arguments in the specific procedure definition match the input arguments passed to the generic procedure. Integer? No. Logical? No. Real? Match! The specific function `average_real` is thus matched at compile time with this particular invocation of the generic `average(temp)`.

Exercise 1: Specific `average` **function for a derived type**

We just went through implementing the specific `average` function for three built-in types: `real`, `integer`, and `logical`. This will make for quite a flexible generic function. However, more complex and real-world apps will likely require encapsulating the arrays in custom derived types, such as the type `Field` that we're now using in the tsunami simulator. Consider this type definition:

```
type :: Field
  real, allocatable :: data(:)
end type Field
```

Your goal for this exercise is to implement the specific `average` function that will accept a `type(Field)` instance as the input argument and return the average value of its `data(:)` component. Can you write this function such that it works regardless of whether the type of `Field % data(:)` is `real`, `integer`, or `logical`?

You can find the solution to this exercise in the "Answer key" section near the end of this chapter.

9.3.4 Results and complete program

Finally, we approach the home stretch. Here's how the output of our program appears:

```
City | Temp.  | Humidity | Wind  | Clear | Total
Code | Score  | Score    | Score | Score | Score
-----+--------+----------+-------+-------+------
EGLL   0.02     0.04       1.00    0.97    0.51
LAX    0.45     0.14       0.72    1.00    0.58
LYBE   0.15     0.13       0.80    0.05    0.28
MIA    1.00     0.00       0.77    0.86    0.66
MMMX   0.41     0.57       0.68    0.47    0.53
NYC    0.10     0.13       0.00    0.41    0.16
OIII   0.55     1.00       0.63    0.41    0.65
SEA    0.00     0.10       0.86    0.58    0.39
SKBO   0.14     0.01       0.50    0.00    0.16
ZGSZ   0.90     0.03       0.80    0.27    0.50
```

From this table, we can see which city has the highest score for each respective variable. For example, Miami (MIA) is the warmest but also the most humid city in the group, yielding scores of 1 and 0 for temperature and humidity, respectively. Tehran, Iran (OIII), has the lowest humidity, yielding the best humidity score, and gets all around decent scores for all other variables. Despite the high humidity, the overall winner is Miami, with a total score of 0.66, followed closely by Tehran, with a total score of 0.65. New York City (NYC) and Bogota, Colombia (SKBO), share the bottom place on the scoreboard, with a score of 0.16. New York City has the lowest score for wind speed and is overall cold relative to the other cities in the group. Bogota, on the other hand, is predominantly cloudy and humid.

To compute these scores, we'll *normalize* the values of each variable such that the lowest value between all stations corresponds to a zero, and the highest value corresponds to a one. To normalize values means to bring them to some common scale. In this exercise, we normalize all values to a scale from 0 to 1. For example, a value of 20 in the range 0 to 50 corresponds to a normalized value of 0.4. The choice here for a normalized range is arbitrary and my personal choice. You could pick any other range, as long as the score that you build makes sense to you and your users.

The following listing shows the complete main program (src/weather_average .f90), including the code that computes the scores for each city and variable.

Listing 9.6   The complete program to compute climate scores for 10 cities

```
program weather_average                          Imports utility functions
                                                 to work on arrays
  use mod_arrays, only: denan, normalize    ◁
  use mod_average, only: average            ◁    Imports the
  use mod_weather_data, only: weather_data  ◁    generic "average"
  implicit none
                                                 Derived type for reading
  type(weather_data) :: dataset             ◁    the data from files
  character(len=4), parameter :: cities(*) = &
    ['EGLL', 'LAX ', 'LYBE', 'MIA ', 'MMMX', &    Station codes
     'NYC ', 'OIII', 'SEA ', 'SKBO', 'ZGSZ']      to process
  integer :: n
  integer, parameter :: nm = size(cities)
  real :: temperature(nm), humidity(nm), &        Arrays to store
          wind_speed(nm), clear_sky(nm)           the averages
  real :: temperature_score(nm), humidity_score(nm), &
          wind_score(nm), clear_score(nm), &      Arrays to store
          total_score(nm)                         the scores

  do n = 1, nm
    dataset = weather_data('data/processed/' // trim(cities(n)) // '.csv')
    temperature(n) = &
      average(denan(dataset % temperature))       Denans then
    humidity(n) = average(denan(dataset % humidity))   averages each
    wind_speed(n) = average(denan(dataset % wind_speed))  weather parameter.
    clear_sky(n) = average(dataset % clear_sky)
  end do

  temperature_score = normalize(temperature)
  humidity_score = 1 - normalize(humidity)        Computing the
  wind_score = normalize(wind_speed)              scores for each
  clear_score = normalize(clear_sky)              variable
  total_score = (temperature_score + humidity_score &
    + wind_score + clear_score) / 4               Total score

  print *, 'City | Temp. | Humidity | Wind  | Clear | Total'
  print *, 'Code | Score | Score    | Score | Score | Score'
  print *, '-----+-------+----------+-------+-------+------'
  do n = 1, nm
```

```
    write(*,'(1x, a4, 3x, 5(f4.2, 5x))') cities(n), temperature_score(n),&
      humidity_score(n), wind_score(n), clear_score(n), total_score(n)
  end do

end program weather_average
```

We take several steps in the main program. First, we loop through each station code, read the data from the file into the `weather_data` type, remove NaNs, and average the arrays. We then normalize the values to the range from 0 to 1—these are our scores. The total score is calculated as the arithmetic average of individual scores. Finally, we print the score table to the standard output.

9.4 Built-in and custom operators

Now that we understand how generic procedures work, we can take the next step and dig deeper into operators—what they are, how they work, and how you can make your own. This is a big topic, and in this chapter we'll take only a small bite. Here, we'll learn how to express the generic functions that we wrote for the weather average calculations as custom operators. This will also serve as a warm-up for the big and powerful topic of custom operators for derived types, which we'll explore in the next chapter.

9.4.1 What's an operator?

An *operator* is a special creature in most programming languages. All expressions are made of some combination of literal constants, variables, function calls, and, you guessed it, operators. Like in math, operators are used to combine values (numeric or otherwise), to compute a new value. In fact, we've been working with operators since chapter 2 without giving them any special mention. Now we'll start paying more attention to them because we'll want to tweak them for special capabilities.

Operators can be unary or binary, depending on whether they take one or two operands, respectively. Take, for example, the arithmetic multiplication operator `*`. This is a binary operator because it's only meaningful to apply it to two numbers; for example, `3 * 5`. Unary operators apply to a single operand. For example, the subtraction operator can be unary (`-5`) or binary (`3 - 5`).

9.4.2 Things to do with operators

There are four main aspects to Fortran operators:

- *Working with built-in operators as is*—We've been doing this throughout this book without hiccups. In fact, the tsunami simulator, and every other miniproject we've worked on so far, relied heavily on number crunching with built-in arithmetic operators. It's no surprise, as that's where Fortran really shines.
- *Invoking a procedure using a custom operator*—You can express a function or a subroutine that takes one or two input arguments as a custom unary or binary

operator, respectively. This doesn't unlock any special powers but may be used to make your code more concise and expressive.

- *Redefining operators for built-in types*—Fortran's strong typing prohibits mixing numerical and character values, unlike, for example, JavaScript, where an expression such as `99 + "problems"` is not only allowed but common. Redefining operators for existing built-in types allows a more flexible, weaker type system in Fortran.

- *Custom operators for derived types*—This is the big and powerful one that we'll explore in the next chapter. As you build your derived types, such as the `Person` type from the previous chapter or the `Field` type from the tsunami simulator, defining built-in operators for these types will allow you to construct whole new sets of rules, essentially extending Fortran's core syntax.

In this chapter, we'll cover the built-in operators (item 1) in more detail, and we'll learn how to express a function or subroutine as a custom operator (item 2). We've used built-in operators extensively since chapter 2 throughout the book but haven't given much attention to what exactly operators are and how they work. Overriding a procedure with a custom operator is more syntactic sugar than anything else. That is, it doesn't add any notable functionality but may make your code easier to read or write, or just prettier. A programmer's happiness matters. Finally, we'll touch on redefining operators for built-in types (item 3) in exercise 2 of this chapter. Custom operators for derived types (item 4), a powerful and interesting feature in their own right, we'll defer until the next chapter.

Back to our weather data analysis app. When we implement the `average` and `denan` functions from listing 9.6 as custom operators, we'll be able to express our main data loop as that shown in the following listing.

Listing 9.7   Applying custom operators to remove NaNs from and average the data

```
do n = 1, nm
  dataset = weather_data('data/processed/' // trim(cities(n)) // '.csv')
  temperature(n) = &
    .average. (.denan. dataset % temperature)          Applies .denan.
  humidity(n) = .average. (.denan. dataset % humidity)  first, .average.
  wind_speed(n) = &                                      second
    .average. (.denan. dataset % wind_speed)
  clear_sky(n) = .average. dataset % clear_sky    ←   We can omit the parentheses
end do                                                 for a single unary operator.
```

Here, `.average.` and `.denan.` are custom operators with the same functionality as functions with the same name. The semantics didn't change, only the syntax—we traded some parentheses for some periods. Note that `.average. .denan. x` (where x is the input array) is not a valid syntax. When chaining multiple unary operators, you must use parentheses to separate two operators. Binary operators don't run into this issue, as they're always separated by operands.

9.4.3 *Fortran's built-in operators*

Fortran comes with a number of built-in operators. Each falls into one of four categories, depending on what type of result they produce:

- *Arithmetic*—These are the most common kind of operators in almost any computer program. They allow you to do arithmetic calculations, such as add, subtract, multiply, and divide numbers. Arithmetic operators work on numeric values and produce a numeric value as a result.
- *Comparison*—These operators let you compare the values of variables to yield logical values, such as True (`.true.`) or False (`.false.`). You can compare numeric or character values (character string comparisons are evaluated based on the integer encoding of Unicode symbols), and the result is always a logical `.true.` or `.false.`.
- *Logical*—These allow you to form logical (Boolean) expressions from two fundamental logical states, True and False. For example, if you'd require both expressions a and b to be True, you'd test for the value of a `.and.` b. If you'd need at least one of them to be True, you'd test it with a `.or.` b. Logical operators always operate on `logical` operands and produce `logical` results. In contrast to all other built-in operators, logical operators are always enclosed in period symbols: `.and.`, `.or.`, `.not.`, etc.
- *Character*—Fortran offers only one operator that works on character strings, the concatenation operator `//`.

There's also the special assignment operator `=`. What's special about it is that rather than returning a value of some data type, it acts to store the result on the right side into the variable on the left side. The assignment operator is by default available for use with all built-in types, as well as user-defined derived types, if the type of the expression on the right side matches the type of the variable on the left side. The assignment can be redefined, just as any other operator can, and to great effect. We'll dig deeper into this in the next chapter, where we'll redefine the assignment for `Field` types in the tsunami simulator to automatically synchronize parallel processors on assignment.

Due to the nature of these operators, there are typical scenarios in which you'll use them. Arithmetic operators are most commonly used in numerical calculations with assignments to new variables. Comparison and logical operators are often used together to test for conditions and criteria in `if`/`else` statements. Finally, character string concatenation is almost exclusively used for text manipulation and I/O.

Table 9.3 summarizes the built-in operators.

Table 9.3   Summary of Fortran's built-in operators, and their meanings

Operator	Kind	Unary or binary	Meaning	Supported types
=	Assignment	Binary	Assign	`integer, real, complex, logical, character,` derived types
+	Arithmetic	Both	Add	`integer, real, complex`
-	Arithmetic	Both	Subtract	`integer, real, complex`
*	Arithmetic	Binary	Multiply	`integer, real, complex`
/	Arithmetic	Binary	Divide	`integer, real, complex`
**	Arithmetic	Binary	Power	`integer, real, complex`
==	Comparison	Binary	Equals	`integer, real, complex, character`
/=	Comparison	Binary	Does not equal	`integer, real, complex, character`
>	Comparison	Binary	Greater	`integer, real, complex, character`
>=	Comparison	Binary	Greater or equal	`integer, real, complex, character`
<	Comparison	Binary	Lesser	`integer, real, complex, character`
<=	Comparison	Binary	Lesser or equal	`integer, real, complex, character`
`.eqv.`	Logical	Binary	Equivalent	`logical`
`.neqv.`	Logical	Binary	Nonequivalent	`logical`
`.and.`	Logical	Binary	Logical AND	`logical`
`.or.`	Logical	Binary	Logical OR	`logical`
`.not.`	Logical	Unary	Logical NOT	`logical`
`//`	Character	Binary	Concatenate	`character`

In total, Fortran provides five arithmetic operators, six comparison operators, five logical operators, and one character string operator.

Comparing logical expressions
Note that Fortran doesn't allow comparing `logical` expressions with the == or /= operators. Use `.eqv.` (equivalent) or `.neqv.` (not equivalent) instead.

9.4.4 *Operator precedence*

An important aspect of operators, and a common source of bugs for novice programmers, is operator precedence. In other words, which operation gets to go first, and which last? Fortran has a few simple rules for arithmetic operator precedence:

1 Exponentiation (**) takes precedence over multiplication (*) and division (/). Example: 2**3 * 2 evaluates to 16 (exponentiation first, multiplication second).

2 Multiplication (*) and division (/) take precedence over addition (+) and subtraction (-). Example: 2 + 3 * 4 evaluates to 14 (multiplication first, addition second).

3 For operators with equal precedence (* and /, and + and -), the operations are evaluated left to right. The order of operations will matter for floating-point arithmetic.

4 Parentheses can be used to control the precedence. Example: (2 + 3) * 4**2 evaluates to 80 (addition in parentheses and exponentiation first, multiplication last).

Comparison operators don't suffer from precedence ambiguity because they operate on numeric or character values, and return a logical value as a result. It's thus illegal to test, for example, 0 < x < 1, like you can in Python; instead you have to test for 0 < x .and. x < 1. Parentheses are not needed in this case, as the order of operations can be determined by the compiler based on the input data types for different operators.

9.4.5 *Writing custom operators*

A custom operator is essentially a procedure under the hood, with an extended syntax that allows it to be used in expressions much like built-in operators:

```
result = a .op. b
```

Once we have a function or a subroutine, it's straightforward to implement it as a custom operator.

> **TIP** Don't confuse the custom operator syntax, .op. with the logical literal constants .true. or .false.. The latter are reserved words and not operators, and they have periods in them for historical reasons.

These are the naming rules for custom operators:

- Operator names must be enclosed by periods: .op..
- Names are restricted to the same character set as variable or procedure names: lower- or uppercase alphabet letters and decimal numbers. Operator names also must not begin with a number.

The main restriction to operators is that they can be either unary, operating on one operand, or binary, operating on two operands. You can't express procedures that operate on three or more arguments as custom operators.

To make a function available as an operator, we write the same interface as we did for a generic procedure, except that for the name of the operator, we use the word `operator`, with the operator name in parentheses, as shown in the following listing.

Listing 9.8   Invoking functions with a custom operator

```
module mod_average
  ...
  public :: operator(.average.)          ◁──   Makes the custom operator
  ...                                          publicly accessible
  interface operator(.average.)          ◁──   Interface block with
    module procedure :: average_int            the operator name
    module procedure :: average_real
    module procedure :: average_logical        Specific procedures
  end interface average                        to be overridden by
  ...                                          the operator
contains
  ...
end module mod_average
```

As you can see, this is almost identical to what we did with generic procedures. The main difference is the special word `operator`, which we need to use to specify that the interface is going to be the operator, and not just a procedure.

9.4.6   *Redefining built-in operators*

To wrap up the chapter, in this section we'll practice redefining Fortran's built-in operators to do something more or other than originally intended. For example, this could involve either of the following:

- *Performing the same operation, but operating on custom types*—For example, we could define the arithmetic addition operation (+) for the derived type `Person` from the derived type. Depending on the application, the result of adding two instances of `Person` type either could be an instance of some new type—for example, `People` or `Team`—or could yield an array of `Person` instances.
- *Modifying the intended operation*—For example, you could redefine the addition operator so it doesn't add numbers but instead multiplies them.

I leave this one as an exercise for you ("Exercise 2" sidebar). It's a fairly new concept, but we've already covered all the pieces you'll need, and it's a matter of putting them together in the correct order.

Exercise 2: Defining a new string concatenation operator

The way we concatenate strings in Fortran is with the // operator. Coming from Python, where it's done with the + operator, it may be convenient to be able to do the same in Fortran. Implement the + operator so that you can concatenate Fortran strings with it:

```
print *, 'Hello' + ' world!'
```

should print Hello world! to the screen.

You can find the solution to this exercise in the "Answer key" section near the end of this chapter.

9.5 Generic procedures and operators in the tsunami simulator

As of the previous chapter, we were already using some generic procedures and custom operators in the tsunami simulator. We'll explore their implementation in depth in the next chapter. For now, I'll give you a taste of what's to come.

9.5.1 Writing user-defined operators for the Field type

In chapter 8, we implemented the tsunami solver using the Field derived type to model physical fields such as water height and velocity. This allowed us to initialize the fields and express the solver equation cleanly and concisely, as shown in the following listing.

Listing 9.9 Main tsunami solver using the Field derived type

```
use mod_field, only: Field          ⟵ Imports the type
...                                     from the module
type(Field) :: h, u, v, hm    ⟵ Declares the Field instances
...
u = Field('u', [im, jm])
v = Field('v', [im, jm])        Initializes fields
h = Field('h', [im, jm])        for water velocity
hm = Field('hm', [im, jm])      and height
...
time_loop: do n = 1, nm
  ...
  u = u - (u * diffx(u) / dx + v * diffy(u) / dy &     Computes the water
    + g * diffx(h) / dx) * dt                          velocity in x direction

  v = v - (u * diffx(v) / dx + v * diffy(v) / dy &     Computes the water
    + g * diffy(h) / dy) * dt                          velocity in y direction

  h = h - (diffx(u * (hm + h)) / dx         Computes the
        + diffy(v * (hm + h)) / dy) * dt    water height
  ...
end do time_loop
```

If you worked through chapter 8, you learned how to use derived types to abstract away complex code into type components and methods. Specifically, in the tsunami simulator, we designed the `Field` type so that each instance carries all the metadata required for tedious bookkeeping, such as array start and end indices, the image indices of parallel neighbor tiles, and so on.

However, what's not immediately obvious from listing 9.9 is how the computation of field instances u, v, and h works under the hood. Notice that here we're using the same code as we did in chapter 7, where we worked directly with coarrays. As you can probably guess by now, my use of built-in arithmetic operators (+, -, *, and /) with `Field` instances didn't come for free. In fact, each of these operators needed at least a few specific functions defined. The following listing provides a sneak peek at implementing the addition (+) operator to add two instances of the `Field` type.

Listing 9.10   Defining the addition operator for the `Field` type

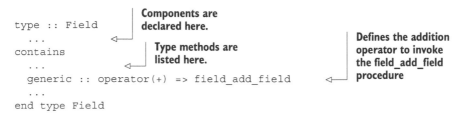

This is the familiar derived type definition block, with one new syntax element—the `generic :: operator()` statement, which specifies a built-in or custom operator and the specific procedure that the operator will invoke. This is just a taste of what's coming.

In the next chapter, we dig deep into defining custom operators for derived types. You'll learn how to use intrinsic operators together with your own custom types to significantly augment the base rules of the language. For the tsunami simulator, this will mean exciting and powerful capabilities, such as applying familiar arithmetic operators directly to instances of the `Field` type, automatically synchronizing parallel images on assignment, and more.

9.6   Answer key

This section contains solutions to exercises in this chapter. Skip ahead if you haven't worked through the exercises yet.

9.6.1   Exercise 1: Specific average function for a derived type

The solution to this exercise relies entirely on what we just learned about writing specific and generic functions, and the syntax about derived types that we covered in chapter 8. If you need to brush up on how to declare derived types and access their components, go back to section 8.2. Here I present the solution and explain how it works.

First, here's the specific function that accepts a `Field` instance as the input argument:

Like with other specific functions, we give this one a unique name.

Accepts a Field type-based instance as the input argument

```
pure real function average_field(f) result(res)
  class(Field), intent(in) :: f
  res = average(f % data)
end function average_field
```

Applies the average to the data component

It may surprise you that this specific function is actually simpler than any of the other three (`average_real`, `average_int`, and `average_logical`). This is thanks to the average of a `Field` type simply being the average of its `data` component. Note that here we don't have to use the specific function name `average_real`. Instead, we can just use the generic `average` and let the compiler do the work of matching the specific function with the input data type. This is a powerful feature of the language—if `Field % data` was declared as an `integer` or `logical` array, the code in listing 9.9 would work as is.

Now that we have the specific function, the rest is easy—we add its name to the generic interface:

```
interface average
  module procedure :: average_int
  module procedure :: average_real
  module procedure :: average_logical
  module procedure :: average_field
end interface average
```

New specific function added to the interface

We can now apply the generic `average` to a `Field` instance, just as we did to built-in data types before, as shown in the following listing.

Listing 9.11 Averaging a real array and a derived type instance

```
program test_average

  use mod_average, only: average
  use mod_field, only: field

  type(Field) :: f

  f % data = [1., 6., 4.]

  print *, average([1., 6., 4.])
  print *, average(f)

end program test_average
```

Assigns data to the Field instance

Averages a real array

Averages a Field instance

This program creates a `Field` instance `f` and assigns a small real array to its `data` component. It then applies the generic `average` to both the real array and the `Field` instance. Compile and run it for yourself to confirm that the two function calls return the same result. You can find the complete program in src/ch09/average_generic.f90 in the listings repo at https://github.com/modern-fortran/listings.

9.6.2   *Exercise 2: Defining a new string concatenation operator*

Like before, we follow the three steps to overriding a function with an operator:

1 Define the specific function (`strcat`).
2 Define the generic interface, this time, to the built-in operator +; point it to the specific procedure `strcat`.
3 Import the new operator from the module into the main program.

The full program is shown in the following listing.

Listing 9.12   Concatenating strings with a + operator

```
module mod_strings

  implicit none

  private
  public :: operator(+)          ←  Makes only the +
                                      interface accessible

  interface operator(+)
    module procedure :: strcat    Generic interface
  end interface                   to operator +

contains
                                              Assumed-length
                                              character strings

  function strcat(s1, s2) result(res)
    character(len=*), intent(in) :: s1, s2  ←  Allocatable character
    character(len=:), allocatable :: res    ←  string as result
    res = s1 // s2                ←
  end function strcat             Concatenates using the
                                  built-in operator; result is
end module mod_strings            allocated on assignment

program strcat                           Accesses the + operator
  use mod_strings, only: operator(+)  ←  from a module
  print *, 'Hello' + ' world'    ←
end program strcat               We can now concatenate
                                 strings using the + operator.
```

We start by writing the specific function `strcat`. This function takes two assumed-length character strings (`character(len=*)`), `s1` and `s2`, as input arguments. The result, `res`, is also a character string, best declared as an allocatable string (`character(len=:), allocatable`). To evaluate the result, we simply use the built-in concatenation operator `//`. We don't have to allocate the result explicitly—we can let the automatic allocation on assignment (introduced in Fortran 2003) do its magic. Once this function is defined, we just need to write an interface for the + operator and let it point to `strcat`.

Voilà! From the main program, we import `operator(+)` from the module and use it to concatenate two strings. While intended more as a fun exercise than a useful one, this solution required a variety of syntax elements from this and earlier chapters. I hope you enjoyed redefining your first built-in operator. What's next?

9.7 New Fortran elements, at a glance

- `interface`/`end interface`—Writing an interface block to define a generic procedure name and list all the specific procedures that it can invoke under the hood
- `interface operator()`—Using a custom operator instead of a function
- `.op. x, x .op. y`—Unary and binary custom operators in action

Summary

- Generic procedures allow you to invoke specific procedures that operate on different data types using the same name.
- Handling different data types requires writing a specific procedure for each type.
- Procedures can be overridden by custom operators for cleaner code.
- Generic procedures are your second layer of abstraction, on top of procedures introduced in chapter 3; use them only when they clearly make your code simpler.

User-defined operators
for derived types

This chapter covers

- User-defined operators for derived types
- Writing a minimal countdown app
- Validating user input
- Synchronization on assignment in the tsunami simulator

Almost any app working with real-world data, or any program more complex than a toy model, will use derived types (classes) to handle abstract data. Operators for arithmetic (+, -, *, /, **) and comparison (==, /=, >=, <=, >, <) are available out of the box for built-in numeric types (integer, real, complex), but not for derived types. For example, to keep track of the calendar date and time in an app, you'd need to compare, add, and subtract datetime instances (data structures that represent date and time). This is where derived types from chapter 8 and generic procedures and custom operators from chapter 9 come together to form a powerful feature of the language: user-defined operators for derived types. Combining these two capabilities will allow you to define what the built-in (and custom) operators mean for any derived type, and in a way extend the syntax of the language.

In this chapter, we'll start by writing a simple command-line app that counts the time between now and some arbitrary date in the future; for example, your birthday. The implementation of the app is centered around a single concept—how to apply an arithmetic operator such as addition or subtraction to a derived type. On this journey, you'll also learn how to parse command-line arguments, validate user input, and work with dates and times. Once done, we'll apply this knowledge to implement an almost complete arithmetic operator set for the `Field` class in the tsunami simulator. Besides being able to express our physics equation in an elegant way like before, we'll also abstract away the synchronization logic in parallel execution mode by defining a custom assignment operator for the `Field` class. You'll leave this chapter with powerful new knowledge that will allow you to extend the built-in arithmetic to arbitrary data types and beyond.

10.1 Happy Birthday! A countdown app

> *Do one thing and do it well.*
>
> —A UNIX philosophy

Our project for this chapter is a minimal countdown app for the command line. Following the old UNIX philosophy, it will do one thing and do it well. The app will read a year, month, and day as command-line arguments input by the user. If the date input is today (according to the local machine time), the app will wish the user happy birthday. Otherwise, it will display the number of days, hours, minutes, and seconds remaining until the user's birthday.

My birthday is on December 10, and running the app on the day of this writing gives me

```
$ ./countdown 2020 12 10
305 days, 4 hours, 41 minutes, and 16 seconds remaining until your Birthday!
```

However, if I wait 305 more days and run the app then, it will greet me as I expect it to:

```
$ ./countdown 2020 12 10
Happy Birthday!
```

Um, that's the whole app. What more do you expect of something that does only one thing?

10.1.1 Some basic specification

For the app to do well the one thing it's supposed to do, it helps to set some specifications so we can plan the implementation:

1 Read a date from user input in the year, month, day form.
2 If the input date matches today's date, print "Happy Birthday!" on the screen.
3 Otherwise, print the number of days, hours, minutes, and seconds until the user's birthday.

4 The app should handle the most likely user input errors, such as no arguments provided, or bad values for year, month, or day arguments.

This specification list is plenty for this exercise. Now for the difficult part—how do we get this thing to work?

10.1.2 Implementation strategy

From our specifications list, it looks like we'll need some clever way to handle date and time data, as well as the time difference. In chapter 8, we learned how to define arbitrary data structures using derived types. We can thus model dates, times, and time difference structures as derived types (or classes)—let's call these `datetime` and `timedelta`, respectively.

Once we have a `datetime` class, we'll need a way to load an instance from user-input command-line arguments, and another from local machine time. Fortran packs a few subroutines that we can use for these tasks. As noted, for the time difference, we'll make the `timedelta` class. We'll also need a way to take the difference between two datetimes. This item is twofold—one is a syntax to define the arithmetic (-) operator for the `datetime` class, and the other is the actual algorithm to do the calculation.

In section 10.2, we'll tackle the date and time data structure (the `datetime` derived type) and how to create `datetime` instances from both user input and current machine time. Then, in section 10.3, we'll implement the time difference or interval structure, the `timedelta` class, and we'll get into the nitty-gritty of defining custom operators.

10.2 Getting user input and current time

In the first part of the implementation, we'll define a `datetime` class and learn how to load it from command-line arguments and from local machine time.

10.2.1 Your first datetime class

The simplest way to model human-readable date and time is by defining a data structure with integer components for each date and time unit. I say human-readable because most of us are quite used to thinking of dates in terms of years, months, and days, and times in terms of a 24-hour clock. A notable example of a simpler, but not human-friendly, time is so-called *UNIX time*, which is a single integer value indicating the number of seconds since 00:00:00 UTC on January 1, 1970. Linux and UNIX-like systems such as macOS use this kind of time internally for timekeeping.

If you're on such a system, you can get the current UNIX time by typing `date +%s` on the command line. Indeed, we'll use a similar measure to implement the difference between two times later in this chapter. Since our app will both expect input from command-line arguments and produce output for a human user, we'll program a date and time structure following the Gregorian calendar, also standardized as ISO 8601 in 1988. Derived types, which we learned about in chapter 8, are the obvious choice for such a data structure. Here's your first `datetime` class:

```
type :: datetime
  integer :: year, month, day
  integer :: hour = 0, minute = 0, second = 0
end type datetime
```

Year, month, and day are required.

Hour, minute, and second are optional.

This is a rather simplified version of a date and time record. It stores time with precision of up to a second, so any fractions of a second are neglected. The same goes for time zones, which we'll ignore for simplicity. Daylight savings? Forget about it. You get the idea—we'll work with the simplest `datetime` instance to accomplish our goal: counting the time between now and the date input by the user.

Note that in the snippet, we initialize the time components (hour, minute, and second) to zero but leave the date components (year, month, and day) uninitialized. This is strictly a UI (user interface) design choice. The user should be allowed to work with the `datetime` class to handle just dates, if time components aren't needed. For example, this approach allows creating a `datetime` instance as just `datetime(2019, 12, 10)`, where the hour, minute, and second components are initialized to zero as the default value. In contrast, there's no obvious sane default value for year, month, or day, if omitted, so we leave them as required components.

With just this one derived type definition, we can import it, declare it, and initialize it to any date we'd like, and print it back to the screen:

```
2019          12          10          0          0          0
```

The following listing shows a program that does that.

Listing 10.1   Creating a datetime instance and printing it to screen

```
program countdown
  use mod_datetime, only: datetime
  implicit none
  type(datetime) :: birthday = datetime(2019, 12, 10)
  print *, birthday
end program countdown
```

Imports the datetime class from the module

Declares and initializes a datetime instance

Prints the datetime instance to screen

This is our first step toward the countdown app. It's a simple, but essential, step—we now have a date and time data structure to work with. Our next stop is reading user input from the command line, and creating the `datetime` instance accordingly.

10.2.2 Reading user input

There are a few different ways for a program to get input from the user. One is the so-called standard input, where the program waits for the user to enter data through the keyboard. This approach is useful when the program's flow depends on users' input. If you're old enough to have grown up with old text adventures such as Colossal

Cave Adventure or Zork, or if you've ever read a choose-your-own-adventure book, they work exactly like this:

- The program asks you a question, and you type in the answer.
- The program then processes the input and acts accordingly.

We explored reading from standard input in chapter 6.

Another approach is to instruct the program to read the input data from files on disk that have been prepared beforehand. We used this liberally in chapters 5, 7, and 9. This approach is necessary when the input data is much bigger than a handful of scalar parameters or character strings; for example, initial fields to a complex simulation program or satellite data streams that come in at set times of the day.

Finally, you can provide input data to the program as command-line arguments, like with many Linux and UNIX command-line programs. This approach is suitable when the input data consists of up to several parameters. A program with a command-line interface can be used as a stand-alone program or as part of a larger, scripted pipeline. Fortran provides subroutines to inquire and read data from the command line, no matter what your operating system is—Linux, Windows, or a UNIX-like system such as macOS. The key subroutine is `get_command_argument`, introduced by the Fortran 2003 standard. It allows you to parse the command-line arguments by position number and store their values into a character string variable. See it in action in the following listing.

Listing 10.2   Reading the date from the command line

Returns a datetime instance →

```fortran
subroutine get_date_from_cli(date)      ◁── A subroutine that will
                                            return date to the caller
  type(datetime), intent(out) :: date
  character(len=4) :: year_arg          Character strings to store command-
  character(len=2) :: month_arg, day_arg line arguments, length 4 for year,
  integer :: year, month, day           and length 2 for month and day

  call get_command_argument(1, year_arg)    Reads each
  call get_command_argument(2, month_arg)   argument into a
  call get_command_argument(3, day_arg)     character string

  read (year_arg, *) year        Converts each argument
  read (month_arg, *) month      from character string to
  read (day_arg, *) day          an integer

  date = datetime(year, month, day, 0, 0, 0)   ◁── Creates a new
                                                    datetime instance
end subroutine get_date_from_cli                  from input values
```

Integer values to convert the character strings into →

This subroutine has no input arguments, and only one output argument, `date`. It's a rather short subroutine; however, it uses two new concepts that we haven't encountered so far in the book. First, we use the `get_command_argument` subroutine to read the arguments from the command-line interface (CLI). What's new about this concept is that it will allow you to provide input parameters to the program at runtime, without needing to recompile the program. The first argument to `get_command_argument` is an integer and refers to the position of the argument on the command line, starting immediately after the program name. The second argument is a character string in which we store the value of the command-line argument. You can see the full description of this subroutine in the following sidebar.

Using the `get_command_argument` subroutine

`get_command_argument` is a built-in subroutine that queries information about command-line arguments passed to the program. It takes at least one and up to four arguments:

- `number`—A non-negative integer number indicating the position of the command-line argument to query.
- `value`—An optional character string in which the value of the command-line argument will be stored. If `number == 0`, the name of the program is stored into `value`.
- `length`—An optional integer that will be set to the number of characters in the command-line argument.
- `status`—An optional integer status. If getting the command-line argument fails, `status` is set to a positive number. If the argument is truncated to fit into `value` (second argument from this list), it's set to -1. Otherwise (success), `status` is set to zero.

Note that there's no implicit conversion of data types from the command line to our program. If you pass integers or reals to the program, `get_command_argument` will always receive them as character strings. You, the programmer, are responsible for explicitly converting them to the data type that you need.

We now have our CLI arguments stored into character string variables. To create a new `datetime` instance, we need them as integers. How do you convert a string to an integer in Fortran? This is where we encounter the second new concept—reading a value from an *internal unit*. This is one of the historical features of Fortran that hails from way back. See, you'd think that you could just do something like `int('42')` or `real('3.1415925')` to get an integer or a real number from a string. However, it's not that easy. To make the conversion, you actually need to *read* a number from a character variable, like you'd do from a text file:

```
read (unit=string, fmt=fmt) var
```

Here, we use the `read` statement to convert a character string, stored in the `string` variable, into a numerical (integer, real, or complex) or logical variable `var`. The second argument, `fmt`, is the formatting string to be used to parse `string`. We'll look into formatting strings in the next chapter in more detail, but for now a default value (`*`) is good enough. Thus, to convert a character string `year_arg` to an integer variable `year`, you'd write `read (year_arg, *) year`, and similarly for month and day arguments. If you're feeling adventurous, you could also write a custom constructor for the `datetime` type that accepts character strings as input, as well as integers.

Note that this subroutine could've been expressed as a function, albeit not a pure one. I chose a subroutine because using a function may imply that no side effects occur. Even though `get_date_from_cli` doesn't modify any other variable in our program, it's not pure by definition because it receives information from the program's environment.

Back to our main program, which we can now write as shown in the following listing.

Listing 10.3   Receiving a date from the CLI and printing it to screen

```
program countdown
  use mod_datetime, only: datetime, get_date_from_cli    ◄─── Imports the class and
  implicit none                                               command-line parser
  type(datetime) :: birthday      ◄───                        from the module
  call get_date_from_cli(birthday)  ◄───             Declares our
  print *, birthday     ◄───                         datetime instance
end program countdown
                                                   Parses the command-
              Prints the datetime                  line argument
              instance to the screen
```

At this point, we can import the `datetime` class and `get_date_from_cli` parser subroutine from the module, declare the `datetime` instance, and initialize it with user-input values. Our app is useful already! However, let's look back at our specification from section 10.1. We need to be able to handle typical cases of invalid user input, such as not enough command-line arguments provided, or values for year, month, or day that aren't meaningful. This will be good to tackle in an exercise, such as the one in the "Exercise 1" sidebar.

Exercise 1: Validating user input

Edit the `get_date_from_cli` subroutine from listing 10.2 to check for the following:

1. Has the user passed at least three command-line arguments to the program? If not, the app should print a short usage message and stop. Hint: use `command_argument_count` to get the integer number of arguments provided to the program.

2. Do each of the year, month, and day arguments have a valid value? If not, print an informative error message and stop. Note that to test for the value of the day, you'll need to determine the number of days given the month and year values. A function to do this is found in mod_datetime.f90 in the source code repository.

The solution to this exercise is given in the "Answer key" section near the end of this chapter.

In this section, we used the built-in `get_command_argument` subroutine to write a simple command-line argument parser. Just using this can get you quite far, but writing a more sophisticated CLI app with many optional arguments and rich documentation can become tedious. Fortunately, there are libraries out there that you could use for this purpose. I describe my favorite in the next sidebar.

Want to write more serious CLI apps?

`command_argument_count` and `get_command_argument` are often more than enough for many simple apps. However, these procedures are low-level tools. If you need your CLI app to receive several different arguments of different types (some of them optional) and to print sophisticated use instructions on the screen, you're better off with a library dedicated to doing exactly that. The Fortran command Line Arguments Parser (FLAP, https://github.com/szaghi/FLAP) is an easy-to-use library for building rich CLI interfaces and docstrings. It's developed and maintained by Stefano Zaghi, an Italian physicist and a true Fortran wizard.

10.2.3 *Getting current date and time*

We got the date from the user input, and now we need to get the current date and time. Fortran provides a subroutine `date_and_time` that gives you access to the current local machine time. Here's how it works, wrapped in a function to return a `datetime` instance:

```
type(datetime) function current_time() result(res)
  integer :: values(8)
  call date_and_time(values=values)
  res = datetime(year = values(1), month = values(2),&
                 day = values(3), hour = values(5),&
                 minute = values(6), second = values(7))
end function current_time
```

Array of eight integers → (annotation pointing to `integer :: values(8)`)

Gets the date and time values and stores them into the array (annotation pointing to `call date_and_time(values=values)`)

Creates a new datetime instance using these values (annotation pointing to `res = datetime(...)`)

This function is short and sweet. We first call the built-in `date_and_time` with the integer array `values` with eight elements. Then, we use several of these elements to create a `datetime` instance and return it as the result. Why is `values` an array with exactly eight elements, and why do we use only six? See the next sidebar for more information.

The `date_and_time` built-in subroutine

`date_and_time` gets the date and time information from the real-time system clock. This is the clock in your computer. There are a few different ways you could use `date_and_time`. The full syntax is

```
date_and_time(date, time, zone, values)
```

(continued)

where

- `date` is a character string of length 8 or larger. If provided, it's populated with the current date in the form `YYYYmmdd` (year, month, day).
- `time` is a character string of length 10 or larger. If provided, it's populated with the current time in the form `hhmmss.sss` (hour, minute, second, millisecond).
- `zone` is a character string of length 5 and has the form `(+-)hhmm`, representing the difference relative to the Coordinated Universal Time (UTC).
- `values` is an integer array of size 8, whose elements are year, month, day, time difference from UTC in minutes, hour, minute, second, and millisecond, respectively.

All four arguments to this subroutine are optional.

10.3   *Calculating the difference between two times*

Finally, we get to the meat of the countdown app: calculating the difference between the two times. There are three necessary ingredients for this to work:

- A data structure to represent a time interval—a `timedelta` class
- A syntax to define a subtraction operator for `datetime` instances
- An algorithm to calculate the difference

At the end of this section, we'll be able to initialize two datetimes and take their difference, which should look something like this:

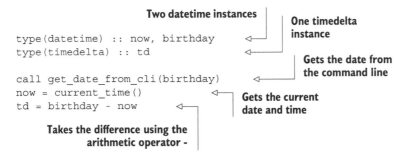

We're already able to declare `datetime` instances and initialize them either from the command line (`get_date_from_cli`) or from machine time (`current_time`). What we don't know how to do yet, and neither does the compiler, is take the difference between two datetimes using nothing but an arithmetic subtraction (`-`) operator and make it return a `timedelta` instance. The next section tackles that problem.

10.3.1 Modeling a time interval

Let's first design a data structure to represent a time interval, or difference. How do we think of time intervals? They can be expressed as a number of days, hours, minutes, seconds, or any combination thereof. You may ask, Why not simply express the time difference as a finite number of days or seconds, like the UNIX time I mentioned earlier? While this is certainly useful for internal calculations, we also need a human-readable format for a time interval to display it as the output of the program. This is where the `timedelta` class comes in. We can use the familiar syntax to create a derived type `timedelta` to model this data structure:

```
type :: timedelta
  integer :: days = 0, hours = 0, &          | All optional, integer
            minutes = 0, seconds = 0          | components
end type timedelta
```

A `timedelta` class is even simpler than the `datetime` class. Here we have only four integer components (days, hours, minutes, and seconds), and all are optional. This makes `timedelta` more flexible than `datetime` as well. If no arguments are provided to the `timedelta` constructor, a zero `timedelta` instance will be created. You may ask why we haven't included the months or years as components as well. It's because both months and years can be of different absolute time lengths. For example, February is always shorter than March in terms of absolute time, and they're both exactly one month. The same goes for leap and nonleap years.

10.3.2 Implementing a custom subtraction operator

We have our `datetime` and `timedelta` classes. The question remains: How can we take the difference between two datetimes using nothing but an arithmetic subtraction operator? Doing just `td = birthday - now` won't work out of the box because a datetime is an arbitrary data structure. To the compiler, it has no intrinsic meaning and is just a sequence of numbers in memory. If we try this, we won't get far:

File name, line number, and column where the error occurred

```
$ gfortran mod_datetime.f90 countdown.f90 -o countdown
countdown.f90:8:7:

    td = birthday - now          The code that
         1                       triggered the error
Error: Unexpected derived-type entities in binary       Error
       intrinsic numeric operator '-' at (1)            message
```

Approximate position where the error occurred

We need to somehow tell the compiler that the operator - has a special meaning for these types, and instruct it on what to do when we try to use it in code. We can do so by associating an operator such as addition (+) or subtraction (-) with a user-defined procedure. Figure 10.1 illustrates the sequence of operations that occur when applying the custom subtraction operator (-) on two datetime instances, a and b.

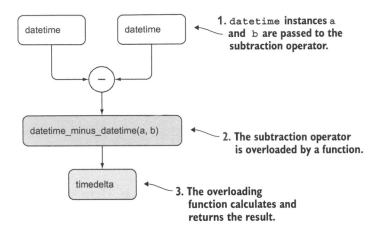

Figure 10.1 Implementing arithmetic operators for derived types in three steps

We first invoke the subtraction operator with the two datetime instances. The compiler determines that a and b are not of built-in numeric types. It looks for any procedure that the - operator is associated with and that matches these data types, and finds datetime_minus_datetime. Under the hood, the compiler replaces the code a - b with datetime_minus_datetime(a, b). This function returns a timedelta instance as the result.

In the previous chapter, you learned how to override operators for built-in (nonderived) data types, as well as how to define your own custom operators. Now we get to see how to associate an operator with a derived type-bound procedure, as shown in the following listing.

Listing 10.4 Implementing the - operator for the datetime class

```
type :: datetime
  integer :: year, month, day
  integer :: hour = 0, minute = 0, second = 0
contains
  procedure, pass(d1) :: datetime_minus_datetime
  generic :: operator(-) => datetime_minus_datetime
end type datetime
```

Type-bound procedure that will be invoked by the operator

Operator "-" is now associated with this procedure.

There are two ingredients here. First, we specify the procedure that will associate the operator with a type-bound procedure, just like we did back in chapter 8. The keyword pass specifies the name of the argument that will correspond to the type instance that's bound. For a refresher on type-bound methods, take a look at section 8.3. Second, we use the `generic :: operator() =>` syntax to specify which operator will be replaced by which procedure. Defined like this, whenever the compiler encounters the `-` operator being applied to `datetime` instances, it will refer to the `datetime_minus_datetime` procedure.

Simple, right? Of course, we still need to write that `datetime_minus_datetime` procedure....

How about custom operators?

In chapter 9, I introduced the concept of custom operators enclosed in periods; for example, `.sub.`. The mechanism used in listing 10.4 isn't restricted to built-in operators and can be used for custom operators as well; for example

```
generic :: operator(.sub.) => datetime_minus_datetime
```

would be a valid statement as well.

10.3.3 *Time difference algorithm*

The simplest algorithm for calculating a difference between two times is to recast the times into a single, common axis, such as number of days since some point in the past. (Recall UNIX time from earlier in the chapter?) Once there, it's straightforward to calculate the difference—it's just a matter of subtracting one numerical value from another. We can then convert this result to a whole number of days, hours, minutes, and seconds, for a user-friendly display.

CONVERTING A DATETIME TO A NUMERICAL VALUE

The trickiest part of this calculation is casting the `datetime` instance to a single numerical value. A floating-point number of days since some fixed point in time is a candidate, because a day always consists of exactly 86,400 seconds. (Let's ignore leap seconds for the sake of this exercise.) Neither a number of months nor a number years would be appropriate because they contain a variable number of days. Real values of hours or minutes could work in theory, but we risk losing floating-point precision for large values (more on this in a bit). An integer number of seconds is another good way to express a time difference, though we'd need to resort to a higher integer kind such as `int64` to avoid overflows. For this exercise, I'll express the time difference as a floating-point number of days since 00:00 January 1 of year 1 AD, as it makes for shorter code. I encourage you to implement a time difference based on an integer number of seconds afterward.

To convert a `datetime` instance to a number of days, we need to go through the following steps:

1 Sum the number of days from all years from year 1 AD up to the previous year. Why not include the current year in this calculation? In this step, we're counting

the days only from whole years. Since the current year is in progress, we'll need to account for it in a separate step. Given a `datetime` instance d1, this calculation can be expressed as

```
sum([(days_in_year(year), year = 1, d1 % year - 1)])
```

Do you remember the syntax for array constructors (or implied `do` loops) from chapter 5? We're using that trick here again. For each value of `year` from 1 to `d1 % year - 1` (previous year), we evaluate `days_in_year(year)` as each element of the array. In the end, we apply the sum to the array. This kind of expression is a concise way to express accumulators (constructs that accumulate values) in Fortran. We haven't implemented `days_in_year` yet, but we'll get to it soon enough.

2 Calculate the current day of the year. We'll implement another function, `yearday`, to do with this task. At this point, we have the total number of days up to today, excluding the current time of the day in hours, minutes, and seconds.

3 In this step, we need to express the current time of day in hours, minutes, and seconds as a fraction of the day. This one is relatively straightforward—all we need to do is convert hours, minutes, and seconds each to a unit of days and add them up.

4 We sum the results of steps 1–3. For modern dates, the number of days since year 1 is quite large, over 700,000 days. At this scale, small numbers such as a second in day units (1/86400) are lost because of the internal representation of floating point numbers in the default (32-bit) real representation. To work around this issue, we cast the whole expression to 64-bit real values by multiplying the result from step 1 by a literal constant `1.0_real64`. This way, small values such as the result of step 3 will be promoted to a `real64` type before being added to the other terms. For a refresher on how type casting (or coercion) works, take a look back at section 5.2.2.

The whole expression then looks like this:

```
                                              The literal constant 1.0
                                              as a 64-bit real number
ndays1 = 1.0_real64                              &   ◁
       * sum([(days_in_year(year),               &        Sums days from
            year = 1, d1 % year - 1)])           &        all previous years
       + yearday(d1 % year, d1 % month, d1 % day) &
       + d1 % hour * h2d                          &   ◁
       + d1 % minute * m2d                        &   ◁    Converts current
       + d1 % second * s2d      ◁                              hours to a fraction
                                                               of the day
```

Current day in the year → (points to `+ yearday(d1 % year, d1 % month, d1 % day)`)

Converts current seconds to a fraction of the day

Converts current minutes to a fraction of the day

In this snippet, `h2d`, `m2d`, and `s2d` are constant real numbers used to convert hours, minutes, and seconds, respectively, to a fraction of the day. Although we could spell them out as literal constants (for example, h2d is just 1.0/24.0), it's useful to have them as named constants, as we'll use them a few more times in this subroutine.

How does the days_in_year function work? Simple—if it's a leap year, return 366, and 365 otherwise:

```
pure elemental integer function days_in_year(year)
  integer, intent(in) :: year
  if (is_leap_year(year)) then
    days_in_year = 366          ◄──────  Leap year
  else
    days_in_year = 365          ◄──────  Nonleap year
  end if
end function days_in_year
```

This function would be more complex if I didn't abstract away the leap year test in its own function, is_leap_year. I'll leave it as an exercise for you. See the following sidebar.

Exercise 2: Leap year in the Gregorian calendar

Two of our functions, days_in_month and days_in_year, need the information about whether a given year is a leap year or not. A leap year is a calendar year that contains one additional day, February 29. How do you determine whether a year is a leap year? A leap year occurs every four years, with a few exceptions. From the United States Naval Observatory website:

> Every year that is exactly divisible by four is a leap year, except for years that are exactly divisible by 100, but these centurial years are leap years if they are exactly divisible by 400. For example, the years 1700, 1800, and 1900 are not leap years, but the year 2000 is.

Using this description, write a function that returns .true. if the input year is a leap year, and .false. otherwise. For convenience, you can use the built-in remainder function mod.

The solution to this exercise is given in the "Answer key" section near the end of the chapter.

The yearday function (step 2 of the number-of-days algorithm) works in a similar way as the accumulator from step 1, except that it accumulates the number of days in the months, up to the previous month, and adds to the result the current day of the month. Here's how the function returns the day of the year:

```
pure elemental integer function yearday(year, month, day)    Year, month, and day are
  integer, intent(in) :: year, month, day                    the input arguments.
  integer :: m
  yearday = sum([(days_in_month(m, year), &                  Sums up the days in the months
              m = 1, month - 1)]) + day                      up to the previous month, and
end function yearday                                          adds the current day of the
                                                             month to the result
```

Combining an array constructor with the sum function is an elegant way to write accumulators in Fortran. For brevity, I don't include the function days_in_month as a listing here, but if you're curious, take a look at the code in the datetime module in mod_datetime.f90 in the repository.

CASTING THE DIFFERENCE TO A TIMEDELTA INSTANCE

Now that we have the code to cast the datetime instances as numerical values, it's easy to take the difference of the two as days_diff = ndays1 - ndays2. However, now we have the opposite problem: we need to cast days_diff as a timedelta instance. Recall that to create a timedelta instance, we need integer values of days, hours, minutes, and seconds. The following snippet from the code casts a number of days into a timedelta instance:

```
days_diff = ndays1 - ndays2          ⟵┐ Takes the difference in days

sgn = sign(1.0_real64, days_diff)    ⟵┐ Gets the sign of days_diff

days = int(abs(days_diff))                               ┐ Converts days_diff to
hours = int((abs(days_diff) - days) * d2h)               │ whole values of days,
minutes = &                                              │ hours, minutes, and
  int((abs(days_diff) - days - hours * h2d) * d2m)       │ seconds
seconds = int((abs(days_diff) - days - hours * h2d &     │
              - minutes * m2d) * d2s)                     ┘

t = timedelta(sgn * days, sgn * hours, &       │ Creates a timedelta instance,
              sgn * minutes, sgn * seconds)    │ preserving the sign
```

The procedure here is reversed relative to the one in the previous subsection. First you get the whole number of days, then the whole number of hours in the remainder, and so on for the hours and seconds. It's a bit tedious, but it works. Once we have days_diff expressed as integer values of days, hours, minutes, and seconds, creating and returning a timedelta instance is easy. Note that we use the built-in sign and abs functions to keep track of whether the time difference is positive or negative, and create a timedelta instance accordingly.

Using the sign and abs functions

The built-in function sign takes two arguments that must both be of integer or real type. sign(x, y) returns the value of x with the sign of y. For example, sign(2, -3) returns -2.

abs returns the absolute value of an integer or real number, which is the non-negative value of the number regardless of its sign. For example, abs(-2) is 2, and abs(7.4) is just 7.4.

THE COMPLETE FUNCTION

We now have all the pieces we need for a calculation of a `timedelta` instance given two input `datetime` instances, and we can put these together into a complete function, as shown in the following listing.

Listing 10.5 Calculating the difference between two `datetime` instances

```
pure elemental type(timedelta) function datetime_minus_datetime(d1, d2) result(t)

  class(datetime), intent(in) :: d1, d2              ←┐  Both input arguments
  real(real64) :: days_diff, ndays1, ndays2, sgn      │  are datetime instances.
  integer :: days, hours, minutes, seconds, year

  real, parameter :: d2h = 24.        ! day -> hour
  real, parameter :: h2d = 1. / d2h   ! hour -> day      Parameters
  real, parameter :: d2m = d2h * 60   ! day -> minute    for converting
  real, parameter :: m2d = 1. / d2m   ! minute -> day    between different
  real, parameter :: s2d = m2d / 60.  ! second -> day    time units
  real, parameter :: d2s = 1. / s2d   ! day -> second

  ndays1 = 1.0_real64                                &
         * sum([(days_in_year(year),                 &
                 year = 1, d1 % year - 1)])          &
         + yearday(d1 % year, d1 % month, d1 % day)  &
         + d1 % hour * h2d                           &
         + d1 % minute * m2d                         &
         + d1 % second * s2d                            Casts the
                                                        datetime
  ndays2 = 1.0_real64                                &   instances to
         * sum([(days_in_year(year),                 &   numeric values
                 year = 1, d2 % year - 1)])          &
         + yearday(d2 % year, d2 % month, d2 % day)  &
         + d2 % hour * h2d                           &
         + d2 % minute * m2d                         &
         + d2 % second * s2d

  days_diff = ndays1 - ndays2         ←┐  Difference between
                                       │  two datetimes in days
  sgn = sign(1.0_real64, days_diff)

  days = int(abs(days_diff))                            Casts the difference
  hours = int((abs(days_diff) - days) * d2h)            in days to a whole
  minutes = &                                           number of days,
    int((abs(days_diff) - days - hours * h2d) * d2m)    hours, minutes,
  seconds = int((abs(days_diff) - days - hours * h2d &  and seconds
              - minutes * m2d) * d2s)

  t = timedelta(sgn * days, sgn * hours, &        Creates and returns a
                sgn * minutes, sgn * seconds)     timedelta, preserving the sign

end function datetime_minus_datetime
```

This function goes through the three steps I described earlier. First, it converts each of the input `datetime` instances d1 and d2 to single numerical measures: number of days since January 1, year 1 AD. These values are stored in `ndays1` and `ndays2`, respectively, and it's straightforward to calculate the difference between the two as `days_diff = ndays1 - ndays2`. This value can be positive or negative, depending on which date-time instance is greater than the other. The difference in days is then cast to integer values of days, hours, minutes, and seconds to be used to create and return a `timedelta` instance. This function is quite complex, using several smaller functions under the hood (figure 10.2).

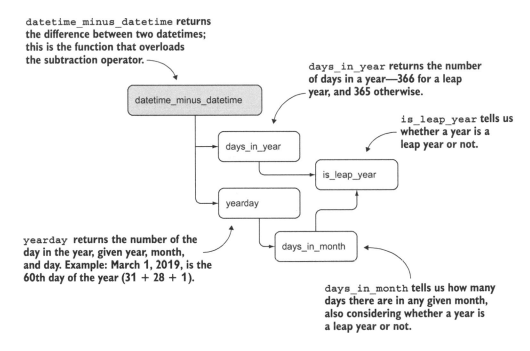

Figure 10.2   Dependency graph for the `datetime_minus_datetime` function

This diagram shows the functions that `datetime_minus_datetime` invokes. `datetime_minus_datetime` uses two functions for its calculations: `days_in_year` and `yearday`. Both functions depend on `is_leap_year`. `yearday` also depends on `days_in_month`, which also needs `is_leap_year`. This is yet another example of the usefulness of breaking down complex calculations into smaller and smaller pieces.

10.3.4   *The complete program*

Finally, we're approaching the home stretch. We now have all the ingredients that our program needs: reading the user-input date from the command line, getting the current local time, and taking the difference between the two times. All that's left now is to test for the values of the two dates and print the message accordingly. The following listing shows the full program.

Listing 10.6 The complete program of the countdown app

```
program countdown

    use mod_datetime, only: datetime, current_time, &          Imports the classes
                            timedelta, get_date_from_cli        and procedures
                                                                from the module
    implicit none
                                                   Declares the datetime
                                                   instances
    type(datetime) :: now, birthday
    type(timedelta) :: td                          Declares the
                                                   timedelta instance
    call get_date_from_cli(birthday)
    now = current_time()                    Gets the current
                                            date and time
    td = birthday - now

    if (now % month == birthday % month &             Prints the
       .and. now % day == birthday % day) then        birthday greeting
      print *, 'Happy Birthday!'                       if same day
    else
      print '(i3, a, 3(i2, a))',          &
         td % days, ' days, ',            &           Prints the countdown
         td % hours, ' hours, ',          &           otherwise, specially
         td % minutes, ' minutes, and ', &            formatted for pretty
         td % seconds, &                              display
            ' seconds remaining until your Birthday!'
    end if

end program countdown
```

Gets the date from user input → `call get_date_from_cli(birthday)`

Computes the time difference → `td = birthday - now`

Since we're testing whether the dates are matching, we actually don't use the timedelta instance for the test, but test for the components of the datetime instances directly. Specifically, the month and day of both datetimes must match for the birthday condition to hold. To test that both the month and day match, we use the built-in function all, which we encountered back in section 5.2.11, the "Exercise 2" sidebar. all evaluates as .true. if all the elements in the logical array are .true., and .false. otherwise. If the month and day of the two datetimes don't match, we use the timedelta instance to report the remaining time in terms of days, hours, minutes, and seconds. Checking for month and day match instead of the timedelta value also saves us from the inconvenient exception that on the day of an actual birthday, the time difference is negative.

Finally, notice that user-defined operators (arithmetic or otherwise) over derived types is yet another layer of abstraction. In this particular scenario, the addition operator + wraps around the type-bound method datetime_minus_datetime, which takes two datetime instances as inputs, which are themselves an abstraction over integer values of year, month, day, and so on. Remember that multiple layers of abstraction add complexity cost to your code—use them only when there's significant benefit to be gained. In this case, our top-level code (the main program, countdown) is quite simple and easy to read and understand. You can get the complete code for the countdown app from GitHub:

```
git clone https://github.com/modern-fortran/countdown
```

If you don't use git, you can download the whole repository as a zip file from http://mng.bz/6QeZ.

> ### Ready for more dates and times?
> If you're ready to step up your date and time game in your Fortran projects, I suggest you check out a more fully featured datetime library at http://mng.bz/oPK2. It provides implementations of datetime and timedelta classes with complete sets of arithmetic and comparison operators that you can start using immediately in your own apps. It contains all the functionality that we implemented in this chapter, and much more.

10.4 Overriding operators in the tsunami simulator

You now have a good idea of how defining an arithmetic operator for use with derived types works. Let's apply this knowledge to implement the full arithmetic for the Field type in the tsunami simulator. We implemented this derived type back in chapter 8, where we used it to model the physical properties of the water flow, such as water surface height and velocity. Using a derived type instead of plain Fortran arrays allowed us to abstract away much of the boilerplate code into the constructor function and type-bound methods. Although I didn't explain how we made the arithmetic operators to work with derived types, we used this concept to code our equations of motion and continuity, just like we did with regular arrays, as shown in the following listing.

Listing 10.7   Excerpt from the Tsunami simulator main time loop

```
time_loop: do n = 1, num_time_steps        ⬅  Iterates for num_time_steps
  ...                                          time steps
  u = u - (u * diffx(u) / dx &
          + v * diffy(u) / dy &             Calculates the new
          + g * diffx(h) / dx) * dt         value of velocity in the x
  call u % sync_edges()                     axis and synchronizes

  v = v - (u * diffx(v) / dx &
          + v * diffy(v) / dy &             Calculates the new
          + g * diffy(h) / dy) * dt         value of velocity in the y
  call v % sync_edges()                     axis and synchronizes
```

```
h = h - (diffx(u * (hm + h)) / dx &
       + diffy(v * (hm + h)) / dy) * dt
call h % sync_edges()
    ...
end do time_loop
```

Calculates the new value of water height and synchronizes

This is the core of the tsunami simulator. First, two equations evaluate the water velocity components u and v in the *x* and *y* axis, respectively, based on the slope of the water surface. The higher `diffx(h) / dx` and `diffy(h) / dy` are, the steeper the water surface in the *x* and *y* directions, respectively, becomes. A steeper water surface leads to an increase in water velocity. The third equation evaluates the water surface height, depending on how much water is coming into or out of the grid cell.

After updating each `Field` variable, we make a call to `sync_edges`. This method updates (or, as we also call it, synchronizes) the edge values with those from neighboring parallel tiles. `sync_edges` is what allows the features of the flow to propagate through from one parallel CPU to another. There are three important points to raise here:

- In serial mode (single core), `sync_edges` does nothing.
- `sync_edges` is required to make the parallel program work in a mechanical sense but is not otherwise meaningful for the physics of the simulator.
- Parallel synchronization of a field is required only when we update the values of that field, not otherwise.

Considering these points, can we find a way to abstract away the explicit synchronization via `sync_edges` in parallel mode? If we're designing tsunami as a library to allow users to design custom fluid dynamics solvers, we shouldn't expect them to also write low-level synchronization calls. Natively parallel code should look the same as its serial counterpart.

Having worked through this chapter up to this point, you have all you need to know to implement the arithmetic operators for the `Field` derived type. We'll go over the details of this implementation in this section. This won't involve any new Fortran features—we'll just apply the existing knowledge from implementing the countdown app to the tsunami simulator. However, we'll also use this opportunity to take it one step further and build the synchronization method (`sync_edges`) into the assignment operator (=) itself! While this involves no new syntax elements, it's a powerful little hack that will allow you to build intricate functionality into mundane statements such as assignments or arithmetic.

10.4.1 A refresher on the Field class

Before we jump into the implementation of type-bound methods operators for the `Field` class, let's refresh our memory on what this class is made of. In a nutshell, the `Field` class is a wrapper around the two-dimensional `data` array that stores the values of the field itself, and a few more components needed for the internal workings of the data structure, as shown here (and in src/ch10/mod_field.f90):

```
type :: Field
  character(:), allocatable :: name            ◁──────── Field name
  integer(int32) :: dims(2), lb(2), ub(2)      ◁───┐
  real(real32), allocatable :: data(:,:)       ◁──┐│  The global dimensions and
end type Field                                    ││  lower and upper bounds of a
                                A two-dimensional array   parallel tile
                                  to store the data
```

With a proper custom constructor, which we implemented in chapter 8 (omitted here for brevity), we declare and initialize our physical fields like this:

```
                                Total grid size in the x
                                      and y dimensions │   Declares water
                                                           velocity and height
integer, parameter :: im = 101, jm = 101  ◁──┘           Field instances
type(Field) :: u, v, h                     ◁────

u = Field('u', [im, jm])     │ Initializes the Field instances
v = Field('v', [im, jm])     │ by passing their names and
h = Field('h', [im, jm])     │ total grid dimensions
```

The custom `Field` constructor is designed to allocate the `data` component with the appropriate range, and to store a few more internal variables mainly needed to instruct the parallel synchronization via the `sync_edges` subroutine. Feel free to look at the implementation of the `field_constructor` function in src/ch10/mod_field.f90.

10.4.2 *Implementing the arithmetic for the Field class*

In section 10.3, we wrote a function that takes the difference between two `datetime` instances, which we then used to redefine the arithmetic operator -. Here, we take the exact same approach, except that we need to put some more leg work in. Take a look back at listing 10.7—we need to implement procedures to define each operator that appears in equations for u, v, and h. We don't need the whole arithmetic set between `Field` and all other types, only those operators that we intend to use. The procedures, operand types, and arithmetic operators that we'll implement are summarized in table 10.1.

Table 10.1   A list of procedures, operands, and operators to be implemented for the `Field` class

Procedure name	Left operand	Right operand	Operator
field_add_field	Field	Field	+
field_add_real	Field	real(:,:)	+
field_sub_field	Field	Field	-
field_sub_real	Field	real(:,:)	-
field_mul_field	Field	Field	*
field_mul_real	Field	real(:,:)	*
field_div_real	Field	real	/
assign_field	Field	Field	=

The operability of `Field` instances with two-dimensional real arrays is necessary because `diffx` and `diffy` functions return two-dimensional real arrays. Note that for the division operator, we only need division of a `Field` with a real scalar, as we divide with grid spacing `dx` and `dy`. If we at any point decided to allow tsunami to have a spatially varying grid spacing (a common approach in both weather and ocean prediction models), we'd need to treat `dx` and `dy` as two-dimensional arrays, and we'd also need a dedicated method for that division. For the sake of this exercise, though, this is good enough. Finally, we'll defer the implementation of `assign_field` until the next subsection.

Let's look at the `field_add_real` procedure, for example. The simplest implementation of this method is to accept a `Field` instance and a two-dimensional real array, and to add the values of the array to the `data` component of the `Field` instance, as shown in the following listing.

Listing 10.8 The `field_add_real` procedure

Since this is a type-bound method, the first argument must be of the type that we're binding to.

```
pure type(Field) function field_add_real(self, x) result(res)
    class(Field), intent(in) :: self
    real(real32), intent(in) :: x(:,:)
    call from_field(res, self)
    res % data = self % data + x
end function field_add_real
```

The second input argument is a two-dimensional real array.

Copies the Field metadata from self into the resulting instance

Assigns values of x to the resulting instance

We use the subroutine `from_field` to conveniently initialize all the internal components of the `Field` class. This step is important because, by default, the `Field` instance `res` comes bare-bones—with uninitialized components and the `data` array not being allocated. Although we could've done that explicitly for more transparency, we'll need to repeat it in every method associated with a user-defined operator. I've thus placed this boilerplate code into a `from_field` subroutine in the same module in `src/ch10/mod_field.f90`. Once `res` is initialized and its `data` component is allocated with the proper range, we add to it the sum of `self % data` and `x`.

Exercise 3: Implementing the addition for the `Field` type

Now that you know how to add a two-dimensional array to a `Field` instance, can you write a similar method that adds the data to two `Field` instances?

Hint: use the `from_field` subroutine to initialize metadata for the result field, like in listing 10.8.

You can find the solution to this exercise in the "Answer key" section near the end of this chapter.

Like we did in section 10.3, the last step to implementing user-defined operators for derived types is to use the generic :: operator() statement in the type definition to instruct the compiler which operators will point to which specific type-bound methods, as shown in the following listing.

Listing 10.9   Associating operators with type-bound methods

```
type Field
  ...
contains
  ...
  procedure, private, pass(self) :: field_add_field, &
                                    field_add_real,  &
                                    field_sub_field, &
                                    field_sub_real,  &
                                    field_mul_field, &
                                    field_mul_real,  &
                                    field_div_real
  generic :: operator(+) => field_add_field, &
                            field_add_real
  generic :: operator(-) => field_sub_field, &
                            field_sub_real
  generic :: operator(*) => field_mul_field, &
                            field_mul_real
  generic :: operator(/) => field_div_real
end type Field
```

Specifies that these are type-bound procedures

Associates arithmetic operators with the specific procedures

This is the same approach that we took in section 10.3.2 and listing 10.4, but now expanded to multiple operators and even more type-bound methods. A user-defined operator can point to multiple different type-bound methods, following the same rules as for generic procedures we covered in chapter 9.

Still missing from listing 10.9 is the implementation of custom assignment (=) that I promised a bit earlier. I'll cover that in the following subsection.

10.4.3 *Synchronizing parallel images on assignment*

The steps for implementing a custom assignment are the same as those for an operator, with a few minor differences. Like other arithmetic operators, assignment is an operation with two operands, one on the left and one on the right. Unlike other arithmetic operators that take two input arguments and return a new value as a result, assignment modifies the value of the left operand in-place. This places a requirement on our method definition—it must be a subroutine (not a function) with the first argument defined as intent(in out):

```
subroutine assign_field(self, f)
  class(Field), intent(in out) :: self
  type(Field), intent(in) :: f
  call from_field(self, f)
  call self % sync_edges()
end subroutine assign_field
```

Field that we're assigning to and is an input and output argument

Field that we're assigning to and is an input argument

Initializes metadata of the resulting field

Synchronizes edges

Like before, here we also use from_field to initialize the field metadata. Since from_field also copies the values of the data component from f to self, all that's left for us to do is synchronize with the sync_edges method. Once we have this method defined, we bind it to the type and instruct the compiler to associate it with the assignment operator:

```
type Field
  ...
contains
  ...
  procedure, private, pass(self) :: assign_field   ⟵──┐ Binds the subroutine
  generic :: assignment(=) => assign_field  ⟵──┐      │ to the type
  ...                                           │ Associates the assignment
end type Field                                  │ operator with the
                                                │ assign_field method
```

There's not much new here except for one tidbit—implementing an assignment requires generic :: assignment(=) keywords instead of generic :: operator(). Otherwise, everything else works the same way as with other operators.

The core of our solver from listing 10.7 now becomes the following listing.

Listing 10.10   Main loop of the tsunami simulator, with synchronization on assignment

```
time_loop: do n = 1, num_time_steps   ⟵──┐ Iterates for num_time_steps
  ...                                      │ time steps
  u = u - (u * diffx(u) / dx &           │ Calculates the new
          + v * diffy(u) / dy &          │ value of velocity in
          + g * diffx(h) / dx) * dt      │ the x axis

  v = v - (u * diffx(v) / dx &           │ Calculates the new
          + v * diffy(v) / dy &          │ value of velocity in
          + g * diffy(h) / dy) * dt      │ the y axis

  h = h - (diffx(u * (hm + h)) / dx &    │ Calculates the new
          + diffy(v * (hm + h)) / dy) * dt │ value of water height
  ...
end do time_loop
```

At first look, this is the same code as in listing 10.7, except for one minor difference—we did away with the sync_edges subroutine calls after each field update. The synchronization is now implicit in the assignment operations for each Field instance. This is not only about having to write fewer lines of code! It's about not having to worry about when exactly we need to synchronize parallel processes, which is a big part of what makes parallel programming hard. It's also about being able to write code that can run in both serial and parallel modes without any modifications.

> **Run it yourself!**
>
> If you've cloned the application's Git repository on GitHub, you can build and run it like this:
>
> ```
> make ch10
> cafrun -n 4 src/ch10/tsunami
> ```

10.5   Answer key

This section contains solutions to exercises in this chapter. Skip ahead if you haven't worked through the exercises yet.

10.5.1   Exercise 1: Validating user input

The best place to validate user input is in the get_date_from_cli subroutine. This way, we don't pollute the main program with various if statements, as shown in the following listing.

Listing 10.11   Validating user input and raising errors if invalid

```
...
if (command_argument_count() < 3) then        First checks that at
  stop 'Usage: countdown YEAR MONTH DAY'      least three arguments
end if                                         are present

call get_command_argument(1, year_arg)
call get_command_argument(2, month_arg)
call get_command_argument(3, day_arg)

read(year_arg, *) year
read(month_arg, *) month
read(day_arg, *) day
                                   Validates the
                                   value of the year
if (year < 1) then
  stop 'YEAR must be >= 1'          ◄
else if (month < 1 .or. month > 12) then       Then validates
  stop 'MONTH must be >= 1 and <= 12'    ◄     the month
else if (day < 1 .or. day > days_in_month(month, year)) then
  stop 'invalid value for DAY'     ◄
end if                                Finally, validates
...                                   the day
```

Relative to our original function, we now have two additional code blocks to validate user input:

1   We use the built-in command_argument_count subroutine to confirm that at least three arguments are passed to the program. Why at least and not exactly three? If there are more than three arguments provided, we can consume the first three and safely ignore the rest. Although this may not be the best UI design, it's simple and it works.

2 After we've converted the three character string values into integers, we check that each value is within the valid range.

Let's try it! Here's the output:

```
gfortran mod_datetime.f90 countdown.f90 -o countdown
./countdown
STOP Usage: countdown YEAR MONTH DAY        Running without any arguments
./countdown -3333 1 15
STOP YEAR must be >= 1                       Running with bad value of year
./countdown 2020 13 15
STOP MONTH must be >= 1 and <= 12            Running with bad value of month
$ ./countdown 2020 2 29
STOP invalid value for DAY                   Running with February 29 on a nonleap year
```

Congrats! Your app now gives some informative feedback when provided with invalid input.

10.5.2 *Exercise 2: Leap year in the Gregorian calendar*

With the help of the built-in function mod, which returns the remainder of the integer division, writing this function is straightforward, as long as we carefully follow the definition of a leap year. A year is a leap year if it's divisible by 4 but not divisible by 100, except when it's divisible by 400.

To test if a year is divisible by 4, we'd test whether mod(year, 4) == 0. We can then use mod in concert with the logical operators .and., .or., and .not. to formulate the leap year test. The following listing demonstrates.

> **Listing 10.12 Function that returns a logical value of whether a year is a leap year**

Integer scalar year is the only input argument.

Elemental will allow invoking this function with scalars or arrays.

```
pure elemental logical function is_leap_year(year)
   integer, intent(in) :: year
   is_leap_year = (mod(year, 4) == 0                &
                   .and. .not. mod(year, 100) == 0) &
                   .or. (mod(year, 400) == 0)
end function is_leap_year
```

Tests for each of the conditions

This function is included in mod_datetime.f90 in the countdown app repository.

10.5.3 *Exercise 3: Implementing the addition for the Field type*

The solution to this exercise is similar to the `field_add_real` implementation from listing 10.8. In fact, this one can be written with one fewer line of code, thanks to both input arguments being Field instances. We follow the same steps as before, initialize the Field metadata using the `from_field` subroutine, then add the data components from two input fields and assign them to the result, as shown in the following listing.

Listing 10.13   Type-bound method to add data from two fields

Two Field instances as input arguments

```
pure type(Field) function field_add_field(self, f) result(res)
  class(Field), intent(in) :: self, f
  call from_field(res, self)                    ◁        Initializes metadata
  res % data = self % data + f % data           ◁        from the self instance
end function field_add_field
```

**Adds data components and assigns
them to the resulting Field**

Like other similar methods, you can find this one in src/ch10/mod_field.f90 in the tsunami source code repository.

10.6   *New Fortran elements, at a glance*

- `generic :: operator()` `=>`—Syntax to associate a built-in or custom operator with a type-bound method of a derived type
- `generic :: assignment(=)` `=>`—Syntax to associate an assignment operator with a type-bound method of a derived type
- Built-in procedures:
  - `command_argument_count`—Returns the number of command-line arguments provided
  - `get_command_argument`—Parses the command-line arguments by position number
  - `date_and_time`—Returns the current machine time
  - `abs`—Returns the absolute value of an integer or real variable
  - `mod`—Returns the remainder of integer division
  - `sign`—Returns the sign of a numerical variable

Summary

- The functionality of derived types can be greatly expanded by implementing custom operators for them.
- User-defined operators for derived types are defined by first implementing a type-bound procedure that takes either one (in case of unary operators) or two (in case of binary operators) input arguments of that type.
- Once the type-bound method is defined, you can use the `generic :: operator()` `=>` syntax to associate an operator (built-in or custom) with that method.
- For user-defined assignments, use the `generic :: assignment(=)` `=>` syntax instead.
- User-defined assignment for derived types is a powerful concept, as it can be used to abstract complex low-level tasks, such as checking the values or parallel synchronization, whenever the data is updated.
- The same operator can invoke multiple specific procedures, following the same rules as for generic procedure resolution from chapter 9.

Part 4

The final stretch

This part of the book covers specialty topics: Fortran interoperability with C, and advanced parallel features, such as teams, events, and collectives.

Chapter 11 will teach you how to interface with existing C code from your Fortran programs. You'll do this by writing a minimal TCP client and server in Fortran, using an existing C library for the low-level networking.

Finally, chapter 12 builds from chapter 7 and covers advanced parallel topics: teams, events, and collectives. Introduced in the latest edition of the language, these features are cutting-edge and will allow you to create innovative parallel algorithms and implementations.

This part of the book is not for the faint of heart. Ideally, you've come here after having worked through at least parts 2 and 3, or you already have significant Fortran programming experience. Either way, you've come this far—the finish line is just around the corner.

Interoperability with C: Exposing your app to the web

11

This chapter covers

- Why invoke C code from Fortran?
- Interfacing with C built-in types, structs, and functions from Fortran
- Writing a minimal Fortran TCP client and server

Pure Fortran is powerful for the numerical and array-oriented computation that's ubiquitous in physical sciences and engineering. However, quite a few things aren't possible in Fortran alone; fortunately, they can be done in a low-level systems programming language such as C. They include reading and writing data to hardware devices, drawing graphics on the screen in real time, and sending data over the internet. Interoperability with C allows a programmer to call C functions from Fortran programs. This is important for two reasons:

- It enables the above-mentioned low-level functionality and gives Fortran access to the C ecosystem of libraries.
- C itself is easily called from many popular programming languages today, such as Python, JavaScript, Go, or Rust. By using C as the interfacing language, Fortran code can be invoked from most other languages. In the real

world, this allows Fortran code to be used within web servers, databases, and real-time graphics.

In this chapter, you'll learn how to use Fortran interoperability with C to write a minimal TCP client and server in Fortran. Through this example, you'll learn not only how to interface C data types and functions from Fortran, but also how to implement simple networking capabilities in your Fortran application. Whether you're developing a remote control panel for your fluid dynamics simulation software, or you want to command a measuring device from your Fortran code, this chapter will give you an idea of how it can be done and show you where to learn more. Keep in mind that this topic is big and thorny. I won't pretend to teach the complete state-of-the-art of Fortran-C interoperability in a single chapter. At the end of this chapter, you'll have the basic knowledge to call C code from Fortran, and hopefully the thirst to dig deeper and learn more.

11.1 *Interfacing C: Writing a minimal TCP client and server*

Some languages are forgiving. The programmer needs only a basic sense of how things work. Errors in the code are flagged by the compile-time or run-time system, and the programmer can muddle through and eventually fix things up to work correctly. The C language is not like that.

—Nick Parlante, *Essential C*

C is a small yet incredibly powerful language. Created by Dennis Ritchie at Bell Labs in the early 1970s, it was the language that took operating systems programming by storm, and, soon after, general-purpose software development as well. It's also one of the most *dangerous* languages out there. C is infamous for being unforgiving to novice programmers because of its minimal yet versatile syntax that can be easily misused if not well understood. Nevertheless, the C ecosystem offers an immense treasury of tools and libraries at your fingertips.

Although Fortran programmers have been writing mixed Fortran and C applications for several decades, the interoperability features were officially introduced into the standard in Fortran 2003, and further improved in later revisions (2008 and 2018). In practice, interfacing C functions with data structures from Fortran boils down to correctly writing the interfaces, which means matching the data types of function arguments. This chapter will teach you very little C. After all, this a book about Fortran programming, and C is a whole other beast. If you have some experience with C, great! Otherwise, don't worry. I'll gently guide you through interfacing with C code from Fortran, and you'll learn all you need to know to do so, without having to learn C on the side. If you want to learn more about C, near the end of the chapter I provide references that I like.

To get your feet wet with interfacing with C from Fortran, we'll develop a minimal TCP client and server. We'll start with an existing C library that's easy to download and install and is well documented. One step at a time, we'll write Fortran interfaces with

C functions that we'll use. With only several function calls, we'll have a working TCP server running as a Fortran program and listening for incoming connections from anywhere in the world. We'll wrap up the chapter by writing a small TCP client, so in the end we'll have two Fortran programs talking to each other over the network.

What is TCP?

Transmission Control Protocol (TCP) is one of the most widely used protocols that power the internet. It allows reliable, error-checked transfer of binary data between hosts (computers) connected on an IP (Internet Protocol) network. TCP is a base transport layer for several different application layers, such as HTTP (Hypertext Transfer Protocol), commonly used to deliver content to web browsers, or websockets, used for responsive real-time networking, such as chat clients or collaborative office tools.

11.1.1 Introducing networking to Fortran

The C programming model is that the programmer knows exactly what they want to do and how to use the language constructs to achieve that goal. The language lets the expert programmer express what they want in the minimum time by staying out of their way.

—Nick Parlante, *Essential C*

While there are easier ways to write networking applications, this example demonstrates well the power of invoking C from Fortran. It's simple enough that we won't get bogged down in the details, and yet intricate enough that we can't implement it with Fortran alone. Except for the native parallelism with coarrays that's built into the language, Fortran offers no networking capability at all. This is where C and its wide array of systems programming libraries come to the rescue.

A fundamental concept in the implementation of computer networks is a socket. A socket is a resource provided by the operating system, and it allows software to access the networking hardware, such as Wi-Fi or Ethernet adapters, to send and receive data across the network. The data that goes through sockets is streams of bytes. A transport layer protocol such as TCP carefully formats packets of bytes into discrete messages. Application layer protocols such as HTTP or websockets are constructed by further formatting of TCP messages. They allow communication with context, which allows for richer applications, such as web pages and chat clients.

For simplicity, we won't interface with sockets directly on the operating system level; we'll use an existing high-level C library instead. There are many libraries out there to choose from, offering various levels of abstraction. For this example, let's use libdill (http://libdill.org), because it's lightweight and easy to install and use. libdill provides a high-level user interface with low-level operations in the operating system. Described as "structured concurrency for C," libdill's main feature is a coroutine, a popular concurrency model in many programming languages. Besides coroutines, libdill also provides easy-to-use interfaces with various networking protocols, including TCP, HTTP, websockets, and others. Perhaps most importantly, libdill is easy to download and

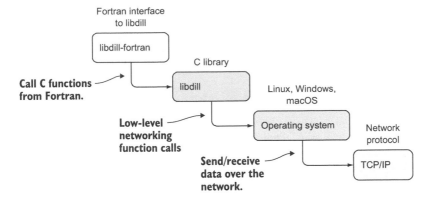

Figure 11.1   The hierarchy in our TCP client-server stack

compile and has great documentation. In this chapter, we'll focus on a small subset of libdill—its TCP stack of functions.

Figure 11.1 illustrates the components of our TCP client-server project. Read this diagram from top left to bottom right. libdill-fortran, the Fortran interface with libdill, will invoke C functions from our Fortran program. The libdill functions will, in turn, make low-level function calls provided by the operating system to send or receive data using the TCP/IP protocol.

As you can probably guess, we'll focus on implementing the top left component from this diagram: libdill-fortran. The libdill C library is already available, and compiling it gives us all the plumbing we need from the operating system to perform TCP networking operations (figure 11.2).

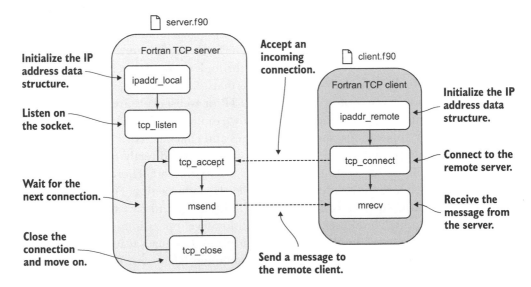

Figure 11.2   Implementing a minimal TCP server and client programs in Fortran

If the function names in this diagram seem a bit cryptic, I hear you! It will all become much clearer as we work through the steps of implementing the interfaces with each of these functions.

11.1.2 *Installing libdill*

Before we write any Fortran code, we'll first download and compile the C library that we'll work with: libdill. You can download the code from http://libdill.org/download .html. This page also includes brief installation instructions. For our work, we won't need to install libdill systemwide. Instead, we'll compile it and take a copy of the compiled library archive file:

Moves into the libdill source directory

Downloads the libdill tarball using curl

```
curl -O http://libdill.org/libdill-2.14.tar.gz
tar xzf libdill-2.14.tar.gz
cd libdill-2.14
./configure
make
cp .libs/libdill.a ..
```

Unpacks the libdill source code

Configures for building

Compiles the code

Makes a copy of the compiled library archive file, libdill.a

Here I used `curl` instead of `wget` (suggested at the libdill website) because it's more likely to already be installed on most Linux operating systems. If you prefer `wget` and have it on your system, by all means feel free to use that instead.

At the time of this writing, 2.14 is the current libdill version, and we'll use that version in this book. However, it's quite possible that you're reading this book years after its publication. If that's the case, you may want to use a later libdill version that may have bug fixes and performance improvements, if available. All the code and Fortran interfaces should still work with a later 2.xx version of libdill, assuming its API doesn't change.

> **Issues compiling libdill?**
>
> Specific versions of some compilers may have difficulty compiling one or more of lib-dill's components. If you encounter any issues, take a look at https://github.com/modern-fortran/tcp-client-server for potential solutions.

11.2 *TCP server program: Receiving network connections*

> *Perhaps the best advice is just to be careful. Don't type things in you don't understand. Debugging takes too much time. Have a mental picture (or a real drawing) of how your C code is using memory. That's good advice in any language, but in C it's critical.*
>
> —Nick Parlante, *Essential C*

Although this quote applies specifically to writing C code (which we won't do here), it's nevertheless important to keep in mind as we go forward with writing the Fortran-C interface.

We'll start by implementing the TCP server first. The heavy lifting of opening and listening on sockets, sending and receiving messages, and the TCP protocol itself will be handled internally by libdill and the operating system, so we won't have to worry about the implementation details of these pieces. What we'll focus on is correctly implementing the Fortran interfaces with libdill functions, and understanding what they do.

Our server will perform the following steps:

1 Initialize the IP address data structure.
2 Open a socket on a given IP address and port number.
3 Listen patiently for incoming connections.
4 On an incoming connection, send a message to the client.
5 When done, close the connection and move on.

To implement each step, we'll write Fortran interfaces with the appropriate C functions (figure 11.3):

- `ipaddr_local`—Initialize the data structure that holds the IP address and port number for the local computer (server).
- `tcp_listen`—Create a new socket given the input IP address structure and listen for incoming connections to it.
- `tcp_accept`—Accept an incoming connection on a socket.
- `suffix_attach` and `suffix_detach`—Append/remove a character string to/from all messages on a given connection to conform to a specific protocol, in our case TCP (not shown in figure 11.3).

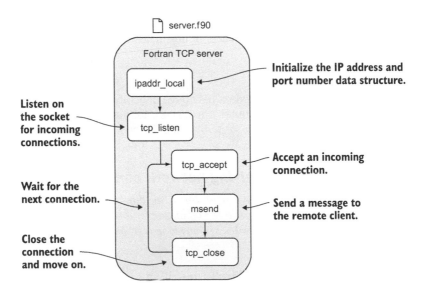

Figure 11.3   Fortran TCP server program, illustrated

- `msend`—Send a message to the remote client that just connected to the server.
- `tcp_close`—Gracefully close the connection and move on.

As you can see in figures 11.2 and 11.3, `ipaddr_local` and `tcp_listen` will be invoked once, when the server program starts up. `tcp_accept` and `msend` will be in an infinite do loop, to allow accepting connections one after another, indefinitely. `suffix_attach` and `suffix_detach`, while not included in the figures for brevity, are convenience functions that will help us format our character strings into valid TCP messages.

We'll tackle these one at a time and learn Fortran-C interoperability along the way. Let's go in order.

11.2.1 IP address data structures

Whenever we write an interface with a C function or struct, we first look at the documentation for that function. Ideally, the C library you work with will be well documented. However, this isn't always the case, and sometimes we need to look at the C source code to see how the function is defined there.

Our first step is to write a Fortran interface with the C struct `ipaddr` in the libdill library. This is the first ingredient we need to get before implementing the `ipaddr_local` (server) and `ipaddr_remote` (client) functions. A struct in C is analogous to a derived type in Fortran (see chapter 8)—an arbitrary data structure with components of built-in or other data types. For the most part, they have a similar syntax and behavior.

Although the functions `ipaddr_local` and `ipaddr_remote` are described in the documentation, the `ipaddr` struct that they use as an argument isn't. To understand how to write a Fortran interface with this struct, we need to look inside the libdill header file. If you installed libdill following the instructions in the previous subsection, you'll find the file here: libdill-2.14/libdill.h. The relevant snippet that gives the definition of the `ipaddr` struct in `libdill.h` is

```
struct dill_ipaddr {char _[32];};
```

Although it may seem a bit cryptic at first, this is a relatively simple struct. It has only one component, an array of 32 characters called _ (underscore). Our task is to define a Fortran derived type that will match this struct. The following listing shows a working Fortran interface, defined in a new module.

> **Listing 11.1   A Fortran interface with the `ipaddr` struct**

```
module mod_dill

    use iso_c_binding, only: c_char          ⟵  Imports the C character
    implicit none                                  type kind parameter
                                                   from iso_c_binding

    private
    public :: ipaddr
                                             Defines a new derived
    type, bind(c, name='dill_ipaddr') :: ipaddr  ⟵  type and binds its name
                                                     to a C equivalent struct
```

```
      character(c_char) :: address(32)          ◁───  This type has only one
  end type ipaddr         ◁────┐                       component, an array
                               │   Closes the type     of 32 characters.
end module mod_dill            │   definition
```

Quite a few things are going on here. First, like any other Fortran code that we aim to reuse, we define this derived type in a module. I chose mod_dill as the module name—mod_ as a prefix following my preferred convention for naming modules, and dill because, well, we're writing an interface with libdill (the dill library).

Second, we import c_char from the iso_c_binding module. Like iso_fortran _env, iso_c_binding is a built-in module that's specified by the standard and provided by the compiler. c_char is a type kind parameter, just like int64 and real64 from iso_fortran_env. Its purpose is to provide the exact type kind to interface with the character in the companion C compiler. A companion C compiler is simply the C compiler compatible with your Fortran compiler, and typically from the same vendor. For example, the companion C compiler to gfortran is gcc, and the companion C compiler to ifort (Intel Fortran) is icc (Intel C compiler).

Finally, we get to our derived type, ipaddr. The opening line of the type definition has a new attribute, bind(). This attribute states that this derived type is meant to bind to an existing C struct, whose name is specified as a keyword argument, name. If this argument is omitted, the compiler will use the name of the derived type (in all lowercase) as the name of the matching C struct. Like its C counterpart, this derived type has only one component, an array of 32 characters. This is where we use the c_char as a type kind parameter to declare the component in the Fortran implementation.

Recall that the original C struct has a component named _ (underscore). Ideally we'd match C variable names exactly in our Fortran interface, for clarity. Although Fortran allows underscores in variable, procedure, and module names, it doesn't allow using one as the first or the only character in a name. To work around this restriction, we can name our component something meaningful. I chose address, as this component will internally store the address and port components of an IP address.

A note on C strings

C has characters, which are always of length 1. Multicharacter strings are represented as arrays of characters. A string in C is terminated with a *null* character, '\0'. This is an important detail to be mindful of as we exchange character strings between our Fortran code and the C functions.

Figure 11.4 illustrates the interface between the Fortran derived type and a C struct.

The ipaddr struct in libdill is used strictly internally. We won't write data to its component directly, and we'll only manipulate it through functions ipaddr_local and ipaddr_remote.

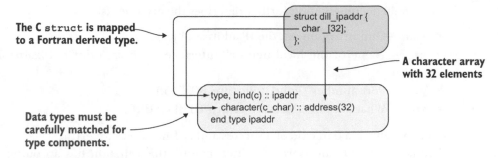

Figure 11.4   Mapping a C struct to a Fortran derived type

You can now compile this module:

```
gfortran -c mod_dill.f90
```

The `-c` option means "compile only, do not link." The compiler will produce the compiled module file mod_dill.mod and the binary object file mod_dill.o. Even though we defined a derived type that binds to a C struct, no C code or compiled object came into the picture. This module doesn't do anything useful yet, as it just defines a simple derived type to interface with a C struct. Let's see how we can use this type to open a new connection.

11.2.2 Initializing the IP address structure

Now that we have a derived type to interface with the `ipaddr` struct, let's create an instance of it. libdill provides two functions to instantiate the `ipaddr` struct: `ipaddr _local` and `ipaddr_remote`. The former is used on the server side, where you want to open up a socket to listen to incoming connections. The latter is used on the client side, where you want to connect to a socket on a remote server.

Unlike the `ipaddr` struct we had to look up in the libdill header file, `ipaddr_local` is described in the libdill documentation pages (http://libdill.org/documentation). Specifically, for `ipaddr_local`, here's the prototype:

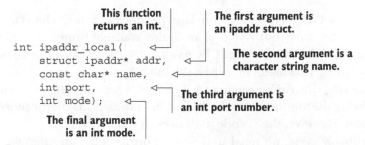

This is the header (or, in C terminology, *prototype*) of the `ipaddr_local` function. The first word, `int`, before the function name, states its type. Inside the parentheses, we have a list of arguments, just like in Fortran functions.

The libdill documentation further describes the arguments:

- `addr`—Output argument; the IP address object
- `name`—Name of the local network interface, such as "eth0", "192.168.0.111" or "::1"
- `port`—Port number (Valid values are 1-65535.)
- `mode`—What kind of address to return (IPv4 or IPv6)

The return value is a 0 in case of a success and a -1 in case of an error.

Unlike all the functions we've written before, this function has an output argument, `addr`. This is required so that a variable can be modified in-place. Recall that in Fortran we use subroutines specifically when we need to modify values of arguments in-place. As C has only functions and no separate concept of subroutines, arguments can be modified in-place by passing them by reference instead of by value. Take note that `addr` and `name` are declared with an * (asterisk) that immediately follows their types (`struct ipaddr*` and `char*`, respectively), while `port` and `mode` aren't. There's an important difference here that we'll dig into shortly.

As for the `mode` argument, libdill defines its possible values as compile-time constants in `libdill.h`:

```
#define DILL_1PADDR_IPV4 1
#define DILL_IPADDR_IPV6 2
```

These constants are defined as C preprocessor macros. When we compiled libdill, the preprocessor first parsed and manipulated the C source files before passing them to the compiler. In this case, the preprocessor replaced any occurrence of `DILL_IPADDR _IPV4` with the literal constant 1 (and likewise with `DILL_IPADDR_IPV6`). For transparency in the Fortran interface with libdill, we'll define the integer parameter with the same name and value, declaring a compile-time constant for IP address mode:

```
use iso_c_binding, only: c_char, c_int

integer(c_int), parameter :: IPADDR_IPV4 = 1
```

Here, we encounter another C-equivalent type kind parameter, `c_int`. This is a Fortran representation of C's int type, and, like `c_char`, is also available from `iso_c_binding`. We'll now be able to invoke `ipaddr_local` by passing `IPADDR_IPV4` as the `mode` argument, rather than having to rcmember to pass the value 1.

If you're wondering why each argument is listed on a separate line, it's merely a choice of style. Listing the arguments on individual lines usually makes for more readable documentation. However, the C code itself doesn't require it.

As you can probably guess, we need to define a Fortran function interface whose return value and arguments will match those of the C function, as shown in listing 11.2.

Types and their representations

We could casually say that C's int and Fortran's integer are the same types. However, this isn't strictly true. They belong to different languages, so even though they seem like they could be similar or equal, they're not. What matters for us, in practice, is that their *representation* in memory is the same. Likewise for C's float and Fortran's real, or C's char and Fortran's character.

Listing 11.2 Defining a Fortran interface to the ipaddr_local C function

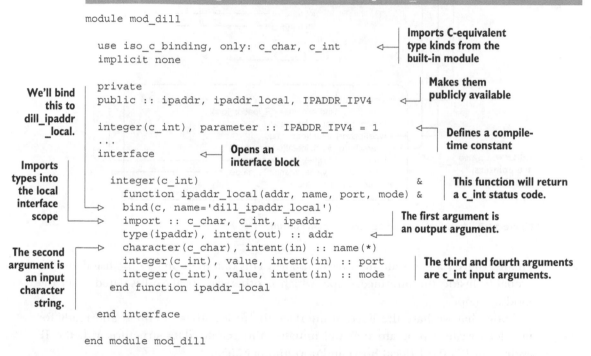

```
module mod_dill

    use iso_c_binding, only: c_char, c_int         Imports C-equivalent
    implicit none                                  type kinds from the
                                                   built-in module

    private                                         Makes them
    public :: ipaddr, ipaddr_local, IPADDR_IPV4     publicly available

    integer(c_int), parameter :: IPADDR_IPV4 = 1    Defines a compile-
    ...                                             time constant
    interface            Opens an
                         interface block

      integer(c_int)                                       &     This function will return
        function ipaddr_local(addr, name, port, mode) &          a c_int status code.
        bind(c, name='dill_ipaddr_local')
        import :: c_char, c_int, ipaddr             The first argument is
        type(ipaddr), intent(out) :: addr           an output argument.
        character(c_char), intent(in) :: name(*)
        integer(c_int), value, intent(in) :: port   The third and fourth arguments
        integer(c_int), value, intent(in) :: mode   are c_int input arguments.
      end function ipaddr_local

    end interface

end module mod_dill
```

We'll bind this to dill_ipaddr_local.

Imports types into the local interface scope

The second argument is an input character string.

There's a lot to unpack here, so I'll go slowly. First, we use the function statement to define the function name and its arguments. This works the same way as with all Fortran functions we worked with before. One key difference is that here we add the bind attribute, like we did when defining the ipaddr derived type. Here, we also specify the name keyword argument in the parentheses, which is the name of the C function that we'll bind our Fortran interface to. Notice that we're binding to the name dill_ipaddr_local, rather than just ipaddr_local. This is because libdill by default adds a prefix dill_ to all its functions to avoid name conflicts with any similar library that may export functions with the same name.

Second, recall that Fortran passes arguments *by reference*, meaning that no new copy of an argument is created inside the function. In contrast, C passes arguments *by value*, meaning that a new copy is created inside the function scope. This means that when the argument in the C function definition is a pointer, we'll interface with it from Fortran as is, because of its default pass-by-reference behavior. However, for regular, nonpointer C arguments, Fortran provides a special attribute, value, which instructs the compiler that the argument is to be passed by value, rather than by reference. Figure 11.5 illustrates this rule.

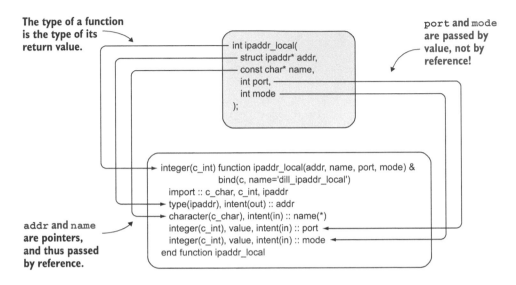

Figure 11.5   Interfacing ipaddr_local from Fortran

Finally, there's a new statement here, import. This statement makes the listed entities available inside the interface scope, which is otherwise local and isolated from the module scope.

Now that we have the Fortran interface to ipaddr_local defined and ready for use, let's write a program that will initialize the ipaddr data structure with the IP address at 127.0.0.1 (local host) and port number 5555.

Listing 11.3   Fortran TCP server initializing only the IP address and port number

```
program server

    use iso_c_binding, only: c_int, c_null_char        ←── Imports C-type kind parameters
    use mod_dill, only: ipaddr, ipaddr_local, IPADDR_IPV4    ←── from the built-in module
                                                                 Imports Fortran
                                                                 interfaces with C
    implicit none                            Declares a return     struct and function
    integer(c_int) :: rc        ←──          code as a C int
    type(ipaddr) :: addr        ←──     Calls ipaddr_local to
                                        initialize the addr instance

    rc = ipaddr_local(addr, '127.0.0.1' // c_null_char, &
                    5555_c_int, IPADDR_IPV4)

end program server
```

We begin by importing two constants from iso_c_binding: c_int, a C integer equivalent, and c_null_char, a special constant that we'll use to terminate C strings. From our new module, mod_dill, we import the ipaddr type and our new ipaddr_local interface.

Our Fortran server program so far has only one function call to ipaddr_local, which stores the IP address and port number parameters in an internal representation that libdill uses. It's at this call to ipaddr_local that we need to be super careful. First, C strings are always terminated with the null character, '\0'. From Fortran, we can do this in a portable way by appending c_null_char to the character string that we pass to the C function. Thus, instead of passing '127.0.0.1' as the second argument to ipaddr_local, we pass '127.0.0.1' // c_null_char. Second, recall that ipaddr_local expects the third and fourth arguments to be of C int type, not Fortran integers! We thus need to cast our arguments to the C int types. We do this by appending the c_int suffix to the value: 5555_c_int. What we're passing as the mode argument is already declared as an integer(c_int) constant, so no explicit conversion is needed here.

Finally, we assign the result of the ipaddr_local function to rc, the integer *return code*. The value of the return code indicates whether the function executed correctly or not. For example, in C and many other programming languages, as well as UNIX and Linux command-line tools, the return code value of zero indicates that the function (or program) finished successfully, that is, without errors. In contrast, a nonzero value, positive or negative, indicates an error, and the specific value of the return code can be used to encode what kind of error it is. If we want, we can explicitly check the value of rc to ensure that the function call worked. This is a common way to do exception handling in C, and we can use it in the Fortran interface as well. The libdill documentation website lists all the error codes that you may encounter while using this library.

IP address and port number values

There's no special meaning behind the value 5555 for the port number. The port number should be no larger than 65535, and not already in use. On most systems, values greater than 1024 are safe to use. Various servers or web frameworks commonly use arbitrary values in development, such as 4000, 5555, or 8080.

You can compile and run this program. If all is good, it will output nothing. We expect this, as the program does nothing but instantiate a data structure and stop. However, currently we don't know if ipaddr is initialized correctly. We'll test that the IP address and port number values have been stored correctly in the next section.

11.2.3 *Checking IP address values*

Testing is recommended. Having made our call to `ipaddr_local`, we have no clue whether it worked or not. All that we know is that the program didn't crash with any error message. After we initialize `ipaddr`, we can use libdill functions to explicitly check for the IP address and port number values stored.

First, let's take a look at the IP address. libdill has a function to read its value from an initialized `ipaddr` struct:

```
const char* ipaddr_str(          ◁         This function returns a pointer
    const struct ipaddr* addr,   ◁──┐      to a character string.
    char* buf);           ◁             The first argument (input)
                                         is an ipaddr struct.
                                    The second argument (input/output)
                                    is a character string.
```

From the libdill documentation, `ipaddr_str` formats the address as a human-readable string.

- addr—IP address object
- buf—Buffer to store the result in, which must be at least `IPADDR_MAXSTRLEN` bytes long

The function returns the `ipstr` argument, which is the pointer to the formatted string.

It seems like there are two ways to obtain the IP address string: by accessing the value through the pointer returned by the function, or by reading it directly from the character string, `buf`. Let's interface this with a Fortran subroutine that will use the character string buffer to retrieve the IP address string, as shown in the following listing.

> **Listing 11.4   Fortran interface to `ipaddr_str`, this time a subroutine**

```
module mod_dill
   ...
   public :: ipaddr, ipaddr_local, ipaddr_str        A subroutine that
                                                       takes two arguments
   interface
      ...
      subroutine ipaddr_str(addr, buf) &          ◁      Let's bind this to
               bind(c, name='dill_ipaddr_str')    ◁      dill_ipaddr_str.
         import :: c_char, ipaddr           ◁
         type(ipaddr), intent(in) :: addr   ◁          Imports C-type kind
         character(c_char), intent(out) :: buf(*)  ◁   parameters into the
      end subroutine ipaddr_str                         local scope
   end interface                       An array of      The ipaddr derived type
                                    characters is the   is the input argument.
end module mod_dill                  output argument.
```

This is the first interface where we use an array of characters as an argument. You may notice a curious detail: this argument is declared with an asterisk (`buf(*)`), rather than a colon like we used in the past for assumed-shape array arguments. This is a somewhat obscure feature of Fortran called *assumed-size* arrays (in contrast to assumed shape) and applies to array or character string arguments to C functions. It's there for easier interfacing with C functions, but otherwise you shouldn't ever use it in pure Fortran programs. To quote the late Walter Brainerd in his book *Guide to Fortran 2008 Programming*: "Do not ask why—just do it."

Note that we could've made this Fortran interface a function as well as a subroutine. A subroutine makes sense when one or more of the arguments are output arguments; however, a subroutine can't capture the return value of a function. In this case, this is okay because we only care about accessing the buffer `buf` as the `intent(out)` argument. The choice between using a function or a subroutine to interface with a C-function also affects the syntax of how the procedure is invoked. Feel free to implement interfaces that best fit your programming style, and make sure that you get the data that you need.

Now that we have a subroutine to get the IP address string from the `ipaddr` struct, how about the port number? Time for an exercise! (See the "Exercise 1" sidebar.)

Exercise 1: The Fortran interface to `ipaddr_port`

It's your turn now! We need to check that the port number is stored correctly when we call the `ipaddr_local` function. We've already implemented the interface to `ipaddr_str`, which returns the character string representation of the IP address. libdill also provides the `ipaddr_port` function, which returns the integer value of the port number associated with the `ipaddr` data structure:

```
int ipaddr_port(
    const struct ipaddr* addr);
```

Implement the Fortran interface to this function and check that it returns the correct value of the port number.

The solution to this exercise is given in the "Answer key" section near the end of the chapter.

Finally, in our server program, we can check that the IP address and port number are stored correctly, as shown in the following listing.

Listing 11.5   Updated Fortran TCP server program

```
program server                          Imports C-type parameters
                                        from the built-in module
    use iso_c_binding, only: c_char, c_int, c_null_char    ←┘
    use mod_dill, only: ipaddr, ipaddr_local,    &
                        ipaddr_port, ipaddr_str, &    Imports our
                        IPADDR_MAXSTRLEN, IPADDR_IPV4    Fortran-C
                                                         interfaces
```

```
implicit none

integer(c_int) :: rc
type(ipaddr) :: addr
character(kind=c_char, len=IPADDR_MAXSTRLEN) :: &
  address_string = ''

rc = ipaddr_local(addr, '127.0.0.1' // c_null_char, &
                  5555_c_int, IPADDR_IPV4)
call ipaddr_str(addr, address_string)

print *, 'Opening socket:'
print *, '  IP address: ', address_string
print *, '  Port: ', ipaddr_port(addr)

end program server
```

Initializes the address string variable

Initializes the IP address and port number

Prints the IP address and port number to the screen

Gets the IP address string to check its value

You can now compile and run this program, and it should print the IP address and port number to the screen:

```
gfortran mod_dill.f90 server.f90 libdill.a \
  -pthread -o server
./server
  Opening socket:
   IP address: 127.0.0.1
   Port:          5555
```

Runs the server program

Compiles and links

The output of the server program

So far, so good! The program compiles successfully and runs without any apparent errors. If you're wondering about the -pthread flag, it enables the use of POSIX threads, a system dependency of libdill. Even though we don't use threads in our Fortran code directly, we include this flag to make the linker happy; that is, so we can build the executable file.

POSIX threads

POSIX (Portable Operating System Interface) threads, often called pthreads, is a concurrent and parallel execution model. It's not intrinsic to any single programming language, but instead is provided by the operating system. It's supported out of the box by most UNIX systems, including macOS, Linux, and Windows using a third-party library. You can read more about POSIX threads at https://en.wikipedia.org/wiki/POSIX_Threads.

11.2.4 *Intermezzo: Matching compatible C and Fortran data types*

Now that you've got a taste of interfacing C-structs with functions from Fortran, it's a good time to go into more detail on compatible C and Fortran data types. I mentioned earlier that C types are different from Fortran types: int is not exactly integer, and `float` is not exactly `real`. What matters, however, is that we have a reliable way to match the compatible data types between C and Fortran such that their internal representation in memory is the same. To that end, a wide array of C-conforming type kind parameters is available out of the box in the `iso_c_binding` module. Table 11.1 lists them all.

Table 11.1 Type kind parameters available in `iso_c_binding` and their corresponding types in C

Base type	Fortran type kind parameter	C type
integer	c_int	int
	c_int8_t	int8_t
	c_int16_t	int16_t
	c_int32_t	int32_t
	c_int64_t	int64_t
	c_int_least8_t	int_least8_t
	c_int_least16_t	int_least16_t
	c_int_least32_t	int_least32_t
	c_int_least64_t	int_least64_t
	c_int_fast8_t	int_fast8_t
	c_int_fast16_t	int_fast16_t
	c_int_fast32_t	int_fast32_t
	c_int_fast64_t	int_fast64_t
	c_intmax_t	intmax_t
	c_intptr_t	intptr_t
	c_size_t	size_t, ssize_t
	c_short	short int
	c_long	long int
	c_long_long	long long int
	c_signed_char	signed char, unsigned char
real	c_float	float
	c_double	double
	c_long_double	long double
complex	c_float_complex	float complex
	c_double_complex	double complex
	c_long_double_complex	long double complex
logical	c_bool	bool
character	c_char	char

As you can see from table 11.1, C has many built-in types, and Fortran's `iso_c_binding` provides type kind parameters to match them.

The C types `bool` and `complex` were introduced in the C99 revision to the C Standard. They may appear as `_Bool` and `_Complex`, respectively, in C code that was meant to be compliant with earlier C standards. You can refer back to this table as you write Fortran interfaces with other C code. For now, you don't need to know any more details about many of these C types and their Fortran siblings. Let's go back to our TCP server, where we'll encounter a few new C types, such as `int64_t` and `size_t`.

C type not supported?

If a C type isn't supported by your Fortran or C compiler, either you'll get a compile-time error or the type kind parameter imported from `iso_c_binding` will have a negative value.

11.2.5 *Creating a socket and listening for connections*

We now have an IP address data structure, and we can initialize its value by calling the `ipaddr_local` function. Let's now use this structure to open a socket and listen for incoming connections. To do this, we'll use the `tcp_listen` function. Like before, we'll first look at the interface of the C function from the libdill documentation:

```
int tcp_listen(
    const struct ipaddr* addr,
    int backlog);
```

- `addr`—IP address to listen on
- `backlog`—Maximum number of connections that can be kept open without accepting them

If successful, the return value is the newly created socket, represented by a single integer value. Otherwise, the return code is -1, indicating an error.

Simple enough! For our example, we'll ignore the backlog—that is, we'll just pass a zero to that argument—but we still need to implement it in the Fortran interface to the `tcp_listen` function:

We'll bind it to
dill_tcp_listen.

This function returns a c_int status.

```
integer(c_int) function tcp_listen(addr, backlog) &
                bind(c, name='dill_tcp_listen')
    import :: c_int, ipaddr
    type(ipaddr), intent(in) :: addr
    integer(c_int), value, intent(in) :: backlog
end function tcp_listen
```

Imports the C-equivalent type kinds into the local scope

The second argument (input) is a c_int integer backlog.

The first argument (input) is an ipaddr struct.

As with previous interfaces, we'll place this one inside the `interface` block in the `mod_dill` module. For simplicity, we won't worry about the `backlog` argument and keeping connections without accepting them. To listen for incoming TCP connections, we'll declare an `integer(c_int)` variable `socket` and add the following line after we initialize our IP address structure:

```
socket = tcp_listen(addr, 0_c_int)
```

This function call instructs the program to listen for incoming connections on a socket at the IP address and port number defined in the `addr` structure. Add this line to the program, recompile it, and run it. The output should be the same as at the end of the previous section. Now we're ready for the fun stuff.

11.2.6 Accepting incoming connections to a socket

We now have our socket open to the world, and we're listening for connections. The C code (libdill) and the operating system will do the work of making the connection happen, so we don't have to worry about that part. Our job here is to accept an incoming connection and do something with it (send a message, for example) once it's established. Back to the libdill documentation; `tcp_accept` accepts an incoming TCP connection:

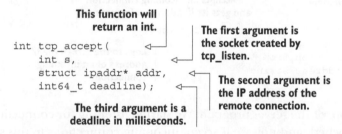

The first argument (input), `s`, is the socket created by `tcp_listen`. The second argument (output) is the IP address structure associated with the remote client—its value will tell us where the connection is coming from. Finally, the `deadline` is a point in time when the operation should time out (abort). According to the libdill documentation, `deadline` having a value of 0 means an immediate timeout, that is, return immediately if the function doesn't succeed. The value of –1 means no deadline—block forever until the function succeeds. For our simple example, blocking until success (`deadline = -1`) will do just fine, and we'll use this value for the deadline through the rest of this chapter. Like before, pay close attention to which arguments are declared as pointers (`ipaddr*`, pass by reference), and which aren't (`s` and `deadline`, pass by value).

This is the first time that we encounter the `int64_t` data type. In C parlance, `int64_t` (short for 64-bit-wide integer type) is known as a *long long*. It's a signed integer type that occupies exactly 8 bytes (64 bits) in memory and is useful for variables whose values can get extraordinarily large, up to about $+/- \, 9 \times 10^{18}$. Like other

C-equivalent type kinds, `int64_t` is available to Fortran through the `iso_c_binding` module as `c_int64_t`:

```
use iso_c_binding, only: c_int64_t
```

Here's the complete Fortran interface to `tcp_accept`:

Imports the C-equivalent type kinds into the local scope

This function will return a c_int.

We'll bind it to dill_tcp_accept.

```
integer(c_int) function tcp_accept(s, addr, deadline) &
                       bind(c, name='dill_tcp_accept')
  import :: c_int, c_int64_t, ipaddr
  integer(c_int), value, intent(in) :: s
  type(ipaddr), intent(out) :: addr
  integer(c_int64_t), value, intent(in) :: deadline
end function tcp_accept
```

The first argument is the c_int socket and is passed by value.

The second argument is the ipaddr struct and is passed by reference.

The third argument is the c_int64_t deadline in milliseconds and is passed by value.

We want the server program to keep accepting connections indefinitely, so we'll place `tcp_accept` in an infinite do loop back in our server program in `server.f90`:

Loops indefinitely

Accepts an incoming connection and gets its IP address information

```
do
  connection = tcp_accept(socket, addr, -1_c_int64_t)
  call ipaddr_str(addr, address_string)
  print *, 'New connection from ' &
         // trim(address_string)
end do
```

Logs to the screen the IP address of an incoming connection

This snippet is the core of the server program. We started listening for connections on the socket that we opened, and now we'll accept incoming connections to this socket. To keep accepting connections one after another, we place this code inside of an infinite do loop. As soon as one incoming connection is accepted and processed, the server will wait for the next one. This also means that the program has no way of stopping on its own, except for unhandled exceptions; otherwise, it would need to be interrupted by the user from the OS (for example, with Ctrl + C in Linux).

Here, we also reuse the `ipaddr_str` interface we implemented earlier to get the text representation of the IP address of the incoming connection. As remote clients connect to your server, you'll be able to see from which IP addresses the connections are coming. Note that at this point, the server program is an intermediate implementation and missing a critical piece—sending a response back to each incoming connection.

11.2.7 *Sending a TCP message to the client*

Finally, on each accepted connection, we'll send a message to the client to let them know the server is alive. Not so fast, though. Recall that the data is just a stream of bytes, and the TCP protocol defines *messages* that are specially formatted packets of binary data. Fortunately, libdill provides a convenience function, `suffix_attach`, to append a suffix to any packet of binary data that we give to it:

```
                    This function returns an int.

int suffix_attach(          <---        Socket to apply
    int s,                  <---         the suffix to
    const void* suffix,     <---
    size_t suffixlen);      <---        Void pointer
                                        to the suffix
         Length of the suffix
```

This is the first time that we encounter the C *void pointer* (void*) as one of the arguments. The void pointer is used to allow addressing variables of different types. In that sense, the void pointer is just an address to a place in memory, but that memory could hold an integer, a float, or a character. The `const` attribute ensures that the value of suffix can't be modified inside the function, analogous to Fortran's `intent(in)` arguments. We could interface the void-typed suffix with any type; however, to format the byte packets into valid TCP messages, we'll append "\r\n"—a carriage return and a new line—to each packet. To that end, interfacing the argument `suffix` with a `character(c_char)` will work fine, using the Fortran interface to the `suffix_attach` function in libdill:

```
integer(c_int) function suffix_attach(s, suffix, suffixlen) &
              bind(c, name='dill_suffix_attach')
  import :: c_char, c_int, c_size_t
  integer(c_int), value, intent(in) :: s
  character(c_char), intent(in) :: suffix(*)
  integer(c_size_t), value, intent(in) :: suffixlen
end function suffix_attach
```

To formulate the suffix "\r\n" in our Fortran code, we need to import these special characters from `iso_c_binding`:

```
...
use iso_c_binding, only: c_null_char, c_new_line, c_carriage_return
character(len=*), parameter :: &
  TCP_SUFFIX = c_carriage_return // c_new_line // c_null_char
...
connection = suffix_attach(connection, TCP_SUFFIX, 2_c_size_t)
...
```

We call the `suffix_attach` function once for any given connection, and every packet sent through that connection will be formatted as a TCP message. If you're wondering why the length of `TCP_SUFFIX` (third argument to `suffix_attach`) is 2 and not 3, it's because libdill (and C in general) doesn't count the null character as a separate character. Even though we pass it here as a three-character string (carriage return, new line, and null character), libdill receives and interprets it as a two-character string.

Now that we have the piece that formats byte packets into valid TCP messages, let's get to actually sending the message to the client. You know the drill—here's how libdill defines the msend function.

Listing 11.6   Header of the msend function in libdill

```
int msend(
    int s,
    const void* buf,
    size_t len,
    int64_t deadline);
```

The function result is an int. → `int msend(`

Input socket on which to send the message → `int s,`

Void pointer to a buffer → `const void* buf,`

Length of the message → `size_t len,`

Deadline in milliseconds → `int64_t deadline);`

And here's its corresponding Fortran interface:

```
integer(c_int) function msend(s, buf, len, deadline) &
            bind(c, name='dill_msend')
  import :: c_char, c_int, c_int64_t, c_size_t
  integer(c_int), value, intent(in) :: s
  character(c_char), intent(in) :: buf(*)
  integer(c_size_t), value, intent(in) :: len
  integer(c_int64_t), value, intent(in) :: deadline
end function msend
```

With these two functions ready, we can now add the new calls to suffix_attach and msend to our server loop to send a TCP message on a remote connection from a client:

```
do
    connection = tcp_accept(socket, addr_remote, -1_c_int64_t)
    call ipaddr_str(addr, address_string)
    print *, 'New connection from ' // trim(address_string)
    connection = suffix_attach(connection, TCP_SUFFIX, 2_c_size_t)
    rc = msend(connection, 'Hello' // c_null_char, 5_c_size_t, -1_c_int64_t)
```

Our connection loop thus far accepts a connection (tcp_accept), parses the remote client IP address (ipaddr_str) and prints it to the screen, attaches a special suffix to format messages following a TCP protocol (suffix_attach), and finally sends a TCP message (msend).

You may have noticed that in the call to msend, we send both the contents of the message as the second argument, and the length of the message as a third argument. At first this may seem tedious and redundant, but it's necessary due to C semantics and how the msend function is designed in libdill. Recall that the message buffer buf is declared as a void pointer (listing 11.6), which is the memory address where the buffer begins, so msend needs additional information about how long the buffer is. If we were designing a higher level Fortran interface with libdill, we could take an extra step and write a wrapper around the Fortran interface to msend, and automatically calculate the length of the message before passing it to msend. Similarly, such a wrapper could automatically append c_null_char to any string that's on its way to libdill. This kind of exercise is beyond the scope of this chapter, but I encourage you to practice by implementing higher level wrappers that are more user friendly.

11.2.8 Closing a connection

There's only one step left before we wrap up and test our little TCP server program— once we send the message, we want to close the connection gracefully. libdill provides a function to do this—tcp_close. Can you help me implement the interface to it? Try exercise 2 in the sidebar.

Exercise 2: Fortran interfaces to suffix_detach **and** tcp_close

You now know everything you need to know to implement the last two remaining pieces of the server code: suffix_detach and tcp_close. These function calls will be necessary to gracefully close the TCP connection from the client. Here's the prototype for the suffix_detach function:

```
int suffix_detach(
    int s,
    int64_t deadline);
```

And here's the prototype of the tcp_close function:

```
int tcp_close(
    int s,
    int64_t deadline);
```

If implemented correctly in the mod_dill module, you'll be able to import these interfaces and call them from the main server loop:

```
connection = suffix_detach(connection, -1_c_int64_t)
rc = tcp_close(connection, -1_c_int64_t)
```

The solution to this exercise is given in the "Answer key" section near the end of the chapter.

Our server loop will now look like the following listing.

Listing 11.7 The main loop that accepts a connection and sends a message

```
do
  connection = tcp_accept(socket, addr_remote, -1_c_int64_t)
  call ipaddr_str(addr, address_string)
  print *, 'New connection from ' // trim(address_string)
  connection = suffix_attach(connection, TCP_SUFFIX, 2_c_size_t)
  rc = msend(connection, 'Hello' // c_null_char, 5_c_size_t, -1_c_int64_t)
  connection = suffix_detach(connection, -1_c_int64_t)
  rc = tcp_close(connection, -1_c_int64_t)
end do
```

That's it! Our server will now accept an incoming connection, send a greeting message to the client, and close the connection.

Let's see how it works from the client side. First, compile and run the server from one terminal session:

```
gfortran mod_dill.f90 server.f90 libdill.a -pthread -o server
./server
 Listening on socket:
   IP address: 127.0.0.1
   Port:          5555
```

In another terminal session, you can use a variety of command-line tools (`curl`, `netcat`, `telnet`) to connect to our Fortran server:

```
curl 127.0.0.1:5555        ⟵───────   Connects to the
Hello                                  server using curl
nc 127.0.0.1 5555          ⟵
Hello
telnet 127.0.0.1 5555      ⟵          Connects to the server
Trying 127.0.0.1...                   using nc (netcat)
Connected to 127.0.0.1.
Escape character is '^]'.              Connects to the
Hello                                  server using telnet
Connection closed by foreign host.
```

Voila! This confirms that our minimal Fortran web server is reachable using language-agnostic networking tools and returns the expected result. All of these tools are available out of the box on most modern Linux distributions. If not, you can easily install them using the system package manager. On macOS, they may or may not be available out of the box but can be downloaded and installed. On Windows, I recommend that you use the recent Windows Terminal or the Windows Subsystem for Linux.

Making TCP requests with `curl`

Our minimal TCP server emits a response as a raw sequence of bytes, without any descriptive headers that are characteristic of HTTP responses. Some newer versions of `curl` may expect an HTTP response by default and may return an error message:

```
curl: (1) Received HTTP/0.9 when not allowed
```

To work around this, invoke `curl` like this:

```
curl --http0.9 127.0.0.1:5555
```

At this point, you should have the following files in your working directory:

- *libdill.a*—A compiled archive file for the libdill library
- *mod_dill.f90*—A Fortran source file containing the mod_dill module, which defines and makes available the following entities: ipaddr, ipaddr_local,

ipaddr_port, ipaddr_str, IPADDR_MAXSTRLEN, IPADDR_IPV4, msend, suffix _attach, suffix _detach, tcp_accept, tcp_close, and tcp_listen

- *server.f90*—A Fortran source file containing the server program that imports the procedures and constants and uses them to listen for incoming connections to an open socket

Now that we've implemented the server, let's write the client program.

11.3 *TCP client program: Connecting to a remote server*

As I mentioned before, to implement the client, we'll need Fortran interfaces to a few new libdill functions (figure 11.6):

- ipaddr_remote to initialize a data structure with the remote IP address and port number
- tcp_connect to connect to a remote socket at a given IP address
- mrecv to receive a message from the server on a successful connection

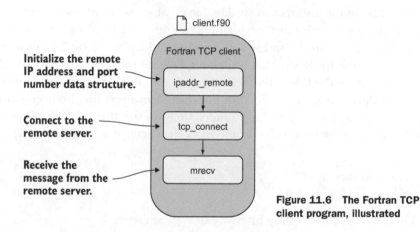

Figure 11.6 The Fortran TCP client program, illustrated

Having gone through the server implementation, writing these interfaces for the client should be straightforward.

11.3.1 *Connecting to a remote socket*

Like we did on the server, first we need to initialize a data structure to hold the IP address and port number. In this case, they'll be the IP address and port number of the remote host to which we'll connect. Here's the prototype of the ipaddr_remote function in libdill:

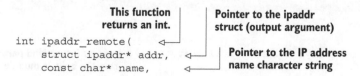

```
int port,                 Integer port number
int mode,                 and mode (IP v4 or v6)
int64_t deadline);    ◄─┐
        Deadline in milliseconds
```

This interface is exactly the same as for `ipaddr_local`, except for the `deadline` argument. As we've implemented this argument in other interfaces, the Fortran interface to `ipaddr_remote` is straightforward:

```
integer(c_int) function ipaddr_remote(addr, name, port, mode, deadline) &
             bind(c, name='dill_ipaddr_remote')
  import :: c_char, c_int, c_int64_t, ipaddr
  type(ipaddr), intent(out) :: addr
  character(c_char), intent(in) :: name(*)
  integer(c_int), value, intent(in) :: port
  integer(c_int), value, intent(in) :: mode
  integer(c_int64_t), value, intent(in) :: deadline
end function ipaddr_remote
```

As in the case of the interface to `ipaddr_local`, which we implemented in section 11.2.2, here we need to watch out for which arguments are passed by reference (pointer to the address in memory), and which by value (a local copy of the argument is made inside the function). Recall that by default, Fortran passes arguments by reference, so any arguments in the C function that are declared with * (denoting them as pointers), can be declared as is in the Fortran interface. However, for the arguments in the C function that aren't declared as pointers, we must use the `value` attribute in the Fortran interface. First, here's the prototype of the C `tcp_connect` function:

```
int tcp_connect(
    const struct ipaddr* addr,
    int64_t deadline);
```

And here's its Fortran sibling interface to `tcp_connect`:

```
integer(c_int) function tcp_connect(addr, deadline) &
             bind(c, name='dill_tcp_connect')
  import :: c_int, c_int64_t, ipaddr
  type(ipaddr), intent(in) :: addr
  integer(c_int64_t), value, intent(in) :: deadline
end function tcp_connect
```

At this point, we can use these interfaces to initialize the `ipaddr` type and connect to a remote socket, as shown in the following listing.

> **Listing 11.8   Fortran TCP client that creates a connection to a remote server**

```
program client

  use iso_c_binding, only: c_int, c_null_char, &    Imports C-type kind parameters
                           c_int64_t              from the built-in module
```

```
      use mod_dill, only: ipaddr, ipaddr_remote, &
                    IPADDR_IPV4, tcp_connect
```
Imports our Fortran interfaces to libdill functions

```
      implicit none
      integer(c_int) :: rc, connection
      type(ipaddr) :: addr

      rc = ipaddr_remote(addr,                        &
                    '127.0.0.1' // c_null_char, &
                    5555_c_int,                 &
                    IPADDR_IPV4,                &
                    -1_c_int64_t)
```
Initializes the remote IP address and port number

```
      connection = tcp_connect(addr, -1_c_int64_t)   ←
```
Creates a new connection to the remote server

```
end program client
```

Similar to the server program, the client begins by initializing the IP address data structure. This time, it's the IP address and port number of the remote host that we're connecting to. As you can see, our remote IP address is the same as the local one initialized in the server program. They're the same because we're running both the client and the server on the same computer, which is a common practice during development.

You can place this program in a new source file; for example, client.f90. Let's compile and run it:

Compiles the mod_dill module file

```
gfortran -c mod_dill.f90        ←
gfortran client.f90 -o client libdill.a -pthread   ←
./client   ←
```
Compiles and links the client program

Runs the client

On its own, nothing should come out of this. Our client simply initializes the remote IP address and connects to a socket at that address. We're also not doing any error checks (by testing the values of `rc` or `connection`), so we don't even know if these function calls succeeded.

Now, open a new terminal session and run the server program in it. From the client terminal, run the client program. You'll see a message come up in the server terminal:

```
./server                              ←
   Listening on socket:
     IP address: 127.0.0.1
     Port:          5555
New connection from 127.0.0.1         ←
```
Runs the server program

Server output on start-up

Server output on new connection from remote client

11.3.2 Receiving a message

In the previous section, you learned how to send a TCP message from the server to a remote client by calling the `msend` function in libdill. We tested that it worked by communicating to the server with command-line networking tools such as `curl`, `nc`, and telnet. What if you wanted to exchange data over the network between two Fortran programs? We need to have a mechanism for receiving a message in the Fortran client program. Now we'll implement mrecv, the sibling of msend:

```
ssize_t mrecv(
    int s,
    void* buf,
    size_t len,
    int64_t deadline);
```

If you look back at the msend prototype in listing 11.6, you'll see that mrecv has exactly the same definition, except for two important differences:

- The return value of the function is now of type ssize_t instead of int. In msend, the function result was just a status code, indicating success or the kind of error that the function encountered. In mrecv, however, the return value is the length of the message. Its type, ssize_t, is the signed variant of the size_t type. It's an integer that can have extremely large values, but, unlike size_t, can also represent negative values. This is useful because with a ssize_t-typed result, this function can return the length of the message if successful, and –1 in case of an error.
- The buffer buf is not a const anymore, which means that its value can (and in this case, will) be written inside mrecv. This has an important implication for our Fortran interface—whereas in msend we declared the buf argument as intent(in), here we'll declare it as intent(out).

With these two considerations, we can proceed to write the Fortran interface to mrecv as

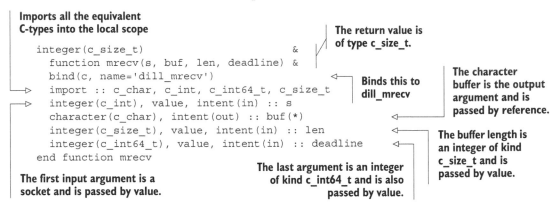

Imports all the equivalent C-types into the local scope

The return value is of type c_size_t.

```
integer(c_size_t)                              &
    function mrecv(s, buf, len, deadline) &
    bind(c, name='dill_mrecv')
    import :: c_char, c_int, c_int64_t, c_size_t
    integer(c_int), value, intent(in) :: s
    character(c_char), intent(out) :: buf(*)
    integer(c_size_t), value, intent(in) :: len
    integer(c_int64_t), value, intent(in) :: deadline
end function mrecv
```

Binds this to dill_mrecv

The character buffer is the output argument and is passed by reference.

The first input argument is a socket and is passed by value.

The last argument is an integer of kind c_int64_t and is also passed by value.

The buffer length is an integer of kind c_size_t and is passed by value.

Interfacing unsigned and signed integers

Whereas C has signed and unsigned (positive only) integers, Fortran has only signed integers. Unsigned (size_t) and signed (ssize_t) C integers are thus matched with the same type kind parameter in Fortran, just c_size_t. Perhaps counterintuitive to its name, c_size_t is signed.

11.3.3 *The complete client program*

The following listing provides the complete program for the Fortran TCP client.

Listing 11.9   Fortran TCP client—the complete program

```fortran
program client

  use iso_c_binding, only: c_int, c_char, c_null_char, c_size_t, &
                           c_int64_t, c_carriage_return, c_new_line
  use mod_dill, only: ipaddr, ipaddr_remote, IPADDR_IPV4, &
                      mrecv, tcp_connect, suffix_attach

  implicit none
  integer :: i
  integer(c_int) :: rc, connection
  integer(c_size_t) :: message_size, msglen = 64
  type(ipaddr) :: addr
  character(c_char) :: message(64) = ''
  character(len=*), parameter :: &
    TCP_SUFFIX = c_carriage_return // c_new_line // c_null_char

  rc = ipaddr_remote(addr, '127.0.0.1' // c_null_char, 5555_c_int, &
                     IPADDR_IPV4, -1_c_int64_t)
  connection = tcp_connect(addr, -1_c_int64_t)
  connection = suffix_attach(connection, TCP_SUFFIX, 2_c_size_t)
  message_size = mrecv(connection, message, msglen, -1_c_int64_t)
  print *, message_size, message

end program client
```

If you now recompile the client program and run it again (making sure the server is still running in the other terminal), you'll see a familiar greeting message:

```
./client
           5 Hello
```

The first item in the output (the numeral 5) is the length of the message (correct!), and the second item is the message itself: "Hello." This is proof that both our client and server work, as the message was transferred correctly using the TCP protocol, even if on the same machine. You can try this exercise on separate computers, and it will still work if the IP address and port number of the server are publicly accessible from the internet.

If you want to take this one step further as an exercise, consider adapting the client and server programs with the get_command_argument subroutine, described in chapter 10, to allow these programs to receive the IP address and port number as command-line arguments.

NOTE   You can download the complete code for this chapter from https://github.com/modern-fortran/tcp-client-server.

11.4   *Some interesting mixed Fortran-C projects*

I'll provide a list here of some of what I think are interesting and useful mixed Fortran-C projects. I encourage you to play with them, explore the source code, and see other possible ways to interface with C code from Fortran:

- DISLIN, a fully featured graphics and data visualization library, with its own interpreter included, and bindings to Fortran and several other languages: https://www.mps.mpg.de/dislin
- Earth System Modeling Framework (ESMF), a mixed Fortran-C++ library for building and coupling parallel Earth system models: https://www.earthsystemcog.org/projects/esmf
- F03GL, a Fortran interface to OpenGL: http://www-stone.ch.cam.ac.uk/pub/f03gl/index.xhtml
- fgsl, a Fortran interface to the GNU Scientific Library: https://github.com/reinh-bader/fgsl
- gtk-fortran, a Fortran interface to GTK for building graphical user interfaces: https://github.com/vmagnin/gtk-fortran/wiki
- NetCDF, for reading and writing self-described, compressed, gridded, multidimensional datasets: https://github.com/Unidata/netcdf-c (C library) and https://github.com/Unidata/netcdf-fortran (its Fortran bindings)
- PLplot, yet another fully featured graphics and data visualization library with bindings to Fortran and many other languages: http://plplot.sourceforge.net
- OpenBLAS, one of the fastest open source linear algebra libraries in the world: https://github.com/xianyi/OpenBLAS

Now that you've gotten this far, what are *you* going to make?

11.5   *Answer key*

This section contains solutions to exercises in this chapter. Skip ahead if you haven't worked through the exercises yet.

11.5.1   *Exercise 1: The Fortran interface to ipaddr_port*

The C function `ipaddr_port` takes the `ipaddr` struct as an input argument and returns the `port` number as a `c_int`. The key to implementing the Fortran interface is to match the argument and the function result data types, as shown in the following listing.

> **Listing 11.10   Fortran interface to `ipaddr_port`**

```
module mod_dill
  ...
  public :: ipaddr, ipaddr_local, &        Makes these functions
            ipaddr_port, ipaddr_str        publicly available for use
  ...
  interface
```

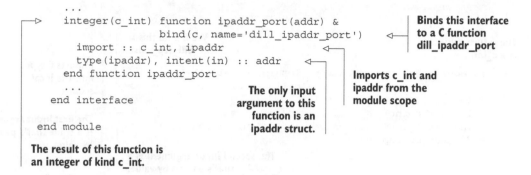

```
...
   integer(c_int) function ipaddr_port(addr) &
                  bind(c, name='dill_ipaddr_port')
     import :: c_int, ipaddr
     type(ipaddr), intent(in) :: addr
   end function ipaddr_port
   ...
 end interface

end module
```

Binds this interface to a C function dill_ipaddr_port

Imports c_int and ipaddr from the module scope

The only input argument to this function is an ipaddr struct.

The result of this function is an integer of kind c_int.

First, the function result is c_int, so we declare it as integer(c_int) on the Fortran interface end. Like before, we specify the name of the C function in the bind attribute to include the dill_ prefix. Second, recall that the function interfaces have their own, local scope, so we need to import them from the module scope using the import statement. The first and only argument is an ipaddr struct, so we declare it in the interface as type(ipaddr), intent(in). Once the function result and arguments are declared, we're done! We don't need to write the function body, as that part is defined in the C source code of the function that we're invoking. The only thing left is to place this function header in an interface block and make it publicly available to be imported from outside of the module.

11.5.2 Exercise 2: Fortran interfaces to suffix_detach and tcp_close

The Fortran interface to suffix_detach requires defining correct types for the function result (c_int) and the arguments (s and deadline). Both arguments are input arguments and are defined as pass-by-value (copy on call). We'll thus declare them with the intent(in) and value attributes, as shown in the following listing.

Listing 11.11   Fortran interface to suffix_detach

The return value is a c_int.

We'll bind this to dill_tcp_close.

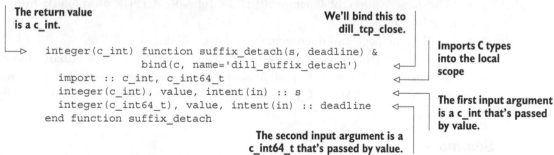

```
integer(c_int) function suffix_detach(s, deadline) &
            bind(c, name='dill_suffix_detach')
   import :: c_int, c_int64_t
   integer(c_int), value, intent(in) :: s
   integer(c_int64_t), value, intent(in) :: deadline
end function suffix_detach
```

Imports C types into the local scope

The first input argument is a c_int that's passed by value.

The second input argument is a c_int64_t that's passed by value.

The interface to tcp_close follows exactly the same pattern, as shown in the following listing.

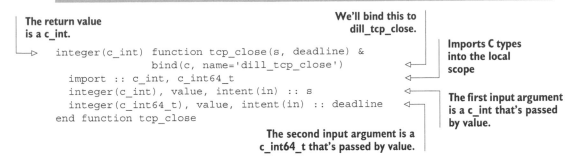

Listing 11.12   Fortran interface to `tcp_close`

```
integer(c_int) function tcp_close(s, deadline) &
                bind(c, name='dill_tcp_close')
  import :: c_int, c_int64_t
  integer(c_int), value, intent(in) :: s
  integer(c_int64_t), value, intent(in) :: deadline
end function tcp_close
```

The return value is a c_int.

We'll bind this to dill_tcp_close.

Imports C types into the local scope

The first input argument is a c_int that's passed by value.

The second input argument is a c_int64_t that's passed by value.

Once you define these two interfaces in mod_dill.f90 and make them publicly available, you'll be able to import them and call them from the server program.

11.6   New Fortran elements, at a glance

- `bind(c)`—A procedure attribute to bind a Fortran procedure to a C function or struct
- `iso_c_binding`—A built-in module that provides C-type kind parameters
- `import`—A statement to make a variable or procedure available inside the interface
- `value`—An attribute that states that the procedure argument should be passed by value, that is, by making a copy on call

11.7   Further reading

- *The C Programming Language*, by Brian W. Kernighan and Dennis M. Ritchie, Prentice Hall Software Series. Many C programmers consider this book a C "bible."
- *Essential C*, by Nick Parlante: http://cslibrary.stanford.edu/101. This concise document is my favorite quick reference material for C.
- "The new features of Fortran 2018," by John Reid (PDF download): http://mng.bz/EdaX.
- libdill home page and documentation: http://libdill.org.
- Chapters 19 ("Interoperability with C") and 21 ("Fortran 2018 enhancements to interoperability with C") of *Modern Fortran Explained: Incorporating Fortran 2018*, by Michael Metcalf, John Reid, and Malcolm Cohen, Oxford University Press.

Summary

- Fortran interoperability with C is built into the language and is defined in the Fortran Standard.
- The C function can be made available to call from Fortran by defining a function interface that binds to and uses data types equivalent to the target C function.

- The `iso_c_binding` built-in module provides data types that are compatible with C types, as well as special characters like carriage return, new line, and null character.
- The `bind(c)` attribute is used to specify that the Fortran interface will match an existing C function; its optional argument `name` allows you to specify which C function to bind to.
- Likewise, Fortran derived types with the `bind(c)` attribute are paired with matching C structs.
- For pass-by-value arguments to C functions (nonpointers), use the `value` attribute in the argument definition in the Fortran interface to make them compatible.
- There are many other C libraries besides libdill that greatly expand on what you can do with Fortran alone.
- You can use Fortran-C interoperability to give your Fortran programs superpowers.

Advanced parallelism with teams, events, and collectives

This chapter covers

- Forming teams of parallel images for different tasks
- Synchronizing execution by posting and waiting for events
- Exchanging data across images using collectives

Parallel programming is ubiquitous in many applications in science and engineering, such as aerodynamics, weather and ocean prediction, and machine learning. Parallel programming lets you distribute work between many CPUs, allowing the program to finish sooner. Distributing the work also reduces the amount of memory needed by the program, so parallelism allows running large programs that otherwise wouldn't fit into the memory of a single computer. Fortran is natively parallel, which means that the syntax used to express parallel programs is built into the language itself.

In chapter 7, your first foray into parallel Fortran programming was through coarrays. They allowed you to distribute the work among multiple CPUs, exchange data between them, and perform the computations faster. In this chapter, we'll take it a step further and explore three new parallel concepts: *teams*, *events*, and *collectives*.

We'll use these new features toward the final implementation of the tsunami simulator that we've been developing in this book.

Teams and events provide advanced means for controlling program flow and synchronization. Collectives allow you to implement common parallel patterns across images without directly invoking coarrays. At the end of the chapter, you'll walk away with the working knowledge to implement advanced parallel patterns in Fortran from scratch, or use them to augment an existing Fortran application. Together, images, coarrays, teams, events, and collectives provide a comprehensive toolbox to express any parallel algorithm that you can think of. This chapter will show you how.

12.1 *From coarrays to teams, events, and collectives*

Chapter 7 introduced the parallel programming concepts in Fortran, including images, synchronization, and data exchange using coarrays. I strongly recommend that you read that chapter before starting this one. Nevertheless, let's refresh our memory on these concepts before we build further on them.

Fortran refers to any parallel process as an *image*. Under the hood, an image can be a process running on a dedicated CPU core or a thread implemented by the operating system. A parallel Fortran program runs on all images, and each image loads its own copy of the program in RAM. The built-in functions this_image and num_images are available. The former returns the number of the current image, and the latter returns the total number of images that are running the program. Each image runs the program independently from all other images until they're synchronized using the sync all statement. These concepts allow us to inquire about images and synchronize them. However, they don't help us regarding exchanging data between images. To do this, Fortran has a special data structure called a *coarray*. A coarray can be *coindexed* to access data on remote images—we can copy data to and from other images by indexing a coarray with the target image number.

Teams, events, and collectives build directly on these concepts. *Teams* let you separate groups of images by different roles, while *events* make communicating status updates between teams (or just images) simple. Consider a weather prediction model, for example. The simulation can't start without the initial data coming in, and the team that writes data to disk needs to wait for the simulation team to finish their part of the job. Posting and waiting for events from different teams is how we can synchronize them. Finally, *collectives* will allow you to perform common parallel calculations, such as sum, minimum, or maximum, without directly invoking coarrays.

As we work on implementing these features in the tsunami simulator, we'll focus mainly on monitoring the time stepping progress of the simulation and extracting some useful statistics about the simulated water height field. Although a real-world application is likely to employ teams, events, and collectives for more complex tasks, such as downloading and processing remote data, writing model output to disk, and serving data to clients, focusing on a simple and minimal task will help us learn and better understand in detail how these features work.

Is your Fortran development environment set up?

In case you opened this chapter before working through the earlier ones in the book, make sure you have your Fortran compiler ready to build parallel code. You'll need recent builds of the GNU Fortran compiler (gfortran) and the OpenCoarrays library. Refer to appendix A for instructions on setting up gfortran and OpenCoarrays. Otherwise, if you're working on a system with access to Intel or Cray Fortran compilers, you're good to go. In that case, specific compile commands and options will be a bit different than presented here. Refer to user documentation of your Fortran compiler for help on how to use it.

12.2 Grouping images into teams with common tasks

Fortran 2018 introduced teams to allow the programmer to assign different tasks to groups of images. For example, if you're computing a weather simulation on 16 images, you could assign them different roles (figure 12.1).

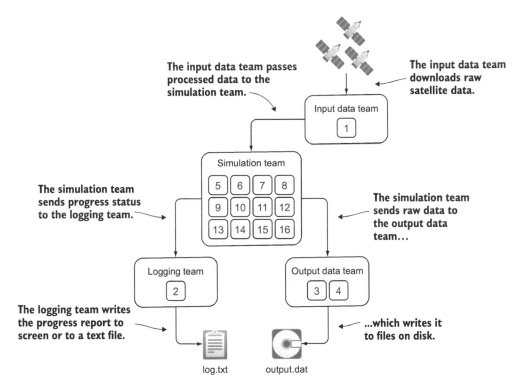

Figure 12.1   A weather model workflow, with parallel images distributed in different teams and each box with a number in it representing one image

In this specific example, the images are distributed in the following setup:

- One image queries a remote server and downloads satellite data when available.
- Another is in charge of monitoring the progress of the simulation and logging appropriate information to a text file.
- Two images are responsible for writing simulation output files to disk.
- The remaining 12 images are churning away with the heavy task of simulation, without getting distracted by other chores.

Let's apply a subset of this pattern to the tsunami simulator we've been developing.

12.2.1 Teams in the tsunami simulator

In this section, we'll use teams to augment our tsunami simulator and assign different roles to parallel images working concurrently. For brevity and to not get bogged down in the details of what the specific roles could be in real-world simulation software, we'll create only two teams: the compute team and the logging team. While the compute team is churning away at the heavy task of number-crunching, the logging team will monitor and report the progress of the simulator. Logging is a relatively light-weight task, so we'll assign only one image to the logging team, and the rest will go to the compute team. Thus, if we run the program on four parallel images, one will be logging progress, while the remaining three will be crunching numbers. This is a simplified variant of the approach illustrated in figure 12.1.

The updated tsunami program that uses teams will look as shown in listing 12.1. This listing shows only the added code relative to where we left off with the tsunami simulator in chapter 10. Don't worry about coding this up just yet; here, I'm merely giving you an overview of what's coming later in the chapter.

Listing 12.1 Introducing teams to the tsunami simulator

```
program tsunami

  use iso_fortran_env, only: team_type        ←  Imports team_type from the
  ...                                             iso_fortran_env module
  type(team_type) :: new_team                 ←  Declares a new
  integer :: team_num                             team_type instance
  ...                           ←  Team number variable that we'll
  team_num = 1                     use to identify sibling teams
  if (this_image() == 1) team_num = 2
  form team(team_num, new_team)   ←  Only the first image
                                     will go to team 2.
  change team(new_team)           ←  Changes the current
    if (team_num == 1) then          team for each image
      ...
    else if (team_num == 2) then
      ...
    end if                ←  The logging    The original simulator code
  end team                   code for team  is assigned to team 1.
                             2 goes here.
end program tsunami
```

All images will go to team 1 by default.

Forms two new teams

Closes the change team construct

This listing summarizes the concepts of forming new teams and switching the execution context between them. First, a team is modeled using a new built-in type, team_type, available from the the iso_fortran_env module. To begin working with teams, we import team_type and declare an instance of it, in this case new_team. We also need a unique integer scalar to refer to different teams by their number, in this case team_num. This variable is used to assign images to different teams. In the form team statement in this example, we assign all images to team 1, except the first one, which we assign to team 2. The form team statement only creates new teams; it doesn't affect the execution.

This is where the change team construct comes in—it instructs all images that execute it to switch to a new team—in this case, new_team. Note that change team is a construct, like an if block or a do loop, and is paired with a matching end team statement.

Within the change team construct, the images are now running in their new teams. We can assign code to be executed to each team by checking the value of the team number. Teams will work on different tasks, and will also need to synchronize and exchange data from time to time.

Figure 12.2 illustrates this process, albeit with a bit different team organization.

The key concepts introduced here are forming new teams (form team statement) and changing the current team (change team construct). The form team statement creates new teams and encodes the information about which image on the current

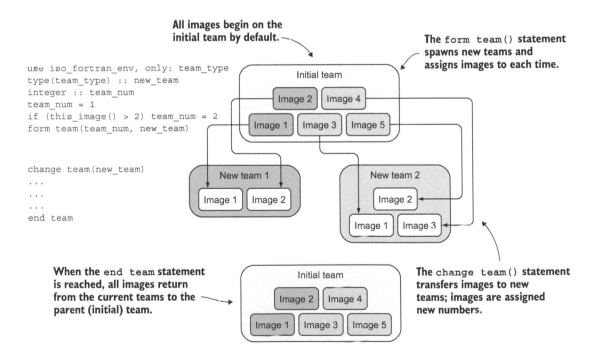

Figure 12.2 Forming and changing teams

team will belong to which new team. The change team construct moves images to the newly created teams. Within the change team construct, the images have new image numbers assigned to them. Teams can work independently from one another, synchronize, and even exchange data.

You may also wonder why we need separate statements for forming and changing teams. We need them because these two operations are fundamentally different in nature: form team instructs the compiler to define new teams and assign images to them, analogous to defining a new function; change team, on the other hand, switches the execution context between already created teams, which is analogous to calling a function. Don't worry if this seems like a lot and not everything is clear yet. We'll go over each element in detail as we work through this section.

> **NOTE** In case you're familiar with MPI programming (discussed earlier in the book), whether in C or Fortran, teams are analogous to MPI communicators.

12.2.2 Forming new teams

Before we dive into the implementation of teams in the tsunami simulator, let's look at the syntax of forming new teams, which will apply to any parallel program that uses them. In the beginning of the program, there's only one team, and we'll refer to it as the *initial team*. All images that run the program start in the initial team by default. If you intend to work with teams at all, the first thing you'll do is form new teams within the initial team using the form team statement. You can make as many new teams as you want. In this example, we'll create two new teams—one for the first half of all images and the other for the rest—as shown in the following listing.

Listing 12.2 Forming two new teams with equal numbers of images

```
program form_team

    use iso_fortran_env, only: team_type      ← Imports team_type from
    implicit none                               the iso_fortran_env
                                                module

    type(team_type) :: new_team      ← Declares a new
    integer :: team_num                 team_type instance

                                     All images will go to
    team_num = 1              ←      team 1 by default.
    if (this_image() > num_images() / 2) team_num = 2    ← The rest will
                                                           go to team 2.
    form team(team_num, new_team)      ← Forms two
                                         new teams
end program form_team
```

Team number variable that we'll
use to identify sibling teams

Besides the basic housekeeping, like importing the team_type from the iso_fortran _env module and declaring the team and team number variables, there are two key elements here. First, we decide how many new teams to create and which images will go to each team. We do this by assigning values to the integer variable `team_num` on every image. Second, we execute the `form team` statement, which creates new teams and internally assigns the images to them. If you compile and run this program, there will be no output. This is expected, as a `form team` statement on its own doesn't emit any output.

A `form_team` statement must be executed by *all* images on the current team. The first `form team` statement in the program is thus always executed by all images in the program. This statement also synchronizes all the images on the team, implying a `sync all` under the hood. (See chapter 8 for a refresher on synchronizing images.) This is the syntax of the `form team` statement:

```
form team(team_num, team_variable[, new_index, stat, errmsg])
```

where

- `team_num` is a positive, scalar, integer constant or expression that uniquely identifies the team to be created.
- `team_variable` is a scalar variable of type `team_type`.
- `new_index` is a scalar integer that allows you to specify an image number that this image will have on the new team.
- `stat` is the integer status code, with a zero value in case of success and nonzero otherwise
- `errmsg` is the character string with an informative error message, if `stat` returns a nonzero value.

`team_num` and `team_variable` are required input parameters. The value of `team_num` across images determines how many teams will be created with the `form team` statement and which image will belong to which new team. If multiple new teams are created, their numbers don't need to be contiguous, but they need to be unique positive integers. `new_index` is an optional input parameter that you can use to specify the number of the image on the new team, which is otherwise compiler-dependent. If provided, the values of `new_index` must be unique and less than or equal to the number of images being assigned to the new team. `stat` and `errmsg`, both optional output parameters, have the same meaning and behavior as they do in the `allocate` and `deallocate` statements in chapter 5. As you'll see throughout the remainder of this chapter, all parallel features introduced by Fortran 2018 have error handling built in.

12.2.3 *Changing execution between teams*

Now that we have two new teams, how do we instruct images on each team to do certain kinds of work? Recall that by default, all images start on the same team. We need to switch each image to a new team to get it to work on a different task. We do this with the `change team` construct. Following the `form_team` statement in listing 12.2, we'll add this snippet:

```
change team(new_team)
  print *, 'Image', this_image(), 'of', num_images(), &
          'is on team', team_number()
end team
```

Reports the image and team number

Switches execution to a new team

Returns to the parent team

Now you understand why change team is a construct—every change team statement must be paired with a matching end team statement. A change team statement instructs all images that execute it to switch to the team specified in parentheses. The code inside the change team construct executes on the new (child) team until the end team statement, when the images return to the original (parent) team. Similar to this_image, which returns the image number, team_number returns a scalar integer value of the current team.

Let's save this program in a file called change_team.f90, compile it, and run it on five images:

Compiles the program using the OpenCoarrays compiler wrapper

Runs the program on five parallel processes

```
caf change_team.f90 -o change_team
cafrun -n 5 --oversubscribe ./change_team
  Image        1 of         2 is on team        1
  Image        2 of         2 is on team        1
  Image        1 of         3 is on team        2
  Image        2 of         3 is on team        2
  Image        3 of         3 is on team        2
```

The output of the program

What's happening here? Each image prints three numbers to the screen: its own image number (this_image()), the total number of images (num_images()), and its team number (team_number()). Let's look at the values in reverse, from right to left. First, we see that there are two images on team 1 and three on team 2. This is what we expected, as we instructed form team to first assign two images (out of five total) to team 1, and the rest to team 2. So far, so good. Second, notice that two of the images report a total number of images of 2, and the remaining three report a total number of images of 3. This means that when executed within the change team construct, num_images() now doesn't represent the total number of images running the whole program, but the total number of images within the current team. Finally, looking at the current image number, it seems that our original images 3, 4, and 5 now have numbers 1, 2, and 3 on their new team. Conclusion: when executed within the change team construct, functions this_image and num_images operate in the context of the current team.

Note that the Fortran Standard doesn't prescribe what the new image numbers on the newly formed teams will be, and leaves the numbering of images on new teams as implementation- (compiler-) dependent. If you need to ensure specific image indices on new teams (or preserve the ones from the initial team), use the new_index argument in the form team statement, described in the previous subsection.

The syntax for the change team construct is

where

- `team_value` is an input scalar variable or expression of type `team_type`.
- `stat` and `errmsg` are optional output parameters that have the same meaning as in the `form team` statement.
- `name` is an optional label for the construct, much like a labeled `do` loop.

At the beginning of a `change team` construct, all images that execute it switch to the team provided in parentheses. Inside the construct, these images execute within the new team. When they reach the `end team` statement, the images automatically synchronize and return to the original (parent) team that they were on immediately before the `change team` statement.

Exercise 1: Hunters and gatherers

Write a parallel program that models a tribe of hunter-gatherers using teams. Form the teams such that this is how they operate:

- Gatherers comprise 1/2 of all villagers, and they go foraging for fruit and vegetables. When they reach their destination, they split into teams of 2 for more efficient foraging.
- Hunters comprise 1/3 of all villagers, and they go hunting. When they reach their destination, they split into teams of 3 for more efficient hunting.
- The remaining 1/6 of villagers are elders, who stay together in the village and rest by the fire pit.

For this exercise, make each team report to the screen:

1 How many villagers are in each team
2 When they leave the village
3 When they engage in an activity

Hint: use a `form team` statement within a `change team` construct to create new teams within teams.

The solution to this exercise is given in the "Answer key" section near the end of the chapter.

12.2.4 Synchronizing teams and exchanging data

We've learned so far, both from coarrays in chapter 7 and from developing the parallel tsunami simulator, that synchronizing images is crucial for writing correct parallel programs. Recall that when we have data dependency between parallel images, one image must wait for data from another image before proceeding with its own calculation. This subsection explains how synchronization of images works within teams, and how to synchronize multiple teams as a whole.

SYNCHRONIZING IMAGES WITHIN A TEAM

The essential synchronization mechanism you learned in chapter 7 was the sync all statement, which placed a barrier in the code at which every image had to wait for all others before proceeding. At the point of a sync all statement, we considered all images to be synchronized. Another option that's available to us, when we need to synchronize the current image with some but not all other images, is the sync images statement. For example, we used sync all in the sync_edges method of the Field type in the tsunami simulator (see section 10.4) to synchronize every image with all other images. Using sync images, we can instead synchronize each image only with its four neighbors, in mod_field.f90, subroutine sync_edges:

```
...
sync images(set(neighbors))         ⟵  Synchronizes with neighbors
                                        before copy into buffer

edge(1:je-js+1,1)[neighbors(1)] = self % data(is,js:je)
edge(1:je-js+1,2)[neighbors(2)] = self % data(ie,js:je)     Copies data into
edge(1:ie-is+1,3)[neighbors(3)] = self % data(is:ie,js)     the coarray
edge(1:ie-is+1,4)[neighbors(4)] = self % data(is:ie,je)     buffer, edge

sync images(set(neighbors))         ⟵  Synchronizes with neighbors again
                                        before copying out of buffer

self % data(is-1,js:je) = edge(1:je-js+1,2)     Copies data from
self % data(ie+1,js:je) = edge(1:je-js+1,1)     coarray buffer into
self % data(is:ie,js-1) = edge(1:ie-is+1,4)     the field array
self % data(is:ie,je+1) = edge(1:ie-is+1,3)
...
```

The same behavior holds in the context of teams: sync all and sync images statements now operate within the team in which they're executed. For example, if you have two teams and you've switched the images to them using the change team construct, issuing sync all synchronizes the images within each team, but *not* the teams themselves. Ditto for sync images. Although this may be confusing at first, you'll get used to it over time as you practice working with teams. Just remember: sync all and sync images statements always operate only within the current team and can't affect the images outside of the team. In the next subsection, you'll see how you can synchronize between teams.

In the sync images snippet, set(neighbors) ensures that we pass unique values of neighbors to sync images. We'll define set in the same module in mod_field.f90, as shown in the following listing.

Listing 12.3   Function `set` to return unique elements of an array

```
pure recursive function set(a) result(res)
  integer, intent(in) :: a(:)
  integer, allocatable :: res(:)
  if (size(a) > 1) then
    res = [a(1), set(pack(a(2:), .not. a(2:) == a(1)))]
  else
    res = a
  end if
end function set
```

> The recursive attribute allows a function to call itself.

> Eliminates nonunique elements from the array, one at a time

This is the first time we encounter the `recursive` attribute. This attribute allows a function or subroutine to invoke itself. The crux of this function is in the fifth line of the listing, where we recursively reduce the array by removing duplicate elements, one by one, using the built-in function `pack`. For a refresher on `pack`, see section 5.4, where we used it for the first time. Note that Fortran 2018—the latest iteration of the language as of this writing—makes all procedures recursive by default, so specifying the `recursive` attribute won't be necessary anymore. I still include it here because most Fortran compilers have yet to catch up with this recent development.

SYNCHRONIZING WHOLE TEAMS

Having established that `sync all` and `sync image` statements operate only within the current team and can't affect the images outside of it, we need a mechanism to synchronize between the teams. Back to our working tsunami example from listing 12.1, where we began incorporating teams for the simulation and logging tasks:

```
change team(new_team)
  if (team_num == 1) then
    ...
  else if (team_num == 2) then
    ...
  end if
end team
```

> Simulation code goes here.

> Logging code goes here.

As logging depends on the data from the simulation team, we need a way to synchronize images between different teams. This is where the new `sync team` statement comes in, as shown in the following listing.

Listing 12.4   Synchronizing images within the initial team using the `sync team` statement

Simulation code

```
use iso_fortran_env, only: initial_team, team_type
...
change team(new_team)
  if (team_num == 1) then
    ...
    sync team(get_team(initial_team))
  else if (team_num == 2) then
    sync team(get_team(initial_team))
```

> Imports the initial_team constant from the module

> Synchronizes with all images that belong to the initial team

```
    . . .
   end if                    ◁─┐  Logging code
end team
```

sync team has been introduced to the language to allow synchronizing images within the parent team without leaving the change team construct. To use it, we need to provide it a team value over which to synchronize. In practice, this will typically be a parent team or some other ancestor team (see the "Exercise 1" sidebar for an example of multiple levels of teams), but can also be the current team or the child team. To refer to a team such as the initial team, which we never defined as a variable, we use the get _team built-in function, and pass it the initial_team constant available from the iso_fortran_env module. Besides the initial_team integer constant, iso_fortran _env also provides the parent_team and current_team constants.

For brevity, we won't get bogged down with the exact code that the logging team will execute. In practice, it could be monitoring the time stepping progress of the simulation team, checking and processing files written to disk, printing simulation statistics to the screen, and perhaps even serving them as a web server. An important element to most of these activities is getting the data from the simulation team.

EXCHANGING DATA BETWEEN TEAMS

I mentioned in the previous subsection that one of the activities the logging team could be performing is monitoring the time stepping of the simulation team. If they're operating independently and concurrently, how can the logging team know each time the simulation team steps forward? To demonstrate the exchange of data between teams, let's send the time step count from the simulation team to the logging team. To do this, we'll make our time step count variable a coarray, and we'll use the team number in the image selector when referencing that coarray, as shown in the following listing.

Listing 12.5 Exchanging data between teams using image selectors

```
integer(ik) :: time_step_count[*]        ◁─┐  Declares time step
...                                          │  count as a coarray
change team(new_team)
  if (team_num == 1) then
    ...
    time_loop: do n = 1, num_time_steps              ┐  Copies n into
      ...                                             │  time_step_count on
      time_step_count[1, team_number=2] = n    ◁──┘  image 1 of team 2
    end do time_loop
  else if (team_num == 2) then
    n = 0
    time_step_count = 0          ┐  Loops        │ Runs this code if
    do                       ◁───┘  indefinitely │ time_step_count
      if (time_step_count > n) then    ◁──┘       has been updated
        n = time_step_count
        print *, 'tsunami logger: step ', n, 'of', num_time_steps, 'done'
```

```
        if (n == num_time_steps) exit
      end if
    end do
  end if
end team
```
◁─┐ **Leaves the loop**
  │ **if we've reached**
  │ **the end**

In listing 12.5, we've declared the `time_step_count` integer coarray, which we'll use to exchange the time step count between the simulation team and the logging team. To send the data, we'll use the usual coarray indexing syntax from chapter 7, with a twist: here, we also specify the team number in the image selector (the values between square brackets). When we write `time_step_count[1, team_number=2] = n`, we're saying "Copy the value of n into the `time_step_count` variable on image 1 of team number 2." This means that the image number is relative to the team in question—image 1 on team 1 is different from image 1 on team 2. On the logging team, we initialize the local value of `time_step_count` to zero, loop indefinitely, and check for its value in each iteration. Every time `time_step_count` is incremented by the simulation team, we print its value to the screen.

While this is a somewhat trivial example—printing a single integer to the screen is not that much work—it illustrates how to effectively offload heavy compute work to other teams. In a real-world app, while the simulation team is busy crunching numbers, one team could be writing the output files to disk, while another could be serving them as a web server. The results of the tsunami simulator won't change with introduction of teams into the code, because they affect only how the code and its order of execution are organized. The simulation part of the code, which is responsible for producing numerical results, is now running in its dedicated team rather than on all images. While teams don't necessarily unlock any new capability relative to original image control and synchronization mechanisms, they allow you to more cleanly express distribution of work among images. This becomes especially important for larger, more complex apps.

12.3   *Posting and waiting for events*

In the previous section, we used teams to distribute work among groups of images. Teams allow us to express some parallel patterns and synchronization more elegantly than we otherwise could by controlling individual images directly. Fortran 2018 introduces another new parallel concept called *events*, provided through the built-in derived type called `event_type`. In a nutshell, you can post events from one or more images, and query or wait for those events from others. Figure 12.3 illustrates how events are implemented in Fortran.

You can read this diagram in any order. An alert event is an instance of `event_type`. Image 1 triggers the alert on image 2 by issuing `event post(alert[2])`. This statement is nonblocking, which means that image 1 can immediately move on with whatever code follows. All instances of `event_type` keep a count of posted events internally. This count is incremented on every `event post` statement, from any image.

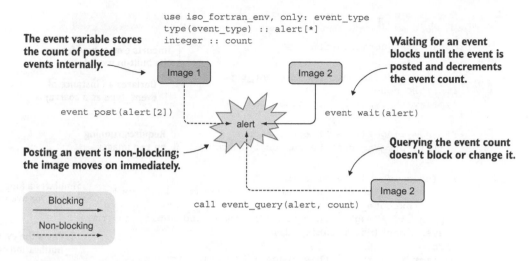

Figure 12.3 Fortran events, where solid and dashed arrows denote blocking and nonblocking operations, respectively

Image 2 issues `event wait(alert)`. This is a blocking statement, which means that image 2 will wait until the alert is posted. When it finally happens, `event wait` decrements the internal event count. Alternatively, image 2 can also poll the number of alerts in a nonblocking fashion with the built-in subroutine `event_query`.

That's all there is to it! Let's first tinker with posting and waiting for events in an example of sending a notification, and then we'll dive into the syntax and rules of events.

12.3.1 A push notification example

In this section, we'll build from our tsunami teams example and use events to post updates from the simulation team to the logging team about data being written to disk. While this is technically doable with coarrays alone, you'll see that events are a perfect candidate for such parallel patterns. Before we jump back into the tsunami, let's see how events work from a simple push notification example.

Sending a notification from one process to another will be important in any scenario in which you have data dependency between processes. Examples include a long-running data mining job by a worker process, waited on by a process whose role is to write a report for the user (see figure 12.1), or waiting for data to become available on a remote server.

This example will demonstrate using events to wait for another image to complete a long-running job. It doesn't matter what the actual job is—here, we'll emulate it by making the image wait for five seconds. When the time is up, the image will send a notification to another image that's waiting for it. The following listing shows the complete program.

Listing 12.6   A push notification example using events

```
program push_notification

  use iso_fortran_env, only: event_type          Imports event_type from
  implicit none                                    the built-in module
  type(event_type) :: notification[*]             Declares an instance of
                                                   event_type as a coarray

  if (num_images() /= 2) error stop &          Requires running
    'This program must be run on 2 images'      on two images

  if (this_image() == 1) then
    print *, 'Image', this_image(), 'working a long job'    Simulates a long job by
    call execute_command_line('sleep 5')                    waiting for five seconds
    print *, 'Image', this_image(), 'done and notifying image 2'
    event post(notification[2])                  Posts the event to
  else                                            notification on image 2
    print *, 'Image', this_image(), 'waiting for image 1'
    event wait(notification)                     On image 2, waits
    print *, 'Image', this_image(), 'notified from image 1'   for notification
  end if

end program push_notification
```

First, we import event_type and declare a coarray instance of it. Like team_type, event_type is also provided by the iso_fortran_env module. An event variable must either be declared as a coarray or be a component of a coarray derived type. Then, from image 1, we post the event by executing the event post statement on the notification variable, with image 2 as the target. This increments the event count in the notification variable, which can now be queried or waited for on image 2. On the other side, image 2 issues the matching event wait statement. This statement blocks the execution on image 2 until image 1 has posted the event.

If you compile and run this program, you'll get

```
caf push_notification.f90 -o push_notification      Compiles the program
cafrun -n 2 ./push_notification                     using the OpenCoarrays
 Image          1 working a long job                compiler
 Image          2 waiting for image 1
 Image          1 done and notifying image 2    Runs the program
 Image          2 notified from image 1         on two images
```

Notice the order of printed lines in the output. The sequence of operations is set by the event post and event wait statements. Because image 1 is working on a long job (here emulated by sleeping for five seconds), image 2 will announce that it's waiting for image 1 before it receives the notification and will print that the message was received only after event wait has executed. The following two subsections describe the general syntax of event post and event wait statements.

> ### Running external (system) commands
> In listing 12.6, I used a built-in subroutine, `execute_command_line`, to run an external command and simulate a long job. On Linux, `sleep 5` means "wait for five seconds." You can run any external command by calling `execute_command_line`. The subroutine will block until the command completes. In general, this is useful for loosely integrating your Fortran programs with external (system) tools and scripts. Fortran itself, however, doesn't provide a way to capture the output (or error message) of the external command. To do this, you'd have to redirect the output of the command into a file that you'd then read from your Fortran program (see chapter 6).

12.3.2 Posting an event

The first step to any work with events is to post them using the `event post` statement, which takes the general form

```
event post(event_var[, stat, errmsg])
```

where `event_var` is a variable of `event_type`, and `stat` and `errmsg` have the same meaning as they do in the `form team` and `change team` statements.

While not strictly required by the language, you'd always want to post to an event variable on another image by coindexing it (indexing a coarray); for example

```
type(event_type) :: notification[*]
event post(notification[this_image() + 1])
```

Posts a notification to the next image

You can post to an event variable as many times and as frequently as you want, with or without matching `event wait` statements. Every time you do, an internal event count for that event variable is incremented. You can also post to an event from more than one image. You'll see soon how this mechanism can be used to make multiple event posts and wait for them only on some occasions.

12.3.3 Waiting for an event

Images posting events is just one side of the transaction. For an image to wait for the event that it owns, it needs to execute the `event wait` statement. This statement has the syntax

```
event wait(event_var[, until_count, stat, errmsg)
```

where

- `event_var` is a scalar variable of `event_type` and has the same meaning as in `event post`.
- `until_count` is an optional integer expression that's the number of posted events for which to wait, with a default value of 1.
- `stat` and `errmsg` are optional output parameters for error handling and have the same meaning as before.

In a nutshell, `event wait` blocks the image that executes it until some other image posts an event to it. If `until_count` is provided and greater than 1, the image will wait until that many events have been posted. On successful execution of `event wait`, the internal event count is decremented by `until_count`, if provided, and by 1 otherwise. For example, this statement

```
event wait(notification, until_count=100)
```

blocks the executing image until 100 events have been posted to the `notification` variable from any other image. Once executed, the internal event count is decremented by exactly 100. Note that this doesn't mean that the event count is always reduced to zero, because remote event posts can keep incrementing the event count before `event wait` has time to return.

Using `event wait` together with the `until_count` parameter allows you to not block on every posted event, but only on some number of events. However, it also illustrates a restriction to `event wait`: it's impossible for the image that listens for events to know how many have been posted without explicitly blocking execution with `event wait`. This is indeed rather limiting. To poll events without blocking the current image, Fortran provides a built-in subroutine `event_query`, which we'll explore in the next subsection.

12.3.4 *Counting event posts*

As you work with events, you'll soon find it useful to query an event variable to find out how many times an event has been posted. The built-in subroutine `event_query` does exactly this

```
call event_query(event_var, count[, stat])
```

where `event_var` is the input variable of type `event_type`, and `count` is the output integer number of events posted. Unlike the `event wait` statement, calling `event _query` doesn't block execution but simply returns the count of posted events. `event_query` is a read-only operation, so it doesn't decrement the event count like `event wait` does. This makes it more suitable for implementation of nonblocking parallel algorithms, as you'll find out in the "Exercise 2" sidebar.

Exercise 2: Tsunami time step logging using events

In the previous section, we used the coarray `time_step_count` to communicate the number of time steps between the simulation and logging teams. In this exercise, use events to keep track of the simulation team's progress and print it to screen from the logging team. For bonus points, implement two solutions, one using an `event wait` statement, and another using an `event_query` subroutine.

The solution to this exercise is given in the "Answer key" section near the end of the chapter.

12.4 *Distributed computing using collectives*

In chapter 7, you learned how to use coarrays and their square bracket syntax to exchange values between parallel images. This mechanism for data exchange is simple and to the point—you as the programmer explicitly instruct the computer to send and receive data between images. For common calculations across many images, such as a global sum or maximum and minimum values of distributed arrays, implementing such parallel algorithms using coarrays directly can be tedious and prone to errors. Fortran 2018 introduced *collective subroutines* to perform common parallel operations on distributed data.

Take, for example, a climate model that predicts the air temperature over the globe far into the future. As a climate scientist or a policy maker, you'd be interested in finding out what the global minimum, maximum, and average value of air temperature or mean sea level was over time. However, if the climate model was running in parallel (almost all of them are!), calculating the global temperature statistics would not be trivial, because every CPU would have the data only for the region that it was computing for. In the simplest implementation, you'd have to do the following:

1 Calculate minimum, maximum, and average values on each CPU for its region.
2 Gather the regional statistics to one CPU.
3 Calculate the global statistics on one CPU based on arrays of regional statistics.

We went through this exercise with a simple dataset back in chapter 7 when we were first introduced to coarrays. Now, collective subroutines (I'll refer to them as *collectives*) can do some of the heavy lifting for you.

12.4.1 *Computing the minimum and maximum of distributed arrays*

Let's try this out in the tsunami simulator. In our working version of the simulator so far, for every time step, we were reporting the time step count to the screen, while the program was writing raw data into files in the background:

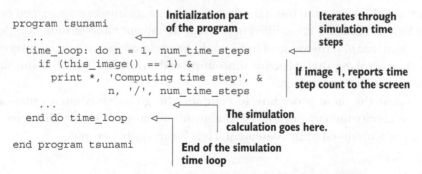

At the beginning of each time step, we print the current time step count and the total number of time steps to the screen. We do this only from one image to avoid printing the same message from all images. Let's augment this short report by adding the minimum, maximum, and average water height value to each print statement. Like in the thought experiment of a parallel climate model, the water height values here are also distributed across parallel images. The following listing shows how we'd calculate global minimum and maximum values using standard collectives co_min and co_max, respectively.

Listing 12.7   Calculating global minimum and maximum values of the water height array

Calculates the collective minimum from hmin on each image and stores it into hmin on image 1

```
...
real(ik) :: hmin, hmax          ◁──┤  Declares temporary
...                                    variables
time_loop: do n = 1, num_time_steps
  ...                                  Calculates the local
  hmin = minval(h % data)       ◁──   minimum on each image
  call co_min(hmin, 1)
                                       Calculates the local
                                       maximum on each image
  hmax = maxval(h % data)       ◁──
  call co_max(hmax, 1)

  if (this_image() == 1) print '(a, i5, 2(f10.6))', &      Prints the current
    'step, min(h), max(h):', n, hmin, hmax                  time step and global
                                                            minimum and
end do time_loop                                            maximum to the
                                                            screen
```

Calculates the collective maximum from hmax on each image and stores it into hmax on image 1

To compute the global minimum of water height, we first calculate the local minimum on each image using the minval function and store it into the temporary variable hmin. Recall that h is a type(Field) instance, so we access the raw values through its component h % data. Second, we use the collective subroutine co_min to calculate the minimum value of hmin across all images. The first argument to co_min is an intent(in out) scalar, and the second argument (optional) is the number of the image on which to store the result. In this case, all images invoke co_min, and only the value of hmin on image 1 is modified in-place. If the image number were not specified (call co_min(hmin)), the value of hmin would be updated in-place on all images. This implies that invoking the collective subroutine will inevitably overwrite the value of the input on at least one image.

We repeat the same procedure to compute the global maximum using co_max. Finally, we report the current time step and minimum and maximum values to the screen using a modified print statement. Here's the sample output:

```
step, min(h), max(h):    1  0.000000  1.000000
step, min(h), max(h):    2  0.000000  0.996691
step, min(h), max(h):    3  0.000000  0.990097
...
step, min(h), max(h):  998 -0.072596  0.186842
step, min(h), max(h):  999  0.072279  0.188818
step, min(h), max(h): 1000 -0.071815  0.190565
```

This was an introduction to the co_min and co_max subroutines by example. In the next section, I'll describe the rest of the collectives and provide their general syntax.

NOTE Collective subroutines are built into the language and are available out of the box, just like the regular functions min, max, and sum.

12.4.2 *Collective subroutines syntax*

Fortran 2018 defines a total of five collective subroutines:

- co_broadcast—Sends the value of a variable from the current image to all others
- co_max—Computes the maximum value of a variable over all images
- co_min—Computes the minimum value of a variable over all images
- co_sum—Computes the sum of all values of a variable across all images
- co_reduce—Applies a reduction function across all images

These cover most collective operations that you'll likely encounter in your work. However, the language won't stop you from implementing your own custom collectives using coarrays and synchronization, should you ever need them. The rest of this section describes co_sum and co_broadcast in more detail. To learn more about co_reduce, the most complex collective subroutine, see section 12.7 for reference.

NOTE If you're familiar with parallel programming using MPI, Fortran 2018 collective subroutines will look familiar, as they're analogs to their MPI counterparts.

Figure 12.4 illustrates how co_sum works when invoked on four images.

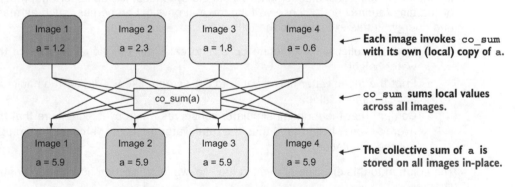

Figure 12.4 A collective sum invoked over four parallel images, with arrows indicating possible data flow directions

In this example, we invoke co_sum(a) on each image, which triggers a summation of values of a across all images. The exact data exchange pattern may vary depending on compilers and underlying libraries, but the point is that you can use this built-in subroutine and not worry about explicitly copying data via coarrays and synchronizing images to avoid race conditions. By default, the result of the collective sum is made available on all images, and the value of a is updated on each image to the global sum value. However, if you need this value on only one image, you can specify it as an argument; for example, call co_sum(a, 3) would compute a sum over all images but update the value of a only on image 3.

The full syntax for invoking co_sum is

```
call co_sum(a[, result_image, stat, errmsg])
```

where

- a is a variable that has the same type across all images. It doesn't need to be declared as a coarray. This is an intent(in out) argument, so its value may be modified in-place.
- result_image is an optional integer scalar indicating on which image to store the result. If omitted, the result is stored on all images.
- stat and errmsg, both optional, are scalar integer and character variables, respectively. They have the same meaning as in allocate and deallocate statements, and allow for explicit error handling.

As you might guess, co_sum, co_min, and co_max are implemented for numeric types only (integer, real, and complex).

Exercise 3: Calculating the global average of water height

In almost all applications of computational fluid dynamics, it's an important property of the simulation code to conserve fundamental physical properties, such as mass and energy. In this exercise, do the following:

1. Use the collective subroutine co_sum to calculate the global average of the water height.
2. Print the mean water height value to the screen, like we did for the minimum and maximum value.
3. Confirm that the tsunami simulator conserves mass by making sure that the average water height (and thus the total water mass) stays constant throughout the simulation.

The solution to this exercise is given in the "Answer key" section near the end of the chapter.

12.4.3 Broadcasting values to other images

While all images must execute the call to co_broadcast, the specified image acts as the sender, and all others act as receivers. Figure 12.5 illustrates an example of this functioning.

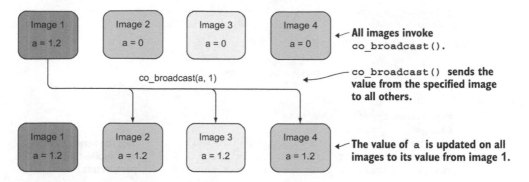

Figure 12.5 A collective broadcast from image 1 to the other three images, with arrows indicating the possible data flow direction

The inner workings of this procedure, including copying of data and synchronization of images, are implemented by the compiler and underlying libraries, so you and I don't have to worry about them.

The full syntax for invoking co_broadcast is similar to co_min, co_max, and co_sum, except that the broadcast variable isn't limited to numeric data types. A subtle but important point about collective subroutines is that the variables they operate on don't have to be declared as coarrays. This allows you to write some parallel algorithms without declaring a single coarray. For an example, take a look at the source code of a popular Fortran framework for neural networks and deep learning at https://github.com/modern-fortran/neural-fortran. It implements parallel network training with co_broadcast and co_sum, without explicitly declaring any coarrays.

Congratulations, you made it to the end! Having now covered teams, events, and collectives, it's a wrap. Work through the exercises, make a few parallel toy apps of your own, and you're off to the races. You should have enough Fortran experience under your belt to start new Fortran programs and libraries, as well as to contribute to other open source projects out there. If you'd like to return to our main example, appendix C provides a recap and complete code of the tsunami simulator. It also offers ideas on where to go from here, as well as tips for learning more about Fortran. The amazing world of parallel Fortran programming is waiting for you.

12.5 Answer key

This section contains solutions to exercises in this chapter. Skip ahead if you haven't worked through the exercises yet.

12.5.1 Exercise 1: Hunters and gatherers

Solving this exercise will require creating three new teams at the beginning of the program: hunters, gatherers, and elders. Furthermore, we'll need to create a yet-to-be-determined number of subteams on each of the hunter and gatherer teams. Let's tackle the first step first, as shown in the following listing.

```
program hunters_gatherers

  use iso_fortran_env, only: team_type
  implicit none

  type(team_type) :: new_team
  integer :: team_num
  integer, parameter :: elders_team_num = 1
  integer, parameter :: hunters_team_num = 2
  integer, parameter :: gatherers_team_num = 3

  real :: image_fraction
  image_fraction = this_image() / real(num_images())

  team_num = elders_team_num
  if (image_fraction > 1 / 6.) &
    team_num = hunters_team_num
  if (image_fraction > 1 / 2.) &
    team_num = gatherers_team_num

  form team(team_num, new_team)

end program hunters_gatherers
```

Sets the team numbers as compile-time parameters

Calculates the fraction of the image number relative to the total number of images

Based on the image number fraction, sets the team number for each image

Forms three new teams

In this part, we're not doing anything new relative to what we learned in section 12.2, except that we're creating three new teams instead of two. The `image_fraction` variable here is used as a convenience to easily assign 1/6, 1/3, and 1/2 to the elders, hunters, and gatherers, respectively.

Now, let's change the team to `new_team` and print a message from one image on each team, as shown in the following listing.

```
...
  change team(new_team)
    if (team_number() == elders_team_num) then
      if (this_image() == 1) &
        print *, num_images(), 'elders stayed in the village to rest'
    else if (team_number() == hunters_team_num) then
      if (this_image() == 1) &
        print *, num_images(), 'hunters went hunting'
    else if (team_number() == gatherers_team_num) then
      if (this_image() == 1) &
        print *, num_images(), 'gatherers went foraging'
    end if
  end team

end program hunters_gatherers
```

Changes context to new_team

Branch that will be executed by the elders

Branch that will be executed by the hunters

Branch that will be executed by the gatherers

Returns context to the original team

Like we learned in section 12.2, we change the team for all images to new_team. Depending on the image number, this will be the elder, hunter, or gatherer team. Inside the change team construct, we check which team we're on by comparing the value of team_number to our compile-time constants for team number. At this point, we only report the activity for each team.

Next, we'll create subteams from each of the hunter and gatherer teams. Specifically for hunters, we'll have the following snippet inside the hunters if branch:

Changes context to the new subteam

Places hunters in subteams of 3

```
form team ((this_image() - 1) / 3 + 1, hunters)
change team(hunters)
print *, 'Hunter', this_image(), 'in team', &
  team_number(), 'hunting for game'
end team
```

Each image reports from its subteam.

Returns back to the hunters team

The code to create and change to subteams for gatherers is similar to that for hunters:

```
form team ((this_image() - 1) / 2 + 1, gatherers)
change team(gatherers)
  print *, 'Gatherer', this_image(), 'in team', &
    team_number(), 'gathering fruits and veggies'
end team
```

Place this code inside the if branch for the gatherers team, and there you have it. If you now compile this program and run it on, say, 12 images, you'll get output similar to this:

Compiles using the OpenCoarrays compiler, caf

Runs on 12 parallel images

Group activity report from each team

```
caf hunters_gatherers.f90 -o hunters_gatherers
cafrun -n 12 --oversubscribe ./hunters_gatherers
           2 elders stayed in the village to rest
           4 hunters went hunting
           6 gatherers went foraging
Hunter              1 in team         2 hunting for game
Hunter              2 in team         1 hunting for game
Hunter              1 in team         1 hunting for game
Gatherer              1 in team         1 gathering fruits and veggies
Hunter              3 in team         1 hunting for game
Gatherer              2 in team         3 gathering fruits and veggies
Gatherer              1 in team         3 gathering fruits and veggies
Gatherer              2 in team         1 gathering fruits and veggies
Gatherer              2 in team         2 gathering fruits and veggies
Gatherer              1 in team         2 gathering fruits and veggies
```

Individual activity reports from each villager on their subteams

In this example, I chose only 12 images for brevity, but this example will work with any number of images (well, up to the limit of your computer's RAM, as each image runs its own copy of the program). Notice that the individual hunter and gatherer activity reports aren't in order, and they shouldn't be—all images execute completely asynchronously, except at `form team` and `end team` statements, where they synchronize (and only with images in their own team). For example, in the outer `change team` construct, the elders, hunters, and gatherers teams run in parallel to one another, and this is the beauty of parallel programming in Fortran.

You can run this program on many images on a single-core computer, and it will run like a traditional concurrent program, which in other languages is accomplished with, say, threading or `async/await`. You can also run this program (unchanged!) on many distributed-memory servers in parallel, and even on computers around the world.

12.5.2 *Exercise 2: Tsunami time step logging using events*

Let's start with the simulation team that's stepping forward through the computation. Recall that in listing 12.5, we used a coarray to copy the time step count from one team to another:

```
if (this_image() == 1) time_step_count[1, team_number=2] = n
```

In this snippet, we sent the value of the local time step n to the `time_step_count` coarray on image 1 of team 2. We did that only from one image, as all images on the simulation team have the same value for the time step count. Now, if we're implementing this using events, this first part is easy. We'll just declare an event variable and use it in the `event post` statement from team 1 to post an event from the simulation team to the logging team:

```
type(event_type) :: time_step_event[*]          ◁──┐  Declares the
...                                                 │  event variable
if (this_image() == 1) &
  event post(time_step_event[1, team_number=2])  ◁──┐

       Posts the event from image 1 on the
       current team to image 1 on team 2
```

That's it as far as posting the event from the simulation team goes. Let's see how we can receive this information from the logging team.

IMPLEMENTATION USING EVENT WAIT

On the logging team, we'll run in an infinite loop and have an `event wait` statement to block the execution. On each event intercepted, we'll increment the counter, print the time step count to the screen, and exit the loop only if we've reached the end of the simulation:

```
...                                    Loops indefinitely
else if (team_num == 2) then
  n = 0                                Blocks until the
  do                            ◁──    event is posted
    event wait(time_step_event) ◁──
    n = n + 1                          Increments the counter
```

```
      print *, 'tsunami logger: step ', n, &          | Prints the time step
                  'of', num_time_steps, 'done'        | count to the screen
       if (n == num_time_steps) exit      <——
   end do                                             Exits if we've reached the
end if                                                end of the simulation
...
```

The advantage to the approach using `event wait` is that we're guaranteed to catch every event that's posted. The downside is that we need to do the counting outselves (n = n + 1), and that `event wait` is blocking the execution. This is fine if counting time steps is the only thing the logging team needs to do. The `event wait` approach thus makes the logging team tightly coupled to the simulation team. Now let's take a look at the alternative solution using `event_query`.

IMPLEMENTATION USING EVENT_QUERY

Here's the solution to the exercise using `event_query`. Rather than blocking execution until each event is posted, we're simply going to query the event count and print it to the screen if its value changed from the previous iteration:

```
...
else if (team_num == 2) then          | Loops
  n = 0                               | indefinitely
  do                        <——                            Blocks until the
     call event_query(time_step_event, time_step_count)  <—— event is posted
     if (time_step_count > n) then
        n = time_step_count
        print *, 'tsunami logger: step ', n, &      | Prints the time step
                    'of', num_time_steps, 'done'    | count to the screen
     end if
     if (n == num_time_steps) exit    <——
  end do                                             Exits if we've reached the
end if                                               end of the simulation
...
```

Increments
the counter (points to `if (time_step_count > n) then` line)

The advantage to this approach is that the counting is handled automatically inside the `time_step_event` variable. This approach is also not blocking, unlike the `event wait` approach. If we needed to, we could carry out some other tasks on the logging team, and in each iteration, the `event_query` subroutine would return whatever the current value of the `time_step_count` was. This approach is thus asynchronous, and some time steps may be skipped if the simulation iterations are faster than the logging.

12.5.3 *Exercise 3: Calculating the global mean of water height*

We'll begin with our existing code in listing 12.7 that computes the global minimum and maximum of water height:

```
hmin = minval(h % data)
call co_min(hmin, 1)

hmax = maxval(h % data)
call co_max(hmax, 1)
```

```
if (this_image() == 1) print '(a, i5, 2(f10.6))', &
  'step, min(h), max(h):', n, hmin, hmax
```

To calculate the global average, we'll follow the same procedure. However, considering that we don't have a collective average function available out of the box, we'll get creative with the collective sum function co_sum. First, to calculate the local average, we'll take the sum of the local array and divide it by the total number of elements. Your first instinct may be to do something like this:

```
hmean = sum(h % data) / size(h % data)
```

Although this is the correct approach, recall that the data component of the Field type is allocated with one extra row and column on each side of the array, to facilitate halo exchange with neighboring images. From the Field type constructor function in mod_field.f90

```
allocate(self % data(self % lb(1)-1:self % ub(1)+1,&    | Allocates the data array with
                     self % lb(2)-1:self % ub(2)+1))    | an extra index on each end
```

Thus, if we were to compute the sum of h % data as a whole, we'd also be including values from the edges of neighbor images, which isn't what we're looking for. Instead, we'll slice the array to go exactly from the lower bound (lb) to the upper bound (ub) in each axis:

```
hmean = sum(h % data(h % lb(1):h % ub(1),h % lb(2):h % ub(2))) &
     / size(h % data(h % lb(1):h % ub(1),h % lb(2):h % ub(2)))
```

At this point, hmean is the local average value of water height on each parallel image. Of course, don't forget to declare hmean in the declaration section of the program. Like with the collective minimum and maximum, we now apply co_sum to hmean to store the sum on image 1, and divide the result by the total number of images to arrive at the average value:

```
call co_sum(hmean, 1)          ←──┐  Computes the collective sum of hmean
hmean = hmean / num_images()          and stores the result on image 1
                               ←──┐  Divides hmean by the total number
                                     of images to get the average value
```

Finally, let's add hmean to the print statement and modify the format string accordingly:

```
if (this_image() == 1) print '(a, i5, 3(f10.6))', &
  'step, min(h), max(h), mean(h):', n, hmin, hmax, hmean
```

If you now recompile and rerun the tsunami simulator, you'll get output like this:

```
step, min(h), max(h), mean(h):     1  0.000000  1.000000  0.003888
step, min(h), max(h), mean(h):     2  0.000000  0.996691  0.003888
step, min(h), max(h), mean(h):     3  0.000000  0.990097  0.003888
 ...
```

```
step, min(h), max(h), mean(h):  998 -0.072596  0.186842  0.003888
step, min(h), max(h), mean(h):  999 -0.072279  0.188818  0.003888
step, min(h), max(h), mean(h): 1000 -0.071815  0.190565  0.003888
```

The rightmost column in the output is our newly added water height average. Its values are constant throughout the simulation, which serves as evidence that our simulator conserves water volume.

12.6 New Fortran elements, at a glance

- Teams, a mechanism to group images by common task:
  - `team_type`—A new type for working with teams, available from the `iso_fortran_env` module
  - `form team`—A statement for creating new teams
  - `change team`/`end team`—A construct to switch images to a new team
  - `team_number`—A built-in function to get the current team number
  - `get_team`—A built-in function to get the team variable, current or otherwise
  - `sync team`—A statement to synchronize images across a common, typically parent team
- Events, a mechanism to organize the flow of your parallel programs around discrete events:
  - `event_type`—A new type for working with events, available from the `iso_fortran_env` module
  - `event post`—A statement to post an event to a remote image
  - `event wait`—A statement to block execution until an event is posted from another image
  - `event_query`—A subroutine to asynchronously count the number of posted events
- Collective subroutines `co_broadcast`, `co_max`, `co_min`, `co_reduce`, and `co_sum`, which implement some common parallel operations
- `recursive`—A procedure attribute that allows a procedure to invoke itself
- `execute_command_line`—A built-in subroutine to run a command from the host operating system

12.7 Further reading

- "The new features of Fortran 2018," by John Reid (PDF download): http://mng.bz/EdaX
- "A parallel Fortran framework for neural networks and deep learning," by Milan Curcic: https://arxiv.org/abs/1902.06714

Summary

- Fortran 2018 introduces new concepts for advanced parallel programming: teams, events, and collectives.
- Teams and events are mechanisms for distribution of work and synchronization, whereas collective subroutines are used for parallel reduction operations, such as sum, minimum, and maximum.
- Teams are used to form distinct groups of images and assign them different tasks.
- At the beginning of the program, all parallel images start in the initial team, and you can create as many teams as you want.
- When you switch images to new teams, all teams run independently from one another until explicitly synchronized.
- Events allow you to express the flow of your parallel program in a more elegant, and, ahem, event-driven style: post events from one or more images, wait for events from others, or just count them asynchronously.
- Collective subroutines allow you to perform some common parallel patterns without directly invoking coarrays.

appendix A
Setting up the Fortran development environment

Before we dive into the code, let's go over the basics of editing, compiling, and running a Fortran program. I'll recommend a few text editors that I like and guide you through setting up the complete Fortran development environment.

If you're familiar with Docker and want to skip all the tedious setup, jump ahead to section A.4, where I describe how to get the Modern Fortran Dockerfile that will get you up and running in no time.

A.1 Editing Fortran source files

You'll write Fortran programs and modules as plain text files. You can edit them in your favorite text editor. Here are some popular choices:

- *Vim* (Vi IMproved, https://www.vim.org/) is lightweight and powerful, although with a steep learning curve for beginners. This is my editor of choice. I picked it up when I first started programming in 2006, and never looked back.
- *Emacs* (https://www.gnu.org/software/emacs) is a powerful and extensible editor, as well as one of the oldest applications still in mainstream use.
- *Atom* (https://atom.io) is a modern, feature-rich, integrated development environment developed by GitHub. Atom also features a built-in package manager for adding third-party functionality to the editor.
- *Visual Studio Code* (https://code.visualstudio.com) is another modern, full-featured integrated development environment, like Atom.

An important feature to look for in your text editor is whether it can highlight Fortran syntax with different colors. All of the editors I've listed can do so, either out-of-the-box or by extension. They're also free and open source, so if you don't have a preferred editor yet, I suggest you try each of them and see which one feels most comfortable.

Fortran source file extensions

Although the Fortran Standard doesn't impose a constraint on what the Fortran source file extension should be, compiler vendors have adopted an almost-general set of rules:

- File names with the suffix .f, .for, or .ftn are interpreted as *fixed-form* (FORTRAN 77 and older) code.
- File names with the suffix .f90, .f95, .f03, or .f08 are interpreted as *free-form*.
- File names with an uppercase suffix (like .F, or .F90) indicate to the compiler that the files should be preprocessed.

All code that we'll write in this book is free-form. Free-form simply refers to a more liberal syntax that was introduced with the Fortran 90 standard. Since all compilers that I know of support .f90 as the universal suffix for free-form code (for example, the Intel compiler by default doesn't support .f95, .f03, or .f08), we'll use this extension throughout the book.

A.2   Setting up the Fortran compiler

There are several high-quality Fortran compilers available. Most are developed and maintained by commercial vendors like Intel, Cray, and others. If you have access to one of these, great! Feel free to use them as you work through this book. Of course, for any compiler-specific settings or usage instructions, you'll need to refer to your compiler's documentation.

Otherwise, a free, open source Fortran compiler is available as part of the GNU Compiler Collection (gcc). For examples and exercises in this book, we'll use the GNU Fortran Compiler (gfortran, https://gcc.gnu.org/fortran). In comparison to other compilers, here are the pros of gfortran:

- Free to download, use, and modify
- Easy to install on most operating systems
- Actively developed
- Implements most standard features, including some from the latest Fortran 2018 Standard

During the writing of this book, more open source compilers have emerged and have still been in active development. In particular, keep an eye out for LFortran (https://lfortran.org) and Flang (https://github.com/flang-compiler/flang).

Linux

On most Linux systems, gfortran is easily installed using the system package manager, without going to an external resource. On DEB-based systems like Debian or Ubuntu, installing gfortran is as easy as

```
apt install gfortran
```

This command resolves the download and install steps for you, and `gfortran` will be available as soon as the command finishes.

On RPM-based systems like Fedora or Centos, you can install gfortran like this:

```
dnf install gcc-gfortran
```

Alternatively, if gfortran is not available through your system's package manager, you can download binaries from https://gcc.gnu.org/wiki/GFortranBinaries.

> **Permissions**
>
> You'll need administrator (root) permissions to install the compiler using the package manager. If you know what you're doing and your username is already on the sudoers list, just prepend `sudo` to the Linux install commands I've provided and you're good to go.

macOS

For macOS, I recommend that you use the homebrew package manager (https://brew.sh). Once you have homebrew set up on your system, installing the Fortran compiler is as simple as

```
brew install gcc
```

This command will install the base GNU Compiler Collection along with the Fortran compiler.

Windows

The easiest way to set up the development environment in Windows is through the Windows Subsystem for Linux. This is an Ubuntu Linux instance that runs natively in your Windows 10 operating system. If your Windows 10 is up to date, you can get the Ubuntu Linux system from the Windows App Store. Once you have it up and running, installing the Fortran compiler is easy:

```
apt install gfortran
```

Otherwise, some people have had success developing Fortran on Windows using Cygwin (https://www.cygwin.com).

A.3   Setting up the MPI library (Message Passing Interface)

In chapter 1, I used an example of data copy between processors to demonstrate the use of MPI for parallel programming. Although in this book we'll focus exclusively on Coarray Fortran (CAF) for parallel algorithms, we still need to install the MPI library, as it's used as a dependency for coarrays when using the GNU compiler (see the "Setting up OpenCoarrays" section).

I recommend either OpenMPI (https://www.open-mpi.org) or MPICH (https://www.mpich.org) as popular, high-quality, and easy-to-use MPI implementations. They're available to install from Linux package managers. For example, if you use Ubuntu or another Debian-based distro, you can install OpenMPI with this command:

```
apt install openmpi-bin libopenmpi-dev
```

On an RPM-based distro like Fedora or Centos, type

```
dnf install openmpi openmpi-devel
```

Once installed, the MPI library provides an executable wrapper around the compiler. If installed correctly, you can verify this by typing `mpif90` at the command prompt:

```
mpif90
gfortran: fatal error: no input files
compilation terminated.
```

Don't worry about this error message. It simply means that `mpif90` correctly invoked `gfortran` under the hood, and that we didn't pass any source files to it.

A.4   Setting up OpenCoarrays

OpenCoarrays (http://www.opencoarrays.org) provides the interface between the GNU Fortran compiler and the underlying parallel implementation; in our case, MPI. You don't need to know much more than this. Think of it as an extension to `gfortran` that will allow you to build and run parallel programs using coarrays.

If you already have access to a compute platform with Intel or Cray compiler suites installed, you won't need OpenCoarrays and can skip to the next section.

Linux

Get the OpenCoarrays release directly from its GitHub repository:

```
git clone --branch 2.9.0 https://github.com/sourceryinstitute/OpenCoarrays
```

The simplest way to get up and running with OpenCoarrays is to build it from source. Given that we already have gfortran and OpenMPI built, compiling OpenCoarrays is relatively straightforward:

```
cd OpenCoarrays
mkdir build
cd build
```

```
FC=gfortran CC=gcc cmake ..
make
make install
```

You'll also need CMake (https://cmake.org) to build OpenCoarrays, as well as root privileges to do a make install on your system.

The latest release of OpenCoarrays is 2.9.0 as of this writing. However, keep an eye on their Releases page (http://mng.bz/eQBG) and download a later version if available.

macOS

Installing OpenCoarrays on macOS is straightforward using brew:

```
brew install opencoarrays
```

Using OpenCoarrays

OpenCoarrays provide two executables:

- caf—A wrapper script for compiling Coarray Fortran programs
- cafrun—A wrapper script for running Coarray Fortran programs

When compiling CAF programs, we'll use caf as the drop-in replacement for our compiler; for example

```
caf array_copy_caf.f90 -o array_copy_caf
```

To run the CAF program, you'll invoke it using the cafrun script:

```
cafrun -n 2 array_copy_caf
```

This command invokes the array_copy_caf program on two parallel processes. If two physical processors are available in the computer, both will be used. Otherwise, cafrun will spawn two parallel threads running on the same processor. These details won't impact the semantics of the program.

Why do we need OpenCoarrays?

Gfortran fully supports the Fortran Coarray syntax of the 2008 Standard. However, on its own, gfortran doesn't yet have a built-in mechanism for parallel computing with coarrays. This means that with plain gfortran, you can compile coarray programs but run them using only a single image (serial) mode. Although this can be useful for early development and testing, we need to be able to run our programs on multiple images in parallel. This is where OpenCoarrays come in.

Note that you only need OpenCoarrays if you work with gfortran. If you're on a system that has the Intel or Cray compiler suite set up, you're good to go with building Coarray Fortran code.

A.5   *Building a Docker image*

If you're familiar with Docker and want to skip all this tedious setup and jump right into action, download the Dockerfile from http://mng.bz/pBZR.

To build the modern Fortran image, type

```
docker build . -t modern-fortran:latest
```

This step will take a while as Docker pulls the base OS image and sets up the image with the compiler, dependencies, and Fortran code from this book.

Once done, if the build is successful, you'll be able to see your new image; for example

```
docker images
REPOSITORY          TAG             IMAGE ID            CREATED
        SIZE
modern-fortran      latest          0e5c745c8928        6 minutes ago
        546MB
```

To run it, type

```
docker run -it modern-fortran:latest /bin/bash
```

and you're off to the races!

appendix B
From calculus to code

I'll take some time here to explain how exactly we go from a partial differential equation to actual Fortran code that will calculate the solution. This appendix gives a foundation for *discretizing partial derivatives* and casting them into computer code.

B.1 The advection equation explained

Recall that our goal for chapter 2 is to write a program that will predict the movement of an object due to steady background flow. The result of the program should be consistent with our sketch in figure 2.2. In the cold front exercise in section 2.2.2, I asked you to calculate the temperature gradient across the front and how fast the temperature in Miami would drop given the propagation speed of the front. When you did the exercise, you may not have realized that you solved the linear advection equation (figure B.1).

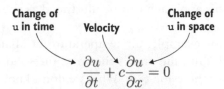

$$\frac{\partial u}{\partial t} + c\frac{\partial u}{\partial x} = 0$$

Figure B.1 The linear 1-D advection equation. u is the advected quantity in space x and time t, and c is the constant advective velocity. u can stand for any quantity, including temperature, concentration of a pollutant, or velocity itself.

This equation states that the rate of change of u in time equals the advective speed c times the spatial gradient of u.

$\frac{\partial u}{\partial t}$ and $\frac{\partial u}{\partial x}$ are the so-called partial derivatives, and they express the change of u in time and space, respectively. If you replace u with temperature, this becomes equivalent to our earlier example of a cold front approaching Miami: the rate of temperature decrease in Miami equals the temperature gradient across the front times the propagation speed of the front. A front with a sharper temperature gradient, or higher propagation speed, will make the temperature drop faster. If we can express this calculation in code, it will work for any quantity.

B.1.1   Discretizing the derivatives

Today's computers can't do calculus. In fact, on the CPU level, they don't do much more than *add* and *multiply* numbers, and move bits and bytes around in memory. Even simple arithmetic operations like subtraction and division are derived from addition and multiplication. How can we solve partial differentials if we have only basic arithmetic? One way is to approximate the partial derivatives with a form that can be expressed with code. This is typically done by *discretizing* the partial derivatives, which expresses them as arithmetic expressions of discrete values.

> **What the heck is discretization?**
>
> Wikipedia defines discretization as "the process of transferring continuous functions, models, variables, and equations into discrete counterparts. This process is usually carried out as a first step toward making them suitable for numerical evaluation and implementation on digital computers."
>
> In simpler words, it's a way to translate a continuous function (such as the one in figure B.1) into numbers that a computer can take in and crunch.

In the cold front exercise, when you calculated the temperature gradient across the front, you used a so-called *finite difference* approach to approximate a derivative. You probably thought something along the lines of this: "temperature gradient equals temperature in Miami minus temperature in Atlanta, divided by the distance between Miami and Atlanta." More generally, this approach can be illustrated as shown in figure B.2.

Take any continuous function u; for example, air temperature in Miami or the height of our blob. This function varies in time and is shown as the solid curve. At the current time (time step n), we know the value of u. What we don't know, and are trying to calculate, is the value of u at a future time (time step $n + 1$). The finite difference approach simplifies the continuous function (curve) with a discrete approximation (straight line). I use the word *discrete* because the line can be determined by the start and end points, which can be represented in computer code.

To draw a connection to our cold front example, here the slope of the red line corresponds to the temperature gradient times the propagation speed. The higher the speed or the gradient, the steeper the straight line would be. The same approach applies to partial derivatives of any quantity, in space or time. We'll use this rule to cast all terms in the equation as discrete variables.

Now that we know this general rule of discretizing partial derivatives, we can apply it to each derivative in the advection equation (figure B.3).

Finite difference of u in time

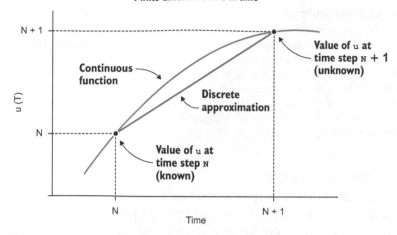

Figure B.2   A finite difference of *u* in time. The time derivative of a continuous function *u(t)* is approximated as the difference between values of *u* at time steps *n+1* and *n*, divided by the time interval between the two points.

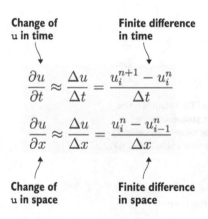

$$\frac{\partial u}{\partial t} \approx \frac{\Delta u}{\Delta t} = \frac{u_i^{n+1} - u_i^n}{\Delta t}$$

$$\frac{\partial u}{\partial x} \approx \frac{\Delta u}{\Delta x} = \frac{u_i^n - u_{i-1}^n}{\Delta x}$$

Figure B.3   Approximating partial derivatives in the advection equation with finite differences. The top equation approximates the change of *u* in time (tendency), and the bottom equation approximates the change of *u* in space (gradient). All terms on the far right side can be represented with variables in a computer program. Discrete time and space indices are shown as n and i, respectively.

Here, we discretize each derivative (time and space) with finite differences. First, we state that the rate of change of *u* in time (*tendency*) can be approximated as the difference of *u* in time divided by the time step ($\Delta u/\Delta t$). In a similar way, the rate of change of *u* in space (*gradient*) can be approximated as the difference of *u* in space divided by the grid spacing ($\Delta u/\Delta x$). On the far right side of each equation, we have the finite difference forms of both the time and space derivatives of *u*. By convention, superscripts *n* and *n* + 1 refer to current and future time steps, respectively. Subscript *i* refers to the position on the spatial grid, which will map to our Fortran array elements in the code.

> ### The order of differencing
> Notice that in time we're doing a forward difference ($u_i^{n+1} - u_i^n$), whereas in space we're doing a backward (upstream) difference ($u_i^n - u_{i-1}^n$). The forward difference in time is the simplest pattern for estimating a value at the next time step (u_i^{n+1}), which is the value we seek. The differencing in space is oriented upstream relative to the flow velocity c. If the velocity is positive, the flow is from left to right. Thus, to capture the object coming in from the left, we need to take the difference in that direction. If the object was moving from right to left (negative value of c), we'd need to switch the differencing in space to $u_{i+1}^n - u_i^n$.

B.1.2   Casting the derivatives into code

Now that we have all our terms written in discrete form, how do we write the code to solve for u at the next time step, u(i,n+1)? Try to reorder the discrete terms we've written so that u(i,n+1) is on the left side and all other terms are on the right side. Can you express this as code? Figure B.4 illustrates my attempt.

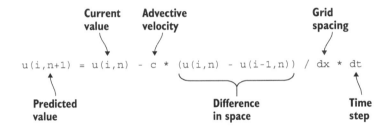

Figure B.4   **A code prototype for our advection solver. To calculate the predicted value** u(i,n+1), **we take the difference in space** u(i,n) - u(i-1,n), **divide it by grid spacing** dx, **multiply by the advective velocity** c **and time step** dt, **and, finally, subtract from the current value** u(i,n).

To me, this is the easiest way to read this equation:

1 Take the difference in space, u(i,n) - u(i-1,n). Analogous to the cold front exercise in chapter 2, this is equivalent to asking, "What's the temperature difference between Miami and Atlanta?"

2 Divide the difference by the grid spacing dx. This gives us the gradient (u(i,n) - u(i-1,n)) / dx; that is, the rate of change in space.

3 Multiply the gradient by the propagation speed c. This gives us the tendency c * (u(i,n) - u(i-1,n)) / dx; that is, the rate of change in time.

4 Finally, we multiply the tendency by the time step and add it to the current value.

Keeping only the present time level in memory

For clarity, I wrote u as a two-dimensional array with dimensions in space (indexed with i) and time (indexed with n). In practice, however, it's memory-consuming to keep all time levels stored in the array, especially when we want to do very long simulations. A simple hack around this is to hold only the present time step in memory, and overwrite the value with the following time step when we compute it. To do so, we can take a two-step approach:

1 Calculate the difference $u(i) - u(i-1)$ for all elements, and store it into an array; say, du.
2 Calculate the new value using the difference from step 1: $u(i) = u(i) - c *$ du(i) / dx * dt, for all elements.

This way, we don't keep every time level in memory, but only the most recent one. This is a common practice in numerical modeling that helps keep a low memory footprint.

appendix C
Concluding remarks

This appendix provides a recap and complete code of the tsunami simulator. It also offers ideas on where to go from here, as well as tips for learning more about Fortran.

C.1   *Tsunami simulator: The complete code*

For closure and as a refresher, let's review the complete tsunami code that we developed together while working through this book:

- In chapter 2, we implemented our first working program, which simply moved the prescribed wave, without changing its shape.
- In chapter 3, we refactored our program from chapter 2 to use a function for finite difference calculation, and a subroutine to initialize the wave shape.
- In chapter 4, we refactored our program from chapter 3 to define the procedures inside of a module. Meanwhile, we used this opportunity to add a few more physics terms to the simulator, which allowed the wave to propagate and evolve more realistically.
- In chapter 7, we used coarrays to parallelize the simulator from chapter 4. This made our program capable of running considerably faster if run on multiple CPUs.
- In chapter 8, we defined the arrays that represented the state of our simulation—water height and velocity—inside a derived type, which allowed us to abstract away low-level boilerplate code. We used this opportunity to also expand the simulator from a 1-D solution to a 2-D solution.
- In chapter 10, we implemented the arithmetic operators for the derived type from chapter 8, which allowed us to work with our derived type instances just like we would with regular arrays.
- Finally, in chapter 12, we experimented with cutting-edge parallel features like teams, events, and collectives. For brevity, I'm excluding the addition of

teams and events for logging, as that served mainly as a proof of concept and doesn't substantially change the essence of the calculation.

What follows is the final state of our simulator. It consists of a total of five source files:

- *tsunami.f90*—The main program that simulates the wave
- *mod_field.f90*—The module that defines the `Field` derived type, the key data structure that the simulator uses
- *mod_diff.f90*—The module that defines finite difference functions, imported and used in mod_field.f90
- *mod_io.f90*—The module that defines the subroutine to write data into a binary file, used in mod_field.f90
- *mod_parallel.f90*—The module that defines utilities for parallel execution

I'll go over each source file in the following subsections. This time around, the annotations in the code describe what the program does on a high level—they don't go into the nitty-gritty detail as before. Feel free to refer back to specific chapters if you need a refresher on how any of the Fortran code here works.

C.1.1 Main program: tsunami.f90

The tsunami.f90 file contains our main program and is shown in the following listing.

Listing C.1 tsunami.f90, the main program of the tsunami simulator

```fortran
program tsunami

  use iso_fortran_env, only: int32, real32
  use mod_field, only: Field, diffx, diffy        Imports the Field derived
                                                  type and finite difference
                                                  functions

  implicit none

  integer(int32) :: n

  integer(int32), parameter :: im = 201, jm = 201       Parameters that
  integer(int32), parameter :: num_time_steps = 1000    describe the grid size
  real(real32), parameter :: dt = 0.02                  and spacing, time steps,
  real(real32), parameter :: dx = 1, dy = 1             and gravitational
  real(real32), parameter :: g = 9.8                    acceleration

  integer(int32), parameter :: ic = im / 2 + 1      Parameters that describe
  integer(int32), parameter :: jc = jm / 2 + 1      the initial position and
  real(real32), parameter :: decay = 0.02           steepness of the wave

  type(Field) :: h, hm, u, v

  real(real32) :: hmin, hmax, hmean

  u = Field('u', [im, jm])          Creates the main data
  v = Field('v', [im, jm])          structures that represent
  h = Field('h', [im, jm])          the water height and
  hm = Field('h_mean', [im, jm])    velocity fields
```

```
call h % init_gaussian(decay, ic, jc)        ⟵┐   Sets the water height values to
                                                │   the initial, perturbed state
hm = 10.                                  ┌─ Writes the initial
                                          │  (time step 0) water
call h % write(0)         ⟵───────────────┘  height data to a file

                                                     Iterates for a set
time_loop: do n = 1, num_time_steps    ⟵───────      number of time steps

  u = u - (u * diffx(u) / dx + v * diffy(u) / dy &
    + g * diffx(h) / dx) * dt
                                                     Computes, updates,
  v = v - (u * diffx(v) / dx + v * diffy(v) / dy &   and synchronizes water
    + g * diffy(h) / dy) * dt                        velocity components
                                                     and water height
  h = h - (diffx(u * (hm + h)) / dx &
          + diffy(v * (hm + h)) / dy) * dt

  hmin = minval(h % data)        │  Computes global
  call co_min(hmin, 1)           │  minimum of water height

  hmax = maxval(h % data)        │  Computes global
  call co_max(hmax, 1)           │  maximum of water height

  hmean = sum(h % data(h % lb(1):h % ub(1),  &
                       h % lb(2):h % ub(2)))  &
        / size(h % data(h % lb(1):h % ub(1),  &    Computes
                        h % lb(2):h % ub(2)))       global average
  call co_sum(hmean, 1)                             of water height
  hmean = hmean / num_images()

  if (this_image() == 1) &
    print '(a, i5, 3(f10.6))', &             Prints the current time step
      'step, min(h), max(h), mean(h):', &    number and water height
      n, hmin, hmax, hmean                   statistics to the terminal

  call h % write(n)    ⟵─┐  Writes the current state
                         │  of the water height into
end do time_loop         │  a binary file

end program tsunami
```

In summary, this program does the following:

1. Imports the derived type and functions that we'll use
2. Declares and initializes simulation parameters
3. Creates and initializes the data structures that represent the water height and velocity fields
4. Iterates for a set number of time steps
5. In each iteration, computes the water height and velocity values for the next time step
6. In each iteration, gathers some statistics about water height and writes the whole field into a binary file

Perhaps the most compelling feature of this program, which was also one of our design goals from the start, is that the program can run correctly in serial or parallel mode without any changes. This is accomplished by defining the low-level code that deals with parallel execution inside the modules on which this program depends. The key data structure we work with is the Field derived type, defined in mod_field.f90. Let's see how this derived type is defined.

C.1.2   *The Field module: mod_field.f90*

The mod_field.f90 module is perhaps the most important, and the heaviest, source file of the tsunami simulator. It defines the main data structure that we use in the main program to carry out the simulation, as well as the low-level boilerplate code needed for the high-level code in the main program to be clean and elegant. The complete module is shown in the following listing.

> Listing C.2   mod_field.f90, the module that defines the Field derived type

```fortran
module mod_field

  use iso_fortran_env, only: int32, real32
  use mod_diff, only: diffx_real => diffx, diffy_real => diffy
  use mod_io, only: write_field
  use mod_parallel, only: tile_indices, tile_neighbors_2d

  implicit none

  private
  public :: Field, diffx, diffy        Opens the type
                                       definition block, with
  type :: Field          <─────────    attributes that follow

    character(:), allocatable :: name
    integer(int32) :: lb(2), ub(2)
    integer(int32) :: dims(2)
    integer(int32) :: neighbors(4)
    integer(int32) :: edge_size
    real(real32), allocatable :: data(:,:)     Type-bound methods
                                               and operators defined
  contains                 <─────────          in this section

    procedure, private, pass(self) :: assign_field, assign_real_scalar
    procedure, private, pass(self) :: field_add_field, field_add_real
    procedure, private, pass(self) :: field_sub_field, field_sub_real
    procedure, private, pass(self) :: field_mul_array, field_mul_real, &
                                      field_mul_field
    procedure, private, pass(self) :: field_div_real
    procedure, public, pass(self) :: gather
    procedure, public, pass(self) :: init_gaussian
    procedure, public, pass(self) :: sync_edges
    procedure, public, pass(self) :: write

    generic :: assignment(=) => assign_field, assign_real_scalar
    generic :: operator(+) => field_add_field, field_add_real
```

```
    generic :: operator(-) => field_sub_field, field_sub_real
    generic :: operator(*) => field_mul_array, field_mul_real, &
                              field_mul_field
    generic :: operator(/) => field_div_real

  end type Field

  interface Field                               Custom procedure to use when
    module procedure :: field_constructor       creating an instance of the type,
  end interface Field                           instead of the default type constructor

contains

  type(Field) function field_constructor(name, dims) result(self)
    character(*), intent(in) :: name
    integer(int32), intent(in) :: dims(2)
    integer(int32) :: edge_size, indices(4)
    self % name = name
    self % dims = dims
    indices = tile_indices(dims)
    self % lb = indices([1, 3])
    self % ub = indices([2, 4])
    allocate(self % data(self % lb(1)-1:self % ub(1)+1,&
                         self % lb(2)-1:self % ub(2)+1))
    self % data = 0
    self % neighbors = tile_neighbors_2d(periodic=.true.)
    self % edge_size = max(self % ub(1)-self % lb(1)+1,&
                           self % ub(2)-self % lb(2)+1)
    call co_max(self % edge_size)
  end function field_constructor

  subroutine assign_field(self, f)                    <───┐
    class(Field), intent(in out) :: self                  │
    class(Field), intent(in) :: f                   Methods that
    call from_field(self, f)                        define the custom
    call self % sync_edges()                        assignment (=)
  end subroutine assign_field                        for the Field

  pure subroutine assign_real_scalar(self, a)   <───┘
    class(Field), intent(in out) :: self
    real(real32), intent(in) :: a
    self % data = a
  end subroutine assign_real_scalar

  pure function diffx(input_field)                    <───┐
    class(Field), intent(in) :: input_field
    real(real32), allocatable :: diffx(:,:)         Thin wrappers
    diffx = diffx_real(input_field % data)          around the diffx
  end function diffx                                 and diffy functions
                                                     from mod_diff.f90
  pure function diffy(input_field)                    <───┘
    class(Field), intent(in) :: input_field
    real(real32), allocatable :: diffy(:,:)
    diffy = diffy_real(input_field % data)
  end function diffy
```

```fortran
pure subroutine from_field(target, source)
  type(Field), intent(in out) :: target
  type(Field), intent(in) :: source
  target % name = source % name
  target % lb = source % lb
  target % ub = source % ub
  target % dims = source % dims
  target % neighbors = source % neighbors
  target % edge_size = source % edge_size
  target % data = source % data
end subroutine from_field
```

Gathers the distributed (parallel) data to a single image, used before writing into a file

```fortran
function gather(self, image)
  class(Field), intent(in) :: self
  integer(int32), intent(in) :: image
  real(real32), allocatable :: gather_coarray(:,:)[:]
  real(real32) :: gather(self % dims(1), self % dims(2))
  allocate(gather_coarray(self % dims(1), self % dims(2))[*])
  associate(is => self % lb(1), ie => self % ub(1),&
            js => self % lb(2), je => self % ub(2))
    gather_coarray(is:ie, js:je)[image] = self % data(is:ie, js:je)
    sync all
    if (this_image() == image) gather = gather_coarray
  end associate
  deallocate(gather_coarray)
end function gather
```

Sets the initial values of water height to a bell shape

```fortran
subroutine init_gaussian(self, decay, ic, jc)
  class(Field), intent(in out) :: self
  real(real32), intent(in) :: decay
  integer(int32), intent(in) :: ic, jc
  integer(int32) :: i, j
  do concurrent(i = self % lb(1):self % ub(1),&
                j = self % lb(2):self % ub(2))
    self % data(i, j) = exp(-decay * ((i - ic)**2 + (j - jc)**2))
  end do
  call self % sync_edges()
end subroutine init_gaussian
```

Methods that define the arithmetic operators for the Field type

```fortran
pure type(Field) &
  function field_add_field(self, f) result(res)
  class(Field), intent(in) :: self, f
  call from_field(res, self)
  res % data = self % data + f % data
end function field_add_field

pure type(Field) &
  function field_add_real(self, x) result(res)
  class(Field), intent(in) :: self
  real(real32), intent(in) :: x(:,:)
  call from_field(res, self)
  res % data = self % data + x
end function field_add_real
```

```
pure type(Field) &
  function field_div_real(self, x) result(res)
  class(Field), intent(in) :: self
  real(real32), intent(in) :: x
  call from_field(res, self)
  res % data = self % data / x
end function field_div_real

pure type(Field) &
  function field_mul_array(self, x) result(res)
  class(Field), intent(in) :: self
  real(real32), intent(in) :: x(:,:)
  call from_field(res, self)
  res % data = self % data * x
end function field_mul_array

pure type(Field) &
  function field_mul_real(self, x) result(res)
  class(Field), intent(in) :: self
  real(real32), intent(in) :: x
  call from_field(res, self)
  res % data = self % data * x
end function field_mul_real

pure type(Field) &
  function field_mul_field(self, f) result(res)
  class(Field), intent(in) :: self, f
  call from_field(res, self)
  res % data = self % data * f % data
end function field_mul_field

pure type(Field) &
  function field_sub_real(self, x) result(res)
  class(Field), intent(in) :: self
  real(real32), intent(in) :: x(:,:)
  call from_field(res, self)
  res % data = self % data - x
end function field_sub_real

pure type(Field) &
  function field_sub_field(self, f) result(res)
  class(Field), intent(in) :: self, f
  call from_field(res, self)
  res % data = self % data - f % data
end function field_sub_field

subroutine sync_edges(self)
  class(Field), intent(in out) :: self
  real(real32), allocatable, save :: edge(:,:)[:]

  associate(is => self % lb(1), ie => self % ub(1),&
            js => self % lb(2), je => self % ub(2),&
            neighbors => self % neighbors)
```

Methods that define the arithmetic operators for the Field type

Synchronizes the array edges on each image with its parallel neighbors

```
    if (.not. allocated(edge)) &
      allocate(edge(self % edge_size, 4)[*])

    sync images(set(neighbors))

    edge(1:je-js+1,1)[neighbors(1)] = self % data(is,js:je)
    edge(1:je-js+1,2)[neighbors(2)] = self % data(ie,js:je)
    edge(1:ie-is+1,3)[neighbors(3)] = self % data(is:ie,js)
    edge(1:ie-is+1,4)[neighbors(4)] = self % data(is:ie,je)

    sync images(set(neighbors))

    self % data(is-1,js:je) = edge(1:je-js+1,2)
    self % data(ie+1,js:je) = edge(1:je-js+1,1)
    self % data(is:ie,js-1) = edge(1:ie-is+1,4)
    self % data(is:ie,je+1) = edge(1:ie-is+1,3)

  end associate

end subroutine sync_edges

subroutine write(self, n)          ◁──┐  Gathers the data to a
  class(Field), intent(in) :: self     │  single image and writes
  integer(int32), intent(in) :: n      │  it to a binary file
  real(real32), allocatable :: gather(:,:)
  gather = self % gather(1)
  if (this_image() == 1) call write_field(gather, self % name, n)
end subroutine write

pure recursive function set(a) result(res)    ◁──┐  Internal function to return
  integer, intent(in) :: a(:)                     │  unique elements of an array,
  integer, allocatable :: res(:)                  │  used in sync_edges
  if (size(a) > 1) then
    res = [a(1), set(pack(a(2:), .not. a(2:) == a(1)))]
  else
    res = a
  end if
end function set

end module mod_field
```

The majority of the code in this module serves to define the `Field` derived type and its methods. The most important methods are the ones that allow the built-in arithmetic operators +, -, *, and / to work with instances of this derived type. These are the methods that are called `field_add_field`, `field_add_real`, `field_sub_field`, and so on. Another important one is the `sync_edges` method, which helps us automatically synchronize the data on each image with its neighbor images on every assignment. Finally, we compute the gradients of our physical quantities—water height and velocity—using the `diffx` and `diffy` functions, defined in mod_diff.f90. Let's see what they look like.

The finite difference module: mod_diff.f90

The mod_diff.f90 module defines the finite difference functions `diffx` and `diffy`. The results of these functions tell us how much the water height and velocity vary in space—that is, how rapidly they change. For a quick refresher on gradients and finite differences, take a look at appendix B. The module is shown in the following listing.

Listing C.3 mod_diff.f90, the module that defines the finite difference functions

```
module mod_diff

  use iso_fortran_env, only: int32, real32
  implicit none

  private
  public :: diffx, diffy
                                              Takes a 2-D real array
                                              as input, and returns
                                              a finite difference of it
  contains                                    in the x axis

    pure function diffx(x) result(dx)     ◄─┘
      real(real32), intent(in) :: x(:,:)
      real(real32) :: dx(size(x, dim=1), size(x, dim=2))
      integer(int32) :: i, im
      im = size(x, dim=1)                              Calculates the finite
      dx = 0                                           difference using whole-
      dx(2:im-1,:) = 0.5 * (x(3:im,:) - x(1:im-2,:)) ◄─┘ array arithmetic
    end function diffx

    pure function diffy(x) result(dx)     ◄──────────
      real(real32), intent(in) :: x(:,:)                 Takes a 2-D real array
      real(real32) :: dx(size(x, dim=1), size(x, dim=2)) as input, and returns a
      integer(int32) :: j, jm                            finite difference of it in
      jm = size(x, dim=2)                                the y axis
      dx = 0
      dx(:,2:jm-1) = 0.5 * (x(:,3:jm) - x(:,1:jm-2))
    end function diffy

end module mod_diff
```

Gets the size of the input array (points to `im = size(x, dim=1)`)

Initializes the resulting array to zero (points to `dx = 0`)

`diffx` and `diffy` are rather similar. The former calculates the difference over the first dimension of the 2-D real array, whereas the latter does so over the second. The gist of these functions appeared as early as chapter 2; however, we wrote them in their final form in chapter 8.

C.1.3 The I/O module: mod_io.f90

The mod_io.f90 file contains a small module that exports one subroutine, write _field, as shown in the following listing.

Listing C.4 mod_io.f90, the input/output module

```fortran
module mod_io

  use iso_fortran_env, only: int32, real32

  implicit none

  private
  public :: write_field

contains

  subroutine write_field(field, fieldname, time)
    real(real32), intent(in) :: field(:,:)
    character(*), intent(in) :: fieldname
    integer(int32), intent(in) :: time
    integer(int32) :: fileunit, record_length
    character(100) :: filename, timestr
    write(timestr, '(i4.4)') time
    filename = 'tsunami_' // fieldname // '_' &
            // trim(timestr) // '.dat'
    record_length = storage_size(field) / 8 * size(field)
    open(newunit=fileunit, file=filename, &
        access='direct', recl=record_length)
    write(unit=fileunit, rec=1) field
    close(fileunit)
  end subroutine write_field

end module mod_io
```

Annotations:
- A 2-D real array containing the data to write to the file → `real(real32), intent(in) :: field(:,:)`
- A character string with the name of the field → `character(*), intent(in) :: fieldname`
- An integer time step number → `integer(int32), intent(in) :: time`
- Constructs the file name
- Opens a binary file for writing
- Writes field into the file → `write(unit=fileunit, rec=1) field`
- Closes the file → `close(fileunit)`

Subroutine write_field writes a 2-D real array into a binary file. It takes three input arguments:

- field(:,:)—A real 2-D array with the data to be written into the file
- fieldname—A character string that contains the name of the field
- time—An integer time step number

fieldname and time are used to construct the name of the file to be written. Once the file name is evaluated, the subroutine opens a new binary file with that name, writes the field array into it, and closes the file.

This subroutine is used from the type-bound method Field % write, defined in mod_field.f90.

C.1.4   *The parallel module: mod_parallel.f90*

The mod_parallel.f90 module provides functions that are used for our parallel computation needs, namely to evenly distribute the computational domain among parallel images and to obtain the index of neighboring images. The complete module is shown in the following listing.

> **Listing C.5   mod_parallel.f90, the module that provides utilities for parallel computation**

```
module mod_parallel

  use iso_fortran_env, only: int32, real32

  implicit none

  private
  public :: num_tiles, tile_indices, &
            tile_neighbors_1d, tile_neighbors_2d

  interface tile_indices
    module procedure :: tile_indices_1d, tile_indices_2d
  end interface tile_indices

contains

  pure function denominators(n)          ◁── Returns denominators of
    integer(int32), intent(in) :: n          an integer number, used
    integer(int32), allocatable :: denominators(:)   internally in num_tiles
    integer(int32) :: i
    denominators = [integer(int32) ::]
    do i = 1, n
      if (mod(n, i) == 0) denominators = [denominators, i]
    end do
  end function denominators
                                         Returns the optimal
                                         number of 2-D images,
  pure function num_tiles(n)          ◁── given the total number
    integer(int32), intent(in) :: n      of images
    integer(int32) :: num_tiles(2)
    integer(int32), allocatable :: denoms(:)
    integer(int32), allocatable :: dim1(:), dim2(:)
    integer(int32) :: i, j, n1, n2

    denoms = denominators(n)

    dim1 = [integer(int32) ::]
    dim2 = [integer(int32) ::]
    do j = 1, size(denoms)
      do i = 1, size(denoms)
        if (denoms(i) * denoms(j) == n) then
          dim1 = [dim1, denoms(i)]
          dim2 = [dim2, denoms(j)]
        end if
      end do
    end do
```

```
  num_tiles = [dim1(1), dim2(1)]
  do i = 2, size(dim1)
    n1 = norm2([dim1(i), dim2(i)] - sqrt(real(n)))
    n2 = norm2(num_tiles - sqrt(real(n)))
    if (n1 < n2) num_tiles = [dim1(i), dim2(i)]
  end do

end function num_tiles

pure function tile_indices_1d(dims, i, n) &
  result(indices)
  integer(int32), intent(in) :: dims, i, n
  integer(int32) :: indices(2)
  integer(int32) :: offset, tile_size

  tile_size = dims / n

  indices(1) = (i - 1) * tile_size + 1
  indices(2) = indices(1) + tile_size - 1

  offset = n - mod(dims, n)
  if (i > offset) then
    indices(1) = indices(1) + i - offset - 1
    indices(2) = indices(2) + i - offset
  end if

end function tile_indices_1d

pure function tile_indices_2d(dims) result(indices)
  integer(int32), intent(in) :: dims(2)
  integer(int32) :: indices(4)
  integer(int32) :: tiles(2), tiles_ij(2)
  tiles = num_tiles(num_images())
  tiles_ij = tile_n2ij(this_image())
  indices(1:2) = tile_indices_1d(dims(1), tiles_ij(1), tiles(1))
  indices(3:4) = tile_indices_1d(dims(2), tiles_ij(2), tiles(2))
end function tile_indices_2d

pure function tile_neighbors_1d() result(neighbors)
  integer(int32) :: neighbors(2)
  integer(int32) :: left, right
  if (num_images() > 1) then
    left = this_image() - 1
    right = this_image() + 1
    if (this_image() == 1) then
      left = num_images()
    else if (this_image() == num_images()) then
      right = 1
    end if
  else
    left = 1
    right = 1
  end if
  neighbors = [left, right]
end function tile_neighbors_1d
```

Returns the start and end indices of a parallel image, in 1-D

As above, but in 2-D

Returns the neighbor indices for a 1-D decomposition

```fortran
pure function tile_n2ij(n) result(ij)
  integer(int32), intent(in) :: n
  integer(int32) :: ij(2), i, j, tiles(2)
  if (n == 0) then
    ij = 0
  else
    tiles = num_tiles(num_images())
    j = (n - 1) / tiles(1) + 1
    i = n - (j - 1) * tiles(1)
    ij = [i, j]
  end if
end function tile_n2ij
```

Converts from a 1-D index n to a 2-D index pair (i,j)

```fortran
pure function tile_ij2n(ij) result(n)
  integer(int32), intent(in) :: ij(2)
  integer(int32) :: n, tiles(2)
  if (any(ij == 0)) then
    n = 0
  else
    tiles = num_tiles(num_images())
    n = (ij(2) - 1) * tiles(1) + ij(1)
  end if
end function tile_ij2n
```

Converts from a 2-D index pair (i,j) to a 1-D index n, used internally

```fortran
pure function tile_neighbors_2d(periodic) &
  result(neighbors)
  logical, intent(in) :: periodic
  integer(int32) :: neighbors(4)
  integer(int32) :: tiles(2), tiles_ij(2), itile, jtile
  integer(int32) :: left, right, down, up
  integer(int32) :: ij_left(2), ij_right(2), ij_down(2), ij_up(2)

  tiles = num_tiles(num_images())
  tiles_ij = tile_n2ij(this_image())
  itile = tiles_ij(1)
  jtile = tiles_ij(2)

  ij_left = [itile - 1, jtile]
  ij_right = [itile + 1, jtile]
  ij_down = [itile, jtile - 1]
  ij_up = [itile, jtile + 1]

  if (periodic) then
    if (ij_left(1) < 1) ij_left(1) = tiles(1)
    if (ij_right(1) > tiles(1)) ij_right(1) = 1
    if (ij_down(2) < 1) ij_down(2) = tiles(2)
    if (ij_up(2) > tiles(2)) ij_up(2) = 1
  else
    if (ij_left(1) < 1) ij_left = 0
    if (ij_right(1) > tiles(1)) ij_right = 0
    if (ij_down(2) < 1) ij_down = 0
    it (ij_up(2) > tiles(2)) ij_up = 0
  end if

  left - tile_ij2n(ij_left)
  right = tile_ij2n(ij_right)
```

Returns the neighbor indices for a 2-D decomposition

```
        down = tile_ij2n(ij_down)
        up = tile_ij2n(ij_up)

        neighbors = [left, right, down, up]

    end function tile_neighbors_2d

end module mod_parallel
```

Much of this code was developed in chapter 7 in support of our parallelization effort for the 1-D tsunami simulator. The rest of it was developed in chapter 8, when we transitioned to a 2-D implementation of the simulator. For brevity, not all code could be covered there, so at the time I pointed you to the GitHub repository instead.

This completes the tsunami simulator project. It's been a long journey, but we've made it. I hope that you can use parts or all of this project in your current or future projects.

C.2 Going forward with the tsunami simulator

While the tsunami simulator we developed is quite capable as is, it's also minimal in terms of features. Here are some open challenges that you can take on to further hone your Fortran programming skills:

- Enable simulation parameters—grid size and spacing, number of time steps, or initial shape of the wave—as command-line arguments.
- Enable nonuniform bathymetry (shape of the bottom), and, even better, implement real-world bathymetry from external data sources.
- Add other physics terms, such as wind stress or bottom friction. (This will take both Fortran programming and independent research skills.)
- Implement writing output fields to self-described NetCDF files using the netcdf-fortran library (https://github.com/Unidata/netcdf-fortran).

C.3 Neural networks and deep learning

Did you know that I rewrote chapter 8 on derived types from scratch? The first draft of the chapter was a bit too busy and got too long, so my editors axed it. However, a Fortran library for neural networks and deep learning came out of it. It's called neural-fortran, and you can find it at https://github.com/modern-fortran/neural-fortran. I even wrote a paper about it—refer back to "Further reading." Study this library if you're interested in how parallel neural networks can be implemented in modern Fortran.

C.4 Online resources

- The home of the Fortran language and its community-developed standard library and package manager: https://fortran-lang.org.
- GFortran online documentation: https://gcc.gnu.org/onlinedocs/gfortran.
- A community-curated Wiki with tutorials, code samples, libraries, and more: http://fortranwiki.org.

- A comprehensive online resource of modern Fortran best practices: https://www.fortran90.org.
- Awesome Fortran, a curated list of Fortran libraries: https://github.com/rabbiabram/awesome-fortran.
- Doctor Fortran, a blog by Steve Lionel: https://stevelionel.com/drfortran. (Steve is a retired senior engineer from Intel who offers insight from the perspective of compiler developers and the Fortran Standard Committee.)
- Degenerate Conic, a blog by Jacob Williams on algorithms, modern Fortran programming, and orbital mechanics: https://degenerateconic.com.
- Bob Apthorpe on modernizing a legacy FORTRAN project: http://mng.bz/QywR.
- Last but not least, the companion blog to this book: https://medium.com/modern-fortran.

C.5   Compilers

- The GNU Fortran compiler: https://gcc.gnu.org/fortran—A must-have for any Fortran developer. Can be installed by the package manager of most operating systems.
- The interactive LFortran compiler based on LLVM: https://lfortran.org.
- Flang, another open source compiler based on LLVM: https://github.com/flang-compiler/flang.
- The Intel Fortran compiler and performance libraries: https://software.intel.com/en-us/fortran-compilers. Although a commercial compiler, you can get a free license for noncommercial use if you're a student, teacher, or an open source contributor.

C.6   Books

So you want to learn more, and you like books. Where to go from here?

- *Modern Fortran Explained: Incorporating Fortran 2018*, by Michael Metcalf, John Reid, and Malcolm Cohen, Oxford University Press, 2018. Considered the Fortran "bible" by many Fortran programmers, including myself. Although quite dry, it's the most comprehensive and complete reference material on the latest edition of Fortran.
- *Modern Fortran in Practice*, by Arjen Markus, Cambridge University Press, 2012. A practical and hands-on book with a variety of fun exercises. This is my top recommendation if you liked this book.
- *Parallel Programming with Co-arrays*, by Robert W. Numrich, Chapman and Hall/CRC, 2018. This book provides a narrow focus on parallel algorithms with coarrays.
- *Parallel and High Performance Computing*, by Robert Robey and Yuliana Zamora, Manning Publications, 2021. Not focused on Fortran, but essential if you're serious about high-performance computing and parallel scalability.

index

RELATED MANNING TITLES

Modern C
by Jens Gustedt

ISBN 9781617295812
408 pages, $59.99
November 2019

C++ Concurrency in Action, Second Edition
by Anthony Williams

ISBN 9781617294693
592 pages, $69.99
February 2019

Parallel and High Performance Computing
by Robert Robey and Yuliana Zamora

ISBN 9781617296468
600 pages (estimated), $69.99
Spring 2021 (estimated)

For ordering information go to www.manning.com